Parents® MAGAZINE'S

The Best Advice I Ever Got

1,023 Fast Fixes, Simple Solutions, and Wise Ideas for Raising Kids

EDITED BY **SALLY LEE**, Editor-in-Chief of Parents Magazine

• FOREWORD BY **ROB REINER** •

RODALE

© 2001 by Gruner + Jahr USA Publishing

First published 2001
First published in paperback 2002

Illustrations © John Ceballos, Kristin Mount
Photographs © Rodale Inc.

Printed in the United States of America
Rodale Inc. makes every effort to use acid-free ∞, recycled paper ♻.

Library of Congress Cataloging-in-Publication Data

Parents magazine's the best advice I ever got : 1,023 fast fixes, simple
solutions, and wise ideas for raising kids / edited by Sally Lee;
foreword by Rob Reiner.
     p. ; cm.
Includes index.
ISBN 1–57954–334–0 hardcover
ISBN 1–57954–664–1 paperback
1. Child rearing—Popular works. 2. Parenting—Popular works.
3. Children—Health and hygiene—Popular works. 4. Children—Care—Popular works.
[DNLM: 1. Child Rearing—Popular Works. 2. Child Care—Popular Works.
3. Infant Care—Popular Works. 4. Parenting—Popular Works.
WS 113 P2283 2001] I. Title: Best advice I ever got. II. Lee, Sally.
III. Parents (New York, N.Y. : 1993)
RJ61 .P2265 2001
649'.1—dc21   00–012330

Distributed to the book trade by St. Martin's Press

2   4   6   8   10   9   7   5   3   1   hardcover
2   4   6   8   10   9   7   5   3   1   paperback

WE **INSPIRE** AND **ENABLE** PEOPLE TO IMPROVE
THEIR LIVES AND THE WORLD AROUND THEM

FOR MORE OF OUR PRODUCTS

WWW.**RODALESTORE**.COM
(800) 848-4735

Parents Magazine's The Best Advice I Ever Got Staff

EDITOR-IN-CHIEF: Sally Lee

PROJECT EDITOR: Kate Lawler

EDITORS: Linda Fears, Mary Mohler

WRITERS: Deborah Baer, Heidi Benson, Diane Debrovner, Dorre Fox, Heather Gowen, Carol Straley, Aminda Jacobs, Linnea Leaver, John Loecke, Lexi Petronis, Betty Wong

Rodale Books Group

VICE PRESIDENT AND PUBLISHER: Neil Wertheimer

MANAGING EDITOR: Kevin Ireland

ART DIRECTOR: Richard Kershner

COVER DESIGNER: Susan P. Eugster

INTERIOR DESIGNER: Tara Long

To our mothers, who have given us a lifetime of great advice: Dorothy Lee, Peggy Lawler, Irene Glassberg, Deane Vedders Mohler, Linda Baer, Ilse Petelinz, Patricia Bruder Debrovner, Judy Fox, Barbara Gowen, Judith Kloeb Heckman, Sharian Leaver, Marlene Loecke, Beth Keenan Petronis, Philomena Straley, Sau Man Wong.

—*the editors*

contents

4: Behavior

5: Development and Learning

6: All in the Family

Resources

foreword

most people know me as an actor and director, but my three young kids know me only as Dad. Being a parent is the best role I've ever had.

I've spent lots of time wondering about my children's future and how my wife's and my own parenting skills will help shape them into the adults they will become. In fact, my wife, Michele, and I are so committed to helping young kids that we launched the I Am Your Child Campaign and Foundation, which raises public awareness about early childhood development and encourages public policy makers to increase spending on early childhood programs. But it doesn't matter how much the government spends if we don't do our part at home as parents.

I don't think we can ever measure the importance of singing and talking to our kids from the very start, or how much family rituals and routines help develop a child's sense of security and ability to understand how the world works.

Research tells us that a child's brain grows to more than 80 percent of its adult size by age 3. We also now know that when you nurture a child with affection and touch, and read and sing to him, you're physiologically causing brain connections. Further, research shows that children who have been properly nurtured and loved, and who have securely bonded and attached with parents or primary caregivers, have a much better chance at achieving success in school, and they have greater self-esteem, making it easier for them to function in society.

That's why this book from the editors of *Parents* magazine is such a terrific service for mothers and fathers. In it, *Parents* readers share great tips on everything from sleep to safety to discipline that have helped them raise their kids. I love the concept of parents passing along ideas to help other parents. And in that spirit, I have a tip of my own to share with you.

Rob Reiner's Allowance Rule: To help my 8- and 6-year-old sons learn the value of budgeting money as well as the importance of helping other people, I've established an allowance policy. Every week, I give them each $7. They're allowed to do whatever they want with $5 of that money, whether they save it or spend it on something they like. They give the other $2 to a charity that they choose.

I hope that ideas like this one will help you be a better parent. I know what a tough job parenting can be, but it's the most important one any of us will ever have. After all, our children's future depends on us.

—Rob Reiner

introduction

i have a confession to make. Even though I'm the editor-in-chief of the largest, most prestigious parenting magazine in the world, when it comes to raising kids, I don't have all the answers. Far from it. Like all concerned parents, I ask a lot of questions and need a lot of help. When my daughter Gracie throws a tantrum in the supermarket because she can't have candy, I turn to my mom for advice. When she got sick with bronchitis last year and simply refused to take her medicine, I called my sister-in-law for help. (She suggested that I invite all of Gracie's dollies to a party and serve up antibiotics in a toy teacup—and it worked!) My daughter, I'm proud to say, was potty trained at an early age thanks to tips I'd read in *Parents* magazine.

The bottom line is that all parents need fast fixes, simple solutions, and wise advice. That's why the editors at *Parents* magazine created this book. In it, you'll find fresh new ideas and sound strategies from moms and dads just like you. We've gathered great ideas for calming a crying baby, teaching a 2-year-old to share, monitoring the media diet of a 5-year-old, and much more. Whether you've just had your first child or you have a family of five, every parent needs good advice—and most every parent has good advice to share.

What's more, we asked day care workers, elementary school teachers, peewee league coaches, and other experts who parent for a living to reveal their shortcuts and secrets. Pediatricians, police officers, and professional clowns all offered their expertise as well. We even asked grandparents and great-grandparents to share the wisdom of their years.

I've learned a lot from this book. Gracie will start school soon, and I already have some great ideas on dealing with separation anxiety, helping her to be a good friend, and teaching her the safety skills she needs to know. As a mom, I will never stop asking questions, but with the help of this indispensable book, I'll have more of the answers. Now, when parents write to ask me how to feed a picky eater or teach a child to swim, I'll have over 1,000 new kid-tested and parent-approved tips and tricks to share.

Sally Lee

your baby

newborn
know-how

1

Congratulations on your new baby! No doubt, you've been eagerly awaiting your first day alone with your little one ever since you found out that you were pregnant. But now that the moment is actually here, you're probably feeling a little nervous. One of the first realizations you'll make as a new parent is that you spend the vast majority of your time engaged in baby care 101: diapering, dressing, bathing, and feeding. And if this is your first baby, these apparently simple activities aren't always as easy as they look.

Your newborn may be more slippery and squirmy than you'd expected, or she may spit up on every clean outfit. She probably cries a lot more than you'd imagined, and she looks so . . . delicate. Not to worry: Even if you've never had a baby before, she's never had a mom either, so you're going to seem just fine to her. The following tips from experienced mothers will help you care for your baby with confidence.

diaper detail

The Perfect Wipe

My doctor advised me not to use baby wipes on my newborn because the chemicals might irritate her sensitive skin. He recommended plain water and cotton balls, but the balls were too messy. So I tried cotton cosmetic pads instead, and they work great. They're handy for traveling too; just presoak them and put them in a sealable plastic bag.

Felicia Scala, Floral Park, New York

Dryer Diapers

When our son, August, was a newborn, he hated to have his diaper changed. He cried every time we undressed him, until we accidentally discovered that changing him on the running clothes dryer soothed him (we held on to him carefully the whole time, of course). The noise, warmth, and vibration seemed to settle him down. Now, we turn the dryer on for all diaper changes.

Tom and Jane Schott, West Lafayette, Indiana

Smiling Faces

My 6-month-old son would never remain still on the changing table unless he could see the picture of the baby on his wipes container. Realizing that more faces might hold his

umbilical cord care

Your newborn's umbilical cord stump will fall off within 2 to 4 weeks. Until then, give your baby sponge baths. To prevent infection and speed healing, wipe around the base of the stump with an alcohol-soaked cotton ball at each diaper change. Since there are no nerve endings there, your baby will not feel any pain. Also try to keep your baby's diaper folded down below the stump so that air can circulate around it. Call your pediatrician if the area looks red, swollen, or infected, or if there is persistent or bloody discharge.

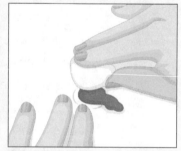

Wipe stump of umbilical cord with cotton ball.

rub-a-dub-dub

Once your baby's umbilical cord stump has fallen off (and his circumcision, if any, has healed), he's ready for his first real bath. You can use either a plastic infant tub or a sink lined with a towel for comfort.

1. Other than the diaper area and spit-up collection under his chin, which you're cleaning often anyway, newborns don't get very dirty. It's fine to give your baby a bath only a couple of times a week.
2. Make sure that the room in which you're bathing your baby is about 75°F.
3. Gather everything you'll need before you begin: mild soap, baby shampoo, cotton balls, a hooded towel, a soft washcloth, and a cup for rinsing.
4. Test the temperature of the bath water on the inside of your wrist.
5. Undress your baby, and slowly slide him into the bath feet first, cradling his head and neck with your forearm and wrist. Your wrist should rest gently under his shoulders.
6. Use your free hand to wet the washcloth. Gently wet his head, then work your way down his body, finishing with the diaper area.
7. Use soap sparingly, if at all. Wipe your infant's most sensitive areas—the face, ears, and genitals—with individual cotton balls.
8. To wash his hair, use only a small amount of baby shampoo or soap. When it's time to rinse off the shampoo, you can use a cup or washcloth.
9. Using baby clippers, try trimming his nails right after a bath, which softens them. Hold each finger and cut following the shape of the fingertip.

attention even better, my 4-year-old daughter and I cut out pictures of babies from magazines, pasted them on the wipes box, and sealed it with contact paper. The box is now covered in smiling faces—and diaper changes are easier than ever.

Claire Piccorelli, *Wappingers Falls, New York*

Fresh Air

Our daughter is quite susceptible to stubborn diaper rash, and we like to give her plenty of time outside her diaper. To prevent accidents, we put her in the bathtub seat on the playroom floor and surround her with books and toys. We can get 15 to 20 minutes of air time by reading books and playing peek-a-boo games with her while her bottom dries.

Mary Cathryn, *Ricker St. Cloud, Minnesota*

Go-Go Changes

I couldn't bear to put my daughter, Rebecca, on those dirty changing tables in public restrooms, and changing pads are never wide or long enough for a baby. I started carrying a spare pillowcase in her diaper bag. It's generously sized, it isn't bulky, and I still use the diaper bag's cushioned pad underneath it. I wash the pillowcase often, and she never has to touch those germy tables!

Shannon Schell, *Tustin, California*

it's my job

baby massage

Your baby may not understand your words yet, but she'll certainly respond to your loving touch, says Lauren McGuinn, a certified massage instructor in New York City. A massage can be an equally enjoyable experience for you and your infant. Choose a quiet, comfortable spot and rub oil on your hands so they'll glide smoothly over your baby's skin. (Use salad oil, since infants love to put their feet and hands in their mouths!)

Legs: Wrap one hand around your baby's thigh and the other around her ankle. Gently squeeze as you slide the thigh hand down to the ankle. Then move the ankle hand up to the thigh, and repeat.

Arms: Grasp your baby's arm with both hands, one above the other. Gently twist your hands back and forth in opposite directions and squeeze as you work them toward the wrist.

Back: Place your baby on her stomach. Put your left hand on her bottom, and with your right hand make a sweeping motion down from the top of her back to meet your left hand.

Chest: Start with both hands at the center of her chest. In a heart-shaped motion, move your hands out to the sides of your baby's chest, down her rib cage, and then back up the center to the starting position.

Stomach: Using your fingertips, "walk" across your baby's tummy from left to right. This can ease gas and colic, and you may feel bubbles releasing under your fingertips.

Face: Because they do so much sucking, infants can carry a lot of tension in their jaws. Make small circles on and around your baby's jawbone with your fingertips to help relieve some of that discomfort.

Face It

When my son was 16 months old, changing his diaper became a challenge. He would squirm and try to get away. I started asking him where his eyes, nose, and mouth were. He got so interested that he stopped trying to get away. I was able to get him changed more quickly, and eventually, he learned all his body parts.

Dahlaine Hampoon, *Santee, California*

Color Coding

My sons are only 14 months apart. You'd be amazed how similar a size 4 and a size 5 diaper look in the diaper bag. We never know which size needs restocking. Now, I streak a marker down the edge of the diapers when I take them out of the package: red for Riley and blue for Casey. It helps with babysitters and visiting grandparents too.

Marilyn Jensen, *New Rochelle, New York*

dressed for success

Squirming Solution

When my daughter, Kaetlynn, began rolling over and trying to climb around, getting her dressed became a trial. I decided to put her in her crib for dressing. She loves to stand and pull up, and I'm able to dress her without worrying about her rolling off the changing table during one of her fast moves.

Christine Heiberg, *Minnetonka, Minnesota*

Ready-to-Wear

As all new parents know, newborns go through several clothing changes a day. To make it easier to pull together a new outfit, I use an over-the-door shoe rack. As I fold the baby's clean laundry, I just place a complete outfit in each pocket (a shirt, pants, socks, etc.) You don't have to search through drawers with an infant in your arms,

star strategy
Marie Osmond

"My baby Matthew's favorite item is plastic keys. He loves to put them in his mouth. I happen to love little plastic toys because you can throw them in the dishwasher or washing machine and keep them really clean."

—singer and mother of seven

Cindy Crawford

"I'm into comfort. I like dressing my baby Presley in cotton leggings, T-shirts, and onesies. I've seen the European stuff and it's so cute, but bloomers and a pea coat are not terribly practical!"

—supermodel and mother of Presley Walker

and it's also helpful for anyone else who might change the baby.

Rebecca Colbath,
East Falmouth, Massachusetts

Out of Sight, Out of Mind

My 10-month-old is at the stage where she's fascinated with her feet and doesn't like having her socks and shoes put on. To make it less of a struggle, I move her to her high chair, where she can't see her feet, while I put the socks and shoes on. The diversion works wonders, and we're ready to head out the door in a lot less time.

Jo Meissner, St. Louis

Pin Down Those Socks

I'm sure I'm not the only parent who has wondered where those tiny socks disappear to in the dryer. To avoid puzzling

the lowdown on spit-up

Worried that your baby is spitting up so much that he may not be getting enough nutrition? A little spit-up looks like a lot more than it really is. To prove that to yourself, pediatrician Katherine Ling-McGeorge, M.D., of Children's Hospital of Michigan, in Detroit, suggests that you pour a teaspoon of water on a towel and see how large the resulting wet spot actually is. Here are some tips to help limit spit-up.

✓ Feed your baby more frequently in smaller amounts, and make sure to burp her regularly during feedings.

✓ If you're using a bottle, angle it so that your baby is getting only milk from the nipple, to prevent her from swallowing excess air.

✓ Support your baby in an upright position in your lap, her stroller, or an infant seat for about 20 minutes after feeding.

✓ Don't overfeed. If your child turns her head away from the breast or bottle, try again later.

over this mystery, I attach pairs with safety pins. It certainly saves sorting time.

Brenda Merken, *Melrose, Massachusetts*

A Better Bib

Our 1-year-old son, Logan, is a real drooler—his shirt used to be constantly soaked! We discovered that bandannas do a better job than bibs of keeping him dry. They're economical, they cut down on laundry loads, and Logan always looks neat (and adorable).

Colleen Warren, *Kingsford, Michigan*

organizing the nursery

Artsy Changing Table

My husband found an inexpensive, antique wooden dry sink at a flea market that we use as a changing table. We had a mattress custom-made to fit the sink area; the cabinets below serve as great storage. It's a sturdy piece of furniture that looks terrific in our child's room. Best of all, when our kid gets out of diapers, we can remove the mattress and use the table as a sideboard in our den.

Sheila Addis, *Philadelphia*

It's a Wrap

After the baby showers for each of my four daughters, I saved some of my favorite wrapping paper and later used it to line each girl's baby-dresser drawers. It looked great, and it was a lovely way to preserve memories of gifts from special friends.

Lynette Kittle, *Tustin, California*

Lighten the Load

Instead of buying a hamper for my baby's room, I bought an inexpensive mesh laundry bag that hangs on a metal frame. When the bag is full, you can take it off the frame and carry it like a duffel bag to the laundry room. It's much easier than lugging a heavy basket or hamper.

Bridget Murphy, *Sea Girt, New Jersey*

baby monitor buying tips

As a new parent, you'll be toting your baby monitor all over the house, so it pays to buy a durable one. We asked Sandy Jones, author of the *Consumer Reports Guide to Baby Products*, what you should look for when you shop.

- ✓ A rechargeable receiver, which will save you up to $50 a year over a monitor that requires regular battery replacement
- ✓ Clear reception. If you change channels from A to B on the receiver and continue to get interference, exchange it for a model with a different channel mix, such as A plus D.
- ✓ A low-battery indicator
- ✓ A belt clip and a flexible antenna, both of which make the monitor more portable
- ✓ Bonuses: a light display that lets you "see" your baby's sounds in addition to hearing them, and a warning light or alarm that signals when you're out of range

Quick-Change Artist

I use king-size pillowcases to cover the changing pad on my table. They fit perfectly, they're easy to put on and remove, and they come in all colors, so I can coordinate them with my son's room.

Hannah Dunne,
West Swanzey, New Hampshire

Sporty Diaper Bag

Rather than use a traditional diaper bag, I bought a vinyl backpack. It has plenty of room inside, small pockets in front for my wallet and keys, and useful outer side pockets (probably meant for water bottles, but great for baby bottles, too). It's more convenient and better-looking than most diaper bags out there.

Tammy Abdelqader,
Rochester, Minnesota

In-Genie-Ous Solution

Those new diaper disposal cans are a great way to cut the mess, but with some brands, you need to buy special bags. I bought one that uses regular garbage bags, which is much less expensive and more convenient—you're never stuck without the right bag when you need it.

Lucy Probert,
Charlotte, North Carolina

Soften the Scent

As my daughter grew, so did the odor of her diaper pail. I tried sachets, deodorant tablets, disinfectant sprays—to no avail. Finally, I discovered an effective odor killer: fabric softener sheets. Putting a few in the pail keeps her room smelling fresh and clean.

Crystal Hiller, Friendship, Wisconsin

helping parents choose baby equipment

Beyond a crib and changing table, what are the most important purchases that new parents make? Annie Rosenberg, of Albee's Baby Carriage Company, in New York City, says that these items are on the top of her customers' lists:

- ✓ Infant carrier
- ✓ Car seat
- ✓ Diaper Genie
- ✓ Glider rocking chair
- ✓ Breast pump
- ✓ High chair
- ✓ Baby monitor
- ✓ Videos for babies
- ✓ Baby swing

moving up

From Bath to Booster

After my daughter outgrew her infant tub, I didn't throw away the large bathtub-shaped sponge that we'd put on the bottom of the tub to make it more comfortable for her. I cut it in half. I placed the larger half on her high chair so she's higher up and won't slide forward. I keep the smaller half in my car to place in the grocery cart seat.

Kathy Petley, *Pittsburgh*

Socks Appeal

My 1-year-old loves to be outside. He just started taking his first steps, but when he's outside, he prefers to crawl. At first I worried about his knees getting scraped on the concrete.

grandmother knows best

I've always found that if you put the plastic bottle of lotion or shampoo in the tub with your baby, the liquid inside will be warm—and more soothing—when you're ready for it.

Evelyn Miller,
Lido Beach, New York

outward bound

Aside from unsolicited comments from grandmotherly passersby ("Is he warm enough/cool enough?"), there's no reason not to take your newborn outside. In extreme temperatures, however, you need to take certain precautions.

1. In the first month, don't take your baby out for a walk if it's hotter than 85°F or colder than 60°F. (A ride to the supermarket in the car is fine as long as the air conditioning or heat is on.)

2. In winter, your baby needs one more layer than you do. Unzip your baby's snowsuit or jacket during car rides and remove his hat and mittens when you go into a store to prevent overheating.

3. In summer, he doesn't need an extra layer. Infants can get overheated easily, and they can't cool themselves down the way adults can.

4. If you're going for a longish walk in the summer, try to go before 10:00 A.M. or after 4:00 P.M., when the sun's rays are less intense. It's okay to take a quick 15-minute walk at peak sun times, but make sure that your baby is wearing tightly woven cotton clothing that covers his arms and legs and that his face is shaded by the baby carriage canopy or by an umbrella.

Then, one day, I found a pair of old white socks that my husband was throwing out. I put the socks on my son, and they came up over his knees. So now, whenever we go outside, he wears his big socks, and he can crawl around without hurting his knees.

Dina Roach, *Lilburn, Georgia*

better
breastfeeding

2

breastfeeding can be a wonderful bonding experience for you and your baby. And, as research shows, it's also one of the best ways to protect your newborn's health—both now and for years to come.

Studies have found that breastfeeding strengthens your child's immune system, helps guard against ear infections and allergies, lowers his risk of sudden infant death syndrome (SIDS), and may even boost his brainpower. For these reasons, the American Academy of Pediatrics recommends breastfeeding for the first year of your child's life.

If that isn't practical, nursing for a shorter period of time—even 2 or 3 months—is still beneficial. Of course, as any mom can tell you, breastfeeding can be physically exhausting, and sometimes painful, especially in the first few weeks. And if your baby won't nurse or simply can't latch on, the experience can be frustrating for both of you. The tips in this chapter will help make you and your baby breastfeeding pros.

getting started

Start in a Quiet Environment

For the first few weeks, I breastfed my son in his bedroom with a CD of lullabies playing. It really helped me relax and focus on what I was doing, so I could trust that my son was getting enough to eat. Only when I was certain that we were both comfortable with our nursing schedule and rhythm did I start to breastfeed while watching TV or when other things were going on around me. By that point, I was much more confident, which made for better feedings.

Gina Lanning, *Euless, Texas*

Make Mini-Goals

Breastfeeding isn't always easy. In fact, the first 2 weeks were really difficult for me: I felt as if all my newborn daughter and I did was cry and get frustrated. My original goal had been to breastfeed for 6 months, but after those first 2 weeks, I reset the goal to 1 month. When I achieved that, I set it for another month, and so on. Setting these short-term goals helped me feel that each month was an accomplishment, and that even if I quit at the end of the month, I had achieved my goal. Every time you nurse your baby, you're doing a wonderful thing, so whether you manage to nurse for 1 day or 1 year, applaud your efforts.

Susan Jervis, *Dundas, Ontario, Canada*

Breathing Lessons

When I breastfed my son, I couldn't believe how much it hurt during the first few weeks, especially when he latched on. But I found that using Lamaze breathing during the first few minutes really helped—it kept me calm and made me focus all of my attention on my son.

Cathy Meisterich, *Yorktown Heights, New York*

Trust Your Instincts

Don't let anyone discourage you from breastfeeding if it's what you want to do. For the first few days after my son was born, he had a very hard time learning to latch on. The nurses in the hospital encouraged me to use a bottle, but I decided to keep trying to nurse. It was very stressful, but I

your baby's first month

The first few weeks with your new baby are an exhilarating time. But they can also be stressful when your infant isn't feeding like you think she's supposed to. These guidelines can help you prepare for your baby's earliest eating habits.

✓ Nurse your baby within 1 hour of giving birth. You should also ask for 24-hour access to your baby while you are in the hospital. This way, you can nurse her whenever she wants and for as long as she wants during those important first days. It's also a good idea to tell the nurses that you intend to breastfeed and ask that they don't give your baby a bottle.

✓ Expect your infant to eat 10 to 14 times in a 24-hour period during the first week. She will also go through a period of cluster feedings—wanting to nurse several times in a few hours. The two most common times for cluster feedings are midnight to 4:00 A.M. and late afternoon to early evening.

✓ Don't wait until your breasts feel full to nurse. Feed your baby when she shows signs of hunger, such as stretching, alertness, mouthing, yawning, putting her hand to her mouth, or *rooting,* where she opens her mouth and turns her head toward whatever is touching her cheek.

✓ Expect engorgement, which happens within a few days after your baby is born. When milk comes in, it can be extremely painful. Apply warm compresses to relieve the discomfort. You may also want to try using a breast pump for a few minutes before you nurse to get the milk flowing and soften the nipples, so your baby can latch on more easily.

✓ Begin feeding on the breast that you ended with the last time, and expect your baby to feed for 10 to 15 minutes on each breast. If she doesn't have at least six wet diapers a day, she could be at risk for inadequate weight gain. She should also have two to four bowel movements a day.

knew that at home, with a little peace and quiet, it would work. My son is now 11 months old and thriving—and I'm still breastfeeding!

Donya Rhett, *Bronx, New York*

Pain Reliever

Before I had my son, I had no idea how painful engorgement could be. A friend's suggestion really helped: I soaked a disposable diaper in hot water and placed it on my chest like a compress while standing in the shower or sitting in the tub. A diaper can hold an amazing amount of water, and it stays warm longer than a washcloth. The heat got the milk flowing almost immediately.

Leslie Johnson, New York City

secrets to better breastfeeding

Ask any mother and she'll tell you: Breastfeeding can be daunting, especially when you first get home from the hospital and you're on your own. But these simple strategies from Cecelia Deslauriers, R.N., a certified lactation consultant in Highland Park, Illinois, can take much of the stress—and discomfort—out of your nursing experience.

Be prepared. Take prenatal breastfeeding classes, call La Leche League for information, or visit a lactation consultant during your pregnancy. "Do whatever you need to do to get your questions answered," says Deslauriers. Building a network of friends and family who have breastfed is also useful for those times when you need advice and support.

Get Dad involved. Have your husband come to a prenatal breastfeeding class so the lactation consultant can explain to him how to position the baby. "The father needs to know this. After all, he'll be there at 2:00 A.M. when Mom and baby are both sleep-deprived and things aren't working right," she says. "He may be the only one who can think clearly enough to position the baby correctly."

Assume the position. Soreness is often a result of incorrect positioning. Sit in a comfortable chair with good support and use a pillow for your arms. For baby to feed, her mouth should be squarely in line with your nipple—you shouldn't have to move your breast to either side. Putting four fingers under your breast, lift it and lightly touch your nipple to baby's top lip. Wait for her to open wide with a yawn, then bring her in close so she is completely latched on and her chin is tucked into your breast.

Soothe sore nipples. A breastfeeding mom's nipples can get dry and cracked. "In the past, women were told to air dry their nipples to avoid soreness," says Deslauriers. "We now know that this doesn't help and may actually make dryness worse." To relieve discomfort, after each feeding, rub on a lanolin-based product, such as Lansinoh, that doesn't need to be washed off before the next feeding.

breastfeeding basics

Trade Off Breast and Bottle

I didn't introduce the bottle until my baby was 3 months old, and by then, she wouldn't take it. With the next baby, I'll start giving some bottles of pumped breast milk within the first month. It will help the baby get used to a bottle—and give my husband a chance to feed her and bond with her early on.

Susan Drumheller, Coeur d'Alene, Idaho

A Daily Diaper Count

As a breastfeeding mother, I need to keep track of how many diapers my newborn son wets each day to be sure that he's getting enough milk. An easy way to do it: I set out eight diapers each morning. As long as they're gone by the end of the day, I don't worry.

Emily Simmons, Athens, Alabama

Watch Your Diet

When I breastfed my daughter, I discovered that many foods—especially acidic ones, such as orange juice and tomato sauce—made her colicky and unhappy. And when I ate broccoli one evening, she was particularly gassy the next day. So, for those first few months, I tried to avoid things that really disagreed

burping 101

Babies often swallow air during feedings. The only way to release this gas buildup is by burping. Depending on how much air your baby swallows, he may need to be burped before you switch breasts. Look to see whether he refuses to go to the other breast, grimaces, or seems uncomfortable. If he is perfectly content, feed from both breasts before burping. Below are the three most popular burping positions.

✓ Hold him in an upright position against your body, with his head resting on your shoulder, then gently pat his back.

✓ Lay him facedown across your knees or forearm, using one hand to hold him safely in place and the other to rub his back.

✓ Sit him up on your knee facing to the side, using one hand to support his chest and chin. With the other hand, rub his back.

how your diet affects baby

Food facts: A breastfeeding mother should eat approximately 500 extra calories a day to keep her milk production up. Try eating nutrient-dense foods such as fruits, vegetables, fish, tofu, and yogurt. At the same time, you may discover that certain foods disagree with your baby when they are passed on through breast milk. While every baby is different, the most common "fussy" foods include dairy products, cruciferous vegetables, anything spicy, and drinks that contain caffeine. You may want to cut out or limit for a while those foods that seem to bother your baby, then try to slowly reintroduce them to your diet.

Is a cocktail okay? New mothers may also want to relax from time to time with an alcoholic beverage. Experts agree that having one or two glasses of beer or wine on occasion is perfectly fine and will not harm your baby. But it's a good idea to minimize the amount of alcohol that gets passed on to your infant by breastfeeding immediately before you drink and then waiting at least 2 hours afterward before you nurse again.

with her. As she got older, I was able to introduce these foods back into my diet without a fuss from her.

Katerina Balint, Bayonne, New Jersey

feeding time!

Forget Following a Schedule

After I brought my son home from the hospital, I tried to follow the feeding schedule that's recommended in many of the books—every 3 hours for 10 minutes on each breast. Pretty soon it became clear that Sam preferred his own schedule, which was whenever and for as long as he wanted. Once I decided to not get too hung up on the rules and to go with Sam's personality, things went much more smoothly.

Nitza Wilon, New York City

Simple Memory Aid

I had trouble remembering which side my son had last nursed on until I had this idea: Since I use a pillow anyway, I started leaving it on the arm of the chair that we were sitting in, on the side he had just nursed on. I never had trouble remembering again.

Cheryl Bayer, *Abingdon, Maryland*

Track Feedings in a Journal

It's amazing how often you must breastfeed in the first few months—it seemed like my son was permanently attached to my breast! Since he didn't nurse according to a schedule, I kept track of his feedings (how often and for how long) by keeping a journal. It also really helped my son's pediatrician see how he was progressing and make sure he was eating enough. Finally, because I wasn't comfortable nursing my baby in public, I found that it worked best to run errands immediately after I fed him. That way, he was content for a few hours and I didn't have to worry about finding a discreet place to nurse.

Nancy Deehan, *Norwood, Massachusetts*

Feed on Demand

Don't try to feed your baby on a schedule; it just doesn't work. With my son, I very quickly learned how to clue in to the fact that he was hungry: He would smack his lips and rub his hands against his mouth. When he was a newborn, we fed pretty much around the clock—there was never more than a 2- to 3-hour break between feedings, and sometimes only an hour break during daytime feedings. What helped me keep my energy up and feel good were two things: I continued to take my prenatal vitamins, and I always had a pitcher of water next to me while I nursed to help quench my thirst.

Julie Ries, *Brooklyn, New York*

pediatrician on call

when mom's on medication

When you're breastfeeding, it's not necessary to tough it out if you have a splitting headache, says pediatrician and *Parents* contributing editor Laura Nathanson, M.D. Many over-the-counter and prescription medications, including acetaminophen and most antibiotics, will not harm a breastfed baby.

But before you get any prescription or take any new drug, make sure that your doctor knows you're nursing. Certain drugs—including those for cancer, sedation, or such chronic conditions as high blood pressure or arthritis—can endanger a nursing baby.

nursing 9 to 5

Reconnecting at the End of the Day

Breastfeeding was a wonderful experience for me and my son Jake. I knew many mothers who stopped nursing before they went back to work because they thought it would be too hard to sustain, but I was determined to continue. After talking to my boss, I found a room where I could pump twice a day. And as soon as I picked up my son at the end of the day, I immediately went home and breastfed. It was such a special time for us to reconnect. Nursing around a work schedule may take a little more effort than bottlefeeding, but for me it was well worth it.

Licia Lichliter, Dallas

Learn How to Multitask

When I returned to work, I tried pumping three or four times a day. Between the setup, cleaning, and pumping time, I felt like I wasn't getting any work done, so I decided to cut back to twice a day. I got more milk at each session and found it

it's my job

survival strategies for working moms

If you're a new mother returning to work after maternity leave, you may be nervous about pumping breast milk at the office. These tips from Carol Huotari, manager of the Center for Breastfeeding Information at La Leche League International in Schaumburg, Illinois, and a mother of six, can help ease that anxiety.

✓ Ask your boss to help you find a discreet place to pump, such as an empty office, a conference room, or a private bathroom. You'll need to pump two to three times a day for 15 to 30 minutes, so discuss with your boss how you'll make up that time.

✓ Wear clothing that's easy to pump in, such as a button-down cotton shirt or a loose pullover, and keep an extra blouse at work in case of spills or leakage.

✓ If you store your milk in a communal refrigerator, keep it in a labeled brown bag.

much less stressful. I also tried to find ways to make use of the time I spent pumping. For example, I scheduled phone calls, using a headset, during these sessions. No one at the other end ever said anything about the sound of the pump, and it helped me get two things done at once.

Catherine Jackson, Pelham, New York

If You Can't Pump at the Office, That's Okay

Expressing milk at the office wasn't an option for me—there was no place to do it, and my schedule didn't really allow it. Still, I wanted to continue nursing. What worked for me was breastfeeding my son in the morning, immediately after work, then at night. During the day, he had formula. My body quickly adapted to this schedule; I didn't even have problems with leaking during the day. My son had no problems adjusting to this mix of formula and breast milk, and we kept it up until he was 8 months old.

Jeanne Skettino, Concord, Massachusetts

save time, money, and stress

Express Milk for Errands

When I began breastfeeding, I was uncomfortable about exposing myself when I had to feed my baby in public. To solve this problem, I started expressing my milk. Whenever I had to run errands, I would put a bottle of milk in a cooler pack. If I went somewhere that I felt was unsuitable for breastfeeding, I just fed her from the bottle.

Diane Washington, Seaside, California

Cut Down on Pumping Time

Because my son often only nursed from one breast at each feeding, I started using a manual breast pump that could be operated with just one hand. (Some require both hands.) With a little practice, I learned how to pump one breast while I cradled and fed my son from the other. I then saved the milk for his middle-of-the-night feeding, which my husband was in charge of. Believe me, it was a huge time-saver—and it helped me get some much-needed sleep!

Jane Lanzillo, Newton, Massachusetts

Easy-Freeze Breast Milk

Every method I used to freeze breast milk was messy, space-consuming, or hard to measure and thaw. Then I heard about the perfect solution: ice cube trays. Each section of the tray holds 1 ounce. Once the cubes freeze, I put them in plastic bags with the date. They defrost quickly in a measuring cup and pour neatly into a bottle.

Sandra Buchalter,
Shoemakersville, Pennsylvania

Share and Save

Most breast pumps caution that they should be used by only one person. But I discovered that a good pump can be very expensive—mine was close to $250. You can buy duplicates of the parts that come in contact with your breasts and the milk, so when I was done with mine, I gave it to a friend to use. She bought the kit of replacement parts and managed to save a lot of money in the process.

Sherri Lerner, Highland Park, New Jersey

the late show

Keep Track of Nighttime Feedings

As a sleep-deprived new mom, I often had trouble remembering exactly when I had last fed my baby. So I removed the face cover from a nonworking clock and hung it over the changing table. After each feeding, I moved the hands to the current time. I didn't have to jot anything down, which helped if I managed to sneak in a nap: My husband could tell at a glance when the baby had last been fed without having to wake me.

Aori Vonada–Miao, Avondale, Pennsylvania

Glow with the Flow

When my children were babies, I made nighttime feedings a little easier by putting a soft blue lightbulb in the lamp by my bed. The gentle glow was just bright enough for me to see by, so it didn't hurt my eyes or wake my husband.

Irina Klein, Ridgecrest, California

Snooze Buster

I was often so tired when I nursed my infant daughter in the middle of the night that I worried I'd fall asleep with her in my arms. To alleviate this fear, I put a timer in her room and set it for 10 minutes when I started nursing. That way, if I did doze off, the timer would wake me up before I fell into a deep sleep. I would then reset it for another 10 minutes until the baby was done on the other side. This little measure gave me peace of mind during some very exhausting nights!

Amy Purdy, Buffalo

A Little Light at a Time

Before my daughter was born, I bought a three-way touch lamp for the nursery. During the night, I could quickly and quietly turn on the dimmest light with one touch as I nursed her, without having to worry about startling her with a bright light. Now that she's older, she enjoys being able to turn on the light by herself when she enters her room and turn it off as she leaves.

Katie Melmer, Edina, Minnesota

sidetracking sibling rivalry

Keep Big Sis Busy

Recently, when our second child was born, I was worried about my 2-year-old daughter's reaction to the amount of time I'd be spending with the new baby—especially when I was breastfeeding. To help Maddi feel special, I emptied out a space in a cabinet within her reach. Each morning, I fill this spot with fruit snacks, cereal bars, coloring books, and other small treats to keep her occupied. Now, I know that Maddi can find anything she needs when I'm busy with the baby, and the cabinet of treasures usually keeps her attention long enough for me to breastfeed without interruption.

Sandi Bruegger, St. Louis

expert help for fussy babies

If your baby fusses after each feeding, the problem may be in the way you nurse her. "Most babies need to nurse from both breasts at each feeding, but switching sides too early may prevent an infant from getting enough hind-milk," says Judy Hopkinson, Ph.D., an assistant professor of pediatrics at Baylor College of Medicine in Houston.

The composition of breast milk changes over the course of a feeding, and hindmilk, which is richer in fat and slows the passage of nutrients through the intestines, flows during the latter part, just before you finish on each breast. Without it, your baby's stomach may empty too fast. This leaves much of the lactose in breast milk undigested, producing gas.

The solution: Let your baby empty one breast completely (she'll lose interest and let go when it's empty) before switching sides. If she doesn't want the second breast, wait until the next feeding to alternate, or pump and save your milk.

Make Both Kids Happy

When I was nursing my second daughter, my 2-year-old daughter always wanted to climb onto my lap. Since it's hard to hold two children while nursing, we played a variation on "Simon says": I'd give her simple commands, without trying to trick her. She enjoyed jumping, rolling, dancing, patting her head—and being the center of my attention.

Suzi Rowe, Colorado Springs, Colorado

Get Everyone Involved

With seven children, I learned very quickly the importance of getting my older children involved with the new baby's care. When I nursed, I had them take turns holding the baby before and after I breastfed, changing diapers, and burping the baby—carefully supervised, of course. This especially helped the next-oldest child, who was often only 2 years older than the new arrival, feel like a big boy rather than be upset that his position as "baby" of the family had been taken over.

Kathy Dillon, Philadelphia

breast pump buyer's guide

Before you buy or rent a breast pump, decide which style is right for you. The guidelines below can help. Then, once you've narrowed the field, choose a model that has the features listed at bottom, advises consumer expert Sandy Jones, author of the *Consumer Reports Guide to Baby Products*.

Hospital-grade pumps are best for moms who need to pump often to maintain a strong milk supply, such as those with twins or triplets. These pumps are also the best option for mothers of premature babies or babies who cannot nurse at the breast immediately, for establishing their milk supply. They are available at rental stores nationwide.

Portable electric pumps copy some of the features of hospital-grade pumps—a variety of suction strengths, dual pumping, and automatic cycling, which mimics the sucking rhythm of nursing. Faster than manual pumps, many electrics are capable of pumping both breasts at once, making them the pump of choice for working moms. Some also offer car adapters or rechargeable battery packs for when you're on the go.

Manual pumps can be a comfortable and discreet option for expressing milk. They're smaller than electric pumps and operate silently. Most allow you to control the vacuum pressure with a pull or squeeze of the hand. Many working moms who have little privacy at their office prefer manuals because they do not make as much noise as other pumps.

Look for these features no matter which pump you decide to buy:

✓ A well-fitting breast shield that's angled for comfortable positioning. It should also provide an airtight seal with no scratchy edges.

✓ Storage bottles and other removable components that are dishwasher-safe

✓ A compact, lightweight design, as well as a discreet travel case for carrying the pump everywhere you go. Cases that have insulated compartments and cold packs for storing milk are a plus.

✓ A toll-free customer support line for getting help

In electrics only:

✓ An optional battery pack or adapter for an auto cigarette lighter outlet

✓ Adjustable suction strength to ensure comfort

✓ Quiet operation for privacy in bathroom stalls or offices

✓ A control knob or fingertip valve that interrupts the vacuum to mimic your baby's natural sucking rhythms—suction bursts every 2 to 3 seconds. Some electric pumps have this feature built in. Automatic cycling can be very helpful, especially when the speed is adjustable.

anatomy of a nursing bra

For a nursing bra that fits and flatters, follow these tips.

✓ To ensure a good fit throughout your nursing months, shop for bras during the last trimester of your pregnancy.

✓ For the most accurate fit, bring breast pads or shields with you and slip them into the cups when you try on the bra.

✓ Look for a bra with roomy cups—the upper sides should be somewhat loose—to accommodate your breasts as they change in shape and size.

✓ Make sure that the band doesn't ride up in the back. If it does, the cups and straps may be too tight. The center of the bra should lie flat against your breastbone.

Feed the Family

When my third child was born, I was a little concerned about how my other two children would react. I didn't want them to feel jealous of their new sister, so whenever it was possible, I breastfed while they were eating lunch or dinner. That way, I could sit at the table and talk to them while I nursed, and all the girls felt like they had my total attention at mealtimes.

Lisa Zaprzalka, *Calcium, New York*

keeping
baby healthy

3

from the moment your baby is born, you're in charge of keeping her healthy and safe. She emerges from the comfort and security of your womb into a world teeming with bacteria, so warding off germs is a constant challenge. A baby's silky-smooth skin is also sensitive and easily irritated. It can look and feel flawless one day, then break out in a rash or scaly patches the next.

Between round-the-clock feedings and diaper changes, you'll no doubt find yourself searching for answers to common problems. What's the best way to prevent diaper rash or treat cradle cap? How do you soothe a colicky baby or deal with your child's first cold? In this chapter you'll find simple, mom-tested solutions to keep your newborn healthy and happy.

colic cures

Head Outside

A little fresh air seemed to calm our colicky son, at least for a while. We also made sure his older sister's video-watching time coincided with his fussiest periods, so she'd feel less left out when we had to tend to him.

Joellen Jones, *Simpsonville, South Carolina*

Try White Noise

I made a tape of the vacuum cleaner and other appliances running. Playing it for my son while I rocked him helped him calm down.

Kathy Belt, *Henderson, Kentucky*

Go for a Ride

A trip in the car can work miracles. Many a night my husband could be found taking our colicky baby daughter for a spin around the neighborhood.

Kim Kotlow, *Franklin Park, Illinois*

Good Vibrations

We strapped our newborn son into his car seat and placed it on top of the clothes dryer—and kept one hand on the seat at all times, of course. I'm not sure if it was the vibrating motion or the hum of the machine, but he calmed down in minutes.

Mary Beth Randall,
Franklin, Massachusetts

grandmother knows best

Whenever one of my four children had a case of prickly heat, this simple remedy brought quick relief. After giving a sponge bath with tepid water, I would shake a little cornstarch on a cotton ball and smooth it under my baby's arms, behind the knees—wherever there were any folds or creases. Using a cotton ball rather than sprinkling the cornstarch directly on the skin also prevented her from breathing in any airborne "clouds" of the stuff. Although I came up with this treatment more than 30 years ago, it's worked well for my grandkids, too.

Shirley McCutcheon,
Plymouth, Massachusetts

skin soothers

Soft Touch

Instead of using my fingers to smooth diaper rash ointment on my daughter, I apply it with a clean makeup sponge. The ointment goes on faster and more

take the ouch out of diaper rash

Until your child has mastered the potty, she's bound to get a case of diaper rash—especially during infancy, when her skin is extra delicate. Here's what you need to know to make it better.

The cause: When you don't change a wet or soiled diaper right away, the diaper holds the urine or feces next to the baby's tender skin. Ammonia in the urine and enzymes in the stool can inflame and irritate the outer layer of skin. And warm, moist environments can breed certain bacteria and yeast. If your baby has diarrhea or takes antibiotics, she may be at risk for a type of diaper rash known as yeast infection.

What the rash looks like: Reddening and/or small bumps on the genitals, buttocks, and lower abdomen. If you see angry red patches, blisters, and/or scattered pimples with whiteheads, especially in the folds of the skin, your baby may have a yeast infection.

Soothing secrets: Frequent diaper changes help. Change soiled diapers as soon as possible and change wet diapers at least every 2 hours during the day. Cleanse and rinse the diaper area, then blot dry. Do not rub; it only irritates your baby's skin. To ease symptoms, smooth on petroleum jelly or zinc oxide. For rash caused by a yeast infection, apply an antifungal cream, such as Lotrimin AF.

When to dial the doctor: If diaper rash doesn't clear up after 3 days of treatment, call your pediatrician. You should also call if blisters appear or if your baby develops a fever.

evenly, and there's less chance of scratching her little bottom with my nails.

Sara Fujimura, West Milford, New Jersey

Diaper Trick

I apply diaper rash ointment straight from the tube to the inside of the diaper. Then I fold the diaper in half and rub the two ends together to evenly distribute the ointment. It's neater and makes me feel that I've minimized the chances of spreading any germs to my daughter by using my hands.

Marla Bazar Sochet, Syosset, New York

Dry Idea

At my pediatrician's suggestion, I bathed my 6-week-old daughter Kerry just before her bedtime as a way of relaxing her. But I was concerned that daily baths might dry her skin. To keep it soft, I applied a little baby lotion after I towel-dried her, but not to her hands or face. This helped prevent her from rubbing the lotion into her eyes or getting it into her mouth.

Cara Blatney, *Darien, Connecticut*

A Treat for Baby and Mom

When each of my three children were infants, I preferred treating diaper rash with A + D ointment rather than zinc oxide formulas. I found the A + D ointment easier to apply because it's not as thick. It also helped soften my hands and left my nails in great condition!

Linda Fears, *Chappaqua, New York*

protect your baby from SIDS

Putting your baby to sleep on her back is the most effective way to minimize the risk of sudden infant death syndrome (SIDS). There are also other precautions you can take that can help your baby (and you) to breathe easier.

✓ Keep the crib clutter-free. To lower the odds of suffocation during sleep, don't use plush bedding such as comforters, pillows, and fluffy blankets, and remove any stuffed animals. Make sure that the crib mattress is firm and flat and that the sheet is tucked in securely at the corners. Dress your baby in a warm sleeper in lieu of a blanket. And check that crib bumpers are tied tightly to side rails.

✓ Breastfeed when you can. Try to breastfeed your baby until she is at least 7 months old, the age when infants are less at risk for SIDS. Scientists are not sure why, but infants who are breastfed at least some of the time are less likely to die of SIDS.

✓ Don't overheat your baby. When a baby is too warm, her risk of SIDS increases. One theory is that heat can make an infant sleep more deeply. If a room is warm enough for you, it's also fine for your baby. But if your baby is perspiring or breathing hard, or if her hair is damp, take off layers of clothing until she is cooler and more comfortable.

✓ Don't smoke. Tobacco smoke may cause an abnormality in the brain that prevents an infant from responding to a lack of oxygen while she's in a deep sleep. Scientists have found that women who smoke during pregnancy are three times as likely to have a SIDS baby as nonsmoking mothers. Exposing an infant to passive smoke can also double her risk.

Grandma's Little Helper

My mother's favorite diaper rash treatment was good old Vaseline, and now I use it every time I change my 3-month-old daughter, Hayley. It seems to soften her skin as well as protect against wetness. She's had diaper rash only once and the Vaseline helped to clear it up in a day. I also try to let her air dry for a few minutes before putting on a fresh diaper.

Debra Princz, *Plantation, Florida*

TLC for Tender Skin

For the first year after my son Caleb was born, I was reluctant to use baby wipes. His skin was so delicate; I didn't want any perfumes or chemicals to touch it. At each diaper change, I simply used plain tap water and a soft, fresh washcloth to clean him. It worked—Caleb never got diaper rash.

Amanda Nadeau, *Brooklyn, New York*

treating cradle cap

Shampoo Strategy

Both of our daughters were born with lots of hair. To treat cradle cap, we put a tiny bit of baby shampoo on a fine-tooth infant's comb and gently combed over the scaly area. When we rinsed the shampoo, the loosened scales were washed away.

Anne and Ben McLaughlin, *Cheshire, Connecticut*

Alternative to Baby Oil

When my son was around 5 months old, he had a really stubborn case of cradle cap. My solution was to grease up his head with Aquaphor, an ointment that's thicker than baby oil, then put him to bed wearing a cotton cap. The next morning, I combed out what I could, shampooed my son's hair and scalp, and then did another Aquaphor treatment at night. After a few days, my son's scalp was clean and smooth.

Donna Campisano, *Livingston, New Jersey*

Gentle Massage

Both my son and daughter had cradle cap as infants. Using a soft-bristle baby brush, I would massage a hypoallergenic soap

pediatrician on call

little babies, big germs

Most illnesses are passed to babies via the hands. Newborns are particularly vulnerable to viruses and bacteria, since they don't start developing their own immunity until the age of about 6 weeks. Until then, they are totally dependent on the immunity that their mothers give them during pregnancy and from breast milk. So, don't think that you're being too fussy if you ask friends and family to wash up before touching your newborn baby. Protect your little one with these tips from pediatrician and *Parents* contributing editor Laura Nathanson, M.D.

✓ Before you let a guest (or another of your own children) hold the baby, ask her to wash her hands with soap and water.

✓ If guests or other children touch their eyes, noses, or mouths or use the toilet, they should wash their hands again before they pick up your baby.

✓ Obviously, adults or kids who are sick with a cold or the flu shouldn't visit.

all over the scalp. Next, I took a cradle cap comb and gently combed the scalp, then rinsed well. This process worked wonders for both children.

Cathleen Straley, *Yardley, Pennsylvania*

germ warfare

Touch Clothing, Not Skin

Having more than one child in the family increases the chances of spreading germs to our 5-month-old son, Graham. When my older boys want to play with Graham but haven't had time to wash their hands, I tell them they can touch areas covered by clothing, but not his bare skin. When the boys have playdates at our house, they give their friends the same reminder.

Loree Sandler, *Glencoe, Illinois*

Quick Cleanups

When my son Evan started teething at 4 months, his hands were always in his mouth. In addition to cleaning his hands at bathtime and during meals, I would wash them with a fresh baby wipe at every diaper change.

Bari Seiden, New York City

Take Along Toys

To minimize our 6-month-old son Connor's exposure to germs, my husband and I wash our hands constantly. I also wash Connor's toys frequently since everything he plays with ends up in his mouth. When we visit friends and family, I

does your thermometer measure up?

Follow our guide to decide which type of thermometer is right for your baby. And remember: When reporting a fever to your pediatrician, always tell him what part of the body you took the temperature from and which thermometer you used.

Mercury rectal thermometer: Can be used from birth. To use, coat bulb with petroleum jelly. Place your baby stomach down; slowly insert thermometer about ½ inch into the rectum. Hold for 2 minutes.

Advantages: Inexpensive; delivers the most accurate reading, which is essential for newborns.

Disadvantages: Fragile; mercury line can be hard to read.

Digital thermometer: Designed for oral or rectal use. It should be used in the rectum for newborns, and under the arm in babies 3 months and older. Hold in place for 2 to 3 minutes, or until thermometer beeps.

Advantages: Easy to read.

Disadvantages: Not as accurate as mercury rectal thermometer.

Instant axillary thermometer: For babies 3 months and older. Lift baby's arm and place thermometer in center of armpit; hold arm snugly against chest.

Advantages: Digital reading takes seconds.

Disadvantages: Less accurate than a mercury rectal thermometer under the arm; costs about $60.

bring along Connor's own toys for him to play with. At least I know that they're clean and I worry less about his picking up germs from other children's playthings.

Nancy Deehan, *Norwood, Massachusetts*

when baby gets sick

Stress-Free Temperature Taking

I've used the same method to take temperatures on all four of my children. I nurse my baby; as he relaxes and focuses on feeding, I carefully insert the thermometer into his rectum. Because he's so content, there's no squirming or fussing. And I feel better knowing that he's comfortable.

Kathleen Raines, *Bluemont, Virginia*

Bottlefeeding Medicine

My daughter Anna started getting ear infections when she was 4 months old. Since she enjoyed drinking from a bottle, my husband and I would put her liquid antibiotic in her baby bottle with diluted fruit juice. When she was colicky,

it's my job

bundling up baby

For quick trips outdoors, even in chilly temperatures, there's no need to bundle up your newborn as if you're taking a trip to the Arctic. "Dress him in layers, plus a hat or hood, to protect him from the cold and wind," says Minneapolis pediatrician Marjorie Hogan, M.D., a spokesperson for the American Academy of Pediatrics. Use a bunting or blanket to keep him cozy; snowsuits are much harder to take off once you're inside a warm car or home, she says.

Babies can regulate their own body heat but are affected by temperature changes more quickly than adults. Indoors, your baby should be dressed in the same number of layers as you are. An easy test: Feel your infant's belly and feet. It's normal for his toes to be slightly cooler than his warm tummy. If both are cool, add another layer.

charting a fever

What does the reading on baby's thermometer mean? 98.6°F is a typical healthy temperature, but a reading slightly lower or higher than 98.6°F can also be healthy. When should you call your pediatrician? Use this simple age-by-age chart as your guide.

Age	Temperature	What to Do
0–3 months	100.2°F or higher	Call your doctor immediately; give baby extra fluids; give infants 2 months and older acetaminophen infant drops
3–6 months	101°F or higher	Call your doctor immediately; give baby extra fluids; give acetaminophen infant drops
6–12 months	102°F (low-grade fever) to 102.5°F (moderate fever)	Give baby extra fluids; give acetaminophen infant drops; call the doctor if the fever is higher than 102.5°F

we'd mix the medication with unsweetened chamomile tea. Drinking her medicine made things less stressful for everyone.

Janet Hurley, *Iselin, New Jersey*

Cold Care

When my daughter Regan was an infant and came down with her first cold, I was frightened because she seemed so congested. To ease her coughing, I took her into the bathroom, closed the door, and ran a hot shower. While I held her, the steam helped to clear the congestion. Sometimes I'd place her in the stroller with her head slightly elevated so that she could rest while the steam worked. I also put saline drops in a bulb syringe to unstuff her nose.

Bridget Murphy, *Sea Girt, New Jersey*

is it spit-up or vomit?

Sometimes it's hard to tell. It's not always the texture and color that make the difference between the two. Spitting up is passive and it's normal. Your baby may dribble out a silver-dollar-size amount of curdled milk or formula. Vomiting is forceful, and it's a signal that your baby is ill. Also, with vomiting, you can see your baby's eyes dilating and watering and his stomach muscles contracting.

If your baby vomits after every feeding or if the vomit is a bright green liquid, call your doctor. There is a chance that he may have an obstruction in his intestine. Or he may have rotavirus, a gastrointestinal virus that almost all children under the age of 3 get at some point. Symptoms for the two conditions are similar, so it's important for your doctor to make the correct diagnosis.

If the stream of liquid spurts forcefully from your baby's mouth (projectile vomiting), your baby might have pyloric stenosis. This occurs when the muscle that encircles the opening to the stomach thickens. As a result, the passageway from the stomach to the small intestine narrows, making it difficult to digest food well. Your baby's stomach churns, making him throw up forcefully. Fortunately, this condition can be treated with minor surgery.

Bathe Away a Fever

I get into a lukewarm bath with my 10-month-old when she comes down with a fever. Being immersed in the water helps to bring down her temperature, and we both have a chance to relax. For fevers 101°F or higher, I give her infant Tylenol drops. To increase her fluid intake, I also nurse my daughter more frequently throughout the day.

Diane Washington, *Seaside, California*

Timing Is Everything

I found that medicines labeled "to be given before or after a meal" were easier to give before a feeding. When my infant's tummy was empty, she was less likely to spit up her medicine, and, because she was hungry, she was more likely to "open wide."

Marianne Straley, *Iselin, New Jersey*

food and nutrition

formulas,
solids, **and more**

4

feeding your baby during her first year of life is quite an adventure. Although it's a treat to bond with your baby when she's just taking formula, the real fun begins with her first spoonfuls of rice cereal, peaches, and sweet potatoes.

Most babies begin solids between the ages of 5 and 6 months, starting with very diluted cereal and working their way up to well-cooked pasta at around 8 months. Whether she chooses to love prunes or spit out peas, your baby's introduction to the joys of eating is guaranteed to produce many picture-perfect moments.

bottle basics

Baby Knows Best

The most important thing to remember about babies and feeding schedules is that the two don't go together! When a baby is hungry, feed him. You'll have the rest of your life and theirs to be on a schedule.

Rebecca Barnett, Oak Park, Illinois

A Clever Bottle System

When my son Bryan was born, we had trouble keeping track of his bottles. They always seemed to fall over in the refrigerator and my husband would put them in a different place than I would. Since formula can only last a few days once opened and mixed, I needed a way to keep the bottles fresh and neat. So, I created a bottle organizer. I took a six-pack cardboard container (like the kind that holds soda bottles) and covered it with blue Con-Tact paper. We place the older bottles in front and the newer bottles in the back row. Now, we always know how many bottles we have on hand and where to find them!

Lori Moriarty, Indian Springs, Ohio

Keep It Cool

My baby got so used to drinking warm formula that he wouldn't take a bottle at room temperature. This became a real hassle when we were out running errands. If I had to do it

grandmother knows best

As a mother who bottlefed her children, I would like to send out a word of support to those women who, for one reason or another, simply cannot breastfeed. I know that it can leave you feeling inadequate—but there's no reason to feel that way. My daughter Krista went through this. After many tries, my infant granddaughter Anna still wasn't wetting her diapers, so Krista decided to try a bottle instead. She and my son-in-law now make meals into a special family time. They both hold Anna very close to their chests, rocking and singing to her. Breastfeeding is wonderful, but it isn't right for everyone.

Karen Brooks, Muncie, Indiana

milk matters

If you plan to switch from breast milk to formula, talk to your pediatrician about which type of formula is best. Here's a look at the basics.

Cow's-milk-based formula: An iron-fortified version is recommended for most infants. It's the best alternative to breast milk. Check with your pediatrician to determine whether the low-iron or regular iron-fortified version is best for your baby.

Soy formula: Uses soy as the protein source. This is ideal for babies who can't tolerate cow's-milk protein or lactose.

Protein hydrolysate: Made with predigested proteins, this is for infants with severe allergies to cow's milk or soy, and those with gastrointestinal problems. It's expensive and should be used only under a doctor's supervision.

Whole cow's milk: This is appropriate only after the age of 1. It's low in iron, so make sure that your toddler gets the mineral from other foods. Switch to low-fat milk only after age 2.

Soy milk and rice milk: Either of these can be used as an alternative to cow's milk for children over age 1, but make sure that the milk is fortified with calcium and vitamin D.

again, I would have given him room-temperature bottles from the beginning.

Laura Owens, Bala Cynwyd, Pennsylvania

minimizing mess

Neater Eater

We love those hard plastic bibs with the gutter at the bottom—they're really great for protecting our baby's clothes. Leo, our 7-month-old son, loves to try to feed himself, but he drops the spoon a lot, and the bib catches it before it can fall to the floor. Also, we've found a vinyl smock to be especially helpful when we don't want to change Leo's outfit after dinner. We slip it on him after he's strapped into the high chair. Some food still manages to sneak in and get on his clothes, but at least he doesn't get totally smeared.

Ken Miller, Brooklyn, New York

A Smarter Bib Fastener

I always had trouble tying bibs on our children. The strings inevitably became tangled, or, if I tied them too loosely, the bib would come off while the baby was squirming. But then my husband found a no-tie method. Simply thread the strings through a plastic cord stop (the kind you see on sleeping bags and Windbreakers) and slide to the right length. You can buy the stops at fabric stores.

Lisa Palmer, *Salt Lake City*

Do the Twist

To make sure that her hair didn't get caught when I tied a bib on my daughter, I secured the bib on the side of her neck instead of at the nape.

Katerina Balint, *Bayonne, New Jersey*

---

it's my job

the lowdown on fruit juice

Fruit juices add a bit of diversity to your baby's palate, but are they necessary in the first year? No, says nutritionist and author Bridget Swinney, R.D. But if you do decide to get your baby all juiced up, follow her advice.

✓ Wait until your baby is at least 6 months old before giving her fruit juice, and always introduce solid fruit before juices.

✓ Avoid citrus juices, such as orange, since they're too acidic for small tummies. Apple and pear juices are also hard to digest. White grape juice is the least likely to cause diarrhea and cramping.

✓ Choose juices with 100 percent fruit whenever possible. Although some juice drinks are fortified with vitamin C, they lack fiber, protein, and other needed minerals.

✓ The American Academy of Pediatrics recommends giving babies no more than 4 ounces of juice per day.

✓ Dilute juice with water (half juice, half water) so that its concentrated sugars won't spoil your baby's appetite for breast milk or formula.

homemade baby food

Want to try cooking up fresh food for your baby? According to Ruth Yaron, author of *Super Baby Food*, you don't need special ingredients or equipment. Here is Yaron's recipe for homemade fruit and vegetable purées.

1. Choose produce as free of pesticides as possible. (Don't cook carrots for babies under 7 months, since they contain too many nitrates.)
2. Wash produce with soap that's specifically made to kill surface bacteria on food.
3. Peel all produce, particularly items with a waxy coating, such as apples and cucumbers, since babies can choke on them.
4. Steam the fruits and vegetables until they're well-cooked and very soft.
5. Purée in a blender until smooth. Scoop into ice cube trays and freeze. When it's mealtime, simply pop a cube out and thaw it in the microwave.

joys and frustrations of feeding

Self-Serve Baby Food

My 9-month-old daughter decided one day that she no longer wanted to be spoon-fed her baby food. But she wasn't ready to hold the spoon, and she had very few teeth. So I spread the baby food onto slices of whole-wheat bread and broke them into tiny pieces so she could feed herself. She loved the freedom, and I was glad that she was still eating well.

Katy Holmes, *Minneapolis*

A Great Way to Eat Together

My husband and I used to feed our son while we ate our own dinner, because we wanted to sit down as a family. But we soon realized how difficult it was to feed ourselves and him at the same time. Whoever was feeding him had to devote full attention to the task or he got mad! Switching off only meant that my husband and I wound up eating cold food. So now, we feed him right before we eat and then put him in his swing chair by the table.

Julie Ries, *Brooklyn, New York*

a solid beginning

From birth to about 4 months, your baby should be fed breast milk or formula. Babies who are fed solids before 4 months are more prone to food allergies and weight problems. At around 4 to 6 months, infants also lose the *extrusion reflex*, which causes them to throw up anything other than liquids. Around this time, babies are also able to sit up with support, hold their necks steady, and move their heads from side to side. Below are guidelines for introducing your baby to solid foods. Keep in mind that breast milk and formula should remain the bulk of a baby's diet until 8 months.

Starting out (4 to 6 months): Choose a time of day when he isn't too hungry or full. Begin with a small amount of iron-fortified rice cereal and blend well with breast milk or formula. Make sure that the consistency is very soupy; he will probably eat only a couple of spoonfuls. Add less liquid each day, and wait until he's about 6 months to try cereal from barley, wheat, or oats.

Fruits and vegetables (6 to 8 months): Start with a few teaspoons of vegetables twice a day, eventually working up to 2 tablespoons twice a day. Try sweeter veggies first, such as sweet potatoes or butternut squash. Bring on the fruit after your baby has sampled a variety of yellow and green vegetables, and again work up to 2 tablespoons twice a day.

No more mush (7 to 10 months): If your baby is showing signs that he wants to eat some of your food, try giving him little bits of toast, well-cooked pasta, or tiny pieces of soft fruits and cooked chopped vegetables. You can also introduce jarred meats.

Finger foods (10 to 12 months): At this point, your baby might insist on feeding himself. Make it easier for him by serving foods such as mashed potatoes, soft casseroles, or even finely chopped chicken or fish. If he's not already, he may want to drink his formula or breast milk from a Sippy cup.

Raise Feeding Time to a New Level

When our daughter was finally ready to sit in her high chair, it was difficult to feed her because she constantly wanted to look down from her new, high vantage point. It was not easy getting food into her mouth when her head was tilted down. To get her to look up, I tied a brightly designed Mylar balloon to the back of the chair that I sat in to feed her. The balloon caught her attention and kept her fascinated throughout her meal.

Allison Wilhelm, Cedar Rapids, Iowa

Sweeten It Up

After I switched my son to formula at the age of 4 weeks, he experienced stomach problems. My doctor suggested that we switch him to soy formula, but when we fed it to him, he would make a horrible face. So, I started to put a little chocolate milk powder into his bottle. After several weeks, I gradually decreased the amount until he was drinking only formula.

Megan Crouch, Trenton, Ohio

Starving for Attention

It was always a challenge trying to feed my infant son and tend to my 2-year-old at the same time. So, I devised a way to keep both of them involved in feeding time. Before I would give the baby a bottle, I would set out a small cup of milk and a cookie on the table for my older son. I would then invite him to come over and sit down next to us and tell them both stories, usually about the two of them. This way, my older son felt involved in caring for his baby brother, and I didn't have to worry about his getting into trouble.

Joan Glaser, Owings Mills, Maryland

choking hazards

Once your child is eating real food, it's very exciting to have him try new things. But be careful! The following are potential choking hazards for children 3 and under:

- ✓ Chunks of meat
- ✓ Nuts
- ✓ Raw apple slices
- ✓ Jelly beans
- ✓ Hard candy
- ✓ Gumdrops
- ✓ Popcorn
- ✓ Raisins
- ✓ Hot dogs
- ✓ Grapes
- ✓ Raw carrots

solid advice

Just a Dab Will Do

When my son Caleb was about 4 months old, he was having trouble sleeping through the night. My pediatrician suggested adding a tiny bit of rice cereal to his bottle before bedtime, and it worked! After that, he had a better night's sleep.

Amanda Nadeau, New York City

Meaningful Munching

When my baby was about 4 months old, I would sit him at the table with us when we ate. After about a week, he started making chewing motions with his mouth. That's when I started him on rice cereal—and now he expects to eat when we do!

Chandra Morris, West Jefferson, Ohio

Read the Fine Print

When I found out that my baby was allergic to soy, I switched to a rice cereal that I thought would be safe. My best advice to parents is to always read the label! I soon dis-

off the shelf:
tips for store-bought baby food

- ✓ Always check the "use by" date on the container.
- ✓ When selecting jars at the grocery store, make sure that the vacuum seal button on the lid is flat. Discard the jar if it has popped up.
- ✓ Store unopened jars at room temperature in a kitchen cabinet.
- ✓ Make sure that you hear a "whoosh" or "pop" when you open the jar, which indicates that it hasn't been opened before.
- ✓ Save leftover baby food in an airtight container in the refrigerator no more than 2 or 3 days and then only if your baby didn't eat directly from the jar. If you feed your baby directly from the jar, you must throw the remainder out; saliva can cause bacteria to grow. If your baby can't eat an entire jar in one sitting, avoid wasting food by spooning out a serving into a separate dish.

babies and food allergies

Babies and toddlers are the most likely to suffer from food allergies since their digestive systems aren't fully developed. Therefore, some experts advise that parents should wait until their child is 6 months old to introduce solids, especially if there is a family history of allergies. The most common culprits? Cow's milk (which you shouldn't feed your baby until 12 months anyway), eggs, soy, wheat, and peanuts.

Always wait 4 to 7 days between each new food you introduce. That way, if your baby has an allergic reaction, you'll be able to identify the cause. Allergy symptoms usually occur within minutes to an hour after eating a particular food and then vanish within 24 hours. They include:

✓ Eczema

✓ Hives/rashes

✓ Runny nose/sneezing

✓ Nasal congestion

✓ Vomiting/diarrhea

If the following symptoms occur, seek medical help immediately. These indicate an intense allergic reaction, otherwise known as anaphylactic shock, which can be fatal:

✓ Wheezing

✓ Swelling of the lips, tongue, or throat

✓ Severe breathing difficulty

✓ Loss of consciousness

covered that although the cereal was labeled "rice," it still contained some soy.

Fran Karoff, Roslindale, Massachusetts

No Mystery Meat, Please

I have a rule about baby food: If I won't eat it, why should I expect my kids to? So, when I bought a jar of baby food meat and was unhappy about how processed it looked, I knew I could never try and feed it to my child. Instead, I gave my son the same meat as we ate, only I chose the leanest pieces, left it unseasoned, and ground it up to a fine paste so he wouldn't choke.

Kim Cinotto, Las Vegas

are baby bottles safe?

You may have heard alarming news suggesting that clear plastic baby bottles are dangerous because a chemical called bisphenol A (BPA) could leach out of heated plastic and into infant formula. Before you throw your bottles out, know that the U.S. FDA maintains that baby bottles are safe. The bottle panic was based on one small study done on lab mice. The FDA says that its on-going reviews have found no problems with normal daily bottle use and no health risks from food containers made of this type of plastic. If you want to be extra-safe, heat formula on the stovetop or use plastic liners.

raising a veggie lover

A Colorful Approach

I started feeding my son cereal at around 6 months old. When it was time to try other foods, I was very careful to start with the vegetables first, so he would not get a sweet tooth and turn them away later. I began with the white foods (homemade mashed potatoes), and I would give each one to him for at least 3 days before starting the next type of vegetable, to be sure that he didn't have an allergic reaction. Next came the orange veggies (such as squash), then the green. Once we had tried all the veg-

food IQ

You want the best nutrition for your baby, but the actual food is only part of the process. Mark Widome, M.D., a pediatrician and *Parents* advisory board member, offers the following advice for safe feedings.

✓ Never microwave a bottle of formula. Not only can this break down vital nutrients in the food but, more importantly, it also heats the milk unevenly, which may burn your baby's mouth. If your baby prefers warm formula, place the bottle in a pan of hot water.

✓ It's okay to mix formula with tap water. Unless you use well water that might be contaminated, you don't need to boil it first.

✓ Don't worry about sterilizing bottles, nipples, and pacifiers. Just toss them in a dishwasher or wash by hand with hot, soapy water.

gies, we moved on to fruit. If he didn't like one, I would try again in a few weeks, and he usually liked it then.

Monica Shirley, Ruston, Louisiana

Trickery Doesn't Hurt

Our foolproof method for getting our 7-month-old daughter to eat vegetables is to feed her a spoonful of fruit followed quickly by a spoonful of vegetables. She tastes the fruit first and doesn't even realize that she's eating the vegetables in the next bite.

Kimberly Irwin, Gruver, Texas

raising a
healthy eater

for kids, good nutrition and good health go hand in hand. Your child's body is developing so quickly that it needs constant nourishment to fuel energy stores, build strong bones and muscles, and boost brainpower. But bad eating habits—junky snacks, fatty fast food, sugary soda—are taking their toll on our kids.

According to the National Center for Health Statistics, in Hyattsville, Maryland, twice as many kids are overweight today than 30 years ago. That's why it's doubly important that you help your children develop a healthy diet early in life. Whether your kids are picky eaters, veggie haters, or sugar lovers, this chapter will show you how to ensure that your children get all the nutrients that they need to grow up big and strong.

making food fun

Just Add Sprinkles

When my son was first starting to eat table foods, it was hard for me to get him to try different fruits. He loved apple slices, but that was it. So, I took him to the grocery store to get a few different bottles of cake-decorating sprinkles. Whenever I gave him a new fruit to try, he would get to choose what kind of sprinkles he wanted and shake a little bit on. Without fail, he would eat the entire fruit every time—and discover that he really liked it.

Leesa Stone, Parker, Colorado

Let Her Watch Herself

I've found a fun way to get my 20-month-old daughter to finish her meals—and even try new foods. She loves watching herself in the mirror, so sometimes, we place a small mirror on the table in front of her so that she can see herself eat. It's improved her eating habits a lot.

Karen White, O'Fallon, Missouri

Add Some Color

To get my 2- and 4-year-olds to drink more water, I put drops of food coloring in their clear cups to make it more fun. I tell them to cover their eyes while I take out my magic wand and say a few special words, and presto—drinks they enjoy!

Erina Lucchesini-Soria, Sacramento

do kids need a multivitamin?

Probably not. The best way for kids to get the nutrients they need is through a well-balanced diet, according to the Children's Nutrition Research Center in Houston. Even picky eaters probably don't need one, since kids don't need to get all their vitamins in one meal—or even in one day.

But if it would make you feel better and help you avoid dinner table battles, giving your choosy child one multivitamin per day won't hurt. Pint-size vegetarians may also benefit from a multivitamin, since they sometimes have nutritional gaps in their diets. Look for a brand that has 100 percent—and no more—of the RDA for each vitamin. The amounts will be on the back label.

the nutrients they need

Your child needs a wide variety of vitamins and minerals each day to build good eyesight, healthy skin, and much more. Here are the USDA's Recommended Dietary Allowances for kids.

Age	1–3 Years	4–6 Years	7–10 Years
Calcium	500 mg	800 mg	800–1,300 mg
Iodine	70 mcg	90 mcg	120 mcg
Iron	10 mg	10 mg	10 mg
Selenium	20 mcg	20 mcg	30 mcg
Vitamin A	400 mcg	500 mcg	700 mcg
Vitamin C	40 mg	45 mg	45 mg
Vitamin D	5 mcg	5 mcg	5 mcg
Vitamin E	6 mg	7 mg	7 mg
Vitamin K	15 mcg	20 mcg	30 mcg
Zinc	10 mg	10 mg	10 mg

SOURCE: United States Department of Agriculture

Make Edible Art

To get my preschool daughter to eat carrots, I ask her to make as many shapes as she can by taking bites out of the carrots. We make smiles, moons, hats, and umbrellas. She has fun while getting some important vitamins and minerals.

Julia Appel, Port Washington, New York

A Fun Way to Eat Fruit

I make "fruit faces" for the kids I care for in my home. I use banana slices for eyes, with a splash of yogurt for the iris and a raisin for the pupil. The nose can be a slice of kiwi, the mouth a slice of melon. Add eyebrows, teeth, or hair with different cuts of fruit, or have the kids make faces of their own.

Louise Marta, Fresno, California

Sensational Seasonings

When I cook fresh zucchini, I top it with a teeny bit of sugar before I steam it to make it more appealing to my 4-year-old son. I also add a dash of soy sauce to the water when I cook frozen broccoli, which cuts the bitter flavor.

Lisa Goldberg, Fairfax, Virginia

sneaky nutrition tips

Thicken Soup with Cereal

My 15-month-old daughter loves chicken noodle soup but refuses to let me feed it to her. To limit mealtime mess and increase nutritional value, I add dry baby cereal to the soup. She can now successfully spoon-feed herself a nutritious meal, and I have less mess to clean up!

Lisa Henderson, Ayr, Ontario, Canada

Make Juice

I use a juicer to get my kids to eat more vegetables. Our favorite combinations are "orange" juice, made with carrots; "green" juice, which includes spinach; and "red" juice, which gets its color from beets. My kids love the flavor, and I feel better because I know that they're getting lots of vitamins and minerals.

Goh Eng-Mui, San Francisco

Choose Cheese

My 3-year-old daughter refuses to eat sliced cheese, so I grate it instead. She sprinkles these "cheese noodles" on everything from scrambled eggs to steamed broccoli.

Christine Richard, Napoleonville, Louisiana

the ugly truth about fast food

It's tempting to fall back on drive-thru meals when you're too busy to cook, but convenience comes with a price. Check out how many calories and grams of fat are in some of your child's fast-food favorites.

Food	Calories	Fat (g)
Biscuit	253	12
Burrito, beef	431	21
Cheeseburger	305	13
Chocolate chip cookie, jumbo	280	13
French fries, medium	320	17
Fried chicken, breast	360	24
Milkshake, chocolate, medium	460	13
Pizza, pepperoni, 2 slices	540	22
Potato, baked, with broccoli and cheese	450	14
Taco salad	905	61

Good-for-You Popsicles

If your kids like frozen pops, try this substitute: Fill the molds with jarred baby fruit and freeze them. My young kids love these treats, and they're healthier than the sweetened pops.

Mandi George, *Los Alamos, New Mexico*

Make a Healthy Sandwich

My husband discovered that our kids actually like spinach if it is layered between cheese on a grilled cheese sandwich.

Carol Jacobs, *Middleville, Michigan*

Something to Hold On To

When my son started eating canned peaches, he had a hard time picking up the slippery pieces. So I put some wheat germ into a plastic bag and added the peaches. I shook the bag to

it's my job

how a pediatrician boosts calcium intake

To build strong bones, kids under age 3 need 500 milligrams daily, 4- to 8-year-olds need 800 milligrams, and 9- to 18-year-olds need 1,300 milligrams. Milk is the best source, but what if your kids hate the stuff? Here's what Houston pediatrician Steven Abrams, M.D., recommends.

"Don't force them to drink milk if they don't want to," he says. "Instead, try strategies like adding low-fat milk to scrambled eggs or sprinkling some cheese on top of baked potatoes." You should also offer your child non-milk foods that are rich in calcium every day. Here are some top choices that kids like.

✓ Plain, fruit, or frozen yogurt

✓ Fortified breakfast cereal

✓ Fortified orange juice

✓ Fortified soy milk

✓ Ice cream

✓ Low-fat mozzarella string cheese

✓ Cottage cheese

✓ Fat-free cream cheese

✓ Custard or pudding

✓ Tofu

coat the fruit, then gave him coated pieces. The nutritious wheat germ makes the peaches easy to grip.

Debbie Rogers, *Waukegan, Illinois*

Make It Smooth

My 4-year-old hates the texture of whole fruits and vegetables, so I serve them to her in purées, blended soups, and fresh tomato sauce. I also keep jars of baby food on hand—such as carrots, squash, and peas—and add them to

portion size planner

Even if your child leaves half her food on her plate, she may well be getting ample amounts of everything you serve her. Here's what is normal and recommended for kids as they grow.

Food	Toddler	Preschooler	Age 5 and Up
Beans	2 Tbsp	¼ c	½ c
Bread	¼–½ slice	½ slice	1 slice
Cheese	1 oz	1½ oz	1½–2 oz
Eggs	½	1	1
Fruit, canned	¼ c	½ c	½ c
Fruit or vegetables, cooked or raw	2 Tbsp	¼ c	1 piece fruit; ½ c vegetables
Meat, poultry, or fish	1 oz	1½ oz	2½–3 oz
Milk and yogurt	½ c (4 oz)	¾ c (6 oz)	1 c (8 oz)
Rice, pasta, cereal	¼ c	⅓ c	½ c

prepared foods such as soups, gravies, and macaroni and cheese.

Brigid Alverson, *Melrose, Massachusetts*

More Fiber

My kids love to have hot biscuits with dinner. To boost their fiber intake, I use half the amount of Bisquick called for on the box and substitute buckwheat pancake mix (from a health food store) for the other half. I do the same thing when I make waffles.

Sally Gilliland, *Brooklyn, New York*

encourage healthy habits

Snack Kits

To keep my kids from oversnacking, I've started making them snack boxes. In the morning, I put healthy snacks such as carrot sticks and pretzels in a different-colored container for each child. As hunger strikes, they can go to the refrigerator and pick something from their boxes. This saves me time and teaches my children how to budget some snacks for later.

Shannon Beesley, *Sandy, Utah*

Give Them Some Control

I created "yuck lists" with my children, which allows them to choose two items each month that they don't have to eat. For instance, my daughter doesn't like potatoes. If they're on her list for that month, I don't put any on her plate during dinnertime. If they're not on her list, then she must eat at least a small portion of them. This approach has made mealtime more enjoyable because the kids have a choice.

Lynda Hamilton, *Oakwood, Ontario, Canada*

Let Him Help

When we cook, I give Eric, our 18-month-old son, his own set of ingre-

10 healthy snacks for kids

1. Grapes*
2. Air-popped popcorn*
3. Nutri-Grain bar
4. Sliced apples, oranges, or pears
5. Broccoli florets
6. Low-fat yogurt
7. Frozen fruit bar
8. Graham crackers
9. Pretzels*
10. Cheerios and low-fat milk

*Do not serve to children age 3 and under

skinny kids

Kids who are underweight can cause their parents just as much worry as those who are overweight, says pediatrician and *Parents* contributing editor Laura Nathanson, M.D. Here's a little advice for handling a kid who doesn't quite tip the scales.

Talk to your doctor. It's possible that your kid is just naturally thin, even if he consumes the right number of calories. Your pediatrician should make sure that your child's height growth is normal and that he has no health problems, such as an overactive thyroid gland.

Offer nutrient-rich foods. Fruits, vegetables, beans, red meat, chicken, cereal, pasta, whole-grain breads, milk, and cheese pack a powerful health punch. Offer your child two or three planned snacks in addition to breakfast, lunch, and dinner, so that he keeps his energy levels high.

Sweeten him up. While high-sugar, empty-calorie junk food isn't good for anyone, it's fine to let your child eat calorie-dense desserts such as chocolate pudding, milkshakes, or dried fruit.

dients and utensils so he can "cook" alongside me. He loves stirring and pouring and mixing. When the real food is done, he is much more likely to eat it because he feels like he has helped.

Rosemary Sargent, *Morrison, Colorado*

Show Them How It's Done

For years, I was the only one in the family who ate vegetables and other healthy foods. One day, I sat down by myself to eat some mushroom and barley soup. Soon, my 5-year-old came over and asked what the "weird things" were in my soup. I told her that she wouldn't enjoy the soup, but she insisted that she would like it. She tried it—and she did like it! Now, whenever I want to introduce a new food into my children's diet, I let them see me enjoying it first. I'd rather have them pleading with me to taste it than me pleading with them to eat.

Gloria Price, *Zichron Yaakov, Israel*

Eliminate the Impulse Buy

When my children were young, they always asked for a treat when we went to the market. So, I saved the colorful produce aisle for last and allowed them to each pick one of anything they wanted. They were thrilled to be in charge! In the checkout lane, they were still proudly holding their treasures of pomegranates and bananas, which made the candy easy to bypass.

Connie Gunkel, *North Kingstown, Rhode Island*

creative rewards

Chart a Course

To remind our preschoolers to eat enough fruits and vegetables, we made a "Five a Day" chart. They cut out pictures of different fruits and veggies and pasted them around the edge of a piece of poster board. They get a mark for each one they eat and a special sticker or treat if they eat five or more. They ask me to "make more" fruits and veggies every day.

Judy Berna, *Jefferson City, Missouri*

A Day of Sugar

Nearly every day, my 8-year-old son would ask if he could have a sugary cereal for breakfast. Since I want my family to start off the day with healthy food, I always said no. Then, I came up with Special Cereal Sunday. My son and I agreed that as long as he eats a healthy breakfast the rest of the week, he can eat his favorite sweet cereal on Sunday. Thankfully, I now enjoy complaint-free mornings all week long.

Darlien Pausch, *Redford, Michigan*

One, Two, Three, Eat!

When my 4-year-old son needs some extra motivation to eat (especially his vegetables), we have a "counting lunch." I arrange food on a plate in various amounts, and he has to count the items in order to eat them. He loves the game, and he sees eating the food as his reward, so he's much more co-operative.

Janine Paolella, *North Beach Haven, New Jersey*

Dip Some Veggies

My children refused to eat vegetables. Finally, I made a deal with them: They only had to eat half the amount of vegetables on their plate, and they could eat them any way that they

veggie Q & A

You know that your kids need to get their share of nutrient-rich veggies every day, but all the choices out there can be confusing. American Dietetic Association spokesperson Sheah Rarback, R.D., who is based in Miami, provides some quick answers to parents' most-asked questions.

Q: Are frozen vegetables as nutritious as fresh ones?
A: Yes. Frozen and fresh vegetables have exactly the same nutrient count, and they might even be a little sweeter, since they're frozen immediately after they're picked. How you cook your veggies, however, does have an effect on their nutrient value. Heat and water both destroy vitamins, which means that quick, low-water methods, such as steaming, are best.

Q: Does lettuce contain fiber?
A: Yes, but not much. There are many other vegetables that are better sources. To figure out how many grams of fiber a day your child needs, add her age to the number 5. Your 6-year-old, for instance, should get 11 grams per day. While ½ cup of lettuce has less than a gram of fiber, peas, carrots, broccoli, and corn all have 3 grams per ½-cup serving. And green beans and potatoes have 2 grams (4 with the skin).

Q: I often make carrot muffins for my kids. Does one muffin count as a serving of vegetables?
A: No. A typical carrot muffin recipe calls for just a cup of grated carrots, which means that each muffin has only about 1½ tablespoons. But every little bit counts, so you're on the right track by adding vegetables to any home-cooked food you can.

Q: I've heard that carrots, corn, and sweet potatoes are bad for kids because they're so sugary. Is this true?
A: No—all vegetables are good for kids! There's a popular theory these days among trendy diet gurus that many carbohydrate-rich foods, including certain vegetables, are unhealthy because they contain natural sugars. But kids need carbohydrates (which are made up of natural sugars) for energy. It's not the same as eating a candy bar, which has empty calories. These vegetables are packed with fiber and disease-fighting nutrients.

help a chubby child

Melinda Sothern, Ph.D., the head of the Committed to Kids pediatric weight loss program at Louisiana State University in New Orleans, deals with children's weight issues every day. Here's her advice on how to help a child lose weight.

Play with your kids. Your child will be more likely to exercise if you do it with him. Take a family bike ride, toss a football in the yard, plan a Saturday afternoon hike, or volunteer to coach his baseball team.

Move the TV. Don't let your child have a television in his room, and don't make the TV the focal point of your family room or den. Set up an attractive, game-filled, TV-free play space inside the house that gives your child room to stretch his legs and run around when he's indoors. You should also set limits on computer time and video games.

Cut the junk. Clear your kitchen of junk food, but don't ban it altogether. Giving your child an occasional treat—a candy bar at the movies or a piece of cake at a party—will help keep those foods from gaining too much significance in his eyes.

Push fluids. Water should always be your child's first choice: Aim for five to six glasses a day. Kids also need to drink two to three glasses of low-fat milk. Several small servings of fruit juice a day is fine, but don't overdo it; and save soda for a once-in-a-while treat.

Make meals more fun. To get your child more interested in eating right, get him involved. Bring him shopping with you and teach him how to read food labels; ask him to toss a salad or help you bake low-fat muffins.

pleased—dipped in brown sugar, ketchup, or barbecue sauce. I think this approach is working because they feel more in control. (Of course, I dish out double portions of the veggies!)
Michele Russell, Bethesda, Maryland

dealing with weight problems

Get Help from a Pro

My 10-year-old son is overweight and was having problems sticking to any kind of eating plan, so I took him to a nutritionist. It was the smartest thing I could have done. She gave me some great recipe ideas for tasty, healthy meals. Now, I

food allergy facts

About 7 percent of young kids have a food allergy. The offending food causes an immune system reaction that may produce eczema, hives, nasal congestion, vomiting, wheezing, facial swelling, stomach cramps, or even loss of consciousness. A child with a very serious food allergy is also at risk for anaphylaxis, a potentially life-threatening condition that makes it difficult to breathe.

The most common foods to which babies and toddlers are allergic are milk, eggs, soy, and wheat. Fortunately, most kids outgrow these allergies by the first grade. Allergies to shellfish, tree nuts, or peanuts are less common but are rarely outgrown—and they cause much more severe reactions. If your child has a food allergy, here are some ways that you can help her deal with it.

✓ Talk about it. Tell her what a food allergy is, and explain to her why it's important for her to avoid the food she's allergic to. The earlier she knows why she can't eat certain foods, the better.

✓ Tell school officials. Once your child is old enough to go to school, write a letter to her teacher explaining the situation. Send copies to the principal, cafeteria manager, and school nurse.

✓ Pack safe food. Make your child lunches from home, discourage trading food at school, and ask the teacher if she'll keep a box of safe treats in her classroom for your child. At home, have separate areas for nonallergenic goodies.

✓ Don't scare your child. Don't make a big deal of your child's food allergies, but be firm. You want to protect her from adverse reactions, but making her scared of her allergy could do more harm than good.

make dishes that include nutritious foods such as broccoli and spinach. My son really likes them and has lost weight.

Eva Amar, Brooklyn, New York

Read the Warning Signs

My daughter was always heavy, but the real wake-up call to me that she needed to lose weight was when she played on a soccer team with other little girls. She couldn't keep up with them on the field, and whenever the coach asked if anyone wanted to sit down, she was always the first to say yes. I signed her up for a kids' weight loss program at a local hospital and she lost nearly 20 pounds.

Laura Murden, River Ridge, Louisiana

Moderation Is Key

One key in helping my 9-year-old son lose weight is letting him have occasional splurges. For instance, if he's going to a soccer team party where he knows there'll be pizza, which he loves, it's not fair to tell him that he can't have any at all. Instead, we make sure that he eats carefully the rest of that day, so that he's allowed to "cheat" and have a slice or two of pizza with his friends.

Cheryl Boraski, *New Orleans*

A Rewarding Offer

Our 5-year-old son underate and was small for his age. To get him to improve his appetite, we cut out pictures of healthy foods from magazines, glued them onto construction paper, and hung them in the kitchen. These were his healthy snack pictures. Every time that he ate a food from the list, he put a star next to it. When he got five stars, he was allowed to pick out a video to rent. This tactic has worked well: He's

kiddie calorie counter

Here's what your children need at every age to fuel them throughout their busy days.

Age	Average Daily Calorie Needs
Birth–6 months	650
6 months–1 year	850
1–3 years	1,300
4–6 years	1,800
7–10 years	2,000
11–14 years (girls)	2,200
11–14 years (boys)	2,500

stealth vegetables

Looking for ways to add extra nutrition to your child's diet? Try one of these undercover methods.

Stir vegetables into meat loaf. Add 1 cup of grated zucchini or carrots for every pound of meat. Each portion packs protein and one-quarter of a serving of veggies.

Shake it up with fruit-flavored shakes. Purée canned peaches, pears, or apricots with milk. Serve with a fun straw so kids can slurp up any fruit that settles to the bottom.

Fool chocolate lovers. Stir dry, finely chopped spinach and one jar of butternut squash baby food into a box of brownies and bake according to package directions. Your kids won't even notice the vegetables.

Hold the mayo. Instead of mayonnaise on that sandwich, try mashed avocado for a delicious alternative.

Make super soups. For a quick shot of vitamin A, substitute carrot juice for part of the liquid in soups, stews, and sauces.

Go green. When preparing family favorites such as baked ziti or lasagna, pack the ricotta cheese mixture with chopped broccoli or spinach for a colorful and nutritious variation.

Pump up pizza. Add puréed roasted red peppers to jarred pizza sauce. Top it with fresh tomato and cheese—they'll never know that their pizza's packin' vitamins.

gained 3 pounds in 4 months, and he's learning to make healthy choices.

Beth Graham, Ashburn, Virginia

Cut Back on Extras

My kids tend to pour tons of sugar on their cereal rather than sprinkling it. So, I put the sugar in a salt shaker; they just use a little bit now, so breakfast is much healthier.

Francine Morasky, Fallbrook, California

Be a Good Role Model

I think that parents need to set a good example for their child if they're trying to encourage her to lose weight. When our daughter needed to lose weight, my husband and I went on a diet with her. If she couldn't eat junk food, neither could we. It helped her a lot. She lost almost 15 pounds, and we both lost weight, too!

Toni Tucker, New Orleans

the kids' food guide pyramid

Here's what kids ages 2 to 6 need to eat each day in order to meet current U.S. Department of Agriculture requirements.

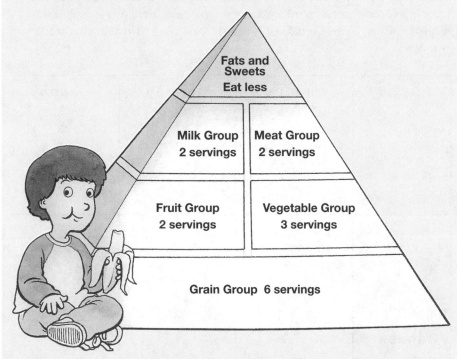

Fats and Sweets
Eat less

Milk Group
2 servings

Meat Group
2 servings

Fruit Group
2 servings

Vegetable Group
3 servings

Grain Group 6 servings

What Counts As One Serving?

Grain Group
1 slice bread
½ c cooked rice or pasta
½ c cooked cereal
1 oz ready-to-eat cereal

Fruit Group
1 piece fruit or melon wedge
¾ c juice
½ c canned fruit
¼ c dried fruit

Vegetable Group
½ c chopped raw or cooked vegetables
1 c raw leafy vegetables

Milk Group
1 c milk or yogurt
2 oz cheese

Meat Group
2–3 oz cooked lean meat, poultry, or fish
(½ c cooked dry beans, or 1 egg, counts as 1 oz lean meat. 2 Tbsp peanut butter count as 1 oz meat.)

Fats and Sweets
Limit calories from these.

Four- to 6-year-olds can eat these serving sizes. Offer 2- to 3-year-olds less, except for milk.

SOURCE: United States Department of Agriculture

charting your child's food consumption

You can use this chart to get an idea of the foods that your child eats over the course of a week. Pencil in the foods eaten each day on the lines below, and color in the corresponding pyramid at the top of the chart. (For example, if a slice of toast is eaten at breakfast, write in "toast" and fill in one grain group pyramid.)

	sunday	monday	tuesday
milk meat fruit vegetable grain	△ △ △ △ △ △ △ △ △ △ △ △ △ △ △	△ △ △ △ △ △ △ △ △ △ △ △ △ △ △	△ △ △ △ △ △ △ △ △ △ △ △ △ △ △
breakfast			
snack			
lunch			
snack			
dinner			

The number of pyramids shown for each food group is the number of servings to be eaten each day. At the end of the week, if you see only a few blank pyramids, keep up the good work. If you notice several blank pyramids, offer more of the foods from the missing food groups in future weeks.

wednesday	thursday	friday	saturday
△ △ △ △ △ △ △ △ △ △ △ △ △ △ △	△ △ △ △ △ △ △ △ △ △ △ △ △ △ △	△ △ △ △ △ △ △ △ △ △ △ △ △ △ △	△ △ △ △ △ △ △ △ △ △ △ △ △ △ △

SOURCE: United States Department of Agriculture

making
mealtime fun

Once upon a time, the whole family gathered around the table every evening for a relaxing home-cooked meal. But times have changed. In today's hectic world, everyone seems to have a scheduling problem. In fact, less than half of American families eat dinner together every night.

Reclaiming the dinner hour is a great way to connect with your busy family. It doesn't have to be a nightly event, it doesn't have to be a feast, and takeout is just fine. If you make the time together a priority, you'll find that you can bond as well over pizza as over pot roast. In this chapter, we've gathered great tips on how to spice up your meals, deal with a picky eater, get your kids involved in cooking, and more.

fun food ideas

No-Scream Ice Cream

My kids love ice-cream cones, but when the ice cream leaks out of the bottom, they no longer want the cone. To avoid the waste—and the mess—I put a tiny marshmallow in the bottom of each cone before filling it with ice cream. The marshmallow keeps the cone from leaking and adds a nice treat at the end.

Bridie Hearne, *Westchester, Illinois*

Baking Buddies

My 3-year-old daughter and I love to bake cookies together. To let her help as much as possible but cut down on the mess, I measure out all the ingredients ahead of time and put them into plastic sandwich bags. When we're ready to bake, she can pour everything in by herself, and she feels proud to be so independent. I don't have to step in until it's time to use the mixer.

Janet Best, *Vienna, Virginia*

how to cook with your kids

We asked Marion Cunningham, author of *Cooking with Children: 15 Lessons for Children Ages 7 and Up Who Really Want to Learn to Cook*, for the basics of introducing kids to the kitchen. Here's her advice.

Start young. The earlier in life you can get the feel of the kitchen, the easier it is to become a good cook. Children may be a little clumsy at first when it comes to chopping and stirring, but they catch on quickly.

Go pint-size. The ideal work surface is waist-high. For children, that's about 30 inches. Since most kitchen counters are 36 inches high, you'll want to have your child stand on a sturdy stool or work at a lower table.

Keep it simple. Work with the minimum number of ingredients and don't give alternate steps. Try not to give too many instructions or warnings, which makes kids timid.

Serve it with pride. Good cooking is something to be proud of. Sharing food he's made fills a child with a sense of accomplishment. Enjoying food together is a great way to bond with your family.

Friday Night Special

In my family, every Friday is fun food night. We make dinner as a family, but we make individual pizzas or tacos or some other do-it-yourself-style food. It's fun for the kids because they get to choose their toppings or fillings, and it's great for us parents because many hands make light work—including at cleanup time!

Mary Beth Griffin, *Hartford, Connecticut*

May I Take Your Order?

My family is never thrilled when we have leftovers. Rather than let the food go to waste, I learned to add some excitement to the night by opening a restaurant. I give the restaurant a name and then write the menu—the contents of the refrigerator—on a dry-erase board. I act as waitress, reading the options aloud, and I let my kids select the dishes they like. Leftovers are a lot more exciting this way.

Lisa Palmer, *Salt Lake City*

Bee Fun

To make eating fun for my 20-month-old son, we play games with his food. For example, sometimes I put some

Parents' 10 favorite family breakfasts

Starting the day off with a balanced meal is important, but nutritious food doesn't have to be boring. Here's a list of our favorites.

1. Buttermilk pancakes with blueberries and maple syrup
2. Toaster waffles with fruit salad and juice
3. Corned-beef hash, served with a mango-orange smoothie
4. Oatmeal with raisins, served with grapefruit halves
5. Scrambled eggs with cottage cheese and tomato
6. Raisin-bran muffins with a banana and milk
7. Homemade granola with yogurt and strawberries
8. Hard-boiled eggs with toast and honey
9. French toast with sliced almonds and applesauce
10. Ham-and-cheese omelettes

food on a spoon and buzz like a bee. The spoon flies around like a bumblebee, eventually landing in his mouth. In another game, I touch the spoon to his cheek or chin and say, "I've got your cheek. . . ." He loves the anticipation, and I can see that he's developing positive feelings about food.

Elisa Zeid, *New York City*

Cone Trick

I am an early childhood teacher with 23 years of experience and I've found a novel way to avoid mealtime battles: Serve it up in an ice-cream cone! Some favorite fillings include sloppy joe mixture, chicken salad, taco filling, yogurt with fruit, and pudding with bananas. Miniature cones are fun for kids; they rarely say, "That's too much."

Linda O'Connell, *St. Louis*

smart solutions

Crust Busting

One day, while making peanut butter and jelly sandwiches, I came up with a great way to trim the crusts. I used the large, round, plastic top to the jar of peanut butter to cut out the bread. It not only gets rid of the crusts neatly, but the round sandwiches are also a treat for my kids.

Beth Veazey, *Baton Rouge, Louisiana*

Instant Breakfast

When school is in session, my kids and I cook a dozen or more slices of French toast at a time. Then we freeze them, two at a time, in sealable plastic bags. On busy mornings, they can enjoy a hot homemade breakfast by popping a couple of slices into the toaster.

Marilyn Lawrence, *Monticello, Iowa*

Berry Healthy

My family is into natural foods, and I never use artificial coloring in anything. My kids love colored frosting on their cakes, however, so I found a great solution. I now make up a big bowl of white frosting and strain frozen raspberries or blueberries, then add the liquid to the white frosting. It

great sandwich add-ons

If your children are shy about trying new foods and you're worried that there's not enough variety in what they eat, try sneaking something fun—and nutritious—into their favorite sandwiches. Here are a few interesting additions to common sandwiches.

✓ Bologna: Add thin-sliced cucumbers; reduced-fat mozzarella or American cheese; bell pepper slices; pickle slices; or tomato slices.

✓ Peanut butter and jelly: Add crushed, drained pineapple; chopped apples; banana slices; grated carrot; chopped dates; raisins; dried cranberries; or wheat germ.

✓ Tuna: Add chopped, cooked egg white; shredded carrot; diced cucumber; shredded zucchini; pickle relish; pine nuts; chopped almonds; or avocado cubes.

looks bright and colorful, it tastes great, and I know it's healthy.

Jennifer Hippensteel, Patterson, California

snack attack

Dinner is in an hour, but your kids have the munchies now. Give them some healthy snacks that won't spoil their appetite.

✓ Banana slices on mini rice cakes

✓ Cold pizza

✓ Cottage cheese with crushed pineapple

✓ Salsa with baked corn chips

✓ Carrot and celery sticks with peanut butter

✓ Chunks of peeled kiwi fruit

✓ Soft cubes of cheese on mini pretzels

Magnet School

I have a hard time keeping my son Jacob busy while I'm cooking. He loves magnets, so I cut out some of his favorite characters from magazines, had them laminated at the local copy shop, and added self-adhesive magnet strips to the back. For less than $10, I filled my whole refrigerator door, and Jacob is enthralled.

Jamie Story, Temecula, California

picky, picky

Hold the Whining

My son was a very fussy eater, and dinnertimes were consumed with trying to get him to eat what the rest of the family was eating and listening

dish it up differently

Kids pay more attention to the food on their plate if you serve it in a fun and interesting way. Try these ideas.

- ✓ Cut slices of American cheese into your child's initials and bake for a minute on a casserole just before serving.
- ✓ Hollow out a multigrain roll and use it as a bowl to serve your favorite stew.
- ✓ Cut cooked salmon into bite-size pieces and serve with toothpicks for easy eating (not for very young children).
- ✓ Mold cooked rice in a teacup. When you invert the cup, the rice will have a cool "mountain" shape.
- ✓ Bake meat loaf in cupcake liners. Later, top with mashed potato "frosting" and carrot shavings.
- ✓ Wrap crescent-roll dough around hot dogs and bake; serve with mustard and ketchup.

to him complain. When he was about 6, I took him aside and explained that from now on, there would be no more complaints about the food at the dinner table. He could check with me while I was making dinner and if it was something he couldn't tolerate, he could make himself a sandwich with a side of carrot sticks (or some other vegetable) and a glass of milk. From then on, dinner was much more pleasant.

Mary Mohler, *New York City*

Hunger Helps

To deal with a fussy eater, you simply have to wait until they're hungry. I've found that when kids are hungry enough (and it doesn't take long), they'll eat pretty much anything you serve them.

Jennifer Abraham, *Castro Valley, California*

messy eaters

Keep It Clean

My 4½-year-old son, Timothy, thinks that bibs are for babies, but he often has trouble keeping clean while eating, especially when he eats messy foods. I have solved the problem by having him wear his plastic paint smock. It's fun for him, and since it completely covers his clothes, he stays clean. All I have to do when the meal is over is wipe down the smock.

Sandra Smith, *Kearney, Nebraska*

Floor It

I found that the best way to reduce mess when feeding an infant is to place an old plastic tablecloth underneath him in front of the high chair. That way, any food that he drops is easy to clean up.

Renee Wirtz, *Lansing, Michigan*

An Artful Solution

Instead of buying an expensive floor mat to place under my daughter's high chair, I made one myself. My 5-year-old son Tylor and I cut pictures of babies, animals, and letters out of

it's my job

entice kids to eat right

Sarah Moulton, host of *Cooking Live* and *Cooking Live Primetime* on the Food Network, is also an editor at *Gourmet* magazine and mother of two. We asked her for advice on making food fun for kids.

Don't force it. "I don't believe in the old-school advice that you have to finish everything on your plate or try everything under the sun."

Give them choices. "I do think it's important to offer a choice of foods to kids. If you're preparing cooked squash and your son won't eat it, have some raw vegetables on hand so that he still gets a balanced meal."

Involve your kids in the kitchen. "There are so many food-related activities that can educate kids about math, science, history, geography, language, and the like. Find the hook that interests them most and use that angle when you cook together."

Be patient. "My grandmother and mother were very sophisticated chefs, yet, until I was about 9 years old, all I ever wanted was hot dogs. I thought that eggs tasted funny. And fish, forget it. But my palate evolved and their skills did leave an impression on me, which encouraged me to become the chef I am today."

cut corners in the kitchen

Marla Bazar Sochet, contributing food and nutrition editor at *Parents* magazine, creates kid-friendly menus every day. She has lots of advice for busy moms who need to save time in the kitchen.

- ✓ Shop smart. Get to know one grocery store really well, and go when it's least crowded. Stock up on pantry items when they go on sale.
- ✓ Take shortcuts on prep time. Hit the salad bar for ready-to-eat veggies, and buy cut-up poultry.
- ✓ Presort groceries. Pack frozen foods in one bag, fruits and produce in another, and pantry items in a third; it will simplify putting them away.
- ✓ Sharpen up. Always keep knives sharpened (and out of reach of kids); food preparation will be easier, faster, and actually safer.
- ✓ Clean as you go. Wash pans, bowls, and utensils as you finish with them; it makes after-dinner cleanup much easier.
- ✓ Enlist your kids' help. It's fun to work together in the kitchen, and children are more likely to eat foods that they've helped prepare.

magazines. We then glued them to construction paper and covered everything with Con-Tact paper, overlapping sheets to make sure that there were no uncovered spots. My daughter just loves it. She looks down at the pictures and shrieks with excitement. It was a fun project for my son, too.

Pamela Coleman, *Kelso, Washington*

Nice Ice

To deal with our messy eater, Max, we put newspaper down on the floor and feed him in his high chair wearing only a diaper. For dessert, we give him a Popsicle made with water instead of juice. He loves the treat, and the melted ice is easier to clean up.

Annie Modesitt, *South Orange, New Jersey*

Table Matters

My toddler has always been an enthusiastic eater. But when he outgrew his high chair and joined us at the dinner table, he dropped food all over his lap. Finally, my mother-in-law suggested that we set him a few inches away from the table. We tried it and it has made all the difference. Because he has to lean over to take a bite, the crumbs can fall back on his plate.

Maureen Belden, *Newburgh, New York*

dining out

Drive-Thru Dinner

When I go to a fast-food restaurant with my two sons, ages 8 months and 2 years, I hate the hassle of standing in line trying to juggle an infant, my wallet, and a tray full of food and drinks, all the while worrying about my toddler wandering off. At the same time, I'd always shunned the drive-thru because I don't like eating in the car. I thought of the perfect solution: I get our meals at the drive-thru window and then bring them inside to eat!

Pam Fields, *Lancaster, South Carolina*

Get a Window Seat

We have four children, ages 8, 5, 3, and 20 months, but this doesn't stop us from eating out at restaurants. We've had the best luck at places with interesting views, such as overlooking

helping hands:
tasks that kids can do

Kids love to help out, but safety comes first in the kitchen. Here's an age-by-age list of chores that are challenging but not too difficult or dangerous.

Ages 3 and up: Gather produce from the refrigerator; wash fruits and veggies; fill measuring cups.

Four and 5 years: Open packages and pour contents into bowls; mix wet and dry ingredients; cut out shapes for pastry or cookies.

Six and 7 years: Use scissors to cut fresh herbs; grate cheese; mash potatoes.

Eight and up: Help do the dishes; set the table; cut up vegetables.

perfect picnic tips

Warm weather means picnic time. Whether you're heading to the beach or your own backyard, you need to take extra precautions to keep food fresh. These tips will guarantee an outing that's safe as well as fun.

Smart Packing

✓ Pack food in shallow containers with tight-fitting lids. Two inches deep is ideal for foods to cool evenly.

✓ Instead of using one big cooler, use two smaller ones: one for salads, drinks, and ready-to-eat foods and the other for raw meat, fish, or poultry, if you plan to grill.

✓ Pack the cooler full to keep it cold: Use freezer packs or ice wrapped in resealable bags to fill in the gaps.

✓ When you're on the road, keep your coolers in the passenger area, not in the trunk, which is usually much warmer.

At the Picnic

✓ Keep coolers in the shade—under a tree or covered with a light-colored blanket.

✓ Use an appliance thermometer to verify that the cooler maintains a temperature of 40°F or less.

✓ Store leftovers in the cooler again within an hour after eating, especially if it's warmer than 85°F outside.

a harbor. The kids have something to distract them, and we can talk about what's going on outside. It's fun and educational, and it passes the time nicely for us, too.

Anita Gaston, *Bluff Point, New York*

Keep the Waitress Happy

Before we go out to eat, I call to make sure that the restaurant has high chairs. To keep my 4-year-old busy, I bring along an old purse that I fill with different goodies, such as crayons and paper, unused keys, old credit cards, and other things that she enjoys playing with. And to keep the waitress happy, I leave a big tip!

Kay Brian, *Brooklyn, New York*

Eat à la Carte

We find it wasteful to order entire meals for our 5-year-old twin girls, and even the kiddie menus aren't always appropriate. Instead, we let them order side dishes à la carte and ask the waitress for two small plates. This way, they can make up their own meals, and we don't waste food or money.

Jackie Forrester, Chicago

Dining al Fresco

My husband and I didn't change our eating-out habits just because we had a baby. We live in California, so now we simply go to restaurants by the beach that serve dinner outdoors. My daughter, Hayley, is 8 months old, and I find that breastfeeding at the table is still the best way to keep her quiet. I have no trouble eating my meal while she's nursing.

Tegan Hopp, Newport Beach, California

Just Desserts

Eating in a restaurant with our 3-year-old daughter was not exactly a relaxing night out—until we came up with the idea of feeding her beforehand. Then, when we get to the restaurant, we order her an ice cream sundae. Not only does she sit happily still the entire meal, but my husband and I also get a chance for conversation with few interruptions.

Josephine Romano, Rocky Point, New York

health

911 guide

kids are always on the go, which means that your child will endure his share of head bumps, scraped elbows, and bruised knees as he grows up. You can protect him from most accidents by creating a safe environment when he's at home or at play. But because you can't be everywhere at once, it's smart to learn basic first-aid skills so that you can treat your child's injuries.

Many childhood emergencies require only at-home care, and this chapter will give you plenty of great tips for soothing your child's minor boo-boos and treating cuts, burns, and more. But one out of every four children sustains an injury serious enough to require medical attention each year, so always call 911 if your child has a serious wound or swallows something poisonous.

boo-boo cures

Make Cuts Less Scary

I have three sons, and they get lots of scrapes and minor cuts. But the sight of blood on the washcloth makes them feel worse than the cut itself. So, instead of a white cloth, I use a red one to apply pressure. I keep it in the freezer so it's handy, and cold, in an emergency.

Becky Keigley, *Crowley, Louisiana*

 pediatrician on call

splinter removal, step by step

Some tiny splinters on tougher parts of the body, such as the soles of the feet or the knees, don't cause irritation and can be left alone, says pediatrician and *Parents* contributing editor Laura Nathanson, M.D. But most splinters should be removed. If you leave one in uncalloused skin, it can get pushed farther in and will only become more difficult to extract. Over time, the area may become infected or the splinter may break into pieces.

Here, Dr. Nathanson offers step-by-step advice on how to remove your child's splinter with the least fuss and the best results.

1. Wash the area thoroughly with warm, soapy water.
2. Sterilize a needle and tweezers in rubbing alcohol. Also, have a bowl of ice cubes on hand.
3. In one hand, firmly hold the part of your child's body where the splinter is located, leaving your other hand free to work. Numb the area by touching it with an ice cube until it just turns white—20 seconds at most.
4. Hiding the needle from your child's gaze, scrape the skin away from the most superficial end of the splinter, then grasp the splinter with the tweezers and pull the splinter out at the same angle at which it entered the skin.
5. Apply an over-the-counter antibacterial ointment, and watch for signs of infection (redness, pus, or swelling).

Call your pediatrician if the splinter is in a delicate area, such as the face, the genitals, or under the nail, or if the splinter is long or in very deep.

why every new parent should learn CPR

Babies and toddlers are at greatest risk of choking: They have a natural tendency to put things in their mouths, they can't chew well, and their upper airways become obstructed easily. Drowning, poisoning, or a severe electric shock can also cause a child to stop breathing. Once that happens, it's only a matter of minutes before the lack of oxygen causes brain damage or death.

Because the clock is ticking while you wait for medical help to arrive, it's best to learn how to clear an obstructed airway and perform CPR yourself. To enroll in an infant/child CPR class, contact your hospital or your local chapter of the American Heart Association or the American Red Cross. Classes typically run for 5 hours, cost about $30 to $50, and cover first-aid, rescue breathing, the Heimlich maneuver, and CPR.

Once you've mastered these lifesaving skills, experts recommend that you get recertified annually and that you practice the techniques so you'll remember what to do in an emergency.

Show It Off

If our daughter gets a scrape from a minor tumble, we ask her to stand up and come over to us. This shows us that she's able to walk. Then we ask her to show us her "owie" and to "wiggle-wiggle, shake-shake" the spot. This shows us she's able to move her injury, and it takes the pain away by turning the situation into a game. Finally, we kiss the "owie" to make it all better.

Melodee Ferreira, Kailua, Hawaii

Wash Away the Pain

To help ease the discomfort of cleaning the many scrapes and cuts that my two active children get, we use a small spray bottle to wash away the dirt. While Daniela or Tony is distracted by the squirting water (or by spraying me), I'm able to thoroughly clean the wound.

Erina Lucchesini-Soria, Sacramento

Soak Off Bandages

I tell my 6-year-old son to peel off his adhesive bandages himself while he's sitting in the bath. The soap and water make it much easier and pain-free.

Helena Ortiz, Brooklyn, New York

Bloody Nose Rx

When my daughter was younger, her nose would often bleed from blowing it too hard. To stop the bleeding, I'd have her sit up and lean forward. Then I'd hold a cold washcloth on her nose while pinching her nostrils closed for 5 minutes without letting go. A humidifier can also help keep nostrils moist and cut down on the number of nosebleeds your child gets.

Rena Barton, New York City

treating a child who has been poisoned

More than 1 million of the reported poisonings every year involve children under the age of 5. Because their small bodies are less able to handle toxins, kids are at greater risk of fatal poisoning than adults.

If you suspect that your child has swallowed a poison (look for empty or spilled bottles, burns around his mouth, or a strange odor on his breath), follow these steps.

1. Locate the substance and its packaging. Remove any remaining poison from your child's mouth with your finger.

2. Call poison control. *Note:* If your child is unconscious, immediately call 911 (or your local emergency center) rather than poison control. Administer CPR if your child isn't breathing.

3. Give them the facts. Provide your child's name, age, weight, medications taken, medical conditions, and symptoms. Give the name of the swallowed substance. If you don't know the name of a prescription drug, give a description, the pharmacy's phone number, and the prescription number. Estimate the amount and time of ingestion.

4. Follow the instructions from poison control or 911. Don't give your child any food, drinks, or medication (such as ipecac syrup or activated charcoal), and don't follow treatment instructions on the substance's package, without first consulting poison control or a doctor. If your child has swallowed a caustic substance, you may be told to give him water or milk to dilute it.

Turning Tears into Smiles

My parents taught me that humor can sometimes be the best medicine. Now, whenever my children, ages 3½ and 2 years, fall and hurt themselves, my husband and I tell them to throw their boo-boos at Daddy. He makes a big deal about getting hit with the boo-boo and falls down. This little trick works every time—they start laughing so hard, they forget to cry over their ouches.

Donna Ozias, *Columbus, Ohio*

ice, ice, baby

A Sweet Treat That Heals

I keep a stash of ice pops in the freezer all year round. This way, when my son falls and hurts his mouth, instead of fighting with him to keep an ice cube in his mouth, I just hand him an ice pop. It's a tasty way to ease his discomfort.

Michele McGowan, *East Meadow, New York*

Reuse Teething Rings

Instead of throwing baby teething rings away when they are no longer needed, put them in the freezer. You'll have an instant, fun-to-hold ice pack to help soothe bumps and bruises.

Sybil McDonald, *Lake Geneva, Wisconsin*

Get Smart with Sponges

I've found an easy way to soothe minor bumps and bruises. I cut a clean sponge into several smaller pieces (approximately 1 inch by 2 inches) and then dip each piece into water before putting them into resealable plastic

20 first-aid must haves

Keep these emergency essentials on hand to help your sick or injured child feel better fast:

- ✓ Sterile gauze pads
- ✓ Sterile adhesive bandages in different sizes
- ✓ Rolls of stretchable sterile gauze (to hold dressings in place)
- ✓ Sterile adhesive tape
- ✓ Cotton balls
- ✓ Large sterile adhesive tape (to use as a sling or for applying pressure to a wound)
- ✓ Antibiotic ointment
- ✓ Antiseptic wipes or antiseptic solution
- ✓ Blunt-tipped scissors (for cutting bandages)
- ✓ Tweezers (for removing splinters)
- ✓ Thermometer
- ✓ Pain relievers, such as acetaminophen and ibuprofen
- ✓ Ipecac syrup
- ✓ Liquid-activated charcoal
- ✓ Petroleum jelly
- ✓ Oral rehydration solution
- ✓ Hydrocortisone cream
- ✓ Antihistamine
- ✓ Calamine lotion
- ✓ Ice pack

bone up on sprains and fractures

Kids' smaller bones break more easily than adults', causing severe pain, swelling, tenderness, and sometimes bruising. If you suspect that your child has a broken bone, call 911 immediately. If your child takes a bad tumble and all you know for sure is that he's in pain, here's how to spot and treat what's wrong.

Injury	What Happens	What to Expect	How It's Treated
Sprain	Ligaments, the strong bands of connective tissue that join bones together, can stretch or tear—often in a fall. Ankles, knees, and wrists are most vulnerable.	Pain, bruising, or swelling of the limb that your child has twisted or landed upon. He may feel a tear or pop when the sprain occurs.	Most doctors recommend RICE (rest, ice, compression, and elevation). Moderate sprains may require an elastic bandage for 2 days after the injury or until swelling subsides. Have your child's coach tape the area if extra support is needed during vigorous activity.
Fracture	A bone cracks, breaks, or shatters due to external pressure.	Severe pain, deformity (if the bone is bent in an unnatural position), or, in rare cases, an open wound. Some breaks are less obvious: If you're not sure, monitor the injured area for 2 days. If pain persists or increases, your child may have a *greenstick* fracture (only one side of the bone is broken) or a hairline fracture (only the surface of the bone is cracked).	Take your child to the doctor for x-rays immediately. The physician may fit a cast around the injured limb or manually reset the bone before casting. Severely fragmented bones require surgery.

Sling Trick

If your child has a broken wrist or arm and you'll be taking him to the ER yourself, immobilize the injured area first. To create a soft arm sling, first place your child's forearm against his chest. Then, get a long piece of gauze, a sheet, or a blanket, Slip one end of the material under the arm and wrap around the shoulder. Bring the other end over the arm and wrap around the opposite shoulder. Secure the splint with safety pins. Apply ice to the area.

bags. I leave them in the freezer until one of my kids gets a boo-boo. The soft, cold cubes are the perfect size for small hands, and they don't drip all over the place either.

Wendy Morley, Northridge, California

A Stay-Put Solution

When my son was learning to walk, he suffered from the typical bumps and bruises—many on his head. Unfortunately, he wouldn't stay still long enough for me to hold a cold pack to his injury. The solution: I used an adult's cooling eye mask with an adjustable strap. The strap kept the mask firmly in place over his bump, and Alex was still free to explore the house.

Melanie Niermeyer, Vestal, New York

Pass the Peas, Please

Instead of ice, I give my toddler a clear, zippered plastic bag filled with frozen peas to ease his bumps and bruises. It's much more interesting and less difficult for him to hold than an ice cube.

Tara Claeys, Arlington, Virginia

Fast-Food Ice Pack

I keep a salad dressing packet (from a fast food restaurant) in the freezer to use on bumps and bruises. It doesn't freeze completely, so it's easy to hold and flexible. Soy sauce packets work well, too.

Sue Davidson, Cary, North Carolina

splinter strategies

First-Aid from Fairies

It used to hurt us as much as it hurt our son to have his splinters removed. Then, my husband came up with the ingenious idea of the Splinter Fairy, who visits our house at night, removing any splinters our child might have. Whenever our son gets a splinter, we put a bandage over it for the rest of the day and "call" the fairy on the phone to let her know that she needs to come to our house that night. Then my husband or I take care of it while our son is asleep. He wakes up the next day, and the splinter is gone.

Kris Bear, Sanford, Maine

Sticky Situation

Instead of probing with a needle to pull the end of a splinter up and away from the skin, I place a piece of Scotch tape over it and pull the tape off. Then, I can easily pull the splinter out with tweezers.

Lisa English,
Columbia, Missouri

A Numbing Effect

My children frequently get splinters from running and crawling on our wood floors. To diminish their pain, I dab a bit of baby teething gel onto the area. It numbs their skin so I have an easier time removing the splinter with a pair of tweezers.

Melissa Chandler,
Carson City, Michigan

it's my job

easing children's "owies"

What's the best way to soothe your child's pain after a bump, bruise, or cut? Distract her, says Mark F. Stegelman, M.D., of Egleston Children's Health Care System in Atlanta. "Distraction is one of the best pain relievers for all sorts of injuries," he says. "The younger the child is, the more easily you can divert her."

At Egleston, doctors keep a "distraction box" handy, which is filled with trinkets designed to keep a child's mind off an injury or potentially painful treatment. Here are some of the kid-tested and approved goodies in their kit.

For babies and toddlers: a pinwheel; a musical mobile; rattles or noisemakers; stuffed animals

For older kids: a bottle of bubbles; rubber doctor's gloves blown into balloons; toy cars; video games

first-aid at your fingertips

Categorize Your Cabinets

My medicine cabinets were a total mess until I found the perfect storage bins: diaper wipe containers. I categorize all of the items (such as first-aid supplies, cough medicine, and pain relievers) and put them in their own containers. I've saved a lot of time by not having to search high and low for what I need, and nothing gets lost behind a bottle or jar.

Amy Gagné, *Kansas City, Missouri*

does your child need stitches?

Are you unsure whether your child's cut is serious enough for stitches? Here's how to treat a basic cut at home—and how to know when you need to bring your child to the doctor or hospital emergency room.

✓ For a superficial cut or scrape, wash it with soap and water and apply an antibiotic ointment and bandage.

✓ For a deeper wound that's bleeding heavily, apply direct pressure with a clean cloth and elevate the wound for 3 to 4 minutes. Once the bleeding stops, gently clean the cut with soap and water or antiseptic wipes. Apply antibiotic ointment, which will prevent infection and reduce the risk of scarring, then bandage the cut.

✓ Call 911 or go to the ER right away if an object, such as glass or metal, is embedded in the laceration (don't try to remove it yourself); if your child continues to bleed heavily after 5 minutes of direct pressure; or if his wound is deep or jagged.

These cuts often need to be closed by a physician; the longer you delay treatment, the greater the risk of infection and scarring. Your child's doctor may apply a topical skin adhesive to close smaller cuts. This seldom requires anesthesia and can be less traumatic for a child than getting stitches. But these adhesives won't adhere to areas of the body that move a lot (such as an elbow or knee) or hold very large wounds together.

✓ If your child needs stitches, the ER physician or plastic surgeon will administer a local anesthetic and then sew the skin together with a surgical needle and thread. Bringing the edges of the wound together encourages the body to seal over the wound itself, which decreases the risk of scarring. Stitches typically stay in for a week or two before a doctor removes them.

first-aid for burns and scalds

As emergency medical services medical director of Children's National Medical Center in Washington, D.C., Joseph Wright, M.D., treats kids' burns and scalds regularly. Here are his best tips on caring for your child's skin.

Type of Burn	Signs	Action	Fast Facts
First degree	Skin is red or bright pink but not broken; there are no blisters.	Rinse in cold water for at least 5 minutes to relieve the burning sensation. To alleviate pain, apply cool, wet cloths (an ice pack is okay for a small wound, but avoid applying it directly to skin); acetaminophen will also help. A light moisturizer, such as one made with aloe, may soothe skin.	Minor burns damage only the top layer of the skin and heal on their own in about a week. Some doctors suggest having your child examined if the burn occurs across a joint, such as the elbow. (There's a slight chance that scarring could affect how the joint works.)
Second degree	Skin is red, tender, swollen, and blistered.	Rinse the burn in cool water; apply cool, wet compresses; and cover the wound loosely with a clean cloth until you can get your child immediate medical help. The doctor will clean the wound, apply an antibiotic ointment, and wrap the area in gauze. Change the dressing twice a day.	Since second-degree burns penetrate deeper into the skin, they can easily become infected. Don't break any blisters. This type of burn will take several weeks to heal.

(continued)

first-aid for burns and scalds (cont.)

Type of Burn	Signs	Action	Fast Facts
Third degree	Skin will look white and leathery or charred.	Call 911 (or your local emergency number). Check to make sure that your child is breathing, and perform CPR if necessary. Remove burned clothing that comes off easily. (Leave anything that sticks to the wound.) Do not apply ice or water. The 911 operator will ask you to describe the burns and will offer additional advice.	All third-degree burns must be treated immediately by a physician, as they do not heal on their own and may require skin grafting. Sometimes a child won't feel any pain, because the burn goes below the dermis and into the tissue under the skin, damaging nerves.

A Handy Babysitter Booklet

When my 1-year-old became mobile, I decided that it was important to provide family members who care for her with emergency information. So, I created emergency-care booklets that include everything from poison control phone numbers to step-by-step CPR instructions. I also explained to them how to care for things like cuts, scrapes, and nosebleeds. Now, when we leave her with relatives, I feel better knowing that they are well-equipped for any situation.

Rebecca Repp, *New Freedom, Pennsylvania*

Bag of Tricks

I always keep a stash of Band-Aids in my purse in case my 16-month-old daughter, Noa, gets a boo-boo. She's more likely to keep the colorful kiddie ones on for longer. I also never leave the house without a rubber bulb syringe in my bag. My

keep vital information handy

You may keep all the pertinent details about your child's health in your head, but will you be able to think clearly or even be the one on duty when an emergency occurs? To ensure that you (or a relative or babysitter) know the emergency essentials, take a few minutes to jot down this important information and post it next to your phone or on your refrigerator. Update it at least twice a year.

✓ Family's name, address, and phone number

✓ Children's names, ages, and weights

✓ Pediatrician's name and office and after-hours phone numbers

✓ Preferred hospital

✓ Insurance information

✓ Allergies to food or medicine

✓ Current medication and dosage schedules

when to call 911

Save calls to 911 (or your local emergency number) for situations when you truly have a feeling that your child might die. Always call if your child:

✓ has swallowed something poisonous,

✓ has a serious burn,

✓ is turning blue,

✓ can't breathe or is breathing with great difficulty,

✓ suddenly becomes extremely lethargic,

✓ is unconscious,

✓ is bleeding uncontrollably,

✓ or breaks a bone and can't move.

toddler's too young to know how to blow her nose, so when we're out and about, I can quickly clean out her runny nose and make her more comfortable.

Alicia Headlam Hines,
New York City

A Kit for the Car

I made my own first-aid kit by filling a small Rubbermaid container with bandages, alcohol swabs, a pair of scissors, gauze, tape, children's medicine, and droppers. I labeled it in large letters with a red marker, so if we're ever in an accident and someone else needs to get the kit, they'll easily spot it in our car.

Brenda Henriquez,
Hingham, Massachusetts

Parental Consent

I think most parents forget and don't leave emergency consent forms with their child-care providers, their babysitters, or even their child's grandparents. I keep a form in our first-aid kit at home, and I always give a copy to anyone who'll be watching my children, in case they ever need medical treatment right away.

Marlynn DePaola, Anaheim, California

I feel sick, mommy

8

Why does it seem like your child is always sick? Kids have immature immune systems and less-than-perfect hygiene, making it easy for them to catch and spread illness-causing cooties. In fact, most kids get 8 to 10 colds in their first 2 years of life alone. If your child is in day care or school, he may get sick even more often, since viruses and other germs spread easily when children are in close contact.

If he's feeling under the weather, give him plenty of TLC, and try some of the smart Dr. Mom sick-day tips in this chapter. We've also gathered the best advice from top pediatricians to help you spot and treat common kids' illnesses—including ear infections, stomach bugs, allergies, and more—so that your child can start feeling better fast.

medicine maneuvers

Tiny Taste

Instead of having my 3-year-old daughter, Alexis, take a big gulp of her medicine, I tell her to taste it with her finger first. Usually, she sees that the medicine's not that bad—she even likes the cherry-flavored ones! Then, I let her hold the medicine syringe herself and help her push the plunger. Giving her some control really seems to take the tantrums out of the process.

Brenda Henriquez, *Hingham, Massachusetts*

Avoid the Tastebuds

When I have to give my 1- and 4-year-olds medicine, I place the medicine dropper in their cheek pouch, then quickly

7 must-know medicine facts

1. Mixing medicine with food is okay if that's the only way you can get your child to take his dose. Medicine that's paired with food or milk will be absorbed less quickly. Some exceptions: Penicillin G and erythromycin, both antibiotics, lose their potency when mixed with acidic foods such as applesauce or juice. Check with your doctor.

2. Crushing tablets isn't always safe. Ask your pharmacist, since some pills may irritate the stomach or medication may no longer work properly if the protective coating is destroyed. Also, have your child swallow, not chew, a crushed tablet. Chewing can interfere with the drug's time-release feature, make the medicine taste bitter, and cause it to stick to your child's teeth.

3. Don't overdo it. If you combine medicine with too much food or drink, your child might have trouble finishing it all and therefore not get the full dosage.

4. Don't freeze or heat medicine to make it taste better. Temperature changes could alter the efficacy of the medication.

5. Never call medicine candy. Your child should not think of it as a treat. Store all medications out of kids' sight and reach.

6. Aspirin isn't for kids. Giving this pain reliever to children under 16 has been linked with Reye's syndrome, a disorder that can cause brain and liver damage and possibly death.

7. Not all teaspoons are the same. Use the dispenser that comes with the drug or a medicine spoon designed for children. Spoons from your silverware drawer could hold too much or too little medicine.

fever facts

While most parents worry when their children get fevers, physicians say that it's generally not a cause for concern. The rise in body temperature helps kill bacteria and viruses more effectively. If you're unsure of how to treat a fever, though, don't hesitate to call your pediatrician. And you should always call the doctor immediately if your feverish child:

✓ has a temperature of 104°F or higher;

✓ is 3 months or younger and has a rectal thermometer reading of 100.2°F, or is 3 to 6 months old and has a temperature of 101°F;

✓ has a seizure, which is common in children under 5 and usually lasts 2 to 3 minutes (Your doctor will advise you on how to care for and prevent future seizures. But if your child seems to have difficulty breathing, is choking, or turns blue, call 911 or your local emergency number immediately.);

✓ has a stiff neck, a sign of meningitis;

✓ will not wake up or is unusually drowsy;

✓ or is irritable, lethargic, or crying continuously or inconsolably.

squeeze. They don't taste it that way, and it's harder for them to spit the medicine out.

Barbara Wagner, Malverne, New York

Mirror Magic

I've found an amazingly simple way to get my 20-month-old to take his medicine: Have him look in the mirror. For some reason, he loves watching himself do this.

Terre Tulsiak, Tampa

Better at Bathtime

When our 9-month-old son gets sick, it's a battle to get him to take his medicine. But we've found that he's much more cooperative when he's taking a bath and distracted by all of his tub toys. The best part is that we can easily rinse off any medicine that drips down his chin.

Jodi Davenport, Indianapolis

Give Medicine a Makeover

I added a drop of red food coloring to my daughter's medicine cup the last time she was sick. It transformed the chalky white liquid to a pleasant pink. Madeline, 4, was enchanted—and she finished the entire dose with a smile.

Joan Morgan, Pelham, New York

Hide It

My 3½-year-old daughter, Hannah, hates the taste of cold remedies. Every time I had to give her a dose of medicine, she'd run to her room to hide. But Hannah loves applesauce, so I sneak the medicine into a spoonful. She gladly takes it and then gets to enjoy the rest of the bowl as a treat.

Regina Ellsworth, Murfreesboro, Tennessee

smart routines

Your Own Medicine Bag

I keep all my children's medications—acetaminophen, ibuprofen, baby decongestant—together with measuring spoons and droppers, dosage charts, Band-Aids, and diaper rash ointment zipped up in a big makeup bag that I received free from a department store promotion. Our kit keeps their medicines together (and safely out of the children's reach), so we can always find just what we need when illness strikes in the middle of the night. It's also handy to grab when we're packing for an out-of-town trip.

Jeanne Sweeney, Arlington, Virginia

No More Misses

When one of my kids would get sick, I'd often forget to bring his daily medicine to the sitter's on my way to work. So, now, I ask the pharmacist to divide the medicine into two jars, and I leave one at the sitter's home and one at ours. It really helps cut down on missed dosages.

Elaine Callahan, Binghamton, New York

Make a Dosage Chart

With three kids, ages 3, 2, and 5 months, keeping track of medicines and dosages is a challenge, so I created a simple chart. On a piece of paper, I made three columns, one for each child. I listed each child's medicines and dosages and taped it to the inside of the medicine cabinet door. Now, there's no confusion, and I can easily update the chart after a doctor visit.

Francesca Raycraft, Severna Park, Maryland

Follow Your Instincts

I've often heard—from my mom and from parenting books I've read—that a parent always knows his or her child best. As a new mother, I was afraid that I wouldn't have that instinct. But when my toddler was sick with a fever and cold symptoms, it kicked in. I'd given her acetaminophen, but by the third day, she was still running a temperature and didn't seem like her energetic, playful self. I knew that something was very wrong and took her to the doctor, who told us that she had pneumonia. Noa got better as soon as she was on medication, but I'm glad I listened to my gut.

Alicia Headlam Hines, New York City

'tame tummy trouble

Sometimes it's hard to know exactly what's making your child sick, since he may be too young to understand or articulate the difference between a burning pain in his stomach and a dull queasiness, for example. But even young kids can provide clues to what's wrong if you ask the right questions, says Houston pediatric gastroenterologist and new dad Bryan Vartabedian, M.D. Here, he offers his best tips for detecting what's behind your child's bellyaches.

What to Ask	What It Could Be	What to Do
"Does it feel like butterflies in your stomach?"	A passing virus can bring on nausea and sometimes a low fever.	Keep your child hydrated with water or a diluted sports drink. If he vomits more than four times in an hour, call your doctor.
"Does it hurt like a knife?"	Constipation typically causes sharp pain, especially at night.	Encourage your child to use the toilet; give him water and fiber-rich foods; avoid constipating foods, such as cheese and pasta.
"Does it feel like your insides are on fire?"	Heartburn occurs when stomach contents back up into the esophagus; the pain is usually higher up, near the ribs.	Avoid giving your child spicy foods, carbonated drinks, caffeine, or big meals, especially right before bed.
"Where does it hurt most?"	An intense, worsening pain on the lower right side could signal appendicitis.	Call your pediatrician immediately if you suspect appendicitis, or if your child refuses to eat, has bloody stools, or has other severe stomach pain.

Easy Temperature Taking

I use an electronic underarm thermometer on my 2-year-old son, Luke. I let him press the button to turn it on, and to convince him to sit still long enough, I tell him to listen for the beeps. When it's ready, we read the numbers aloud together and he gets to press the beeping button again to turn it off.

Kendall Mallette, Chicago

Carry-Along Cold Relief

When my 6-month-old son got a cold, I was sick of running for tissues every time he sneezed. So, I took a basket with a handle and filled it with all the essentials: tissues, saline drops, Vaseline for his sore nose, and liquid hand sanitizer. That way, I could easily tote everything around the house.

Julia Ferguson, Vienna, Virginia

tender, loving treatment

Body Painting

When my 3-year-old daughter, Emily, got the chicken pox, she didn't like me to put calamine lotion on her, even though she was miserable and itchy. One day, I gave her an oatmeal bath and afterward had an idea. Emily loves to fingerpaint, so I poured some calamine lotion into a small bowl and asked her to fingerpaint every dot on her body. She loved it! We finger-

grandmother knows best

Hiccups are no fun, and there are lots of tricks for getting rid of them. One sweet technique that I used on my four daughters—and now my grandkids—is to give the hiccuping child ⅛ to ¼ teaspoon of dry table sugar. Doctors have told me that swallowing the sugar overstimulates nerve endings between the throat and diaphragm, stopping the spasms. And since all kids love sugar, it's often an easier way to end hiccups than trying to get them to hold their breath or sip a glass of water.

Maureen Conroy,
Babylon, New York

painted a couple of times a day, and the remaining days of her chicken pox were a breeze.

Nancy Kolada, Saskatoon, Saskatchewan, Canada

Cooling a Fever

When one of my children develops a high fever, I dampen a large towel with tepid water and wrap it around his or her bare shoulders, back, and chest. We sit together for a few minutes and the fever usually drops significantly. This trick makes it more comfortable for my kids to rest and easier for me to administer their medicine.

Donna Earl, Old Bridge, New Jersey

Fuss-Free Oatmeal Baths

When my son had the chicken pox, it was quite a challenge to get him to lie down in the bathtub long enough to get any benefit from oatmeal baths. I started giving him ice pops as a way to keep boredom at bay, and two pops turned out to be the recommended soaking time.

Janet Baumann, Murrysville, Pennsylvania

Clear the Air

My 6-year-old son and I used to often wake up with headaches, and I couldn't figure out why. Then, I read a book

does your child have asthma?

Asthma affects 5 million children in the United States, but many kids go undiagnosed because symptoms vary in severity and mild cases may be mistaken for a cold or allergy. If your child persistently shows the following symptoms, talk to your doctor. If the doctor doesn't diagnose asthma but the symptoms continue, consider seeing a pediatric allergist. Signs of asthma include:

✓ a nagging, dry cough that won't go away

✓ frequent episodes of rapid breathing or shortness of breath

✓ a wheezing sound when your child breathes

✓ a feeling of tightness in her chest

✓ symptoms that worsen at night or sometimes after vigorous activity

meals that heal

Though your child may not have much of an appetite when he's sick, try to get him to eat. The better nourished he is, the faster he'll recover. These comfort foods can help.

If Your Child Has:	Serve:
Constipation	Prunes or prune juice to stimulate bowel function; high-fiber foods, such as fresh apples, oranges, carrots, and celery; water to keep stools regular
Diarrhea	Clear fluids, such as water, broth (for kids over age 1), or electrolyte solutions, to prevent dehydration. (Avoid juice and soft drinks; the sugar can worsen diarrhea.) Serve a normal diet that includes such binding foods as rice, ripe bananas, and cooked veggies.
A fever	A regular diet, but since feverish kids generally eat very little, add dips, sauces, or butter to increase every bite's caloric density. Also give plenty of fluids.
A sore throat	Hot noncaffeinated tea with honey (but only for children over age 1); high-calorie ice-cream smoothies
A stuffy nose	Warm foods, such as chicken soup, which acts as a vaporizer, loosening nasal mucus

about mold and mildew allergies, which can trigger headaches. I put a dehumidifier in each of our closets to reduce mold-causing dampness. I close the closet doors at night but let them air out during the day. And we sleep with the windows slightly open every night. It has helped tremendously—no more headaches!

Kim Bloom, *Huntington Beach, California*

Steamy Solution

When my son has a cold and his stuffy nose makes it difficult for him to sleep, I turn on a humidifier in his room. I add a pinch of baking soda to the water, so it steams faster. If he wakes up in the middle of the night and still can't breathe, we go into the bathroom for a steam bath. I close the door, turn on the hot shower, and sit with him in there for about 15 minutes. The warm, misty air usually clears his nose enough so that he can go back to sleep.

Helena Ortiz, *Brooklyn, New York*

keep kids healthy

Bye-Bye, Germs

I used to have a hard time getting my 2½-year-old son to wash his hands with soap. To demonstrate that we do this in order to kill germs, I put a dash of black pepper into a bowl of water and told him that it was some germs. Then, I squeezed a little liquid soap into the water, which caused the black specks to move to the rim of the bowl. I explained that the germs go

spotting ear infections

Ear infections, know as otitis media (inflammation of the middle ear), are most common among babies from 6 months to 1 year old. But plenty of older kids get them, too. More than 35 percent of children will suffer through three or more bouts before they turn 4. Telltale ear infection signs include:

✓ Pain. Your child may pull on her ear, or become fussy and irritable, especially at meals and bedtime.

✓ Fever. It ranges from 101°F to 104°F.

✓ Drainage. You may see yellow or white fluid draining from your child's ear.

Take your child to the doctor, who may prescribe antibiotics to treat the infection or suggest that you use acetaminophen and warm compresses to relieve your child's pain. Because persistent ear infections can lead to hearing loss, which could cause speech delays, it's important to get your child treated right away. Once on antibiotics, your child should feel better within a few days.

get smart about antibiotics

When your child has a cold or the flu, don't bother asking your pediatrician to prescribe antibiotics, since they won't help. Antibiotics target and kill bacteria, not viruses. Administering them unnecessarily can produce strains of bacteria that are resistant to medication. To prevent the spread of these "superbugs," take these steps.

- ✓ Follow dosing instructions and give your child the complete course of the prescription, even if he's feeling better. If you don't, surviving bacteria can multiply and cause a relapse.
- ✓ Ask your doctor to tailor the prescription, if possible, to fit your and your child's schedule so you don't miss a dose.
- ✓ Ask your pediatrician to prescribe the antibiotic that can be taken for the shortest duration.
- ✓ If there's a choice, have your doctor prescribe a narrow-spectrum antibiotic, which works against fewer strains of bacteria, rather than a broad-spectrum one, which targets many strains. The more bacteria that are exposed to antibiotics, the greater the chance that a strain will develop resistance.
- ✓ Use the antibiotic only for the prescribed illness. Never give your child or other family members leftover medicine.

away when the soap touches them. Now, he washes his hands with soap without a struggle.

Christine Borrello, *Novi, Michigan*

Handy Hygiene

My 1-year-old son hates to have his hands washed. To make it more fun for him, I bought a spray bottle and filled it with soap and water. I spray his hands, then wipe them off with a warm washcloth. Now, he actually puts his hands out to get them cleaned!

Christine Pohow, *Rockford, Illinois*

Vitamin C Boost

To improve their immunity, I give my children a daily multivitamin. During the cold season, I also make sure that they get ample vitamin C in their diets with orange juice, strawberries,

when to keep kids home from school

Your child wakes up on a weekday morning complaining that she doesn't feel well. Should you send her to school or keep her home? Beverly Nelms, R.N., a school nurse at Westcreek Elementary School in Fort Worth, Texas, offers these guidelines to help you decide.

Fever: Keep your child home if her temperature is 100°F or higher. She should be fever-free without medication for 24 hours before returning to school.

Cold: If your child feels well aside from a minor cough or sniffles, send her to class. Pack extra tissues in her school bag, and encourage frequent hand-washing to prevent the spread of germs.

Ear infection: As long as she isn't feverish or in pain, your child is ready for school 24 hours after her infection is diagnosed and she's begun taking antibiotics. (Viral cases, though, don't require drugs.)

Chicken pox: Your child will no longer be contagious when all her lesions have crusted over (usually a week after the first blister appears). The hands usually take longest to heal.

Stomachache: It could be a virus or simple indigestion. Encourage your child to use the bathroom. Keep her home until she regains her appetite and has normal bowel movements.

and cantaloupe. To fight germs when we're out and about, I keep a supply of baby wipes in my purse so I can frequently clean my children's hands.

Jodi Fiore, *Sicklerville, New Jersey*

Sippy Solution

To tell my two children's Sippy cups apart, I put a rubber band around my older child's cup. This way, they don't get confused and fight over each other's drinks, and if one of them is sick with a cold, he doesn't share his germs with the other child.

Tara Claeys, *Arlington, Virginia*

childproof your home

9

from the moment when your child learns to crawl, usually at around 8 months, your home becomes a wonderful obstacle course for him to explore. But hidden hazards can make your house a danger zone as well. Your child's natural curiosity will prompt him to open bathroom cabinets, touch the knobs on the stove, peer over windowsills, or put small objects in his mouth.

The best way to safeguard your baby? Get on your hands and knees and crawl around for a kid's-eye view of the surroundings. You'll be amazed to discover the many troublesome temptations around your house that you hadn't noticed standing up. You also can use the smart childproofing steps in this chapter to spot and eliminate potential dangers in every room of your home.

home improvements

Secure Your Furniture

One day when my 4-year-old son was playing in his room, he managed to knock down a heavy dresser, along with the 10-gallon aquarium on top of it. He had been swinging on the dresser doors, which must have gotten the water splashing with enough force to tip everything over. The shattered glass cut his arms and legs, and he needed several stitches. I never thought I would need to secure such a heavy piece of furniture to the wall, but kids love to climb. Dressers, armoires, shelves, and bunk beds should be secured with brackets that screw into the wall.

Amie Truett, *Frenchtown, Montana*

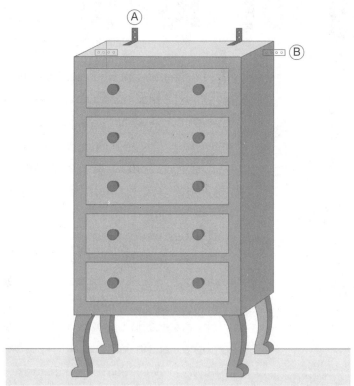

To secure a heavy piece of furniture such as a dresser, you can screw L-brackets to the top of the dresser, then screw the brackets to the studs inside your walls (A). Or, if you'd rather not damage the surface of the furniture, screw flat brackets to the back of the dresser so that about half of each bracket extends beyond the edge of the piece. Then, screw through the exposed part of the bracket and into the wall (B).

nursery know-how

The nursery is the first room in your home that you'll need to childproof. Even though it may still be several months before your baby is crawling or walking (and getting into trouble), furniture such as cribs and playpens, where your child will be spending most of his time, can pose significant hazards. Here are important features to look for and precautions to take.

Cribs

✓ Slats should be no more than $2\frac{3}{8}$ inches apart, secure, and intact.

✓ Make sure that the mattress fits snugly in the crib frame, with no more than two fingers' width between the mattress and sides of the crib.

✓ Frequently check to see that crib sheets fit by pulling at the corners and sides. Sheets can shrink after washings, and a baby can become entangled and suffocate if he pulls off an improperly fitting sheet.

✓ Choose a crib that has a solid headboard and footboard, with no cutouts that could trap a baby. Also, the corner posts should extend no more than $\frac{1}{16}$ inch above the panels, and the pieces should be attached with secure hardware.

✓ Do not place your child's crib, or any other baby furniture, near a window or window cord.

Playpens

✓ A mesh model should have top rails that lock automatically. Otherwise, they can fall down and form a pocket that can suffocate a baby.

✓ Look for mesh netting with openings smaller than $\frac{1}{4}$ inch; and on a wooden playpen, the slats should be no more than $2\frac{3}{8}$ inches apart.

Changing Tables

✓ To prevent falls, look for models with a safety strap.

✓ Keep supplies accessible in the table's drawers or shelves, so you can keep one hand on your squirmy baby and still grab what you need.

Listen for Doorbells

As an extra precaution, we hang bells on the doors of our home that need to stay closed for our toddler's safety, such as the basement door and those near stairs. The ringing alerts us if someone is opening the door. We hang bells on our front and back doors, too.

Mary Montes, *Trenton, New Jersey*

safety checks

In the Kitchen

✓ Try to keep toddlers out of the kitchen while you're cooking; use a safety gate.

✓ Turn all pot handles to the back of the stove, and make sure that appliance cords do not hang over the edges of counters.

✓ Install child safety locks on drawers and cabinets, but as an added measure, store dangerous items in a locked cabinet high above your child's reach.

✓ Remove stove dials and replace them with childproof caps.

✓ Keep kids away from a hot oven; the metal door can cause a serious burn.

✓ Place hot foods and drinks away from the table's edge; do not use tablecloths or place mats around babies and toddlers.

In the Bathroom

✓ Set your water heater's thermostat to 120°F or lower.

✓ Install showerheads and faucets that have anti-scald technology, and install a soft guard over the faucet to protect against bumps on the head.

✓ Place nonskid decals or a mat inside the tub to prevent slipping.

✓ Put a lid lock on your toilet to keep curious toddlers out.

✓ Store medicines and other dangerous items such as razors or cleaning products in a locked cabinet.

✓ Unplug your hair dryer and curling iron after each use and keep them out of kids' reach.

✓ Never leave a young child unattended in the bathroom.

No More Pinched Fingers

When my twin boys were able to close doors, I needed a way to keep them from pinching their fingers. So, I put a folded towel over the tops of our doors near the hinges. It's inexpensive and temporary; we do this in hotel rooms, too, to keep the kids from locking themselves in the bathroom.

Lynn Wilson, *Ripley, Ohio*

Around the House

✓ Install safety covers on all unused outlets; also place furniture in front of outlets to keep them out of your child's sight.

✓ Use cord covers to tuck loose electrical cords against a baseboard so children can't pull, chew, or trip on them.

✓ Don't overload an extension cord or outlet with more appliances than it is designed to handle.

✓ Install window guards on all windows; don't rely on screens to keep children in. And wrap window blind cords high above your child's reach.

✓ Install safety gates at the top and bottom of each staircase.

✓ Place covers over metal radiators, fireplaces, and exposed pipes to prevent burns.

In the Garage and Backyard

✓ Replace your automatic garage door with a system that won't close if it senses a child in the way.

✓ Keep automotive, gardening, and laundry products in their original containers and out of your child's reach.

✓ Always remember to empty buckets after use.

✓ Never leave children unattended near a pool—even a small, plastic wading pool, which should be emptied after use. Enclose your pool with a fence that's at least 5 feet tall and has a self-locking gate.

✓ Lock any out-of-the-way freezers, coolers, or trunks, which can be intriguing hiding places for children who may suffocate in them.

✓ Secure the doors on washers and dryers so that children cannot open them.

Cut and Wrap Cords

Even though I made sure to cut the loop in my miniblind cord and tuck the slack above the window's valance, my 2-year-old daughter Julie still managed to reach the cord by climbing on our sofa. She wrapped the string around her neck—thank goodness I found her in time. Now I know that cutting the loop isn't enough. I've replaced most of

our home's miniblinds with shades or bound up the cords'
slack with rubber bands so there's no way the kids can undo
them.

Patricia Jandeska, *New Lenox, Illinois*

it's my job

fire escape plans

Keeping matches out of your child's reach and routinely checking the
batteries in your home's smoke detectors are smart fire safety moves.
But creating—and practicing—an escape plan is also essential to
helping your family survive a fire. "Children need to be taught to get
out of the house in an emergency," says Jim Amy, a fire protection
engineer and father of a 2-year-old, from Findlay, Ohio. "When kids are
frightened, they may make the mistake of hiding in what seems like a
safe place, like their bed or a closet." Here, Amy, who inspects businesses
and homes for fire hazards, suggests lifesaving precautions that every
parent must follow.

Set a 2-minute limit. Flames and smoke can become deadly in
seconds. Explain to your child that as soon as she smells smoke or hears
an alarm, she should calmly leave the house as quickly as possible on
her own—even if it means leaving behind toys or a pet. The goal: to exit
in 2 minutes.

Plan an escape route. Draw a floor plan and map out an exit for
your child from her bedroom and other areas of the house. Each room
should have both a primary and an alternate means of escape. If the
exit is through a window, make sure that your child is able to reach
the sill, open the window, and safely drop to the ground or onto an
adjacent roof.

Practice often. At first, you may have to physically walk your child
through the route and out of the house. Conduct fire drills at least twice a
year, sometimes practicing at night. Agree on a meeting place outside,
such as a tree or mailbox. And plan on every family member leaving the
house immediately—someone can call the fire department later.

Sofa Solution

We now stuff towels into the seat cracks of our recliner. My 5-year-old daughter was climbing on our sofa, which has built-in recliners on each end, when her foot slipped. She cut her leg on a metal part of the reclining mechanism inside the seat

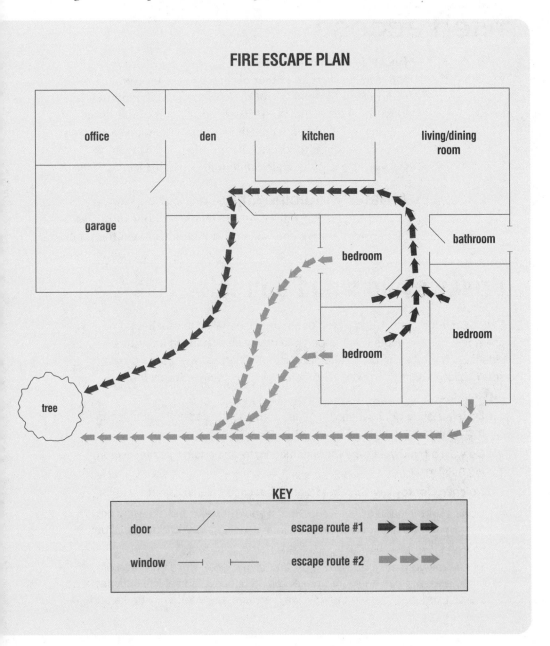

FIRE ESCAPE PLAN

office   den   kitchen   living/dining room

garage   bathroom

bedroom   bedroom

tree   bedroom

KEY

| door | escape route #1 |
| window | escape route #2 |

and needed stitches. I've heard of kids getting caught under the footrest or pinching their fingers. But parents need to also check the seat cracks for sharp ends.

Bridget Gaertner, St. Louis

limited access

New Doorknob

We store cleaners and other dangerous substances in our bathroom closet. To childproof the closet, my husband installed a new doorknob about 6 inches from the top of the door. By the time the children were tall enough to open the door, they were old enough to know what products are dangerous.

Gayle Schaming, Grimsby, Ontario, Canada

A Safer Medicine Chest

We'd thought that our cough medicine was out of our toddler's reach, but she climbed onto a high shelf to get the bottle

driveway do's and don'ts

Each year, more than 100 children under age 5 are killed in off-street collisions, car accidents that happen in a driveway or parking lot or on a sidewalk. The most common accident occurs when a driver backs over a small child. To safeguard your child from driveway danger, follow these precautions.

✓ Do tell another adult when you're about to use the car, so he or she can make sure that your child is kept at a safe distance.

✓ Do walk around your car before getting in, to be certain that no children are nearby.

✓ Do check for toys, which could signal that children are around.

✓ Don't start the car until you've looked in your rearview and sideview mirrors. Buckle up and look again. Continue checking as you slowly pull out of your driveway.

✓ Don't park your car in the driveway, if at all possible. Children like to play in the area and can be injured or killed if an unoccupied vehicle rolls backward. If you must park in the driveway, engage the emergency brake and lock the car doors.

and twisted off the childproof cap. She's fine, but we now keep all medicines and other potential hazards (including vitamins, ointments, and bug spray) in a small suitcase with a combination lock.

Liza Drewry, Fort Worth, Texas

Lock Exercise Equipment

My toddler cut his finger reaching for the chain of my mom's stationary bike. His 5-year-old brother had gotten on it and was pedaling while the adults were in another room. We should have been watching the kids more closely, but to prevent further accidents, my mom now keeps a lock on the bike's chain and wheel. The kids know that only she is allowed to touch it.

Pam Karnes, Bloomsburg, Pennsylvania

Protect Your Plants

We have a number of large plants in our home that were especially enticing to our son while he was learning to walk. He'd grab handfuls of soil and try to eat it, and I was constantly cleaning up after him. I was close to giving my plants away when my husband created a cover for each pot. He screwed two wooden slats across the inside of the pot, making sure that the screws were hidden by the lip. Then he nailed precut slats across the top, leaving spaces big enough to water the plants but too small for little fingers.

Lisa Chang, Austell, Georgia

sibling safety

A Reverse Playpen

When my son Matthew was 3, he was starting to play with small toys. Our second son, Graham, then 8 months, was just starting to crawl. The boys share a room, so I needed to find a way for Matthew to play with his toys, which present a choking risk to his little brother. We made the playpen the place to play with small toys. Graham was content crawling and exploring his baby-proofed room, and Matthew enjoyed having a place to play that wasn't isolated from everyone else.

Marilyn Powell, Nanaimo, British Columbia, Canada

childproof your backyard

Kids need a safe place to play outdoors, and what better setting than your own backyard? But your yard can contain surprising dangers, such as the lawn mower, the barbecue grill, gardening tools, and pesticides. Follow these safety measures.

✓ Keep small children indoors when someone is mowing your lawn. A child could be run over, or he could fall off a ride-on mower, get his hands or feet caught in moving blades, or be hit by debris or small stones kicked up by the machine.

✓ Don't let children under age 9 use any gardening tool with a sharp edge, such as a trowel or shears.

✓ Minimize your use of pesticides on your lawn; keep kids inside when they are being applied and off the treated lawn for 24 hours, until the product has dried.

✓ Store fertilizers and pesticides in a locked cupboard or shed.

✓ Keep children away from barbecues, even after you're done grilling, since the charcoal may still be hot.

Give Big Siblings a Test Tube

Because my 3-year-old now plays with toys that might be a choking hazard for her baby sister, my pediatrician taught her an easy way to "test" her toys. If the toy fits through a toilet-paper roll, it's too small for her little sister to play with. Since my older daughter loves to color and paste, we took a paper-towel tube (which is the same size) and decorated it with markers and colored paper. Now, when she wants to share her toys with her little sister, she checks first to see whether the item fits through her tube. It's safe only if the toy is too big.

Jeanine Gatto, San Marcos, Texas

Teach Infant Safety

When I was pregnant with my youngest son, Ryan, my then-3-year-old son, Adam, and I made a "little things" jar out of an empty, family-size peanut butter jar. We put all the small playthings that posed a potential choking hazard for a baby, such as rubber balls and toy parts, into the jar. This not only made it easier to keep track of these items but also made Adam aware, well ahead of time, of the types of things that would be unsuitable for our new baby to play with.

Tammy Maxey, *Midwest City, Oklahoma*

safeguard your yard

Create a Driveway Safety Zone

Our 18-month-old son, Ian, is a very active boy who loves playing outside. But there's a blind spot in our driveway where it curves around the back of the house, and we worried about accidents. So, we made our own traffic safety sign with a few pieces of wood and some cardboard. It says "Slow: Ian at Play," and we place it in the middle of the driveway to warn visitors

holiday hazards

Before you deck the halls with glittery lights, mistletoe, candles, and other festive decorations, do a quick safety check of your home. Because you might be distracted by shopping, wrapping gifts, cooking, or other activities during the holidays, you'll want to take precautions beforehand to make sure your children are safe. Here are some ideas.

✓ Before you put up any holiday lights, check for frayed wires or broken sockets; don't even think of using real candles on trees.

✓ Look for a Christmas tree with supple, deep green needles; water it regularly to keep the needles moist.

✓ Set your tree well away from radiators and the fireplace.

✓ Hang small or breakable ornaments and any food or foodlike decorations—candy canes, gingerbread men, plastic apples, artificial berries—high on the tree.

✓ Keep ribbons on presents short: a small child can wrap a long ribbon around her neck and choke.

✓ Make sure that candles in menorahs or on dining tables are well out of the reach of little hands.

✓ Keep children away from potential poisons, such as holly, mistletoe berries, and amaryllis; alcoholic drinks, such as eggnog, and cigarette butts left over from parties; artificial snow spray; fire salts; and prescription drugs belonging to visiting family members.

that he is outside. This way, drivers have no choice but to stop, and we have one less thing to worry about.

Mischelle Guthrie, *Augusta, Georgia*

A Better Gatekeeper

My 2-year-old son seemed to be able to open any lock we put on our gate. To keep him from opening the gate and wandering outside our yard, I secured the gate with dog leash clips. They work great. My son can't open them, but I can—with one hand. I attached them to the fence with a short chain, so they don't get lost in the grass. Now, my toddler can safely explore the backyard without going too far.

Marcia Stubstad, *Fargo, North Dakota*

Watch Out for Hot Spots

I no longer let our daughter out in the yard without her shoes. One hot, sunny day when she was 2, Caroline was wearing only a bathing suit and toddled up our house's angled metal cellar door. She burned her feet and her bottom when she fell. We've since repainted the cellar door white to make it less heat-absorbent.

Patricia Giercyk, *Lake Hiawatha, New Jersey*

safety solutions for special situations

Party Favors

Our daughter, Sammy, is our first child, so our condo was anything but baby-proofed. When she turned 6 months old, we thought it'd be a great reason to throw a half-year birthday party—but with a baby-proofing theme. When our guests arrived, they were each assigned a small baby-proofing job, such as installing outlet covers, putting a lock on the basement door, hanging cabinet locks, or resetting our hot water heater to 120°F. After we had cake, my brother, who's an emergency medicine technician, gave us all an infant CPR refresher course. The gifts followed the theme: Sammy received a bump guard for the bathtub spout, a safety gate, and baby-safe toys. Everyone was happy to help, and we had a great time.

Erin Ficociello, *North Chelmsford, Massachusetts*

growing a kid-safe garden

To your curious toddler, the plants and flowers in your garden can look pretty enough to eat. Therefore, it's important to closely supervise your child and to teach her to never eat anything growing in your yard or in the wild without your okay, says Ted Maclin, who coordinates the Children's Garden Program at the Brooklyn Botanic Garden in New York City. "Be especially careful of plants with shiny berries, which are often poisonous," he says.

Your local nursery can help you identify potentially toxic plants to keep out of your home or yard, or you can call your local poison control center for a list. Maclin offers these guidelines to help you choose kid-friendly plants to grow (and toxic ones to avoid) in your garden.

Poisonous Plants

✓ Azalea

✓ Calla lily

✓ Delphinium

✓ Foxglove

✓ Jimsonweed

✓ Lily of the valley

✓ Monkshood

✓ Narcissus, jonquil

✓ Nightshade

✓ Potato (the leaves are toxic)

✓ Rhubarb (the leaves are toxic)

Kid-Safe Plants

✓ Allium

✓ African violet

✓ Blueberry

✓ Daylily

✓ Lilac

✓ Marigold

✓ Nasturtium

✓ Pansy

✓ Rose

✓ Snapdragon

✓ Strawberry

Friendly Inspection

Although my neighbor and I are vigilant about our children's safety, we double-checked each other by doing a room-by-room inspection of both our homes. It was very helpful to have another parent's perspective, especially because our daughters, who are friends, like to explore and play with different things.

Cindy Henry, *Denton, Texas*

Sound Advice

When it was time to move into our new house, my 4-year-old daughter was eager to help, but I was worried that with so many people coming and going she might get hurt. So that our friends and family would know where she was despite all the commotion, I put small bells on her shoes. They worked perfectly: Everyone could hear my daughter, even if they couldn't see her over what they were carrying.

Sherry Griffin, *Galt, California*

Use Detectors

A home carbon monoxide detector installed outside our bedroom probably saved my baby's life. One day, when he was just 1 month old, I noticed the detector read 32 ppm (parts per million). Within minutes, it climbed to 42 ppm. At first, I thought it was malfunctioning, but when I reset it, the reading was still 42. I called the fire department. The dispatcher told me to get out of the house immediately. When the firefighters later checked out the house, they discovered lethal levels of carbon monoxide in the garage, which is right below our bedroom (the baby usually slept there, too). Exhaust fumes from the car must have seeped upstairs. Without the detector, we might have lost our son.

Kristine Daversa, *Wingdale, New York*

outdoor and car safety

10

It's a fact: 90 percent of serious injuries to children can be prevented by taking a few safety precautions, according to Heather Paul, Ph.D., of the National Safe Kids Campaign, based in Washington, D.C. That includes buckling kids securely into their car or booster seats, making sure that they hold your hand as you cross the street, watching out for hazards at the playground, and dressing them in the right clothes to guard against the winter chill or the summer sun.

The smart tips in this chapter will help you protect your children from outdoor dangers as well as help make your outings easier on everyone. Follow our expert advice on car seats, pedestrian safety, playgrounds, and more.

out and about

Hat Trick

To keep a hat on my 7–month-old son, I always carry two hats with me. He inevitably pulls the first one off, and while he's busy examining that one, I slip the second one on his head. It works every time.

Jennifer Gleason-Sichel, Sherman, Connecticut

Facing Up to the Cold

To protect my son's cheeks in the winter, I apply moisturizer to his face before letting him play outside. I use one that

cold comfort

If your older child will be spending a lot of time outside sledding, skating, or building snowmen in the winter, encourage him to come inside often to warm up. Also watch for the following hazards.

Winter Woe	Telltale Signs	What to Do
Frostnip	Red skin may tingle or feel numb	Soak the affected area in warm water.
Frostbite	Pale or mottled blue skin, often on the fingers, nose, and ears; may feel painful or totally numb	Don't rub the skin; that can cause further injury. Immerse the area in warm—never hot—water. Call the doctor if the skin doesn't regain normal color or sensation within 10 minutes.
Hypothermia	Confusion, drowsiness, shivering; this rare drop in core body temperature can occur if your child falls through ice or is exposed to extreme cold.	Remove wet clothing, wrap your child in dry blankets, and take him to the ER immediately.

contains sunscreen, since kids can get sunburned even in the winter. I also give him some warm tea to drink before heading out into the cold. This at least ensures that he'll have to come back inside soon to use the bathroom and warm up.

Helena Ortiz, Brooklyn, New York

cool it!

On hot days, be sure to give your child plenty of fluids to drink, to help combat the listlessness, irritability, and headaches that can signal dehydration. Offer her a drink every few hours. Keep in mind that not all beverages are created equal and that foods such as ice pops and fruit contain lots of water, too. Here's the lowdown on some common refreshments.

Thirst Quencher	What You Should Know
Fruit	Contains 80 to 95 percent water, as well as vitamins and fiber
Ice pops	More appealing than plain water, but don't overdo it, since they often contain artificial flavorings and sugar
Juice	Be careful with this sugary favorite, since too much can lead to cramping, bloating, and chronic diarrhea in small children.
Soda	Often high in sugar and in caffeine, which has a diuretic effect, robbing the body of necessary fluids
Sports drinks	Okay if your kids like the taste, but not necessary; normal play does not result in a loss of electrolytes that water can't fix
Water	The best drink, since it has no sugar, caffeine, or artificial flavorings

Keeping Kids Hydrated

To make sure that my son and I always have water readily available when we travel, I refill empty water bottles three-quarters of the way and freeze them. When we go out, I take the bottle and add a little tap water to help it thaw. The melting ice provides us with cold water on the go.

Monica Parkhill, Lindsay, Texas

playtime strategies

A Shore Thing

When we head to the beach, we bring along an inflatable wading pool for our 3-year-old daughter. We fill it with water and put an umbrella over it. She has fun in the water while staying close by, and the shade offers extra sun protection.

Pat Wood, Amsterdam, New York

sunscreen savvy

According to the American Academy of Dermatology, 80 percent of harmful sun exposure occurs before age 18, and one bad sunburn in childhood doubles the risk of developing skin cancer later in life. That's why you must take steps to protect your child's skin not only at the beach but also at the playground, in your backyard, or when you're walking in town, even on overcast days. Follow these key rules for successful sun protection.

1. Buy the right formula. Check the label to make sure that your child's sunscreen protects against both UVA and UVB rays. Look for such ingredients as titanium dioxide, zinc oxide, or Z-Cote, which block ultraviolet radiation completely, and choose a sunscreen with an SPF of at least 15. Kids' formulas are usually hypoallergenic and safe even for babies.

2. Apply early and often. Apply a thick layer of sunblock under your child's clothes and on her face half an hour before she goes outside. Don't forget easy-to-miss areas such as the tops of her ears, feet, and hands. Reapply every 2 hours.

3. Teach good sun habits. Teach your kids to slip on a shirt, slop on sunblock, and slap on a hat whenever they're in the sun. To encourage your child to reapply, choose a kid-friendly colored sunscreen.

bug-proof your kids

Kids are bound to attract an occasional bug bite or sting each summer. To protect your child from pests, use an insect repellent that has a concentration of no more than 10 percent DEET (but never apply it to a baby under 6 months old). Spritz the repellent on your hands first, and rub onto your child's exposed skin, avoiding the eyes, mouth, and any scrapes or cuts. Avoid applying repellent to a small child's hands, since she may put them in her mouth. Wash the repellent off once your child comes indoors. Here are other pest-proofing tips.

✓ Don't let your kids play in swampy areas or near garbage cans.

✓ If your children will be playing outdoors for extended periods of time, dress them in long-sleeve shirts and long pants tucked into socks.

✓ Avoid using scented soaps, lotions, sunscreens, and hair care products on your child, as they can attract mosquitoes and bees.

✓ Teach your child to walk away slowly if she ever comes upon a hive, nest, or swarm, and never to swat at insects, which makes them more likely to attack.

✓ Get in the habit of checking your child for ticks after she's played outside. Pay special attention to the back of the neck and hairline, the armpits, and behind the ears and knees. Don't forget to check your pets regularly, too.

Made in the Shade

No canopy or shade over your child's portable playpen? If you'll be using the pen outdoors, stretch a fitted crib sheet over the corners. You can enjoy the sun, and your baby will be protected from dangerous rays.

Tracy Celentano, *Rochester, New York*

Dressed for Success

When I take my sons, Jack, 3, and Matthew, 18 months, to the park, I don't let them wear sandals, no matter how warm it is outside. The rule is, they must wear sneakers, so they don't slip or cut their toes.

Kate Jackson Kelly, *Pelham, New York*

Bug Off!

My kids are in the habit of wearing hats outdoors, to help keep them warm in the winter and to shield them from the sun during

treat poison ivy

If your child is going to be playing outdoors in a grassy or wooded area, make sure that he knows how to spot—and avoid—poison ivy, oak, and sumac, cautions Lawrence Schachner, M.D., professor of dermatology and pediatrics at the University of Miami School of Medicine. If your child touches one of these plants, apply cold-water compresses to the area every 2 hours and use a hydrocortisone cream to ease discomfort.

"The lines or patches of red, swollen, itchy blisters take about a week to heal," says Dr. Schachner. "Take your child to a doctor if his rash is severe."

Teach your child this reminder about plants to avoid: "Leaves of three, let them be." To identify each of the common poisonous plants, keep the following characteristics in mind.

Poison ivy: Three notched, shiny leaves with a red stem; grows as a vine, bush, or plant, usually east of the Rocky Mountains.

Poison oak: Three hairy leaves per stem, which look like tiny oak leaves; grows as a shrub mainly in the Southeast, and as a tall shrub or vine in the West.

Poison sumac: Tall shrub often found in swampy areas of the Southeast; has two parallel rows of 6 to 12 small, smooth-edged leaves with one leaf on top.

the summer. But I've found an unexpected benefit of this habit: During insect season, I spray bug repellent on their hats, rather than their faces, since the ingredients can be irritating to young skin.

Amy Zintl, New City, New Jersey

car seat safety

Seat Swapping Solution

Having two cars and only one car seat means that we often have to transfer it from one vehicle to the other. My husband and I came up with a system for when we're in a hurry to move the car seat but we don't have time to install it properly. We turn the safety seat sideways, so it's obvious that it's not belted into the car securely. That simple precaution could protect our child from a dangerous oversight.

Valerie Haveman, Chattanooga, Tennessee

Hooray for Car Seats!

To keep my toddler from fussing when I put her in her car seat, I've developed a little routine. I cheer, "Hooray, you're in your seat!" She raises her hands to clap and cheer along, which allows me to snap in her belt buckle. Once she's snug in her seat, she gets a big kiss, and we're on our way!

Alicia Headlam Hines, New York City

install car seats safely

If you have trouble making heads or tails of your child's safety seat, you're not alone. According to the National Safe Kids Campaign, 85 percent of car seats are used incorrectly.

Hal Karp, a certified child-passenger safety technician in Dallas, often performs car-seat safety checks and teaches families about the right way to buckle up. Here are the most common mistakes parents make and how to avoid them.

✓ The safety seat is too loose. It often takes two people to correctly install a car seat—one to hold it in place while the other person fastens it tightly with the car's seat belt. The test: You shouldn't be able to move the safety seat more than 1 inch in any direction.

✓ The car seat's harness isn't snug. You may need to adjust the straps of the harness depending on what your child is wearing. If you can fit more than one adult finger between the harness and your child's collarbone, it's too loose.

✓ The seat is facing the wrong direction or angle. An infant must ride in a rear-facing safety seat until he is at least 1 year old and weighs 20 pounds or more. The rear-facing seat should also be at a 45-degree angle to the ground. If your car's backseat is slanted, you may need to insert a rolled-up towel under the front of the safety seat to get the right incline.

✓ The child is in the wrong seat or not in a safety seat at all. Your toddler must ride in a forward-facing car seat until he weighs 40 pounds or reaches the height and weight limits of the seat. Then he should ride in a booster seat, since he's still too young and too small to be safely secured by the car's seat belt alone.

✓ Parents are using a secondhand seat. A car seat that is more than 6 years old may no longer work properly, especially if it has been in an accident. To be safe, invest in a new car seat for your child.

ask **Peggy Post**

riding in a friend's car

Q: My 7-year-old son sometimes goes on outings with his friend's family. Once, when I came along, I noticed that the parents were rather lax about having the kids use seat belts and sit in the back. How can I make sure that my son is safe in their car?

A: Your child's safety is too important a topic to avoid, so be honest with his friend's parents. Tell them that you are trying to teach your son to always use a seat belt and ride in the backseat. In fact, until he's 8 years old or 60 pounds, your son should also use a booster seat. Ask the friend's parents if they would please help by making sure that your son always rides belted in a booster seat (which you'll provide) in the backseat of their car, too—for consistency's sake as well as safety.

Bringing up the topic with the other parents may start a discussion about car safety. If so, you can share any information you may have, but be careful not to lecture. A bossy attitude is likely to offend.

Starter Kids

I tell my four kids that the car won't start unless everyone is buckled into their safety belts or booster seats. If anyone tries to sneak out of the restraints or squeeze out of his car seat while the car is in motion, I slowly and safely pull over and remind them that the car won't move unless everyone is secure. This rule may slow down our trip, but at least my little passengers are safe.

Donna Earl, Old Bridge, New Jersey

Eat and Ride

To keep my kids from trying to get out of their car seats, I drop a few Cheerios along the side of the seat (after making sure that it's very clean, of course). They're usually too busy picking out the little O's to think about wanting out. This trick works in the stroller, too.

Tonya Rutherford, Lynnwood, Washington

Take Your Positions

To keep our 2-year-old daughter safe while we unpack groceries from the car, we taught her to stand near a wheel and not budge. It works great: She feels proud each time she takes her position by "her" wheel, and we know exactly where she is, so we're able to keep a close eye on her.

Teryl Mandel, Portland, Oregon

enjoy the ride

I Can See Clearly Now

After my son was born, I hated driving our van anywhere because I couldn't see him in his backward-facing car seat. Backseat mirrors are designed to be attached to a car's rear window, but that is too far away to work in a van. Instead, I found that the clip-on mirrors designed for car sun visors work great. I clipped one on to the metal supporting the backseat headrest. Now, when I look in my rearview mirror, I can see my son's smiling face.

Christine Yeary, Brookville, Ohio

Changing Scenery

To give my baby something interesting to look at while he sits in his rear-facing car seat, I took an old bedsheet, drew designs and faces on it with permanent black and red markers, and draped it over the backseat. Every so often, I rotate the sheet so he can look at different scenes while I drive.

Julie Mulopulos, Mundelein, Illinois

Music Makers

My 3-year-old and 15-month-old daughters love to listen to music in the car. And to make our trips more fun, I keep a pair of maracas in the car. When it's time for the girls to get into their car seats, I say, "Everybody grab your instruments." Once they're buckled in, they have fun jamming along to the music.

Brenda Henriquez, Hingham, Massachusetts

Travel with Treats

In addition to keeping snacks handy in the car, I also have a stash of toys in the backseat that my daughter is allowed to play

teach your child street sense

Almost from the day your child begins to walk, you'll need to help him learn safety rules that will prevent accidents on the street. Follow these age-by-age guidelines.

Ages 4 and under: An adult should always accompany a toddler or preschooler outside. Nevertheless, you should teach him to do the following things.

- ✓ Play away from streets or driveways.
- ✓ Walk only where it's safe (on the sidewalk), and stop at the curb or edge of the driveway.
- ✓ Refrain from chasing a friend, ball, or pet into a street or driveway.
- ✓ Cross the street only with an adult.

Ages 5 through 9: Kids this age are especially vulnerable to pedestrian injuries because they're eager to be independent, and parents may overestimate their abilities. A child under the age of 10 should not be permitted to cross the street alone, but it's wise to teach him these basic safety rules anyway.

- ✓ Stop before entering a roadway or crossing a driveway.
- ✓ Look left, right, and left again before crossing.
- ✓ Obey all pedestrian markings.
- ✓ Never cross when an emergency vehicle is coming, even if the light is green.
- ✓ Never enter the street from between parked cars or from behind a bush, mailbox, or tree.
- ✓ Never cross behind a vehicle that is backing up.

Ages 10 and older: While middle-school kids have mastered the skills needed to cross a street alone, they still need to be frequently reminded of good pedestrian behavior. Teach your child these road rules.

- ✓ Cross at a corner or crosswalk, never diagonally or in the middle of the block.
- ✓ Check for other traffic when a car stops to let you cross.
- ✓ Try to make eye contact with the driver of a stopped or turning car before crossing; don't assume that he sees you.
- ✓ Watch for vehicles turning into or backing out of a parking space or garage.

with only when she's sitting in her car seat. She loves the treats, and I give them to her only when she behaves in the car.

Sarah Windham, Norwood, Massachusetts

street smarts

Practice Makes Perfect

To prepare my toddlers to learn how to cross the street, we play "stop and go" during our walks around the neighborhood. First, we walk around the block without crossing any streets. I say "Stop," and we all stop together. After a few seconds, I say "Go," and the game continues. Then when we approach a street or alley, I make it a point to say "Stop," look in all directions, then say "Go" when we've all decided it's safe and clear.

Margaret Deuser, Chicago

Stroller Solution

My 3-year-old son is very active and hates to sit still for long, especially in his stroller. If he wants out, instead of fighting with him, I let him push the stroller down the street for a while. That usually tires him out, and he'll often ask to get in again within minutes.

Tracie Beideman, Miami

Red Light, Green Light

My 2- and 5-year-old boys were always running ahead of me. To keep them in control, I devised a simple game: If I say "Red light," they must stop immediately; "Yellow light" means slow down; and "Green light" means that they can keep going. The boys know that if they don't follow our traffic rules, they'll get their "driver's licenses" taken away—and have to stay by my side for the rest of the trip.

Kelly Haack, Omaha, Nebraska

Walk This Way

When I'm pushing my 21-month-old in his stroller, I can't hold on to my 5-year-old son's hand at the same time. We've developed a routine to solve the problem. He now grabs on to the stroller handle, and as long as I can see his hand there, I know that both of my kids are safe when we're out walking.

Kesia VanPelt, Lawton, Oklahoma

Sign Language

On our walks around the neighborhood, I always try to point out letters and numbers on signs to my 2-year-old. Even at this early age, he's able to recognize letters and knows how to read a stop sign. When we see a big red sign, he always stops to spell out the letters. The game teaches him the basics of letters and of traffic.

Kendall Mallette, Chicago

Avoiding Stranger Danger

I taught my kids a simple rule about strangers: "You may talk, but never walk." I explain to my children that before going anywhere without me or their dad, they must come and tell us. Their occasional "chats" with strangers are always just that—they know they can't go anywhere without checking with us first.

Karen Johnson, Bedford, New Hampshire

playground safety

You might assume that since playgrounds are designed for kids, they must be safe places for children to play in. But the disturbing truth is that every year, more than 200,000 children are treated in hospital emergency rooms for playground-related injuries, most often resulting from falls. There are no mandatory safety standards for public playgrounds, so it's up to you to ensure that your child plays it safe. Follow these steps.

✓ Make sure that the playground has a protective surface made of rubber, fine sand, pea gravel, or wood chips to cushion falls. It should extend at least 6 feet around the play equipment.

✓ Check for protruding hardware or sharp edges.

✓ Steer your child to age-appropriate equipment. A toddler or preschooler can safely play with activity panels, tot swings, small slides, spring rocking animals, sandboxes, and crawl tunnels.

✓ Don't let a child under age 5 play on equipment higher than 4 feet; a school-age child should not use equipment that exceeds 8 feet in height.

✓ Don't let your child wear scarves, bike helmets, or clothing with drawstrings, which can get caught on equipment and pose a strangulation hazard.

✓ Always closely supervise your child when she's at the playground. Be ready to jump in and play along to make the activity safer.

smart shopping rules

It's every parent's nightmare: One minute, your child is right beside you at the store or supermarket; the next minute, you can't find her. It's easy for parents and kids to lose track of each other in crowded places. Fortunately, a curious child rarely strays far. A trick: If you're at a busy department store, get down and look for your child's feet. And teach your child to follow these important safety rules.

✓ Ask a safe adult, such as a woman with kids or the closest cashier, for help. (A police officer may not be around, or it may be too hard for your child to spot a badge several feet above her head.)

✓ Speak up. Teach your child to say, "My mom's lost. Can you help me find her?" A child over age 3 should also be able to memorize her full name, address, and phone number. Teach her your full name, too. (It's not Mommy.)

✓ Stay in the area. Emphasize that your child should never leave the store or mall or go to the parking lot—it would be harder to find her. Also, teach your child to yell "No!" and take three steps back if an unknown person asks her to go with him.

Name Plates

My 20-month-old twins each wear an identification bracelet—not because we can't tell them apart, but in case they ever get lost. They're still too young to be able to recite their full names and address.

Marlynn DePaola, *Anaheim, California*

healthy teeth

it's never too early to start thinking about your child's dental health. Even though baby teeth eventually fall out, keeping them clean and cavity-free will help your child have a bright, beautiful smile when his adult teeth come in. That's why instilling good habits—brushing, flossing, regular dentist visits—at a young age is so important.

But teaching a stubborn preschooler to handle a toothbrush or wrangling a reluctant second grader into the dentist's chair is easier said than done. The parent-tested and expert tips in this chapter will offer you great ways to soothe teething pain, get your kids to brush regularly, find a kid-friendly dentist, and make office visits more fun.

teething tricks

Cool Solution

When my daughter was teething, she refused to use a teething ring or other toys to help alleviate her discomfort. Finally, I found a solution: I put a few ounces of juice in a baby bottle, then placed it in the freezer upside down so the juice would rest in the nipple. (Put a napkin under the bottle to absorb the drips before it freezes.) Danielle loved her "bottlesicle," and I felt better knowing that she had some relief.

Hallie Kemper, Valley Glen, California

Traveling Teether

I live in a rural area and have to drive around a lot to get my errands done. This is murder on my teething daughter, because her chilled teething rings warm up by mid-trip. I bought a small cooler for the car and packed it with ice, along with an assortment of teething toys. Now, Miranda gets a fresh teething ring every time she needs it.

Dawn Savory, Otis, Massachusetts

choosing a dentist

Share a Chair

I found a dentist who let my 2-year-old, Nicholas, sit on my lap in the chair. As a result, he was less frightened and more cooperative, and the visit went smoothly.

Tracey Johnston, Howard Beach, New York

Cater to Kids

Our dentist has found a fun way to illustrate the concept of tooth decay. He shows my son a pair of plastic teeth and places little rubber bugs on them. Then, he gets to knock them off with a toothbrush. Now, it's easy to get my

health alert: baby bottle tooth decay

Believe it or not, your child's bottle can be hazardous to his teeth. When a baby falls asleep with a bottle in his mouth, the sugars from the formula, milk, or juice pool in his mouth and feed bacteria that collect around the teeth. The resulting enamel erosion, tooth discoloration, and decay can rot baby teeth and jeopardize the health of permanent teeth. If your child needs something to suck on at night, give him a bottle of plain warm water.

how to ease teething pain

Between 4 months and 7 months, you'll probably notice two little red swellings at the front of your baby's bottom gums—a sign that his first teeth are coming in. Your normally cheerful child may have occasional periods of crankiness, crying, excessive drooling, or an urge to chomp on something hard. Also, he may suffer from a low-grade fever. Fortunately, most teething trauma ends within a few weeks, when the teeth push through the gums. Try these tested tips to soothe a cranky teether.

✓ Stock up on safe chewable toys. (Any toy that has breakable parts or is smaller than the circumference of a toilet paper roll is a choking hazard.)

✓ Gently rub your baby's gums with a clean finger or give her a chilled hard rubber teething ring.

✓ A non-aspirin baby pain reliever will soothe pain and reduce fever. If your child's fever is over 101°F, call your pediatrician.

✓ To help baby relax and feel better, rock her, sing to her, or play her favorite music.

✓ Never rub alcohol on a baby's gums. Even a small amount can be harmful. Instead, try a children's oral analgesic in topical gel form.

son to go to the dentist. I just tell him we're going to attack the cavity creeps.

Candy Salli, *Cranston, Rhode Island*

Tempt with Treats

I found a dentist who likes to give away a lot of prizes before, during, and after checkups. Just knowing that she'll get to choose fun toys makes the dentist's office less threatening to my daughter.

Lynne Bertram, *San Francisco*

no-fear office visits

Read All about It

To prepare my son for his first dental visit, we read a book about going to the dentist that explained how he helps keeps teeth clean and shiny. The first visit went so well that my son asked me to stay in the waiting room the next time!

Kristin Hogue, Downingtown, Pennsylvania

Find a Friend

My older son told my younger son dentist horror stories, so he was terrified to go to the dentist. To help make him feel better, I let him pick out a special stuffed animal from the toy store to go with him for checkups. Taking along his protection puppy really makes him feel better.

Fran Swerdlow, Fairfield, Connecticut

Getting to Know You

To get my son comfortable with going to the dentist, I staggered his dental visits. On the first visit, he looked around the office. At the next, he got his teeth counted. By the time we got to the cleaning, he was used to the whole process.

Sam Davies, Phoenix, Maryland

Set an Example

I took my son to the dentist with me for several of my checkups. When it was his turn, the process wasn't such a mystery, and he felt comfortable.

Dianne Rocheny, New York City

finding a child-friendly dentist

Your child will be ready for his first visit to the dentist between his first and second birthdays. You may have a wonderful dentist yourself, but unless a sizable amount of his practice is dedicated to children, you'll probably want to find a pediatric specialist for your child. Call the American Dental Association (312-440-2617; www.ada.org) or the American Academy of Pediatric Dentistry (312-337-2169; www.aapd.org) to get a recommendation for an accredited dentist in your area.

toothbrush tactics

Add a Dash of Humor

I recite a funny poem as we brush. My toddler looks forward to hearing the poem every day, so she can't wait to brush.

Johanna Harris, Bloomington, Minnesota

Let Your Child Choose

To encourage my 5-year-old to brush longer, I let her choose her own toothbrush and flavored toothpaste at the super-

teach tots to floss

Brushing alone can't clean teeth and gums thoroughly. To head off tooth decay and gum disease, your child needs to floss as well. Here, Laura De-Carlo, a dental hygienist in Brooklyn, New York, offers her inside tips.

✓ Start early. You can even try on children as young as age 2. Explain that flossing protects teeth and gums, just like brushing.

✓ Be reassuring. Show your child how flossing works on your own teeth so he can see that it doesn't hurt. Brush the floss across his arm or gently wrap it around his finger so he can see how it feels. To make the task more appealing, let him choose his own colored or flavored floss.

✓ Lend a hand. Always help your child floss so that he does a thorough job and doesn't harm his gums. Consider using a flossing tool, which is easier for a child to handle.

market. Sometimes, I even let her get two kinds so that when she's bored with one, she can switch to another.

Judy Fox, *Marblehead, Massachusetts*

Turn Up the Volume

To get my 5-year-old to brush for 3 minutes, I play a tape of songs that lasts for just that amount of time. She knows that when the tape is over, she can stop. But usually, she wants to do it all over again!

Molly Brown, *Toronto, Canada*

brushing battles

Talk to Me

Brushing my 2½-year-old daughter's teeth each night was a battle until I started talking to her teeth. While I'm brushing, I search for friends in between her molars. Of course, she must open her mouth wide so our friends can hear me. My daughter loves it and now requests that I talk to her teeth in the middle of the day!

Julie Walburg, *Alexandria, Kentucky*

Do It Together

My very independent 3-year-old loves to brush his teeth but insists on doing it himself. Trying to help him do a thorough job usually brought on a temper tantrum until I discovered this trick: After he brushes alone, I give him my toothbrush and let him brush my teeth while I brush his. This bolsters his "big boy" image and gets the job done at the same time.

Wyndie Prestwich, *Snowflake, Arizona*

Taking Turns

When it's time for my 2½-year-old to brush her teeth, she always wants to do it herself—which means that her teeth won't get clean. To keep both of us happy, I let her start the job herself and then give me a turn; then, I let her finish. That way, there are no fights, and I know that the job is done properly.

Mary Groezinger, *Hanover, Illinois*

Doll Dentist

My 2-year-old daughter resisted all of our attempts to brush her teeth, even if we offered to let her brush them herself. But she

brushing basics, age by age

Birth to 18 months: Rub your baby's gums with a thin, wet washcloth once a day. When his teeth emerge, rub each side of each tooth as well.

Eighteen months to 3 years: Buy your child his first toothbrush. Choose a brush that's labeled for children 1 to 4 years old and that has a small, rounded head; soft bristles; and a wide handle that's easy for little hands to grip. Brush your toddler's teeth with water after meals. Replace your child's toothbrush every 3 months.

Three to 6 years: By now, your child can use a fluoridated toothpaste; avoid tartar control formulas, which may irritate his mouth. Use only a pea-size amount of toothpaste; too much fluoride can lead to fluorosis, a discoloration that will affect a child's adult teeth. Make sure that your child brushes for a minimum of 2 minutes at each session.

Six years and beyond: At age 6, many kids can start brushing on their own; just stand by to make sure that your child brushes his whole mouth for at least 2 minutes. Many children begin to lose baby teeth around the age of 6 and will avoid brushing loose teeth, so watch carefully to make sure that your child is doing a good job.

using dental sealants

A dental sealant is a plastic coating brushed onto the chewing surfaces of molars that protects them from plaque and cavity-causing acids. The pits and fissures of decay start in childhood, so it's worth considering this simple, painless procedure for your child. Judy Ann Taylor, D.D.S., a pediatric dentist in Brooklyn, New York, offers tips on making the decision.

✓ If you have a family history of early decay, consider sealing your child's teeth in toddlerhood, as severe decay in childhood can harm permanent teeth. (Sealants are usually applied at age 6, when permanent teeth erupt.)

✓ Some dentists only apply sealants to permanent teeth that are beginning to decay; others use it as a preventive measure before decay starts. Check with a few dentists to find out what the best choice is for your child.

✓ If your child has allergies, check with your pediatrician or allergist before going forward with sealants.

✓ Before the procedure, have the dentist brush your child's teeth with the sealant brush so she can see that it doesn't hurt.

enjoys brushing her dolls' teeth, so I asked if she would like one of them to brush her teeth, too. She loved the idea, and now I help Dolly handle the brush. Better yet, she even lets her doll brush her teeth for a longer period of time than she ever lets us.

Kathryn Miller, *Pittsburgh*

A Family Affair

To entice my 4-year-old to brush, I have him watch his older sister. He wants to do everything she does, so he's more than willing to follow!

Joan Levine, *Fredericton, New Brunswick, Canada*

healthy habits

Make Some Magic

To encourage my 3-year-old to rinse between meals when we can't brush, I bring along a bottle of magic water that I tint with food coloring. He's so eager to rinse with his special water that he asks for it himself.

Tracy Busey, *Madison, Wisconsin*

Eat Your Veggies

Our best trips to the dentist are those where nothing happens. We've kept tooth problems at bay in our children by limiting candy consumption and making sure that they eat lots of nutritious foods, such as raw vegetables. A dentist once hugged me because he was so impressed by my kids' healthy teeth!

Janna Abbott, *Charleston, South Carolina*

tooth fairy tales

We asked *Parents* readers what the tooth fairy leaves under their children's pillows.

The tooth fairy pays $3 per tooth in my house, but according to one of my son's classmates, she pays more across town—$5 each!

Roberta Hanlon,
Westwood, New Jersey

Our tooth fairy leaves whatever change was in Dad's pocket. Last time, it was 58 cents!

Lindsay McConnell,
Santa Cruz, California

Once, the tooth fairy left her size-six gold shoes here. She was so tired and her feet were hurting so much by the end of the night that she took them off and forgot to put them back on. She called and said that my daughter could keep them!

Jacquie Coffin,
Olathe, Kansas

My son adores reading, so the tooth fairy got him a Captain Underpants book. Next time, she's going to write a message with a silver glitter pen inside the book she leaves.

Beth Squier,
Stamford, Connecticut

One night, the tooth fairy left a silver charm bracelet. Each time a tooth came out, a new charm appeared under the pillow!

Jocelyn Levine,
Thorn Hill, Ontario, Canada

"mommy, my tooth is loose!"

At the age of 5 or 6, your child will start to lose her baby teeth. Here's how to deal with this exciting milestone.

✓ Encourage your child to wiggle and jiggle her loose baby tooth.

✓ Soothe sore gums with ice or teething gel.

✓ Don't worry if a baby tooth hangs on after the permanent one has pushed through. It will fall out on its own eventually.

✓ If the baby tooth doesn't fall out after the permanent tooth fully emerges, see your dentist. He may have to extract the baby tooth to keep the new tooth properly aligned.

✓ After your child's tooth falls out, have her put it under her pillow for the tooth fairy!

Strike a Compromise

To get my 6-year-old daughter to floss, I made a deal with her. If she flossed with me after dinner, I'd move her bedtime up an extra 5 minutes—which is an eternity to a child. So far, it has worked like a charm.

Robert Fox, *Salem, Massachusetts*

 pediatrician on call

tooth grinding

Tired of the daily grind? Many children under age 6 grind their teeth in their sleep or when they're doing quiet activities, says pediatrician and *Parents* contributing editor Laura Nathanson, M.D. This habit, known as bruxism, is a way of relieving stress. Though it may seem (and sound) harmful, it's unlikely that a young child will damage his teeth, as children have very flexible jaws that distribute the force throughout the mouth. If a child is older and has permanent teeth, make an appointment with your dentist. If he's concerned about damage from bruxism, he'll make a special protective plate that your child can wear at night or during the times of day when he's most likely to grind his teeth.

making the most of

doctor visits

12

because of all the vaccinations that your baby needs, you'll probably see his health care provider more often in the first year than any other time. These appointments will give you and the physician a chance to discuss your child's growth, nutrition, and development. That's why it's essential to choose a provider who is open to answering any of your questions and who will make little patients feel at ease.

Hopefully, your child will come to love his pediatrician with time, but he'll probably have a hard time at first understanding why the doctor is poking and prodding him. To make checkups easier and more pleasant, follow the smart tips in this chapter.

finding dr. right

Bonding Is Key

When you interview doctors, try to get a sense of how they make you—and your child—feel. I chose my daughter's doctor because of how good she is at comforting Nicole. Before the exam, she often asks for a hug and takes the time to talk to her. Our doctor lets Nicole hold the instruments that she'll be using, and she examines Nicole's stuffed animals, too. I think the extra attention makes all the difference.

Tracy Engel-Hickam, Reno

No Unnecessary Tests

Our pediatrician won us over when he told us that he wouldn't prescribe antibiotics without solid justification. He's also against conducting tests, such as drawing blood or taking

choosing a pediatrician

An ideal time to look for a pediatrician is when you're still pregnant. But you may find yourself hunting again for a health care provider if you switch health insurance plans or move. Whenever you search, look for someone you and your child can feel at ease with, as well as an office staff that is friendly and supportive. Here are some questions to ask when interviewing a new doctor for your child.

✓ What insurance plans do you participate in? What fees do you charge for an average visit? When must payments be made—at the time of the visit, or when billed?

✓ How do you feel about . . . ? (You may have strong feelings about breast-feeding, antibiotics, or sharing your bed with your child, for example. You'll want to make sure that you and your doctor share similar philosophies on at least the major concerns.)

✓ Are you board certified? What hospitals are you affiliated with?

✓ How do you handle after-hours emergencies? What's your call-in policy? Do you charge for these phone consultations?

✓ What is the average waiting time for an appointment? How much time is allotted for each visit?

✓ Who will examine my child if you are not available?

5 ways to get the most from each appointment

Prescriptions, vaccines, sleep and diet changes: You may get hit with a lot of information during your child's medical checkup. And, unfortunately, if your provider has a waiting room full of other patients (as most docs do), you may have only a few minutes to address your concerns. Elizabeth Pruett, R.N., a pediatric nurse practitioner in Portland, Oregon, offers these tips for making the most of your time.

Think ahead. Your doctor or nurse practitioner will likely want to know about your child's milestones since her last visit. Take a few moments to think about your child's health from head to toe and to jot down any concerns that you might have. Also jot down any current medications.

Take notes. During the visit, be sure to write down important information, such as the names and dosages of any medicine being prescribed. It's okay to ask your provider to slow down, repeat things, or give you information in writing.

Ask the right questions. Your health care provider should have no problem answering simple questions such as "Does Susie need a multivitamin?" or "Is that rash normal?" while also examining your child. But if your concerns are more complex—you're concerned about a risk of asthma, or your child has been acting up at school—it's best to call ahead so that your provider can schedule extra time into your visit or set up another appointment with you.

Keep your own records. Because you may switch providers often, it's your job to keep track of your child's medical history and immunizations. Don't rely on your provider to always have that information.

Schedule wisely. The first appointment of the day is generally better than the last. And consider timing a checkup during your child's best hour, when she's well-fed and rested.

chest x-rays, unless they're necessary. He realizes that these procedures can really scare kids.

Cindy Felberg, *Albuquerque, New Mexico*

Someone Who Understands

My daughter was born 2 months early, and I chose my current pediatrician because her own child was also born prematurely and was about Miranda's age. She really understood my fears and concerns.

Myra Cocca, Indianapolis

Get Personal
I stayed away from a large, impersonal office. My daughter's doctor has a small practice with just herself and a nurse practitioner. That way, she really gets to know my daughter. At bigger offices, you might have to see a different pediatrician at every visit.

Alicia Headlam Hines, New York City

ease your child's fears

Read about It First
I have several storybooks about going to the doctor that I read with my 18-month-old daughter. I substitute her doctor's name for the one in the story and add or omit details to suit our needs. We always finish our story hour with a reminder that the doctor is our friend.

Stephanie Walsh, New Providence, New Jersey

Let Your Child Play Doctor
When our 2-year-old needed four stitches, I worried that he'd never want to see a doctor again! But his stuffed Mickey Mouse had a similar accident that also required four stitches (from Dr. Mom). When we brought C. J. in for a follow-up visit, we paid special attention to how the doctor removed the stitches so that C. J. could perform the same procedure on Mickey. The doctor even sent us home with a pair of surgical gloves.

Tami Skillingstad, Okanogan, Washington

Get Rid of the White Coat
Sometimes, a white lab coat is what frightens kids most, because they associate it with the hospital. My 14-month-old son sees a doctor whose staff wears bright colors or Looney Tunes uniforms. Or you can ask your doctor to remove his white coat before he sees your child.

Lisa Bates, Warren, Ohio

A Toy Kit That Teaches

To ease our son's fears, we bought him a toy doctor's kit with a stethoscope and other instruments. He loves giving his stuffed animals checkups, and he's much less afraid of his pediatrician now.

Donna Zangari,
Lancaster, Pennsylvania

Acknowledge His Fear

When my son was 16 months old, he had to receive stitches for a cut, and now, he cries at every doctor visit. But I let him know that it's okay to be scared and that I'm close by. Sometimes, I think kids just need reassurance that you'll be there.

Abegaile Valencia,
Royal Palm Beach, Florida

Special Treatment

Plan something special to do after the doctor's appointment, such as getting an ice-cream cone or going to the park. Talk about the upcoming treat during the visit, so that your child will focus on that instead of on what the doctor is doing.

Dorothy Kazebokowski,
Milwaukee

Dolly Needs a Checkup

I told my daughter that her dolly wasn't feeling well. My daughter explained the doll's symptoms (which were her own) to the doctor. He examined both the doll and my daughter (so the doll wouldn't be scared). Before I knew it, we were on our way—with no tears.

Yolanda Leon, Trenton, New Jersey

your child's health record

Even though your pediatrician keeps your child's medical and growth information on file at his office, it's smart to have your own set of records too. Jotting down a few facts at each doctor visit can prove invaluable when your child must be examined by a different physician, such as at the ER. Your records don't have to be fancy; a simple notebook will do, or your pediatrician may give you a "baby book" for this purpose. You can also use the handy "Your Child's Medical Diary" resource found on page 431. Here are the stats you should keep track of:

✓ Date of each doctor visit
✓ Reason for visit
✓ Baby's weight
✓ Baby's height
✓ Baby's head circumference
✓ Vaccine received
✓ Baby's reaction
✓ Diagnosis
✓ Treatment
✓ Doctor's comments

shot schedule

While you may have heard scary stories about children getting sick from vaccines, these cases are rare, according to the American Academy of Pediatrics. Still, you should talk to your child's doctor if you have concerns about reactions to the vaccinations on this list. Note: kids with health conditions such as seizure disorders, food allergies, or neurological problems may need to delay or avoid certain vaccines.

Child's Age	Vaccine
Birth–2 months	Hepatitis B (1st in series)
1–4 months	Hepatitis B (2nd)
2 months	DTaP or DTP (1st), Hib (1st), polio (1st)
4 months	DTaP or DTP (2nd), Hib (2nd), polio (2nd)
6 months	DTaP or DTP (3rd), Hib (3rd)
6–18 months	Hepatitis B (3rd), polio (3rd)
12–15 months	Hib (4th), MMR (1st)
12–18 months	Chicken pox
15–18 months	DTaP or DTP (4th)
2–12 years	Hepatitis A (required in selected states only)
4–6 years	DTaP or DTP (5th), polio (4th), MMR (2nd)
11–12 years	Hepatitis B (4th), MMR (3rd), chicken pox (if not given previously)
11–16 years	Diphtheria, tetanus

Key: DTaP: diphtheria, tetanus, acellular pertussis; DTP: diphtheria, tetanus, pertussis; Hib: *Haemophilus influenzae* type b; MMR: Measles, mumps, rubella

Video Doc

To minimize my daughter's fear of going to the doctor, I videotaped my older son's visit to the pediatrician (with the doctor's permission, of course). Before her appointments, my daughter and I watch the tape together and talk about what's going on. Seeing what happened during her brother's checkup helps her understand exactly what to expect during her own visits.

Misty Yoon, San Jose, California

taking the pain out of shots
Tell the Truth

It's better to be honest with your child if a procedure will be uncomfortable. If you tell him that it won't hurt and it does, he'll be less likely to trust you and even more fearful in the future.

Kristi Smith, Palestine, Texas

Bring a Treat

If your doctor doesn't give something to little patients, pass a treat to her so she can give it to your child. That way, your toddler will learn that bravery has its rewards.

Katie Wernerstrom, Springfield, Oregon

Talk It Up

I'm scared of needles, but I make sure not to show that I'm upset when my daughter gets a shot. Instead, I have a positive attitude: I've taught my daughter that doctors are nice, fun people who help you feel better and give you stickers. She looks forward to her checkups now.

Chaka Ivey, Vallejo, California

Keep Your Kid Guessing

I've found a way to keep my 4-year-old son from getting too upset or frightened during painful procedures such as shots. After the doctor explains what he's going to do, I produce a small wrapped gift from my pocket. We make a game out of guessing what it is; sometimes, the doctor even joins in. By the time we unwrap the package, the worst is over. We leave with smiles instead of tears.

Bruce Hanway, U.S. Naval Station, Rota, Spain

pediatrician on call

charting baby's growth

Besides vaccinating your baby at well-child visits, your pediatrician will use the early checkups to measure her growth. Growth chart percentiles may be a big topic of conversation among the other parents in your playgroup. But just because your neighbor's burly baby is "off the charts" and your little one is on the small side doesn't mean that you're doing anything wrong. By definition, half the population is below average on measurements of height and weight, says pediatrician and *Parents* contributing editor Laura Nathanson, M.D. "The rate of your child's growth is most important—not how she compares with other children," she cautions. Here, Dr. Nathanson offers some points to consider.

✓ Percentiles are only half the story. Your doctor will measure your child's height and weight at each well visit to make sure that her growth is steady. Even a tiny baby can still be healthy. Any unusual speeding up or slowing down of growth could signal a problem.

✓ Genes determine your child's tallest height. If your baby is below average, it's likely because being short runs in your family. A well-balanced diet will help her reach her genetically programmed height.

✓ Size isn't everything. Children who grow up to be shorter than average are usually normal, happy, intelligent youngsters. Studies show that height has little effect on self-esteem.

special strategies

Stress-Free Waiting

To keep my five children entertained while we wait at the doctor's office, we play "scavenger hunt." I make a list of 10 simple items (such as a tree or a red truck). Then, my kids search the magazines and books in the waiting room for pictures of the items. As they find them and show them to me, I check them off the list. The first child to find all the items wins.

Sheila Kelly, *Shirley, New York*

Remember Your Records

I jotted down the dates of my son's vaccines in the little book that our pediatrician gave us. I made it a point to keep it in his diaper bag, so I would never forget to bring it along to his many well-baby visits.

Kendall Mallette, Chicago

kids in the ER

Few kids get through childhood without a visit to the emergency room. In fact, a child is admitted to an emergency department somewhere in the United States every second—most often, due to a fall-related injury. Here's what to do if your child has to go to the ER.

1. Stay calm. Your injured or sick child will already be scared. If you panic, you will only frighten him further. Keep your cool so that you can better assess the situation.

2. Call your child's doctor first if it's not an emergency. Your pediatrician may be able to examine your child in his office. Or he may decide to meet you at the ER, or he may confer with the ER physicians by phone.

3. Keep close by. If at all possible, insist on being present during your child's ER exams and procedures. He'll need you to comfort him, and since you know what's normal behavior for your child, you'll be a valuable resource to the doctors.

4. Be honest. Don't downplay medical tests and procedures. Reassure your child that he's being well taken care of, even if things may be unpleasant and scary at the moment.

5. Support the ER staff. It's important for you to ask questions and get answers, but try not to get defensive or hostile. You child needs to feel that you have faith in his doctors and the treatment he's getting.

behavior

easing separation anxiety

13

the sobbing, the screaming, the desperate pleas for you to stay: When your child is in the throes of separation anxiety, it's enough to break your heart into a million pieces. Many children first experience this stage between 8 and 12 months of age, when they begin to understand that people are individuals and there is only one Mommy or Daddy. The panic often reappears when kids are preschoolers, and it can come and go for years when daily routines are disrupted.

The important thing to remember is that it's perfectly normal for your child to want you by her side: Learning how to be independent is part of her emotional development. Whether your child is having a difficult time letting go of you or a favorite security object, these creative tips will help ease the pain.

easier goodbyes

A Pocketful of Kisses

To ease our daughter's separation anxiety, we put pretend kisses in her pocket before we leave the house in the morning. We blow a kiss or two into her pocket and close it up so they won't escape; that usually stops her crying. We tell her that if she gets lonely at nursery school, she can reach inside her pocket and a kiss will be waiting. Her teacher has seen her reach for kisses during the day.

Nikki Coleman, Bronx, New York

Let Her See You Go

When our daughter was just a baby and I was still working outside our home, my husband would stand at the door with her and have her wave and say "Bye-bye." She got used to it, and whenever we would leave her with a babysitter, she would do the same thing. This has become a must now, and she's almost 4. It really helped her to see that I was leaving, not just mysteriously disappearing. Now, she knows that I always come back.

Jennifer Fitzgerald, Royal Oak, Michigan

Time It Right

I had a hard time getting my 3-year-old son to sleep by himself in his own bed. When it came time for me to leave after reading him a story, he would cry. So, I started letting him set an egg timer for 15 minutes. When the 15 minutes were up, it was time for me to go. It was really hard for him the first few nights, but within a week, he was telling me that I had to leave when the timer went off.

Rebecca Chase, Ogden, Utah

Soothe Upset Feelings

My 4-year-old son would throw tantrums when I left him with his babysitter. Generally, he always insists that he's a big boy and can do things by himself, so we sat down and had a mommy-to-big-boy talk. We talked about how it was okay for him to miss me and feel sad, but big boys do just fine without their mommies for a little while. He seemed to really understand.

Karen O'Connell, Boston

when new parents have separation anxiety

Children aren't the only ones who experience anxiety; parents can also feel the pain. Whether you're going back to work or simply going out for the day, leaving your infant for the first time can be tough. While there's no magic technique for defusing your distress, there are a few strategies that can help.

✓ Remember that it's harder for you. Babies aren't upset about being with strangers until they're around 9 months old, so your 2-month-old infant isn't yet feeling any distress at being separated from you. In fact, some babies are so at ease with other adults that their parents are disturbed that they don't make a fuss.

✓ Choose the right caregiver. If you're the least bit worried about your baby's safety, it will be harder for you to separate. But it's important to remember that no one can be as perfect as Mary Poppins: You should have realistic expectations of your infant's sitter.

✓ Phone home. Keeping in close contact with your baby's caregiver will make you feel more relaxed; just make sure she knows that you'll be calling often because you're feeling anxious. Chances are that she's experienced this before. As you become more comfortable with the routine of checking in, you'll probably feel less of a need to call so frequently.

daytime connections

Picture This

My husband and I rearranged our schedules so that one of us would always be home with our 8-month-old son, but we found that he would cry and miss the absent parent. To remedy this, we hung 16- by 20-inch pictures of us. Now, when he cries for Mom or Dad, we take him to his photo gallery for a quick peek. He laughs and squeals with delight when he sees the pictures. It also makes us feel better to know that we're with him, even when we're away from home.

Heather Snyder, *Quarryville, Pennsylvania*

A Letter a Day

When I go on trips out of the country, it's difficult and expensive to call home. To help my two children cope during my absence, I leave each of them a letter for every day that I'll be gone. I write about what I'll be doing that day and include a joke. It helps the time pass more quickly.

Mary Fowler, *Albany, Oregon*

Get Together and Do Lunch

I've found a wonderful family-owned day care about five blocks from where I work. My 2-year-old son's caregiver is very kind in allowing me to spend my lunch hour with him. It's much easier to part in the mornings when we know that we'll see each other during the middle of the day.

Lauren Westergard, *Portland, Oregon*

it's my job

relieve kids' anxiety

To end the crying game when you say "Bye-bye" to your child, try these tips from Eve Burkhardt, Ph.D., a family therapist in Westchester, New York.

✓ Keep the goodbyes short and sweet. Your toddler is superattuned to your emotions, so if she sees that you're upset, she'll be upset, says Dr. Burkhardt. Instead of a long-winded "Mommy's going to miss you so much!" every time you leave, say goodbye quickly and matter-of-factly.

✓ Do a trial run. Practice saying goodbye, then come back in an hour. The next day, appear again after 2 hours, and so on. Soon enough, your child will realize that even though you say goodbye, you always come back.

✓ Give her mementos. The soft sweater you wear that your child loves to stroke can help ease the pain of separation anxiety. "A tangible object makes her feel like she's holding on to a part of you while you're gone," says Dr. Burkhardt.

✓ Stay in touch when you're away. "Make a tape of yourself reading a story to her that she can listen to while you're gone," suggests Dr. Burkhardt. Another idea: Call her when you're away at work or doing errands, and tell her that you've left a surprise for her somewhere in the house. By the end of the conversation, she'll be so excited to find the surprise that she'll have forgotten about the fact that you're not home with her.

Parents' guide to calmer mornings

The predictability of daily routines soothes anxious toddlers. If your child screams and cries when it's time for him to go to preschool, these tactics can make your mornings go more smoothly.

1. Get up early enough that you don't have to rush. Keep the mood upbeat—this isn't the time to start arguing over what's for lunch or which shoes to wear.
2. To establish a routine, have your child do the same tasks in the same order each morning, such as getting dressed, eating breakfast, and brushing his teeth.
3. Don't turn on the television; use precious morning time to eat breakfast together and talk about the fun day that's ahead.
4. If you work outside the home, make a connection between your child's going to preschool and your going to work.
5. Create goodbye rituals that you can repeat every day, such as singing a special song on the way to school.

Daily Surprises

It was a continuous battle to get my 4-year-old son to stay at day care. He would sob and hold my arm tight. So, every day, I put surprises in his pocket—simple things like quarters, chocolates, and small pictures. It's a good way of showing him that, even though we're apart, we're still communicating. It has worked wonders.

Amy Gray, Great Falls, Montana

Make It into a Game

We found a great way for our 3-year-old son to get through the day without us, almost tear-free. He stays at home with a sitter, so we have preplanned times when one of us will call from the office: after he eats his lunch and after he takes his nap. Then we play a quick game: We make silly guesses about what he had for lunch or what he dreamed about during his nap. Our sitter tells us that he really looks forward to these calls and is still smiling when he hangs up.

Stefanie Stein, Hartville, Ohio

bye-bye to blankies and pacifiers

Make It Smaller

My son held on to his larger-than-average blankie for the longest time. It started getting holes from being snuggled and washed too often. I whipped out my sewing kit and, rather than fixing up the tears, I made it into a smaller, more manageable (and better-looking!) blankie. A month later, I made it into an even smaller blankie. Eventually, it was so small that he could keep it in his pocket for comfort.

Anna Hughes, New Castle, Pennsylvania

Wean Him Slowly

Just after our son turned 3, we slowly weaned him off of his pacifier. First, he wasn't allowed to suck on it in the car. Once he got used to that, we didn't let him have it when he watched television. Then, the pacifier could only be used in his bedroom, and, finally, only during naps and at bedtime. It took a long time and lots of patience, but he finally learned to live without it.

Beth Fernandez, Mystic, Connecticut

Let Him Decide When He's Ready

My son was 2 years old when he decided that he no longer needed to carry around his favorite object—a scrap of soft fur from an old hat. For the longest time, he'd rub it against his cheek while he sucked his thumb. One day, he simply put the fur on a shelf and never picked it up again. Soon after, his thumb sucking stopped too. He just needed some time to figure out what worked best for him.

Beth Petronis, Albuquerque, New Mexico

Stay Cool—And Offer a Reward

Both of my daughters hung on to their pacifiers well past 3 years old. As much as we agonized that they were too old to be sucking on them, we tried not to make a big deal out of it. Instead, we casually—but consistently—told them that it was almost time to put them away for good. We also told them that they could sleep in big-girl beds when they gave them up

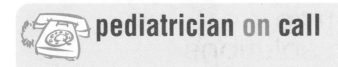

help for thumb suckers

Babies and toddlers often unconsciously turn to their thumbs when they're feeling stressed. Don't worry too much, says pediatrician and *Parents* contributing editor Laura Nathanson, M.D. It's actually a healthy way for your child to comfort himself. Children usually stop the habit on their own, but sometimes they need their parents' encouragement.

Give reminders. Make your child aware of his thumb sucking, but not in a way that makes him feel guilty or like he's done something wrong. Simply ask, "Did you know that you're sucking your thumb?" Your child should be willing to try to give up the habit; pressure from you may only make him rebellious and uncooperative.

Reward him. Chart his progress on a calendar and give him small rewards—such as stickers, shiny new quarters, or extra stories before bedtime—for each day of no thumb sucking.

Keep his hands busy. If you notice him sucking his thumb, encourage him to do something else with his hands, such as play with construction toys, cuddle a stuffed animal, or put together a jigsaw puzzle.

Make it less appealing. Wrap a plain adhesive bandage on your child's thumb: It's unobtrusive and flesh-colored, but not especially tasty.

entirely. As soon as our youngest got rid of her pacifier, we rewarded the girls with bunk beds!

Christy Zang, *Olathe, Kansas*

Throw a Goodbye Party

To help our 3-year-old son get rid of his pacifier, we announced that it was time for a going-away party for it and had him pick the day. We made sure to prepare him for what it would be like to say goodbye, and we talked about what a big boy he was. At the party, we had pizza and cupcakes, and then it was time for the big moment: My son went to the garbage and threw his pacifier away! He occasionally asked where I thought his "nucky" had gone, but overall, he was able to part with it without difficulty.

Lisa Kolstad, *Middletown, Connecticut*

tried-and-true
separation solutions

The Disappearing Mommy

I used to try to sneak off after dropping my 3-year-old son at day care, but the teachers told me that he felt abandoned and would cry when he discovered that I was gone. Now, I'm careful to make sure that he knows I'm leaving, without overdoing it. It makes us both feel better.

Lisa Stevenson, *Boulder, Colorado*

Soothing Substitutes

Ever since I first brought my son home from the hospital, I've kept the same teddy bear and blanket in his crib. Now, they really help him with transitions to new places: Wherever he goes, Teddie and Blankie go too. It gives him some comfort when he has to be away from me.

Paige Goode, *Melbourne, Florida*

Get Enough Sleep

My 4-year-old daughter gets cranky and anxious if she doesn't get 11 hours of sleep every night. She latches onto my leg and just won't let me leave her at day care. So, I make sure that she goes to bed on time and gets all the sleep she needs. She's able to deal with my leaving much better when she's rested.

Denise Collins, *Tucson*

introducing your baby to her sitter

To test out the chemistry between your baby and a new caregiver, try these tips.

✓ Allow yourself an extra hour or two before you leave so that the three of you can spend some "getting to know you" time together.

✓ Let the sitter talk to the baby without touching or reaching out for her.

✓ Once your baby seems at ease, put her on the floor to play with a favorite toy. The sitter should slowly come forward and play with the toy too. You can gradually move back.

✓ Leave the room quietly and see what happens. If your baby doesn't notice that you've left, the introduction has gone well.

keep kindergartners calm

Cece James, a teacher at Serendipity Day School in Albuquerque, New Mexico, uses some creative methods to help her students feel better when their parents leave.

- ✓ Have them write a letter to Mommy. Or draw a picture, or make a craft just for her. Spending time on a gift for a parent is better than feeling sad that the parent isn't there.

- ✓ Wave from the "goodbye window." "It can help for children to see their parents actually getting in their cars and leaving—it makes them feel like they have some control over the situation by being the ones to say goodbye," says James. After the parent has pulled away, the child understands that it's time for play.

- ✓ Sympathize. Acknowledge the child's sad feelings. "I say, 'Sometimes, I miss my mommy too,'" James says. Not only does this validate the child's feelings and make him feel better, but it also builds a bond between him and the caregiver.

comfort for clingy kids

Encouraging Independence

My 14-month-old son insisted on being held while I vacuumed; he didn't like being away from me for a minute. To help him gain some independence (and let me vacuum without a 27-pound toddler in my arms!), I bought him his own vacuum cleaner toy. He loves it: He now vacuums right beside me.

Megan Crouch, *Trenton, Ohio*

Let Him Show You Around

My 4-year-old would throw fits when I left him at day care, so I started sticking around a little longer when I took him there in the morning. I would ask him to tell me different things about the toys, the rooms, and the crafts out on the tables. After a few weeks of this, he didn't mind it so much when it was time for me to leave him. I think he started to realize that any place he knew so much about couldn't be that bad.

Pamela Moore, *Tampa*

Jodie Foster

"My focus is so completely on my son. Even if I get a lot done in the day, I just can't think about anything else but him. You have to be okay with the fact that some stuff is going to suffer, and what's going to suffer is the job. It's never going to be your child."

—actress and mother
of Charles

Find a Friend

When my daughter, Christina, was 3, she seemed permanently attached to my leg: It terrified her to let go of me! My mother convinced me that a regular companion (besides me) might help her be less dependent. One day, I invited the toddler daughter of a friend over, and, after a little hesitation, Christina let go of me and started to play. Soon enough, the two became the best of friends and, as Christina gained a little independence, she stopped needing to be next to me at all times.

Debbie Trott, Fayetteville,
North Carolina

discipline

do's and don'ts

disciplining your children is probably one of the most challenging jobs you do as a parent. It can be especially difficult when your kids behave in ways that drive you nuts—like when your oldest child hits her little sibling or when your kids turn your living room into a three-ring circus. You may feel like throwing a tantrum yourself sometimes, but try to stay calm and realize that your kids need you to set limits for them in order to learn what's appropriate behavior.

Discipline is more about teaching right from wrong than it is about punishment. The tried-and-true tactics in this chapter will help you encourage your children to do what you ask—without yelling.

14

keep it positive

Recognize Good Behavior

Every so often we hold an "appreciation day" to honor a member of our family. On that day, the honoree receives his favorite meal and plenty of praise. Most recently, one of our sons was honored for being a great big brother. It helps us all focus on the positive.

Renee Brown, Missouri City, Texas

No More No's

Rather than telling our 2-year-old Luke no every time he does something wrong (which would only teach him to say no all the time, too), my husband and I have tried to say, "That's not a good choice." Also, we make an effort to point out his good deeds as well. So, when he helps clean up or plays nicely, we say, "You made a really good choice."

Kendall Mallette, Chicago

Discipline in Private

I've learned that it's best to praise kids in public and correct in private. While it's important to correct and direct our children, it's really not other people's business. Disciplining a child in front of others—even an aunt or grandparent—can embarrass and demean the child.

*Janna Abbott,
Columbia, South Carolina*

Present a United Front

My husband and I try to discuss and agree upon methods of discipline before implementing them with our kids. Our advice: Never get into a conflict with each other over punishment in front of your children. They'll find it confusing and be more likely to challenge you when you lay down the law in the future.

Donna Earl, Old Bridge, New Jersey

grandmother knows best

During one of my 3-year-old granddaughter's fits of anger, I lay down beside her ranting, railing body and said, "Wow! Can you show me how to do that?" Amazingly, she calmed down and began her instructions on how to kick and yell. Then, she arose from her position and helped me adjust my "tantrum pose." We laughed as she moved my arms and legs while giving additional directions.

*Sue Turner,
Coeur D'Alene, Idaho*

timeout mistakes parents make

Every parent uses time outs, but do you know how to do it right? Camilo Ortiz, Ph.D., a clinical psychologist and researcher at the State University of New York at Stony Brook, has conducted many parenting classes at community centers to help moms and dads develop better discipline strategies. "Timeouts help interrupt a child's bad behavior and give a cooling-off period when a meltdown is about to happen," he says. But in order for this discipline tool to be effective, you must follow a few simple rules. Here, says Dr. Ortiz, are five common pitfalls to avoid.

1. Making timeout fun: Your child won't view timeout as a punishment if she has fun things to do during it. Find a boring spot in your house that doesn't have a lot of distractions, such as a bathroom, a laundry room, or a chair in the hallway. "The more boring a timeout is, the better," Dr. Ortiz says.

2. Giving your child attention during the timeout: Silence speaks louder than words. Therefore, don't talk to or lecture your child during a timeout. Kids will take negative attention over being ignored any day. Even if your child starts protesting, ignore him until the timeout is over.

3. Making empty threats: Never threaten to put your child in a timeout unless you have the time and energy to follow through—even if he acts up and resists. Avoid unrealistic statements like "If you don't stop, you'll be in timeout all day."

4. Making timeouts either too short or too long: A child under the age of 3 is too young to really understand the concept of a timeout, so simply remove your toddler from the situation in which he's misbehaving. For older kids, timeouts should last just a few minutes: 3 minutes for a 3-year-old, 4 for a 4-year-old, and up to 5 for kids 5 years and older.

5. Not having a backup plan: If your child refuses to go to her timeout chair or leaves too soon, you can tell her that you'll now add another minute to the timer. You can escort or carry her to the timeout spot, but don't get into any discussions. Just tell her that she must stay in the chair. If she still refuses, take away a coveted privilege and drop the timeout.

Delay the Dispute

If one of us is disciplining our kids and the other disagrees, we let the person doing the disciplining follow through. But then, my husband and I talk about it as soon as possible and try to come up with how we will deal with this behavior in the future.

Mary Kay Healy, Hebron, Connecticut

setting limits

Time Is on Your Side

To avoid the tears and arguments that usually arise when we have to end one of my 3-year-old son's favorite activities, we use the stopwatch on my husband's wristwatch. We tell him how many minutes he has left to play, and when the beeper goes off, he knows that it's time to stop whatever he's

when mom and dad disagree

He thinks you're too strict with the kids. You think he's a wimp. One thing's for sure: It's natural to get into occasional spats with your spouse over discipline. "We've all inherited different philosophies on child rearing from our own parents," says John Gottman, Ph.D., professor of psychology at the University of Washington, in Seattle, and a member of the *Parents* advisory board. So, how do you and your spouse parent successfully as a team? This advice can help.

It's okay to have different styles. Your children can actually benefit from this. Seeing you approach conflicts differently than your spouse helps your children learn to deal with issues from more than one perspective.

Always present a united front. While it's healthy to have different parenting styles, it's important to keep overt conflicts out of the picture. Arguing about discipline in front of your kids forces them to take sides. "Children tend to take responsibility for marital strife," says Dr. Gottman. Try to negotiate with your spouse on hot-button issues, such as bedtime or hitting, beforehand.

Find a compromise that you can live with. You don't have to meet halfway on every discipline issue. Sometimes, compromise can mean agreeing to go Dad's way on some things. Your kids just need to get the message that both parents support the decision. You can even compartmentalize your responsibilities: Mom's in charge of homework and Dad is in charge of meals and bedtime.

doing. It's worked so well that I got the same watch for my birthday.

Stacy Schwab, Philadelphia

Be Consistent

My husband's job requires him to be away from home for long stretches of time. I've learned that it's important for my kids to know what to expect from me when Dad's not around. When my husband first left, I backed off sometimes on discipline: I felt sorry for my kids because I knew that they missed their daddy. But when I did that, I noticed a negative change in the way my children reacted to me and others. Follow the same routine as when you're both home. I believe that this makes kids feel secure.

Mikie Hoeye, Fort Polk, Louisiana

Give Your Child a Choice

When our 4-year-old acts up, my husband or I look her in the eye and calmly ask her one question: "Easy way or hard way?" If she won't stop yelling in the store, for example, I say, "The easy way is to use your quiet voice and we have fun shopping. The hard way is if you keep yelling, we go home now and no videos today." Then, I wait for her answer. So far, she has always picked the easy way—with a sly smile. Letting her decide her actions allows her to feel a part of the discipline process, and we never have to raise our voices.

Janet Thomson, Hanover, Maryland

stop yelling

Show Them That You Mean It

I used to be a yeller, but I found that it only made me seem out of control. Plus, by raising my voice, I felt that I was teaching my child to raise hers, too. Now, I speak with a firm voice and facial expression. My child knows that when my eyebrows go up, I'm serious. If you look and sound determined, your kids will quickly learn when you mean business!

Elsa Rabe, Slidell, Louisiana

Have a Little Fun

To get our kids to cooperate without having to resort to anger, we use something called the family fun jar. Here's how it works: When our children listen the first time that we make a calm request, they are given a penny to put into a jar. If they don't listen, they have to take a penny out. When the jar is full, they get to choose a fun family activity, such as camping in the backyard, staying up late telling ghost stories, or anything they choose.

Cate Alexander, Stow, Ohio

the latest on spanking

According to a *Parents* magazine reader poll, 72 percent of moms and dads say that they spank in certain situations. While many parents still approve of spanking as a disciplinary tactic, the number is down from 94 percent who favored it in a 1968 poll. Most child development experts, however, are clearly opposed.

The American Academy of Pediatrics recently took an official stance against spanking, stating that it has negative consequences and is no more effective than other approaches. Some experts feel that positive discipline techniques, such as pointing out what your child does right and praising him, are most effective in getting children to behave. Spanking may lower self-esteem and teach kids that force is a way to solve problems. In fact, studies have linked spanking to increased aggression in preschool- and school-age children.

Pick Your Battles

Choose the three things your kids do that bother you the most—for example, hitting each other, jumping on the furniture, yelling in the house. Concentrate on disciplining them just for these three behaviors and let everything else go (except for situations in which your kids are in danger, of course). This way, they won't turn a deaf ear when you discipline because you won't be nagging them so frequently.

Julie Hummel, Galt, California

Make Eye Contact

Our 3-year-old has a hard time listening. Now, when we want him to do something, we gently turn his face so that he's looking us in the eye. With his full attention, we can ask questions or discipline him, then have him repeat what we've said so that we know we've been heard.

Elaine Snyder, Olean, New York

Take a Time Out

When I'm ready to lose it, I give myself a time out. If the kids are running wild but are not in any danger, I'll hide in the bathroom for 3 or 5 minutes. A little time alone allows me to pull myself together. Then, I can eval-

listen to me!

We polled moms and dads who logged on to the Parents.com Web site about their toughest discipline challenge, and the hands-down winner was "My child doesn't listen to me."

Children of all ages chronically ignore instructions and refuse to cooperate. To encourage your kids to listen, you have to be a good role model. Offer them your ear when they have something to say. Avoid lectures, and involve your kids in creating solutions. Here are five other ways to encourage your kids to do what you ask.

✓ Describe ("These blocks need to go back in the toy box") instead of criticizing ("Do I always have to ask you to put your blocks away?").

✓ Be specific ("Please pick up the books on the floor" rather than "Clean up this mess").

✓ Ask them to repeat what you have told them.

✓ Offer limited choices ("Would you like a bath or a shower?") instead of giving orders ("You have to take a bath right now!").

✓ Try to give your undivided attention when your kids are talking to you.

uate the situation and decide what needs to be done. Also, briefly removing yourself from the chaos may give the children the time they need to sort things out or regain their composure. The role reversal also tends to shock my kids and lets them know that I'm really upset.

Christine Koch, *Abbotsford, British Columbia, Canada*

Follow Through

If you don't do what you say you're going to do when your children act up, they're never going to take you seriously.

Beth Bernstein, *Thousand Oaks, California*

Think First

When I find myself wanting to shout at my 4-year-old son, I stop and ask myself, "Is he hungry? Tired? Too warm or cold?" Usually, there's a reason why he's acting up. It's amazing how his behavior improves after a quick snack or nap.

Lisa Yowell, *Arvada, Colorado*

Give Some Notice

I let my twins have three strikes before sending them to time out. At first, I'd often get to the point where the boys had to be sent to their room. But now, the prospect of punishment is usually enough to keep them in check. If I see them fighting over a toy, I'll say, "That's one." Usually, that's all it takes to nip the misbehavior in the bud.

Marisa Kaplowitz, Denville, New Jersey

proper punishments

Do More with Chores

I don't give extra chores as punishment—talk about a way to make a child hate helping out around the house! But if my 4–

the rules of rewards

Though rewards and bribes aren't inherently bad, you should use them wisely. Children who expect a reward for every task that they complete are bound to be frustrated when prizes don't appear, or think that unrewarded activities aren't worth doing. Here are some guidelines to help you keep the treats under control.

✓ Praise is often reward enough. Young children are highly motivated by a parent's recognition and approval. Giving your child affection and generous verbal praise for cooperative behavior can go a long way toward encouraging more good deeds.

✓ Recognize exceptionally good deeds. If your child has just spent an entire morning running errands with you with few complaints or upsets, a reward is appropriate.

✓ Use incentives, not bribes. Bribes usually arise out of desperation: You promise your toddler a new toy if she sits still at the restaurant, for example. An incentive, on the other hand, marks consistent progress, encourages kids to change their habits for the long term, and is agreed upon in advance rather than negotiated in the moment.

✓ Use the right-size rewards. If you're asking for your child's cooperation at bathtime, for example, an extra story when she's done is an appropriate prize. Promising a new toy the next day is too far removed and unrelated to the evening activity.

biting basics

Toddlers occasionally bite their playmates or their parents not because they're trying to be vicious but because of their natural curiosity and lack of language skills. They don't know that biting hurts people. When a toddler is fighting for a toy or vying for attention, or simply wants his own space, he may use his teeth to express himself. Here's how to manage and discourage the habit.

✓ Let him know that you disapprove. Give the injured party more attention: Offer to kiss the boo-boo, ask if she's okay. Then, tell your toddler in a firm tone, "No biting people. Biting hurts." Never punish your child by biting back.

✓ Offer an alternative. Teach your child to come to you for help the next time he gets angry. You can teach him to say "I don't like that!" rather than retaliating with his teeth.

✓ Don't bite your child in play. If you say "I'm gonna eat you up!" and put his toes or fingers in your mouth, it's natural for your toddler to try it on someone else.

✓ Offer a biting substitute. Give your toddler a washcloth to bite on. Explain that people aren't for biting, but if he gets frustrated, he can bite the cloth instead.

year-old has a privilege taken away as punishment, he can earn the privilege back by doing a household chore beyond the ones be does anyway.

Gae Piotti, *Newark, Delaware*

Smart Sibling Strategy

My 6-year-old would occasionally lose his temper and hit his 8-year-old sister. She knew not to hit back, but just having him apologize and go to time out didn't seem like enough of a punishment. To teach my son a lesson, I let my daughter choose a favor for him to do for her, such as straightening her room. It helped my daughter feel as though she had some power in the situation and gave my son time to reflect on his behavior. After a couple of incidents—and time spent doing favors—the hitting stopped.

Connie Gunkle, *North Kingstown, Rhode Island*

discipline for your little one

Setting limits during your child's first 3 years is critical and, of course, difficult. How, for example, do you get your toddler to understand that she can't throw sand at her playmate in the sandbox? The key is to teach your child which behaviors are and are not allowed. Here's an age-by-age guide.

Age	Problem	Solutions
Infant	Your baby cries incessantly.	Respond to her crying, which is your infant's only way of communicating. Make sure that her needs (for sleep, nourishment, changing, and comforting) are met. Don't worry—you can't spoil an infant.
8–9 months	Your baby wreaks havoc exploring the living room.	Setting limits at this age means keeping your curious child safe. Child-proof your home, remove dangerous and breakable objects, and provide baby-safe substitutions, such as a low kitchen cupboard filled with plastic containers, for her to explore.
1 year	Your baby is drawn to what's off-limits, such as the TV, the VCR, the stove, and electrical outlets.	Begin setting limits in earnest, now that your child is aware of the forbidden and is intentionally testing you. Respond consistently whenever your baby tries something dangerous (a firm "No, that's hot" for example); offer interesting, safe alternatives.
1–2 years	Your child becomes increasingly defiant and loves the word *no*. Tantrums are becoming more regular.	Stop saying no so much yourself, since toddlers imitate adults. Instead of asking her whether she wants to do something, steer her in the right direction by saying "Let's go take a bath" and walking her to the tub. When your child throws a tantrum, make sure that she's safe and can't hurt herself, and then leave the room, telling her that you'll be back when she's calm.

(continued)

discipline for your little one (cont.)

Age	Problem	Solutions
2–3 years	Your child responds to *no* by trying to negotiate.	Make certain limits nonnegotiable. If your kids are clear that arguing will get them nowhere, they might not bother. Focus on enforcing those limits that are most important to you. And keep explanations short and simple. If you try to reason too much with your kids, they are sure to reason back.

The Power of Consequences

Our 3-year-old, Steven, first gets a verbal reprimand. Then comes a warning with a consequence ("If you hit your brother with your tractor again, I'll have to take it away") or the removal of a privilege (watching videos or a favorite TV show). A few months ago, at the playground, Steven chased some older kids into the street. I told him that if he ran into the street again, we'd have to leave. He pushed his luck, and I carried him home immediately. I only had to do that once.

Jennifer Chu, Redlands, California

Write from Wrong

Our family developed a form of discipline that's actually educational. When our children were old enough to read and write fairly well, whenever they misbehaved, they had to sit down with a volume of the encyclopedia and copy from it. The number of pages they had to copy depended on the infraction. When finished writing, they would have to give us an oral report on what they had learned. By the time my older child was 13, she knew quite a bit of volume A. Her younger sibling has watched her agonize over many pages and so far has had fewer behavior difficulties.

Karina Spencer, Seattle

sleep-tight tips

15

is "Mom, I can't sleep" or "There are monsters under my bed" a nightly refrain from your first grader? Is your 8-month-old still waking up several times a night? Does your toddler refuse to take a nap? You're not alone. Sleep problems are surprisingly common in today's kids.

Studies show that up to 60 percent of children in the United States are sleep-deprived. If your child is one of the statistics, it's time for you to reform bad bedtime habits. Teaching your child to be a good sleeper—from infancy all the way through grade school—is crucial for his health. Kids literally need sleep to grow, since human growth hormone is released at night. Ample shut-eye also bolsters their immunity, helps them do better in school, and fends off crabby moods. Here are some great tried-and-true tips to help your child, no matter what age, sleep like a baby.

better sleep for babies

Baby Tape

I recorded my infant's coos, gurgles, and laughs onto a cassette, then recorded soothing music over it. We play the tape for him every night when we put him to bed. The sound of his own voice relaxes him and helps him sleep.

Paul Currier, Huntington, Vermont

TV Trick

We finally decided to let our 14-month-old cry it out for a few nights. To make the minutes between checking up on her easier to bear, we turned up the volume on the TV, which distracted us a bit from her wails. By the third night, she knew that her crying would be to no avail, and within a week, we were all getting a good night's sleep.

Anne-Marie Welsh, Erie, Pennsylvania

Turn It Off

When our 8-month-old baby was still waking up several times a night, I took the night-light out of his room. He has no trouble sleeping through the night when the room is completely dark. We're also careful to enter the bedroom in the dark and close the door quickly to keep out any light.

Lisa Gonzales, Dalton, Massachusetts

Traveling Bed

We used an infant bassinet with wheels on it for both of our kids when they were newborns. We'd put the baby to sleep in our room, then wheel him into the hallway just outside our room when we were ready for bed. That way, he was close by for nighttime feedings but he wasn't awakened as my husband and I talked in bed. He slept much better—and so did we.

Sally Gilliland, Brooklyn, New York

grandmother knows best

Bedtime could be hectic when our 8 grown-up children were kids, since they were close in age and they were all sharing rooms. What worked for me was something so basic that it probably sounds old-fashioned. I established a routine—say prayers, read a story, have a drink of water, and then turn out the lights—and I was very firm about sticking to it. As much as my children fought it at first, I didn't give in. It was partly desperation, because my husband and I needed some quiet time to ourselves each night.

Mary Lou Egan,
Silver Spring, Maryland

Save the Crib for Nighttime

People are amazed when I tell them that my daughter was sleeping through the night when she was 10 weeks old. The key was something that my mom taught me when I brought Abby home from the hospital. Whenever it was practical, I had her take naps in her bouncy chair or in a cradle in the living room, and I only put her in her crib at night. That way, she

Parents' guide to baby bedtime mistakes

Most babies are ready to sleep through the night by 3 to 4 months—if their parents let them. These common mom-and-dad errors can turn your baby into a poor sleeper.

Being a slave to your baby monitor: If your baby cries when you put her down at night and you rush in to comfort her each time, she'll never learn to soothe herself to sleep. (Of course, if your child is sick or in distress, you need to help her.) Turn down the monitor so that you don't hear every whine and whimper; when she really cries, wait it out for 5 minutes before you go in to check on her. Tomorrow night, extend the check-in interval to 10 minutes, and so on.

Extending nighttime feedings: Your child is ready to give up middle-of-the-night feedings once she reaches about 12 pounds. If she's much heavier than that and is still crying for food at 2:00 A.M., it's a learned behavior. Instead of whisking her out of bed for a feeding, give your child a chance to put herself back to sleep.

Rocking baby to sleep: If you do this frequently, your baby will begin to depend on being in your arms to doze off. If she tends to fall asleep when you give her a bottle or nurse her, gently wake her up before you place her in her crib.

Putting her to bed with a bottle: When your baby falls asleep drinking a bottle, formula can pool in her mouth, leading to tooth discoloration and decay. Sleeping with a bottle also increases her risk of ear infections.

Confusing days and nights: She'll never be able to sleep through the night if she doesn't learn the difference between dark and light. To help your child organize her natural sleep rhythms, keep her room light in the morning and during daytime naps. And don't leave a light on in her room at night.

quickly learned to associate her crib and her bedroom with nighttime sleeping.

Mimi Lynch, Melrose, Massachusetts

Wean from Midnight Meals

By the time that my son was 9 months old, he still wasn't sleeping through the night because he'd need an early morning bottle. Over the course of a week, I gradually cut down on the formula and added water. Within a few days of getting a water-only bottle, he stopped waking up for his 4:00 A.M. feeding.

Ricki Mendolez, Jersey City, New Jersey

snooze strategies for older kids

Sweet Smell of Mommy

My 3-year-old daughter Rachel started having a hard time going to sleep after her baby brother was born. One evening, as I was lying with her in bed trying to get her to doze off, I took off the shirt I was wearing and said, "Here, sleep with Mommy's shirt and it'll keep me close all night." It worked like a charm. Now, Rachel picks a shirt from my T-shirt drawer each night to sleep with, and she goes to bed without protest.

Arlene Shusteff, Deerfield, Illinois

Bedtime Pass

My husband and I were having a hard time getting our 4-year-old son to stay in bed. He would come out every 10 minutes to show us an imaginary boo-boo, ask for a glass of water, give the kitty another kiss—it went on and on. Finally, my husband laminated three "tickets" for our son to use each night; he has to give us one ticket each time he comes out of his room. Just knowing that he's allowed to come out, and having to decide when it's really important, has helped Jordan immensely. His requests have diminished greatly, and we're all more relaxed at bedtime.

Cindy McKinley, Milford, Michigan

Easy-Access Water

If your child doesn't have a table near his bed, attach a drink holder (the kind that you hang on a car window) to his head-

toddler naps

Most kids are ready to give up morning naps at around 18 months, but experts say that toddlers still need a 1- to 2-hour afternoon rest between the ages of 2 and 3. Jodi Mindell, Ph.D., a child psychologist at St. Joseph's University in Philadelphia, recommends that your child settle down at the same time and in the same place each day. Don't let him sleep in the car or in his stroller, which could disrupt his schedule. Most toddlers are ready to settle down soon after lunch. Keep the routine short—a quick story, then let your child go to sleep, in his clothes, in a dark room. If your busy toddler says that he's not sleepy, insist that he have some quiet time in his bed anyway. Even if he doesn't fall asleep, he'll benefit from resting.

board. That way, he has ready access to a cup of water if he's thirsty after he goes to bed

Randy and Deborah Gremmer, *Brit, Iowa*

"Time for Bed" Alarm

We stumbled upon a great way to end bedtime battles. My husband sets his watch alarm for 7:15 P.M. When it goes off, we call out, "Jammy alarm!" Our kids know that that's the time to change into pajamas and start the bedtime routine. Sometimes, we even pair off with the kids and have a race to see who can get into their pajamas first.

Jill Cyra, *Cincinnati*

Start on the Floor

To ease my child's transition from crib to bed, I placed the mattress on the floor at first. If my son fell out of bed in the middle of the night, he fell only a few inches, onto a pillow that I had placed on the floor. Once he got used to the mattress, we moved it onto the bed frame.

Liza Judd, *Kelowna, British Columbia, Canada*

An Innovative Night-Light

An aquarium (safely secured to the wall) is the perfect night-light. The company of the fish, the glow of the light, and the rhythmic sound of the heater help my 2-year-old son fall asleep without a fuss.

Kristine Morris, *Monroe, Ohio*

Have a Reward System

To make bedtime easier, we keep a chart on each of my children's doors. After they accumulate 10 stars for going to bed without too much fuss, they earn an extra bedtime story.

Kathy Fenton, Hartford, Connecticut

Filled with Love

To keep my kids in bed at night, I have each of my sons pick a favorite stuffed toy at bedtime. I give the toys a big hug and a kiss and say that I'm filling them up with a night's supply of love. If the boys wake up at night and think that they need me, they know that they can squeeze their toys and get a dose of Mommy love.

Lisa Romo, Modesto, California

Home Away from Home

When we're away from home, the minute that we get to our hotel room, I show my son where he's going to sleep. I always bring his quilt with us and put that, along with a stuffed toy he has selected for the trip, on his bed. By the time he's ready for sleep, he feels comfortably at home.

Louise Goldstein, Ithaca, New York

Pint-Size Pedicure

When my daughter was 4, she went through a phase where she would come into our bed in the middle of the night. Finally, I came up with an idea that worked. For every night that she slept in her bed all night, I told her that I would paint one of her toenails—she could pick out whatever color she wanted. If she got out of bed, I'd remove the polish from one of her toes. The polish made her feel special, and it allowed her to track her progress. By the end of a few months, she consistently had all 10 toes polished!

Kristi Stone, Houston

how much is enough?

Is your child getting the right amount of sleep? Kids gradually need less snooze time as they get older. Here's what your child should log each day.

1 to 3 months: 15 to 16 hours

6 months: 15 hours

12 months: 13 to 14 hours

2 years: 13 hours

5 years: 11 hours

6 to 11 years: 9½ to 11 hours

"mom, I had a bad dream!"

Nightmares are especially common among preschoolers because they still can't distinguish between imagination and reality, but scary dreams can strike at any age. And just about anything can provoke one, from a Snow White video to a picture book to anxiety or stress—a stern teacher at school or a new baby brother, for instance. We asked the American Academy of Pediatrics for the best ways to deal with bad dreams.

✓ If your child wakes up from a scary dream, calm her down by holding her and letting her tell you about it.

✓ Figure out ways to combat her fears if she has bad dreams regularly. Gently question her about what might be bothering her ("Are you nervous about your new bed?" "Did the book about the witch scare you?"). This strategy can prevent stressful feelings from building up.

✓ Don't allow her to watch television or videos right before bed, and carefully monitor what she does watch during the day. Even an advertisement or a cartoon can contain images that scare a small child.

morning time

Bright Idea

Our 2-year-old daughter was waking up and calling for us at 5:00 every morning. We were exhausted. So I set up a light-timer in her room and attached it to her night-light. We set it for 6:15 A.M. and told her not to call us until her night-light went on. Now, she goes back to sleep if she sees that her light isn't on yet.

Susan Forgey, *Livermore, California*

Use Blackout Shades

I bought blackout shades for my son's room to keep the sun from shining in and waking him up. That way, it stays dark—and he stays asleep—until I roll up the shades each morning.

Marjorie Rollens, *Bridgehampton, New York*

Make Wake-Up Calls Easier

My daughter is cranky all day if she's awakened too abruptly in the morning. To make it easier, I walk into her room

best bedtime stories

Reading your child a book before bedtime is a terrific way for both of you to calm down after a long day—and to ensure sweet dreams. Nancy Landon, owner of the Brewster Bookstore in Brewster, Massachusetts, has been recommending bedtime books to parents for 20 years. Here are her favorites.

Picture Books for Young Children

Goodnight Moon, by Margaret Wise Brown. A perennial favorite that even babies love.

Time for Bed, by Mem Fox. This simple, gentle tale is filled with lovely animal illustrations by Jane Dyer.

Mouse Mess, by Linnea Riley. A charming story about a mouse who sneaks into the kitchen for a midnight snack.

How Do Dinosaurs Say Good Night? by Jane Yolen. Kids get a kick out of this funny book about 10 sleepy dinosaurs.

Chapter Books for Older Kids

Now We Are Six, by A. A. Milne. By the writer of Winnie the Pooh, this much-loved classic is filled with fun, memorable rhymes and poems.

Mary Poppins, by P. L. Travers. Most kids know the movie, but the book is even better. Each chapter is a self-contained bedtime story.

My Father's Dragon, by Ruth Stiles Gannett. A delightful fantasy about a boy and a baby dragon.

The Milly-Molly-Mandy Storybook, by Joyce Lankester Brisley. Girls will especially love these sweet tales of a little girl growing up in a rural English village.

The Adventures of Buster Bear, by Thornton Burgess. Your kids will also enjoy the other books in this series, about characters such as Bobby Raccoon, Johnny Chuck, and Grandfather Frog.

quietly singing a song, increasing the volume as I approach the bed. That way, she isn't startled out of sleep, and she loves to cuddle with me on the bed as I finish the song.

Christine Richard, *Napoleonville, Louisiana*

moving out of the family bed

Warm Up

My son shared our bed until he was 7 months old. Since it seemed that he craved the warmth of our bodies, I placed a heating pad in his bed before putting him to sleep. Just remember to take the pad out before you put the baby in his crib!

Tina Azeff, Skippack, Pennsylvania

co-sleeping safety

"A crib is the safest place for babies to sleep, but if you're going to use a family bed, take the same precautions that you would in a crib," says John Kattwinkel, M.D., chairman of the American Academy of Pediatrics task force on infant positioning and sudden infant death syndrome (SIDS).

✓ Have your baby sleep on his back to lower his risk of SIDS.

✓ Do not use quilts or comforters, which can suffocate an infant; keep your pillow well away from your baby's face.

✓ Use a firm, flat mattress and allow no space between the mattress and headboard.

✓ Consider using a co-sleeping crib, which attaches to the side of your bed but lets your infant have his own safe space.

✓ Never put your baby to bed with you if you've been drinking.

Earlier Works Better

The earlier your child sleeps in his own bed, the sooner he'll develop the skill of putting himself to sleep independently. We found that it was much easier for our child to make the transition out of our bed when he was still an infant.

Rebecca Anlas, Midland, Michigan

Midnight Strategy

When my son was 1, my husband and I wanted him to sleep in his crib. So, we'd wait until he had fallen asleep with us, then move him to his room. By waking up in his own bedroom, he got used to sleeping by himself. After a month, he was able to fall asleep in his crib from the start.

Shelly Williams, Woodbridge, Virginia

nightmares and monsters

Spray Them Away

I purchased a spray bottle, filled it with water, and told my daughter that the bottle contained anti-monster spray. Now, when she is frightened at night, she sprays a fine mist of water to chase away whatever is scaring her.

Valerie Dinetti, Hot Springs, Maryland

pediatrician on call

sleepwalking solutions

Kids who sleepwalk are in a state halfway between dreaming and deep sleep, says pediatrician and *Parents* contributing editor Laura Nathanson, M.D. Doctors aren't sure why certain children sleepwalk, but they do know that the habit affects more boys than girls and tends to run in families. How can you help your child if he's a sleepwalker? Here's Dr. Nathanson's advice.

✓ **Play it safe.** Put a night-light on in his room and leave a light on in the hallway. Keep his regular sleepwalking path clear of toys and furniture; you should also secure a gate across the top of the stairs each night.

✓ **Don't wake him up.** A sudden jolt to consciousness would be alarming and disorienting and might make it difficult for him to fall back asleep. Simply guide him back to bed.

✓ **Keep it quiet.** Don't mention the sleepwalking to your child the next morning. It will only embarrass him and make him anxious.

✓ **Take action.** It's not easy to prevent sleepwalking, but there are several strategies that can help. Keep your child on a regular schedule, with plenty of exercise, and put him to bed early so that he gets enough sleep. Try setting your alarm clock for 15 minutes before your child usually sets forth, then go into his room and gently wake him up. This may reset his biological clock, helping him make an easier transition from dreaming sleep to deep sleep.

Stay Out!

My 3- and 4-year-old boys share a bedroom, and the imaginary monsters have been quite a disturbance. So, my husband and I made a sign to hang on the outside of the kids' door that reads: "No Monsters Allowed, Property of Anthony and Thomas." It worked like magic, and we all started to get some sleep.

Tracy Sinaguglia, Brampton, Ontario, Canada

Sweet Dreams

To minimize my daughter's bad dreams, every night, before we go to bed, we talk about "the good stuff." We list all the fun things we did that day, such as going for a walk, doing a puzzle, or playing outside. Thinking happy thoughts helps her relax.

Heidi Jenkins, *Hackettstown, New Jersey*

Put It on the Floor

My 3-year-old daughter was always afraid that there were monsters under her bed. I came up with a good solution: I removed her bed frame from her room and left her box spring and mattress on the floor. Now that there's no space for monsters to hide, she falls asleep easily.

Melissa Geoghegan, *Thorndale, Pennsylvania*

potty
success

earning to use the potty is a milestone in your child's life, and it's meaningful for you, too. You probably can't wait to put the changing table in storage and toss the diaper pail. But toilet-teaching can be an extremely frustrating phase, so be patient.

Most kids are ready to be trained between the ages of 2 and 3. As any parent who has gone through the process will tell you, it can take from weeks to months. The most important strategy, say experts, is to let your child decide when he's ready.

Studies show that many kids who start before 18 months aren't fully trained until age 4, while children who start around age 2 will be fully taught by age 3. Daytime control usually comes first, and getting kids to stay dry through the night can take much longer. The tips in this chapter will give you great ways to cope with the unique challenges of toilet-training.

getting started

Start an Evening Routine

When my son was 17 months old, I started putting him on the potty each evening while I ran his bath. The sound of the running water seemed to encourage him, and within a few nights, we had success. I made a big deal out of his accomplishment and kept up the routine of having him go at that same time every evening. Slowly, we added more trips to the potty throughout the day. I used this method successfully with all three of my kids.

Shannon Turner, Stevensville, Maryland

Timing Is Everything

The biggest secret to success is waiting until your child is ready. If children can't follow several directions in a row and can't keep a diaper dry for 4 hours, they probably aren't up to the task. We waited until my daughter was 2½ years old. We didn't pressure her, but we encouraged her every step of the way. She was fully trained in less than a week.

Angela Hutson, McKinney, Texas

Keep a Consistent Schedule

Be consistent: Plan on having at least 3 solid days to focus on toilet-teaching without interruptions. I taught my daughter by putting her on her potty chair every hour. I kept a close eye on the clock to keep track of when she usually went; this helped avoid accidents later. To help keep her still when she was on the potty, I read her stories.

Leanne Ivie, Modesto, California

Give Your Child a Hug

When my youngest daughter was 2, she was afraid to use the potty. To help her get over this, we started the "magic hug"—I would put my arms around her while she was on the potty.

5 signs that your child is ready

Most kids shows signs of potty-training readiness around the age of 2. The key to success, say experts, is not to push or force your child. He's probably ready when he:

1. Can stay dry for several hours during the day, and wakes up dry in the morning and from naps

2. Has bowel movements at predictable times

3. Asks to be changed when he has soiled or wet a diaper

4. Takes an interest in the bathroom habits of other family members

5. Asks to use the toilet or potty

how to pick a potty

Here's what parents should look for when they buy a potty, advises consumer expert Sandy Jones, author of the *Consumer Reports Guide to Baby Products*.

Floor Potties

✓ A basic design with a smooth surface for easy cleaning

✓ A raised front section or flexible, soft shield that acts as a splash guard for boys

✓ Slip-resistant pads on the base that keep it from sliding as your tot backs into it

✓ If the pot fits inside a seat, it should slide out effortlessly or lift out from the top with no hitches.

✓ A model that doubles as a step stool when the lid is shut is a bonus.

Toilet Seat Adapters

✓ Easy attachment to the adult toilet seat, as well as a secure fit to help steady the child

✓ Smooth edges with no pinch points

She felt secure, which helped her relax and focus on going to the bathroom. This strategy really helped make the transition to using the toilet easier.

Denise Samartano, *Clinton, Connecticut*

encouraging success
Let Your Child Do It His Way

Don't be surprised by anything that happens when you potty-teach. My oldest son was 2 and had the unusual ritual of taking off all his clothes before having a bowel movement. I was surprised the first time he did this, but I didn't express any emotion because I wanted him to do it his way. I never tried to persuade him to change this routine, and he stopped stripping down on his own after 6 months. The key is to help your child as much as possible, but don't stress him out about it.

Angela Brown, *Greenbrier, Arkansas*

Make the Potty a Pleasant Experience

We found that encouragement worked well with our four daughters—one even liked it when we applauded. If an accident did occur, we never scolded. Instead, we told our children that it happened to everyone and that they were doing a great job. One of my daughters really enjoyed having a stack of picture books next to her potty chair. It kept her sitting longer and helped her associate going to the potty with her favorite stories.

Lynette Kittle, Hilo, Hawaii

Give Easy Access

We put the potty right next to our daughter's bed. We felt like it took some of the pressure off by allowing her her own space, and she could get to it quicker, especially first thing in the morning and at night.

Anne and Ben McLaughlin, Cheshire, Connecticut

Get Dolly in on the Act

My 2-year-old daughter didn't want to stop playing to use the potty. To encourage her, I told her that she needed to teach all of her dolls how to use the toilet, too. We took one of these "friends" into the bathroom each time, so my daughter could give a step-by-step demonstration. In no time, she was telling me each time she had to go because she was so excited to teach her dolls.

Gina Rodriguez, Fullerton, California

grandmother knows best

More than 30 years ago, when I potty-trained my four children, I used a trick that made the whole process very easy. I let my kids run around in just underpants inside the house and, if it was summertime, outside in the yard as well. Not having regular pants on makes children more aware when they're wet; less clothes also means that it's easier for a child to get to the potty on time—and makes less laundry for the mom when accidents happen. I've helped my children train several of their own kids using this same technique, and it still works like a charm!

Peggy Lawler, Hamden, Connecticut

small rewards

Prize Bag

I was desperate for anything that might motivate my then 3-year-old daughter to use her potty. I finally found success when I bought a gift bag and filled it with lots of little toys and trinkets from a party supply store. Each time she successfully used the toilet, she got to pick an item from the bag. A week and a half later, the bag was empty—and she was fully trained.

Dawn Ciardi, *Quincy, Massachusetts*

Make a Potty Poster

My daughter was almost 3 before she was completely trained. She loved stickers, so, to motivate her, we made a "potty poster," which we decorated and hung in the bathroom. Every time she used the toilet, she got to pick a sticker for her board. She was so excited to get a new one that training became a snap.

Shari Zemmol, *Huntington Woods, Michigan*

Parents' toilet-teaching basics

Ease her into it: To get your child used to the idea of a potty, start by letting her sit on it fully clothed while you explain what it's for. Try reading a book to her or singing a song to keep her sitting on the potty for a longer amount of time.

Start a routine: Once your child is comfortable with the potty, bring her in to use it when she shows signs of needing to urinate or have a bowel movement. You should also have her sit on the potty at regular intervals during the day: when she wakes up, after meals, and after snacks. If she doesn't go after a few minutes, take her off the potty. Don't worry if she has accidents or doesn't go in the potty very often at first.

Praise her successes: Be positive even if she's making slow progress. Saying things like "That was a good job of pulling your pants down" or "I'm happy you told me that you needed to use the potty" will keep your child motivated. When she has accidents, clean them up in a matter-of-fact way, but don't criticize her.

Be a good model: Your child may be very curious about how other family members go the bathroom. Let her observe an older sibling using the toilet, or let her stand in the bathroom with you while you use the toilet.

Superheroes to the Rescue

Three months after my 3-year-old son was urinating in the potty, he still wouldn't use it for bowel movements. Desperate, we tried one last thing: Cameron loved action figures, so we took him to the store and let him pick two out. When we got home, we left them in their packaging but hung them on the bathroom towel bar, where he could see them. We told him that he could have each of them after he successfully went in the potty twice. It worked like a charm: Two days later, he had two new toys, and we never had an accident again.

Kathy Noel, Portland, Connecticut

dealing with accidents

Nighttime Strategies

After the first time that my newly potty-trained son wet his bed at night, I realized that I never again wanted to fumble around for clean sheets at 2:00 in the morning. So, I bought another waterproof mattress pad, covered it with a fitted sheet, then put it on top of the waterproof pad and sheet already on his bed. That way, when he wet the bed, I just pulled the top layer off and had a clean sheet and pad underneath. During those first few weeks, it really helped me—and my son—get back to sleep quickly.

Shelley Chatfield, Fairfield, Connecticut

Quick-Change Artist

I protect my son's bed by putting two half-size mattress pads made for a crib on top of his sheet. They have tabs that tuck under the mattress. When my son has an accident in the middle of the night, I just take off the pad that's wet, rather than having to change the whole bed.

Rhonda Bastian, Whitehall, Pennsylvania

Special Sleeping Pants

My 4-year-old daughter has not yet mastered staying dry at night, so I buy her cotton bedwetter pants from a catalog. They come in sizes big enough for older children and make cleanup in the morning a snap. Since my daughter has been wearing the pants, she's had more dry mornings. I think that taking the pressure off of her has made a tremendous difference.

Renee Schmitt, Lake City, Florida

potty fears

A big, cold toilet can scare a child, especially when you're trying to get your kid to make the move from her potty chair to the toilet. For expert advice, we went to a pro: day care worker Kara Crowley, of the Goddard School day care center in West Long Branch, New Jersey, who supervises a class of 2- to 3-year-olds.

✓ "Sometimes the flushing sound scares a child, especially if it's loud. I've found that even after a few times, though, kids learn to love flushing the toilet. Our kids look forward to using the toilet just so they can flush it."

✓ "I've had lots of kids who are afraid of falling into the toilet when they first sit on it. I'll hold a child's hand while she's on the toilet or sit down next to her and talk to her to take her mind off of her fear."

Staying Dry in the Car

To help my 2-year-old daughter with potty-training when we are on the go, I keep a small plastic potty seat in the car with a plastic grocery bag lining the inside. After she uses it, I just tie up the bag and toss it out. Not only is cleanup a snap, but having the potty in the car also helps reassure my daughter— and makes for fewer accidents.

Christine Enders, Villanova, Pennsylvania

special tactics

A New Way to Color

To get my son excited about potty-teaching, we put a few drops of food coloring (his choice of color, of course) into the toilet bowl so he could see it change color as he went. When it was time to train our daughter, we did the same—except we sat her on the potty facing backward, so she could see. It may sound gross, but it worked for us!

Vicki Stocking, Chapel Hill, North Carolina

Pretty Pants

My daughter didn't want to switch from disposable training pants to cotton ones because they were plain-looking. So, we picked

what the experts say about bedwetting

Don't be concerned if your child wets his bed until kindergarten or even after, says pediatrician and *Parents* contributing editor Laura Nathanson, M.D. A child's bladder and nervous system are often simply not developed enough yet, so that he can't wake himself out of a deep sleep when his bladder is full. Or he may have an especially small bladder; in some cases, bedwetting is genetic.

The good news is that the problem in young children gradually disappears. Here, Dr. Nathanson gives you strategies to deal with your preschooler who is still outgrowing nighttime wetting.

Be reassuring. Bedwetting can be embarrassing for a child because it makes him feel like a baby. Remember that he's not doing it on purpose, nor can he control himself. The best thing a parent can do is not make a big deal about it. Change your child's pull-up pants or the sheets cheerfully and matter-of-factly, without blaming him. If you or your spouse wet the bed as a child, let your child know. Hearing that Mommy or Daddy had the same problem may make him feel better.

Don't disturb his sleep. Waking a child up to go to the bathroom in the middle of the night—a strategy that can be effective for older bedwetters—won't help a preschooler. Limiting fluids before bedtime at this age doesn't work well either; it often feels like punishment to a young child for something he can't help.

Don't set her up for failure. Reward systems, such as sticker charts, that may have been effective for you when you toilet-trained your child are unlikely to work for bedwetting, since the child has no control over the problem.

See your pediatrician if:

✓ Your child has been dry at night for months and suddenly starts wetting the bed regularly. There may be an underlying medical problem such as a bladder infection or diabetes, or your child may be undergoing emotional stress.

✓ Your child is 6 or 7 and has still not had a dry night. This is the age at which bedwetting becomes a problem. Your pediatrician can do a thorough exam to rule out any serious bladder disorders and may suggest that you try a bedwetting alarm.

out some sponges in the shapes of animals and used them to stamp her cotton pants with fabric paint. Now, she always makes it on time to the potty so she doesn't mess up her pretty pants.

Melissa Simmons, Draper, Utah

The Santa Solution

Sometimes, it's the littlest things that encourage a child to potty-train. Our daughter was 2½, and although she had no problem peeing in the potty, she wouldn't try having a bowel movement. After much begging and pleading from me, all it took was my husband walking in the bathroom and saying, "You can do it, Whitney. Even Santa goes in the potty!" Maybe it was the fact that Christmas was right around the corner, but she heard it loud and clear—and potty-teaching was smooth sailing from then on.

Amy and Tim Wyman, Charlestown, New Hampshire

The Traveling Potty

When our daughter was first learning to use the potty, she would urinate before her nap but would wait until we put her down in her crib to poop in her diaper. One day, I left her bottom bare and put her in the crib with the potty seat (it was a sturdy type that couldn't tip over). Sure enough, she used her potty. After following this schedule for several days, we moved the potty to the bathroom and she had no problem adjusting.

Anita Wells, Charlottesville, Virginia

Try Target Practice

When I was trying to potty-train my eldest son, my stepmother suggested that I put Cheerios in the toilet and challenge my son to sink them. He thought it was so fun that he was eager to go to the bathroom every time. Although I found myself constantly explaining to guests why we had a box of cereal in the bathroom, it really did work, which is all that matters.

Angel Tack, Deerfield, Ohio

Easier Cleanup

I keep my child's potty chair clean with the help of disposable coffee filters. Line your child's potty with one. It makes cleaning up a bowel movement quick and easy.

Kristina Brew, Bayside, New York

help for older bedwetters

Overnight Parties

Don't let bedwetting restrict a child's activities. My son is 12 and has wet the bed on and off for the last 9 years. Whenever he was invited to a sleepover, we talked to the parents beforehand and sent along a plastic mattress cover and an extra sheet and pajamas with my son. Other parents were always very understanding of the situation—and my son was never the subject of teasing from his friends.

S. Soho,
Windsor, Vermont

Set a Clock

To help my 7-year-old daughter stop wetting the bed, we spent a few weeks waking her up during the night to pinpoint the most common time that she wet the bed. We found that it usually occurred around 3:00 A.M., so we set an alarm for her and made it her responsibility to get up and go to the bathroom. This helped give my daughter some control over the situation and made it easier for her to wake up dry in the morning.

Marla Payne,
Keokuk, Iowa

Invest in an Alarm

Our pediatrician recommended a bedwetting alarm system for our 6-year-old. At the first sign of wetness, the alarm went off, waking her up. We'd immediately get up with her and take her to the bathroom. Miraculously, after 2 nights, she stopped wetting the bed, making it well worth the $50 we spent.

Lisa Green,
Auburn, New York

Be Supportive

My 8-year-old son still wets the bed. His pediatrician reassured us that many children still do at this age and that my son will probably outgrow it as he gets older. We make sure not to criticize him and instead focus on praising him when he doesn't wet the bed. In the meantime, Pull-Ups training pants help keep him dry at night.

Cathy Reynolds,
Tampa

mood
meltdowns

your toddler has a tantrum in the cereal aisle; your 5-year-old gets up on the wrong side of the bed; your 8-year-old goes into a major sulk when you tell him that he can't have those $100 sneakers. Welcome to parenthood.

You'll notice crabbiness most in toddlers, but it's normal for kids of all ages to have bad days, bad moods, and an urge to test limits. Children have only just begun to develop the cognitive skills to make sense of—and control—their emotions. That fact, coupled with a limited attention span, results in what seems like wild mood swings.

What makes a normally cheery child suddenly give way to a roaring fit of fury? In a word, frustration. The trick is to help kids learn to express their emotions while keeping one hand on the volume control. Here are tips from parents who have come up with effective strategies for meltdown maintenance—and damage control.

parenting in public

Bragging Rights

I've found a simple trick for keeping my 16-month-old calm on shopping trips. Whenever she starts to lose her patience, I pull out "Mom's brag book," a small photo album that I keep in my purse. She loves looking at the pictures of herself, and it keeps her occupied so I can get to the checkout line in peace.

Lauren Banks, Fitchburg, Wisconsin

Just Leave

When my child loses it in public, we leave the location immediately—even if I have to desert a full cart of groceries or ask for a doggie bag in a restaurant. I didn't see immediate re-

it's my job

cheer up crabby kids

How do you cope when your child is having a terrible, horrible, no-good day? We asked someone who deals with grumpy children every day. Cynthia Travers is an early childhood teacher at the Children's Aid Society, which provides home, recreational, educational, and health services to New York City's neediest children and families.

Be a good observer. Think about what has happened in your child's day in the last few hours. Did Grandma just leave after a weeklong stay? How did he sleep last night? Is his little sister sick? If you're able to pick up these blues clues, you'll be able to talk to your child about the specific problem.

Empathize. Tell your child that he's not alone. When the problem is not so serious, Travers sometimes has a child in her class discuss it with other kids. More often than not, someone will respond, "That happened to me too!," which makes the child feel better.

Pick your battles. If your child merely woke up on the wrong side of bed, give him space. Don't be a stickler about rules. Choose to let minor things go.

Divert your child's attention. Pull out that new toy you've been hiding away in the closet. Or do an activity that you know your child loves, such as baking banana bread or looking through family albums.

sults when I started this, but I hung in there. We now have a wonderfully behaved 6-year-old.

Danita Schimming, *Olathe, Kansas*

These Precious Things

In the grocery store, I allow my girls to pick one thing they really want, such as a favorite cereal, chips, or a snack for their lunch (no gum or candy!). Once they have chosen, that's it. If they whine, the item goes back on the shelf. I let them hold it while we shop and put it on the conveyor belt at the register.

Jeanette Akright, *Dunlap, Illinois*

How Sweet It Is

If I'm taking the kids grocery shopping, we sometimes hit the bakery first so they have something delicious to munch as we go along. The bonus is that if they have a snack in hand, it makes it easier for me to say no later on in the store.

Sue Heitzman, *Fond du Lac, Wisconsin*

Mall Meltdown

My son once had a horrible tantrum in the mall. He was having a great time playing in the common area, but I had to tell him that it was time to go. He began screaming so loudly that I was afraid people might think I was kidnapping him! I just bit my lip, fastened him into the stroller, and pushed him through the mall to the parking lot. It would have been much easier—and less embarrassing—to give in, but in the long run, it's a bad idea. I think he realized that screaming doesn't work, because he hasn't done it again.

Tammi Price, *Crofton, Maryland*

it's my job

when your child lashes out

"Hitting and kicking are not that common in 3- or 4-year-olds," says Edward Christopherson, author of *Beyond Discipline: Parenting That Lasts a Lifetime*. "If your child reacts this way when she's frustrated, she's learning that behavior from someone around her."

Parents who spank and yell tend to have more aggressive children, he notes. Also ask yourself whether a sibling, a playmate, or even television show characters are modeling the kind of behavior you're seeing in your child. Here are some ways to help stop it.

✓ Give your child an immediate timeout whenever she hits or kicks.

✓ If she's learned this behavior from a classmate or friend, try to keep her away from that person for a while.

✓ Make sure that you're not unintentionally rewarding her. If she hits her brother because she wants his cookie, for example, and she ultimately ends up with the cookie, she's getting a payoff for her bad behavior.

✓ Teach her the right way to ask for what she wants.

home remedies

Picture This

By the time that bedtime rolls around, my 3-year-old daughter is invariably grouchy. To change the tone of the evening, I hand her a funny photo I once took of her "grumpy" face, and I ask her if she can get any grumpier than the face in the picture. We usually wind up giggling together as she tries out silly faces in front of the mirror. Before we know it, the bad mood has vanished.

Teresa Cantwell, Cary, North Carolina

Dressing Duels

Getting my daughter dressed was a daily battle. So, we started playing "department store." She "shops" for her outfit, choosing "new" clothes from her closet, with my help. I act like a saleswoman and call her Madam. When she has selected an outfit, I help her get dressed. These days, she's ready in no time flat. She loves the attention and feels so grown-up that she forgets all about fussing.

Susan Walters, White Oak, Pennsylvania

6 surefire tantrum tamers

1. Sing a soothing song.
2. Rock him gently.
3. Let him punch a pillow.
4. Give him an object with a soothing texture, such as a fuzzy stuffed animal or a fleecy blanket.
5. Go outside and listen to the birds chirp.
6. Stare into his eyes and take deep breaths. He'll eventually do the same.

Room for Improvement

If one of my children is in the middle of a tantrum, I tell them that they can go into their room and scream all they want and come back when they are done. Even my 23-month-old son understands this and cooperates. When they are finished letting out their frustrations, they come out and talk about what was bothering them, which seems to help them deal with their anger better the next time.

Laurie Callahan, Ann Arbor, Michigan

"I Want to Be Alone"

When my daughter has a meltdown, sometimes she just wants to be left alone for a few minutes. She likes to "hide" in a corner or in her toy tent until she is calm and feeling better. Then, she's ready to jump right back into things.

Janet Phillips, *Danville, Virginia*

alternatives to time out

Recorded History

You can't argue with a tape recorder, as I discovered the first time I taped my 4-year-old whining. When I played his performance back to him, he was genuinely startled. His eyes grew wide and he looked embarrassed. "Is that what I really sound like?" he said. It's made a big difference.

Vicky Mylniec, *Los Gatos, California*

Give Me a Hug

Getting my 3-year-old to take a timeout can be a challenge. When her temper is at its worst, I ask whether she wants a timeout or a hug. She usually opts for the hug, which is really what we both need at the time.

Michele Kosek, *Clifton Park, New York*

be nice!

Kids can say the darnedest things. And sometimes, their words can cut like a knife. When your child throws some zingers your way, instead of blurting out "Don't you dare say that to me!," try these strategies.

Situation: You won't let her have candy before dinner.

Zinger: "I hate you!"

Your reply: "I understand that you're angry that you can't have your candy right now, but your words hurt my feelings, and we try not to hurt other people's feelings."

Situation: He wants to cross the street by himself, but you won't let him.

Zinger: "You're stupid! I don't need a mommy!"

Your reply: "You wish you made the rules, not me. But in our family we don't say things like that to each other."

Situation: She doesn't want to leave a playdate.

Zinger: "You're not my friend!"

Your reply: "You're upset that it's time to go home. It's okay to be angry with me but not to say mean words. Time to get your jacket on."

toddler tempers

Here are some time-tested ways to defuse an emotional hurricane in your 1- to 2-year-old.

- ✓ Avoid frustrating situations. Examples: giving your toddler toys that are too advanced for her abilities, expecting her to sit quietly for long periods, or concentrating for too long when learning new skills.

- ✓ Be consistent. Toddlers thrive on order and routine, and they do best when they know what the limits are.

- ✓ Keep snacks on hand. Like anyone else, your child is more likely to be cranky if she's hungry.

- ✓ Encourage naps. A tired child has a shorter fuse.

- ✓ Distract her. When you feel the tension rising, introduce a fun game, read a book, put on some music and dance, or simply go outside.

Tickle Time Out

Like many children, my 4-year-old son gets upset when he doesn't get his way. One day, I announced that we had a new rule. He isn't allowed to scream or hit me when he gets mad—instead, he has to tickle me. Within a few minutes, he calms down, and then we're able to discuss what upset him. He still gets mad at me once in a while, but it doesn't last long.

Dave Noble, *Oak Park, Michigan*

Tender Touch

When my daughter loses her cool, we softly rub her back, the back of her head, or even her arms. The physical contact makes it hard for her to concentrate on her tantrum antics.

Heather Germano, *San Diego*

Speak and Spell

My 2-year-old son gets into his share of trouble. But rather than leave him alone to cry and scream, I sit with him and have him recite his ABCs for me. When he's done, we talk about what went wrong and what behavior I expect of him. It's nice to accomplish something instead of letting him cry. And the task of concentrating on his ABCs helps him calm down.

April Phillips,
Fort Huachuca, Arizona

To Laugh or to Cry

When young children are in tantrum mode, there's usually a fine line between screaming and hysterical laughing. So, I use humor as a defuser. Toddlers are easy, because they have a short attention span. I've found that tickling, funny faces, and swirling around like a dancer works well.

Ann Morales-Ear, *Staten Island, New York*

your emotions

Keeping It Light

When one of my children is having an outburst, I calmly tell her that I am not changing my mind, and I leave the room but stay close by. If she's not able to calm herself, I go in and try to voice her feelings for her by saying, "You're feeling frustrated and angry because you can't have a cookie." If all else fails, I try a joke. Sometimes, I throw myself on the floor and say, "I want a BMW! Right now!" My daughter usually looks at me in shock and says "Mom!"—and forgets her own tantrum.

Michelle Fondin,
Falls Church, Virginia

soothing solutions

When your child loses it, he needs you to stay calm. Here are some ways to help him regain control—and help you keep a lid on your temper.

- ✓ Use a gentle tone. If your child is yelling, simplify your own language and speak in a quiet voice. Don't let your child whine or use baby talk.

- ✓ Limit choices. Although your child may get angry when he feels that he has no control over a situation, he can also become overwhelmed by having too many options. For example, don't say, "What would you like for lunch?"; instead, say, "Would you like a peanut butter or a tuna fish sandwich?"

- ✓ Get closer. Physical closeness is very comforting. Let him sit in your lap or sit close to him while he tries to calm down.

- ✓ Give fair warning of change or transition. Instead of saying "We're leaving right now!", try "We're leaving in 10 minutes, right after you finish your drawing."

- ✓ Laugh it off. Turn the battle into something silly. When your toddler is hopping mad, why not hop?

- ✓ Count to 10. It's a very low-tech way for you to calm down, but it works.

Tough Love

I think that it's important to speak calmly but stand your ground. You must also be consistent and willing to follow through with your discipline. Never say things that you have no intention of doing, such as "I'm going to leave you there and go home if you don't get up."

Jamie Rivington, Monterey, California

brothers
and sisters

18

thinking about trying for baby number two—or three, or four? According to parents and experts alike, having more than one child definitely has its rewards. Many moms and dads report that after the first child, loving and raising the next is easier and more fun.

If you have several kids already, or if you grew up with siblings, you know what a valuable playmate and ally a brother or sister can be. But as each new family member arrives, it also takes older siblings a little time to understand that Mommy and Daddy's love increases, not decreases. This chapter will help you decide whether and when to have another child, figure out the best way to tell your older children about a new brother or sister, and turn sibling rivalry into sibling revelry.

when should you have another?

Gauge Your Child's Readiness

We waited until our son was fairly independent. He was 4 years old when our daughter was born. He had made friends and could do a lot for himself. As a result, my husband and I weren't overwhelmed by caring for two babies. If you're unsure when to have a second, consider this: Just as your love multiplies, so will your strength and patience.

Tracey Adams, Holland, Ohio

Wait a While

We decided to wait until our first child was 2 or 3 before we even considered getting pregnant again. We wanted to give our daughter a chance to have some time with us on her own. Another reason to wait: Toddlers are wonderful and exciting, but they run you ragged. It's hard to deal with morning sickness and exhaustion when your little one is screaming "Mommy!"

Maggie Huffman, Wichita, Kansas

how many years apart should siblings be?

Though there's no spacing that will guarantee ideal family dynamics, there are medical reasons to avoid having kids less than 18 months apart.

Research shows that babies who were conceived in the optimal spacing of 18 to 23 months after a previous birth were the least likely to be born premature, have a low birth weight, or be a small size for their gestational age. Babies who were conceived 6 months after a previous sibling's birth were most likely to be affected. Researchers speculate that mothers need time for their reproductive systems to fully recover from having a baby.

What if you become pregnant after recently giving birth? It's even more important that you take care of yourself. Quit smoking immediately, refrain from drinking alcohol, eat a balanced diet full of vitamins and protein to gain proper weight, exercise regularly and moderately, reduce stress, and seek prenatal care as early as possible.

Do It All at Once

If you're thinking about having another child, do it when your first is a baby, so that your children will be close in age. They'll have common interests, and you can get a moment's peace while they play with each other. Plus, you're finished with diapers in a few years!

Amy Mullins, Elkton, Maryland

new-sibling stress

Practice Makes Perfect

To prepare my older children for the birth of my fourth baby, we acted out the scenario several times with dolls. I started out the scene with the "children" dolls playing and the "mommy" doll announcing, "It's time for the baby to be born." Then, the "grandparent" dolls came and took the children dolls for a special night with them. We had practiced so well that on the big night, my 2½-year-old was the first one out the door with his suitcase and toothbrush in hand.

Christine Moleski, Tallahassee, Florida

Let Big Brother Announce It

When my husband and I learned that I was pregnant with our second child, we wanted to tell our friends and family the news in a way that included our 3-year-old son. We came up with the idea of putting the announcement on a kid's T-shirt that Trevor could wear. We used iron-on letters and patches and fabric paint to write, "I'm gonna be a big brother." Trevor loved wearing the shirt around town, and everyone enjoyed receiving the news in such a fun way!

Renee Richmond, Bear, Delaware

star strategy

Marie Osmond

"I think the more kids you have, the more joyful your life is. When I had my first child, I thought, 'How am I ever going to love another baby as much as I love this one?' Then, my second came along, and I realized that your capacity to love increases with each child. I always wanted to have a big family—I had eight brothers, and it was fun. Big families teach you to get along, to share, to be a helper."

—singer and mother of seven

who's the baby here?

His new little sister has only been in the house for a week, and suddenly, your 5-year-old is crawling into the baby's crib and sucking on her bottles. What should you do if your child experiences this type of regression back to babyhood? Indulge him, say experts, but only for a few minutes. Let him get his fill of rolling around the crib and pretending that he's the baby. It won't hurt to play along if he asks you to. But once it gets out of control or uncomfortable, tell him that he's "played baby" long enough and that it's time to be a big boy again. Suggest that you and he go do a "big boy" activity together, such as read a story or color, and always be sure to praise big-kid behavior.

Make It a Pleasant Surprise

To help my 3-year-old son adjust to the arrival of his baby sister, I used a grab bag. Anytime he helped me care for the new baby, he was allowed to fish for a surprise from the bag. The items included small toys, books, and snacks. It helped him get involved in his sister's care and fostered a positive attitude during a tough transition.

Lisa Kirby, Mebane, North Carolina

Celebrate the Older Siblings

Whenever I bring a gift for a new baby, I always bring small gifts for the older siblings as well. I also make sure to congratulate them along with the parents so they don't feel so alienated. After all, it's the whole family's celebration.

Debbie Jacobs, Muncie, Indiana

Kids Can Share Lessons

At some time, all parents wonder if they'll have the energy for two. My patience sometimes wears thin, but my 4-year-old is able to help a lot and give her 19-month-old sister things I never could—the opportunity to be silly and imaginative—and the baby reciprocates by teaching her lessons, such as sharing and loyalty.

Margy Nicklas, Saint Marys, Pennsylvania

sharing a room

Let Them Fall Asleep Together

Our daughter was 3 years old when her sister was born. To help them both get a good night's sleep, we put them to bed at the same time. Then, when the baby woke up during the night for her feeding, I brought her into our room, where we had a cradle set up. The arrangement worked smoothly—except that our 5-year-old son started asking for another baby because he had no one to sleep with!

Suzanne Schenker, Tinton Falls, New Jersey

Be Careful Not to Rush It

Moving our newborn into our toddler's room was disastrous. The baby's crying kept my then 22-month-old daughter awake, which put her in a foul mood the next day. To remedy the situation, we put the baby to sleep in her crib only during naptimes. At night, she slept in a bassinet in our room. It wasn't until the baby slept through the night— at 6 months—that we put her to bed in the same room as her sister.

Tanja Brewer, Clinton, Kentucky

extra! extra!: breaking the news to an older sibling

Whether your older child is 18 months or almost a teen, telling her that a new addition to the family is on the way can be exciting, yet nerve-wracking. Depending on the age, here's what to say and when to say it.

Ten to 18 Months: Although at this age she may not understand what's going on, it's still important to let her know that changes are on the way. Keep it simple. Tell her, "You're going to have a baby brother or sister."

Toddler: You can wait until the second trimester, but keep in mind that the earlier you tell her, the more time she has to adjust to the idea. Keep reinforcing that this baby is going to be very lucky since he or she will have a great big sister. You may even want to visit a baby of a friend or relative to show her what to expect.

Preschooler: Whenever you feel comfortable telling her, do so. But be prepared for a lot of questions about where the baby is coming from and how it got inside you. Reading books such as *Arthur's New Baby Book* or *Little Bear Is a Big Brother* will help her to adjust.

Five and up: You can tell her whenever you're ready. Experts suggest approaching it in a grown-up way. Let her know that you have some important news for her—that you're pregnant, and she is going to have a little brother or sister.

Give Each Child His Own Space

When our second son was born, our first was 5 years old. To help ease the transition and to make the room special for both kids, we decorated each side of the room differently: sports posters for our older son and Mickey Mouse for the baby. It really helped our older child that part of the room was still all his own.

Tammy Cruse, Pierre, South Dakota

Don't Assume the Worst

Our daughter was 22 months old when we moved the baby into her room. My biggest concern was that they would wake each other up at night, but for the most part, it didn't happen. My daughter slept through all of the baby's feedings, and he usually stayed asleep during bedtime rituals with her. When they did wake each other, my husband and I worked as a team: I nursed the baby while he soothed our daughter back to sleep.

Michelle Woodworth, East Rochester, New York

Stagger Their Bedtimes

The best way to get my children to sleep is to put them to bed at different times. We put our older child to bed first; then I rock the baby to sleep in the living room. By the time I put him to bed, our daughter is in dreamland, and she doesn't even wake when her brother cries in the middle of the night.

Tess Leary, Cape Neddick, Maine

Let Your Child Help Decorate

When it is time to move your children into the same room, have your older sibling participate in the transition as much as possible. Let him help choose the new bedding for the baby, or have him show you where he wants the crib to go. If you let him help make decisions about his sibling, your child will be better prepared for the change.

Jervaun Trier, San Diego

special time for everyone

Plan a Monthly Date

I was having a hard time carving out one-on-one time with each of my kids—ages 11, 9, and 4 years old—so I started

settle squabbles

Getting a little tired of the bickering? Fights between siblings can get pretty dirty, as Colleen Fagan, a nanny in Philadelphia for 12 years, can attest. Here's her strategy for playing referee but not becoming a contestant.

1. Stop the argument. If the children are hitting or are especially upset, separate them until they're calm enough to talk.

2. Have them sit down together. Give each of them a chance to tell their side of the story. If one child becomes accusatory ("She started it!"), direct him back to just telling his side of the story by saying, "I'm not interested in who started it. I just want to know exactly what took place."

3. Ask for input on how they could resolve their argument. If they're fighting over what television program to watch, maybe they could alternate. The one child could watch his show for that day, and the other could watch hers the next day.

4. Have them hug.

5. From that point on, whenever you observe them playing nicely, praise them by saying, "This is how brothers and sisters should treat each other."

It's Your Day. Once a month, either my husband or I make plans with one of our children. It doesn't have to be an expensive outing or take the entire day; usually, it's something that really appeals to that particular child. I've taken my kids putt-putt golfing, to their favorite restaurant, and shopping for shoes and ice cream sundaes. As your children grow up, they will cherish the special attention you give them.

Jenny Heidel, Cincinnati

Give Grandma a Turn

One way to make your kids feel special is to have a grandparent or other close relative take a few siblings once a week for the day. That way, you can spend the day focusing on one child. The best part? Your other children won't feel deprived—they'll have a wonderful time with Grandma!

Nicole Chmielewski, Milwaukee

teach brothers and sisters to share

When it comes to sharing Mom's time, siblings really have no choice in the matter. But what about bikes or toys? Here's how you can avoid squabbles over material possessions.

✓ Choose family activities that involve sharing, such as gardening or working on a puzzle. This teaches kids how each family member can use the same items (such as a rake or puzzle pieces) to accomplish one goal.

✓ Assure younger children that sharing doesn't mean giving the item up forever. Demonstrate by saying, "Brian is going to play with the ball for 15 minutes, and then you can play with the ball for 15 minutes." Set a timer. When the child's time is up, hand the ball to the other sibling.

✓ Set up ground rules for the whole family. An example might be that any toy left lying around in the living room may be used by anyone. If the item is placed in a specific place, however, special permission from the owner is required to play with it.

✓ Make sure that kids know that certain possessions will be secure. Assure them that they never have to share their favorite blankie or stuffed bear.

Get Creative with Quiet Time

I am the second-oldest of seven kids and fondly remember my mom always making time for each of us. One way she did this was taking advantage of quiet time. Whenever we were all supposed to be napping or reading in our rooms, my mother would sneak one of us out to spend time with her. I always looked forward to those times alone with Mom.

Rebecca Cavendar, Wichita, Kansas

Make Shopping Time Special

I've found the grocery store to be a great place for bonding with my two kids. I alternate, taking either my 5-year-old son or 2-year-old daughter with me. They each like spending time alone with me while we pick out our groceries, and at the same time, the other child gets to stay home and play with Dad.

Penny McBride, Free Soil, Michigan

Take Advantage of Bedtime

What works well for my husband and me is making time for each child at night. After we've put the kids to bed, we take turns with each one, either reading a story together or just cuddling. It's now one of my favorite parts of the day.

Kim Pirrie, Sioux City, Iowa

Make a "Coffee" Date

Once a week, on a rotating basis, I put two of my children to bed and allow one to stay up for an extra 10 to 15 minutes. We make hot chocolate or decaffeinated tea and just visit. It's nice for the child to have the opportunity to talk without his fellow siblings interrupting him or competing for my atten-

it's my job

a mom of multiples on nurturing individuality

In the middle of carpooling, changing diapers, and cooking dinner, it might be difficult to remember that each of your children has a very unique personality. How can you nurture each one? Amy Schiffman of Woodmere, New York, is a mother of triplets, twins, and a single. Here's her advice for attending to each child's interests.

✓ Spend blocks of time with your kids. "I spend all day with the triplets, so when the twins and my oldest son come home from school, I usually let our caregiver take care of the triplets for the rest of the evening," Schiffman says. "It's the other kids' turn then."

✓ Recognize when one child needs special attention. "They go through phases, and you can usually pick up on who needs a little more individual time with you," she says.

✓ Cater to each kid's interest. "My oldest son and one of the twins attend an art class together. They really get a lot out of it," Schiffman says. "However, the other twin is more interested in sports. To prevent him from feeling left out, I take him to the playground or just talk to him during the time the other two are in class. I think he really needs that extra time with me."

tion. I learn more about them than I would in a week of busy carpools and activities. And the happy smile at bedtime is a good indication of time well spent.

Connie Gunkel, *North Kingstown, Rhode Island*

Learn Together

One way that I find one-on-one time with my quadruplets is through "water baby" classes. I take the two girls for one 5-week session (a caregiver and I each hold one, making sure that we trade off from time to time). Next session, it's the boys and me.

Julie King, *Ankeny, Iowa*

good
manners

19

let's face it: In our fast-paced society, courtesy and politeness don't seem to be as important as they once were, especially among kids.

But the truth is, good manners never go out of style, and your children need them to function in the world. And although social graces certainly don't come naturally, you can instill them in your kids with a little patience and a lot of persistence.

Even toddlers can master the concept of asking for something instead of grabbing it. Once a child gets a little older, she's ready to learn etiquette basics such as behaving politely at a restaurant, saying hello to an adult, or thanking a friend for a gift. For innovative and effective ways to teach your child good manners, read on.

thank you!

A Gentle Reminder

My 4–year-old and I devised a system to remind him to say thank you. I would simply tap him on the shoulder when he forgot. This was less embarrassing than always asking him to say thank you. And it worked. As time went on, I gave him fewer and fewer taps.

Rebecca Walker, Camden, Alabama

Note Worthy

Whenever my kids get a present for their birthday or a holiday, the first thing I do is reach for the thank-you notes and have them write one. Not only does it take very little time, but it's also a good lesson in gratitude. I believe that writing really teaches them to appreciate the time and energy that the giver put into the gift. As they've gotten older, showing gratitude in ways like this has become second nature to them.

Lorraine Glennon, Brooklyn, New York

raise grateful kids

All parents want to be appreciated by their children, but it's up to us to help our kids learn this important quality, says psychologist and *Parents* contributing editor Ron Taffel, Ph.D. Here's how.

✓ Express gratitude yourself. Children are born copycats, so the more they see you show appreciation, the more they'll do it too. That means not forgetting to thank the cashier at the grocery store, or your child for being on his best behavior at the movies.

✓ Describe what you've done. Instead of demanding an instant thank-you for the birthday party that you spent weeks planning, explain to your child exactly what you did. It's amazing, says Dr. Taffel, how kids react when they're presented with the facts. Many times they simply don't comprehend how much work their parents do for them.

✓ Do sweat the small stuff. Sure, you expect a word of thanks for a big-ticket item like a new baseball mitt, but you shouldn't let kids off the hook when you get them a cup of juice or help with their homework.

✓ Make yourself and your spouse the center of attention. Teaching your child to honor your special days (birthdays, wedding anniversary, Mother's Day) helps them understand that life is a two-way street.

ask **Peggy Post**

help for shy children

Q: When I take my 6-year-old daughter to visit relatives and it's time to leave, she won't hug and kiss anyone or say thank you or even goodbye. I can see how insulted they are by her standoffishness. How can I encourage her to show her appreciation?

A: Kids often experiment with ignoring manners in order to see what's truly expected of them, but they may have no idea that they're hurting someone else's feelings. If your child is going through this phase, you might tell your relatives that it's an area you're working on with her, and reassure them that she loves them. You don't have to push a child to kiss or hug when she doesn't want to, but it's important for her to learn to say goodbye and thank you. Try to help her see how her actions make your relatives feel sad. Let her know that taking the time to speak to people makes them feel special.

Photo Op

I've found an easy way for my young kids to participate in sending thank-you notes, even though they can't write yet. I keep a box of spare photos of the children. They pick a photo that they like and glue it onto a folded piece of construction paper. I write a simple thank-you inside and then they sign their names. The notes are a big hit with family and friends.

Carla Coburn, *Grand Rapids, Michigan*

A Special Thanks

I want my children to know that any act of kindness can be a reason to say an informal thank-you or to do something nice in return. For example, I might say, "Grandma read so many stories with you, what can we do for Grandma to say thank you?" or "It was so nice of Jim to invite you to play at his house, what can we do to say thank you?" These situations give my children a chance to be an active part of a thank-you process.

Catherine Romo, *Fort Myers, Florida*

Learn by Example

If I see a child speaking respectfully to an adult or taking the time to say thank you, I tell my two boys how impressed I am by it. And whenever I see another child behaving in a rude or inappropriate way, I make sure to point it out to my sons and tell them that I don't like that kind of behavior. I think they get the message loud and clear.

Carin Pratt, Washington, D.C.

practicing politeness

No More Interruptions

To teach my two young children not to interrupt me or other adults while we are talking, I asked them to stand next to me and hold my hand whenever they have to tell me something. This physical gesture is an easy way for them to silently get my attention, and it's a gentle reminder for me to give it to them as soon as I can.

Penny Friedman, Virginia Beach, Virginia

Make It a Game

I found a great way to review simple manners with my 3- and 4-year-olds. I describe a situation and ask, "What would

grandmother knows best

When our three children were in grammar school, we had a hard time getting them to address adults in the neighborhood by their names. No matter how often we'd remind them, they'd say "Hi" but be too shy or forgetful to say "Hi, Mr. Smith." One summer, we started the name game. Every time one of the kids greeted a neighbor by name, we put a dime in a jar for them. At the end of each month, they could take the dimes they earned and buy something. I guess it was old-fashioned bribery, but by the end of the summer, the problem was solved. Their confidence around grown-ups really improved. Today, my kids are all outgoing, polite adults themselves!

Peggy King, Stamford, Connecticut

you say?" For example, you are walking down a crowded street and accidentally bump into someone. What would you say? You are at a friend's house and their mother asks if you want another cookie. What would you say? This is a fun and instructive way to spend 10 minutes.

Martha Tisdale, McLean, Virginia

Encouraging Remarks

I constantly found myself saying "don't, don't, don't" when my 4-year-old did something that I thought was rude. Then, I discovered that encouragement works much better. If she says, "I'm thirsty. Could I please have a drink?," I say, "When you ask so nicely, I'm happy to give you a drink." Children thrive on praise and will repeat the behavior that merits it.

Patricia Elton, Austin, Texas

Make It a Team Effort

I let my 5-year-old's grandparents and caregiver know which manners we're working on each week. When I drop David off at his grandparents, I might say, "Please remind David to say please and thank you." When I pick him up from day care, I might ask, "Did David stay sitting down during lunch? We've been practicing that at home." The continuity has really helped him learn.

Jan Woodyard, Madisonville, Tennessee

teaching gratitude

A Thanksgiving Reminder

In an effort to teach my children about gratitude, I made an "I'm thankful" poster to display in our living room during the month of November. I glued a paper turkey to the bottom edge of the poster and cut out colorful paper feathers that sit next to it. Whenever children or adults feel in the mood, they can write the things for which they are thankful on the feathers and glue them to the turkey. By the time that Thanksgiving rolls around, our turkey has a beautiful tail of feathers and our kids have learned an important lesson in giving thanks.

Carrie Wall, Huntington Beach, California

no more restaurant nightmares

It's unrealistic to expect restaurant outings to run smoothly every time you eat out, especially when one of your dinner companions is your toddler. Here's how to make the process less of an ordeal for your family and your fellow diners.

Pick the right place. Casual restaurants at off-peak hours are always a safe bet—the service will be quicker and the staff will most likely be more accommodating. Hint: Kid-friendly restaurants often have place mats instead of tablecloths, a row of high chairs, and a kids' menu.

Plan ahead. Just because your toddler is in a good mood when you enter the restaurant doesn't mean things will stay that way, especially if he's hungry. One solution: Call the restaurant and get them to set up a table and take your order ahead of your arrival, so you can sit down and eat the moment that you walk in the door.

Bring some activities. Have props on hand just in case you have to wait for a table or service. Board books, crayons, action figures, and other small toys are good tools for diverting a toddler's attention.

Check out the sights. If you can't phone ahead to order your meals, then as soon as you've placed your order, take your toddler for a stroll. By the time that you get back to the table, the food should be there and your child will be ready to eat.

Know when to bail. If your instincts tell you that your child has passed the point of no return, cut your losses and get out. If you've already ordered, ask that the food be boxed to go.

Just Because

To help my family be grateful for how much we have, I started a "just because" activity. Once a month, we do something special for someone "just because." We bring a tray of homemade cookies to a neighbor or make place mats for a local nursing home. We look forward to it each month. Best of all, my 10- and 12-year-old are reaping the joy that kindness brings.

Dorothy Kohls, *Muncie, Indiana*

table manners

Dinner Table Harmony

I hate constantly telling my kids to mind their manners at the table, which makes everyone crabby. So, at the beginning of each week, we talk about one skill that we want to work on, such as not talking with a full mouth. After that, we're only allowed to use body language to correct one another. If one of my kids starts talking with a full mouth, I just point to my closed mouth. It's more fun this way because no one feels picked on.

Kathleen Bartels, *Hewitt, Texas*

Practice Makes Perfect

I encourage my children, who are 7, 9, and 11, to practice their table manners by planning a special dinner and inviting grandparents and other relatives to attend. Each child is assigned special duties, such as setting and clearing the table, and each one is expected to use his best table manners.

Judy Best, *La Porte, Indiana*

Stop Reaching!

My 6- and 8-year-old children were often reaching for things at the table rather than asking for them properly. In desperation, I told them that we would have to do something to help them remember: Each time they reached for something, I'd

? ask Peggy Post

good table manners

Q: My husband and I want our children to have good table manners. But ever since our kids were little, family mealtimes have been a struggle. We're constantly harping on them to keep their elbows off the table, use their forks instead of their fingers, and so on. Is there anything we can do to make meals more pleasant while still teaching the kids manners?

A: You might try a more upbeat approach, since children tend to respond better to positive rather than negative feedback. As often as possible, praise your children's successes: "I like how you're sitting so nicely, Jack." Don't feel that you have to jump on every mistake, but when you do decide to correct your children, do it with a brief and gentle reminder: "Elbows, Melissa." Instead of trying to reform your kids overnight, concentrate first on a couple of the stickiest problems, then move on to others.

kid-friendly formal affairs

There's no telling how your kids might behave when you include them in special events like weddings. But the prospect of less-than-perfect manners doesn't mean that they should automatically be excluded either. The following tips will help make your next formal affair more kid-friendly.

✓ Tantrum-proof your child. If you fear that your kid may become tired and cranky halfway through the evening, make arrangements for her to attend only the first couple of hours, then take her home or back to a babysitter at the hotel.

✓ Entertain them. To avoid total meltdown, keep toddlers and preschoolers busy with board books, crayons, and paper. Older children can be distracted with books, a deck of cards, or even a disposable camera.

✓ Dress for success. An early dress rehearsal gives you a chance to spot problems (a scratchy lace collar or uncomfortable shoes) in time to make changes. It also lets your child warm up to the idea of wearing clothing that she doesn't wear every day.

✓ Keep your sense of humor. No matter how carefully you prepare, something is bound to happen. Just keep telling yourself that someday, it'll make a great family story.

deduct 10 cents from their allowance. I kept a pad and pencil by the table to record the deductions. It didn't take long before they were regularly asking politely for food to be passed.

Beth Jacobsen, *Chicago*

Something to Chew On

Helping my 4-year-old learn to chew with his mouth closed took patience and lots of reminding. But his behavior improved greatly when I came up with an incentive. Whenever Jason completed a meal and only had to be reminded twice to chew with his mouth shut, we would call one of his grandparents and he could announce his accomplishment to them. We slowly went to one reminder and then to none. His grandparents' praise reinforced for him the value of good table manners.

Jennifer Dukes, *Davenport, Iowa*

promoting appropriate behavior

Play Mouse

It's great to have groups of children over to play, but their voices get very loud. When this happens, I calm things down by suggesting that the children pretend to be mice. It works like a charm, every time.

Janet Lindsey, Tarzana, California

The Write Stuff

When one of my children performs an especially thoughtful deed, I write a short note on a bright sheet of paper and put it on his pillow. The notes help to reinforce nice behavior and build self-esteem.

Jennifer Young, Kansas City, Missouri

it's my job

an etiquette teacher's tips on proper introductions

In this ultracasual day and age, figuring out how your kids should address your adult friends can be tough. Sure, they call your college roommate whom they've known forever by her first name, but how should they refer to a neighbor or their friends' parents? For the definitive answer, we went to St. Louis–based etiquette consultant Maria Everding, whose nationwide program, Pretty As A Picture, teaches children proper manners, poise, and style. Here's the scoop.

✓ "In general, if the person in question is old enough to be a parent to your child, your child should refer to them as Mr., Mrs., Miss, or Doctor. I know this is formal, but I consider it a sign of respect. It shows that your child recognizes that he's not at the same age level as the person that he is speaking to."

✓ "The old rule that children should speak only when spoken to no longer applies. Your child should show an interest in talking to your adult friends."

grandmother knows best

I think that dinnertime is the most important time for the family. When I was a young parent in the 1940s and 1950s, my husband ran a dairy, so we were up early, and we ate dinner early, always with our two children. The dinner table is where I taught them manners, such as not slurping soup, saying "Yes, please" and "No, thank you," and asking to be excused from the table. It is also the best place to teach the fine art of conversation; children can practice talking like young men and ladies every day!

Anita Guyton, *Bloomfield, Connecticut*

Say It Nicely

My son thinks everything "stinks!" It's not necessarily a bad word, but it's also not the nicest thing to say. Every time he utters it, I remind him how boring it is to hear the same thing over and over, then ask him what he really wants to say. For example, if he says that a movie stinks, I encourage him to describe instead why he didn't like the story or the cast. It's helping him break this bad habit.

Amanda Loecke, *West Des Moines, Iowa*

Compliments Work Wonders

Part of teaching manners is showing kids how to be thoughtful. I give out compliments as often as possible and encourage other family members to do the same. The more we do this, the easier it becomes. We praise each other for simple things such as helping out with a chore, being a good sport, or remembering to say thanks for a kind act.

Catherine Bach, *Topeka, Kansas*

5

development
and learning

raising
kids who care

20

teaching your children good values is one of the most difficult tasks you'll face as a parent. Qualities such as honesty, kindness, charity, and spirituality can be fuzzy concepts for kids to grasp, especially if they get conflicting messages from schoolmates, friends, and the media.

So, how can you raise a kid with character? Start at home. Give your child daily lessons about right and wrong from the time when he's very young, and try to be a great role model for him. Get your kids involved in the community as well: Activities such as a canned food drive, a children's service at your church, or a cleanup day at a local park will teach children about compassion.

The terrific parent-tested tips in this chapter can help you raise an empathetic, moral, and socially conscious kid.

charity begins at home

Start a Food Basket

To teach my kids, ages 7 and 12, to share with others who are less fortunate, I placed a visible reminder in my kitchen. We have a large basket that we fill with nonperishable food items to donate to the town's crisis center. Every time that we go shopping, we pick up a few extras for the basket, and when it's full, we carry it to the crisis center and begin again.

Margaret Fretwell, Old Fort, North Carolina

The Gift of a Good Book

Each month, my 7-year-old son brings home book order forms from school. Many of the books are relatively inexpensive, so instead of just buying one or two books for him, we also purchase a few to donate to charity. My son is thrilled to pick out books that he thinks other kids will like—and I feel good knowing that we're helping out families less fortunate than ours.

Kathryn DeWitt, Shoshoni, Wyoming

Help Older Folks

We have an elderly neighbor who has difficulty getting around. A few years ago, I started asking my two sons to go over early in the morning on days when it snowed to shovel her walk. I explained to them that this was a favor to her, and they shouldn't take any money if she offered it. They feel proud of their job looking after our neighbor, and they're learning the value of helping out another person just because it's a nice thing to do. Now that they've gotten a little older, they volunteer to mow her lawn in the summer as well.

Margaret Thormann, Winnetka, Illinois

Keep the Spirit of Giving Alive

To make sure that our kids don't lose the giving spirit of the holidays, some friends and I came up with a way to focus on the importance of sharing with others throughout the year. Before our monthly get-togethers, each child uses part of his allowance to buy an item for our "giving box." The category changes each month: It might be beach toys in the summer or school supplies in the fall. In December, we take the box to a charity.

Debbie Weidler, Lititz, Pennsylvania

service-savvy kids

It's never too early to teach a child the value of helping others. In fact, Mike Mc-Cabe, vice president of programming for Youth Service America in Washington, D.C., and a father of three, regularly brings his 5-year-old daughter on volunteer projects. Here are his tips for raising a socially conscious kid.

Read books that encourage volunteering. In addition to classics such as *The Giving Tree* by Shel Silverstein, more and more kids' books today focus on generosity. "My daughter has both Arthur and Berenstain Bears books that focus on characters performing community service. She loves being able to equate the work she does to help others with what her favorite characters do," says McCabe.

Be a model yourself. Kids are three times more likely to volunteer if they have a role model who does. Take them with you on one of your service projects (making sure that there is something age-appropriate for them to do).

Be creative. Service can be fun—and it doesn't have to take a lot of extra time or money. "We've had kids who made service projects part of their birthday party by making extra sandwiches for the homeless," says McCabe.

Celebrate their accomplishments. After your child's service work is done, affirm the good job she did by talking about how it made her feel, and find out what she learned from it.

Keep it up. Encourage your child to keep a service log where she can record what she's done and track her hours. Both you and your child can be proud when you look back on what she's accomplished. It's also nice to take pictures of your child at her service sites and keep the photos in a special album.

A Simple Way to Share

We often get requests for nonperishable food for the needy. To make sure that I always have enough on hand, I look for and use "buy one, get one free" coupons. After each shopping trip, I put the free items on a special shelf in our basement. When my kids need food for school, church, or charity organizations, they shop from the shelf. This way, I know that we always have plenty to share, and I don't have to make extra trips to the store.

Kathy Merwin, Hudson, Ohio

easy ways for kids to act now

✓ Put kids in charge of your household's recycling effort and ask them to find ways to reduce waste and reuse items around the house.

✓ Help plant flowers and trees in your yard or at a park or school that is looking for volunteer planters.

✓ Clean up and collect trash around the neighborhood or at the local playground, river, or park.

✓ Have a garage sale or lemonade stand and donate profits to charity.

✓ Organize classmates for a larger project, such as painting a mural over graffiti or cleaning up a vacant lot.

Toy Drive

To help my 8- and 10-year-old daughters learn about caring and sharing, I had them sort through their toys and decide which ones they could live without. Then, we boxed up the toys and gave them to the preschool at our church. It was a great way to teach them how to make decisions while helping others at the same time.

Stacy Romo, Philadelphia

helping your community

Music Practice

Every few weeks, in lieu of my daughter's regular music practice, I take her to visit her great-grandmother in a nursing home. She brings her violin and practices there, much to the delight of the residents. My daughter gains valuable experience performing before an audience, and the residents are refreshed by the presence of a young child making music. It always ends up being a great practice session.

J. E. Kral, Pelham, Alabama

Open Your Home to Others

Last year, we took part in the Fresh Air Fund, an organization that places inner-city children in homes in the country. For 2 weeks, a 6½-year-old boy from the city stayed with us, and it was a real learning experience for my kids, 6-year-old twins and a 3-year-old. While it was rocky at points—the kids fought like all kids are apt to do—it had many positive results. My kids really got a lesson in sharing their things, understanding people from different backgrounds, and opening their home to someone new. We're already looking forward to this summer: Our Fresh Air friend is coming back for another 2 weeks.

Michelle Dennigan, Wilton, Connecticut

Give during the Holidays

As a single mom with three boys—ages 5, 9, and 11—it's often hard to find time to volunteer. This past year, however, I made a commitment to myself to find a way to serve others during the holidays. Together with a coworker, I helped organize a collection for 25 families at a homeless shelter. The best part was going shopping with my kids for the one child we "adopted." They were so excited and really thought hard about each item they bought him, even the small things for his stocking. I was proud of their generosity, especially when I read one of their letters to Santa. It said, "I don't want much this year, just be nice to the people in the shelter." It was such a good feeling to help others—and it really taught the boys and me how lucky we are.

Diane Ferguson, Elliot, Maine

finding volunteer opportunities

These Web sites and toll-free numbers can help put you in touch with your local volunteer center and fill you in on child-friendly service opportunities near you.

✓ www.servenet.org

✓ www.ysa.org

✓ www.americaspromise.org or (888) 559-6884

✓ (800) VOLUNTEER (that's 800-865-8683)

Or contact your local YMCA, 4-H club, church or synagogue, or community center.

A Little Help for the Homeless

In a big city, you often become immune to people begging for money on the streets or subway. But whenever my 6-year-old sees someone asking for change, she insists that we help them. Because I want her to grow up with a sense of empathy for others, I always oblige. Sometimes, it's whatever change we find in our coat pockets; other times, it's a dollar—whatever it is, Abby insists on giving the money to the person herself. It really makes me feel good to see her want to help so many people.

Diane Debrovner, New York City

Visit Older Members of the Community

When my youngest child was 4, I decided to deliver meals to the homebound elderly in my town. Taking Kevin along was a marvelous lesson in helping others. And the seniors really

it's my job

how to raise a spiritual child.

Imparting your child with a sense of spirituality isn't always serious business. In fact, according to Reverend Cynthia O'Brien, a minister at Smith Memorial Presbyterian Church in Portland, Oregon, and mother of a 1-year-old daughter, it's often the little things that will help you raise a child with a healthy attitude about religion.

✓ At church or temple, encourage your child to participate by explaining what is happening during the service, holding her and dancing together during the songs, and helping her follow along in the Bible or Torah, even if she can't read. Talk to your minister or rabbi about ways to make the service appeal to kids.

✓ Set up playdates with other families who share your values, and introduce your child to older members of your house of worship. Although they may be shy around them at first, children often become friends with seniors who can act as mentors and role models.

✓ Attend potluck suppers or volunteer to make goodies for the annual bake sale. Or, encourage your child to donate her own money to special programs, such as disaster relief, that your congregation may be sponsoring. "Kids love putting money in the offering plate. It really makes them feel like they are an important part of the church family," says O'Brien.

enjoyed talking to a young child for a few minutes. It was a win-win situation for all.

Brian Wentz, Saint Joseph, Missouri

Make Helping Others a Lifelong Lesson

I've tried to raise my 9-year-old son to be a good person, and part of that is teaching him to help others. Ever since he was little, we've gone food shopping together, then donated some of what we buy to a shelter. Even though we don't have a lot ourselves, this has given my son a sense of how important it is to help others. I think it's a lesson he's really taken to heart—in fact, he recently gave away some of his lunch at school because another child had nothing to eat.

Rene Garcia, Los Banos, California

Find a Custom-Fit Charity

One of the best ways to motivate a child to donate her time and money is by finding a cause that really interests her. My daughter loves animals, so whenever we sell books to a secondhand store, we've made a habit of giving the money to our local animal shelter or an animal rights group. What's also worked for our family is doing things together, such as a recent walk to raise money for AIDS charities. Not only are you a good role model for your kids, but it's also a great way to fit in some quality time together.

Lorraine Glennon, Brooklyn, New York

spiritual strategies

Family-Friendly Service

We take our two sons, ages 9 and 3, to a special children's mass every Sunday. It includes a children's choir, kids acting as ushers, and a homily directed to their interests. As a result, my kids really feel involved in the mass and love going to church.

Patricia Wrotniak, Mount Vernon, New York

Front Row Seat

Children often get bored in church when they can't see what's going on. When I moved up to the front with my 2½-year-old daughter (with her sitting in the aisle so she could see the

Vanna White

"I'm a very spiritual person, in the sense of quiet meditation and believing in God. I think one of the greatest things I do to show my children love is saying prayers with them every night before they go to bed."

—Wheel of Fortune *hostess and mother of Nicholas and Giovanna*

altar), she immediately became interested in the service.

Maura Parker Quinlan, Atlanta

Keep Kids Busy

When my 2-year-old daughter started having a hard time sitting quietly through church, I created a "church bag" for her. I bought a canvas tote and fabric paints and helped her decorate it. I filled it with a container of crackers, a Sippy cup of water, a stuffed animal, crayons, and paper. My daughter loves these quiet activities, and they really keep her entertained during the parts of the service that don't hold her attention.

Gretchen Mousel, Canton, Michigan

Focus on Good Behavior

We found that following a routine before and during the service was the best way to teach our young son proper church behavior. First, we'd budget an extra 10 minutes into our morning to "get the wiggles out." He knew that he had to get all the noise out before church because he was expected to be quiet while we were there. Then, we'd talk about proper church behavior, such as using his quiet voice. Finally, we'd praise him for his good behavior the minute that church was over, making sure to tell him what he had done well.

Jean Hawn, Detroit

Go on a Tour

The moms in our "play and pray" group asked our priest to give the group, which includes children from birth to age 5, a tour of the church. The kids were able to explore freely and even got to play the organ. Our priest talked about the different parts of the church and service and answered questions. The tour helped the kids feel more comfortable in church— and it even led to fewer disruptions.

Sheri Terbovich, Pickerington, Ohio

is honesty the best policy?

Q: My 3-year-old daughter recently got a present from an adult friend of ours, and when she unwrapped it, she announced that she already had that particular doll. I don't want to encourage her to lie, but how do I explain why she can't say something like that even if it's true?

A: The polite "lie" to spare someone's feelings is too sophisticated and confusing a concept for very young children, who can't distinguish between that kind of "socially correct" deceit and untruthfulness in other situations. Help your daughter prepare for this type of situation by warning her that people might give her something she already has, and by telling her that the best thing to say is simply "Thank you very much!" if they do. Explain that the reason she would say thank you is that the gift givers have tried hard to pick out something she would like, and that it might hurt their feelings if she showed that she didn't like it or told them that she already had it. You could also tell your daughter that if she does receive duplicate gifts, you and she will go to the store and trade it for something she doesn't have.

Take Advantage of the Nursery

I've been taking my 21-month-old daughter to church since she was only a few months old, but recently, she's had a hard time sitting through a whole service. Now, I let her stay for the first part—hymns, announcements, and the children's story time—and then I take her to the nursery. This way, she gets to experience being in church with adults, but for a shorter period of time so she doesn't get bored. At the nursery, she likes playing with the other kids, and I get to enjoy the rest of the service without disruptions.

Tracey Jones, Waterford, California

Home-Based Spirituality

I wanted to have a blessing ceremony for my newborn son but felt awkward about having it in a church, since we do not participate in an organized religion. Instead, I had all of our family over for dinner and asked each to bring a poem or letter to read about their hopes and dreams for him. Our homemade ceremony was beautiful, and after it was over, I collected the poems and letters and put them in an album with each participant's picture. As my son grows up, I hope that he can turn to this collection to understand how blessed he is to have such wonderful people in his life.

Trina Zeljak, Carlsbad, California

the value of values

Be a Role Model

I believe that if we as parents model good behavior, then kids will automatically pick it up. I never lie in front of my kids; even letting them hear me tell a white lie gives them permission to do it themselves, which isn't okay. The same goes for cheating: If there's a kid's menu for kids under 12, I won't let my 13-year-old order from it. And if someone makes a mistake when giving me change, I always point it out and return the extra money.

Mary Manning, Point Lookout, New York

A Lesson in Lying

Whenever I catch my 6-year-old in a lie, I am sure to sit down with him and ask him why he lied. He eventually tells us the truth, and we then talk about why lying is wrong. Approaching the subject head-on and explaining why telling lies is bad seems to work: He's been fibbing less and less in the past few months.

Grace Lenchyshyn, Saint Adolphe, Manitoba, Canada

Pet Power

If you can, I've found that getting a pet for your child can be a wonderful—and a learning—experience. Taking care of something smaller and totally dependent on her teaches a child a valuable lesson in kindness and responsibility. Of course, Mom and Dad may have to help, but a child can be in charge of making sure that a dog or cat gets enough water, food, and exercise.

Elena Lewis, Milford, Connecticut

Set House Rules

We have several rules that apply to both kids and adults in our house, including being kind to each other, respecting other

teaching respect
for other people's property

Q: My 5-year-old daughter wandered into our neighbor's yard and picked a bunch of her flowers, even though I've told her many times not to take other people's property. Should I have made her return the flowers and apologize or just hope that my neighbor didn't notice?

A: Think of this as an opportunity to teach your daughter both honesty and the art of apologizing. Tell her that because she took something that doesn't belong to her, she must say that she's sorry. Explain that the neighbor must have put a lot of care into her garden and is likely to be upset. Have your child practice a simple apology, and then go with her to pave the way. You might say to the neighbor, "Jenny has something she needs to talk to you about."

Depending on your daughter's verbal and social skills, you may have to help her tell what happened and prompt her to say that she's sorry. You might brain-storm ahead of time to see how your daughter could make it up to the neighbor, perhaps by giving her a new flowering plant or a little gardening gift. This isn't strictly necessary, but it would be a nice way to demonstrate to your daughter the importance of tending carefully the various relationships in her life.

people's property, and taking personal responsibility for what we do and say. If one of our children breaks another child's toy, he must replace it; if he acts rudely, he must apologize. I think that this is the most basic way to teach our kids that everyone in this world is important and that no one has the right to be mean, impolite, or unkind to others.

Martha Ladyman, Austin, Texas

Make Family a Priority

To raise our children with good values, we spend lots of quality time together as a family so that they learn proper morals and beliefs. We set aside special times each week to spend together—time for them to tell us what's on their minds and for us to help them out with problems they may be having

what values do you try to instill in your children?

"Strength and perseverance. They're what made me succeed."

—*Vanessa Williams*, *actress, singer, and mother of Melanie, Jillian, and Devin*

"Respect for other people and honesty. If you hold on to those values, you'll come out ahead."

—*Harrison Ford*, *actor and father of Ben, Willard, Malcolm, and Georgia*

"I hope my daughter develops a passion for something as she gets older, like I have for dance. I also want her to be strong and self-sufficient, which is how I was raised."

—*Jasmine Guy*, *actress, dancer, and mother of Imani*

"People have never regarded me as a great actress or a great beauty, but I've always tried to go beyond those notions and prove myself. I want my kids to do the same."

—*Jamie Lee Curtis*, *actress and mother of Annie and Thomas*

"I want my daughter to know that she doesn't have to conform to one ideal of what a woman should be."

—*Rene Russo*, *actress and mother of Rosie*

in school or with friends. By letting our children know that we are there for them and by staying consistent with what we expect, they will grow up to be responsible adults.

Kathy Dillon, *Philadelphia*

money matters

Banking Basics

To help my 7-year-old son learn the value of money, I gave him an old checkbook from a closed bank account and started Mommy's Bank. Every week, he deposits his allowance and records it in his register. Whenever we go shopping, he brings his checkbook along and decides on his own whether he wants to spend money on a new toy. He's learning how to be a responsible consumer, and it's a great way for him to practice addition and subtraction.

Terri Gross, *Commack, New York*

Help Wanted

My children, ages 9, 4, and 2, must do certain chores each week and don't get an allowance. So, to give them the chance to earn spending money, I made a job board. The board lists a variety of extra chores—such as watering the plants or cleaning up the playroom—that they can do around the house. Besides letting them earn money, this system has helped build their self-confidence and taught them the importance of hard work.

Michelle Hortenberry, *Cincinnati*

A Lesson Learned

My kids were constantly asking me for money: to go to the movies, to buy a soda, even to pay late fees at the library. I was beginning to feel that they had no appreciation for what things cost or where money came from, so I came up with a plan. We started giving them a $10 allowance each week, but out of that, they had to pay their own expenses. I'll never forget the look of horror on my 10-year-old's face when she had to pay $9 for a video she returned late. From then on, every tape has gone back on time.

Mary Hickey, Montclair, New Jersey

Encourage Giving

Every week, my 7-year-old son saves 50 cents from his allowance to donate to a charity. When it adds up to $25, I

giving kids an allowance

Most child experts agree: The sooner kids learn the value of money, the better. And one of the best ways to teach money management skills is by giving your child an allowance. Of course, children must be competent enough to understand the power—and risk—that goes along with handling money, and that usually takes place when a child starts elementary school. Here are some things to keep in mind if you decide to give your child an allowance.

✓ Consider how much. While the amount that parents give varies, $2 to $5 is a typical weekly allowance for children 5 to 6 years old. No matter what you give, be consistent: Give the same amount on the same day each week.

✓ Set rules. Let your child know if there are certain things that he is not allowed to buy with the money, and determine a set amount each week that he should save.

✓ Encourage generosity. At this age, kids are very open to learning values we teach them about money. This is the perfect time to talk about the importance of sharing what we have with others and to set up a system so that part of his allowance goes to charity.

✓ Don't link the allowance to chores. Regular jobs around the house should be considered part of being in the family, not something for which your child expects to be paid.

match it, and then he chooses who to give it to from a list of charities for kids. Last year, it went to the Hole-in-the-Wall Gang Camp for kids with cancer. He likes knowing that his money is helping other children—and he was really pleased when he got a letter of thanks from the camp in the mail.

Jeffrey Saks, *Chappaqua, New York*

Try a Layaway Plan

When my kids see a game, toy, or book that they would like to buy, I encourage them to save until they can afford it. But when my daughter wanted a doll that we weren't sure would still be around in a few months, we put it on layaway. Each week, she paid a portion of the cost until it was paid for. It was hard for her to wait, but it really taught her patience and the value of money. It also works to make your own layaway plan if the store doesn't have one: Buy the toy or game, then keep it tucked away until your kids pay for it in full.

Lynette Kittle, *Hilo, Hawaii*

best friends

21

there's nothing quite as heartwarming as seeing your child invite the new kid in the neighborhood to join in a game of tag, or watching him share his favorite toy with his "very best friend in the whole world."

Making friends may seem natural for kids, but it often takes practice to get it right. And although we once thought that children didn't develop true friendships until they reached the preschool years, studies now show that kids develop close bonds as early as age 1. By ages 3 and 4, these relationships are vital to your child's self-confidence, and they provide him with much-needed comfort during the early school years. No wonder the calendars of most families today are booked with playdates for their little ones.

Use the creative tips in this chapter to help your little social butterfly make friends, learn to share, have successful playdates, and more.

easy ways to make friends

Take a Class

I joined a parent/tot class at our local community center to help my 3-year-old make friends. We really got to know some of the mothers and their children and were soon invited to join a mom's group. It's been a lifesaver: We meet once a week for 2 hours, and the kids get to play while we talk and help each other out with parenting concerns. It's been a great way to expose my daughter to a group of friends whose parents I like and approve of.

Aileen Schaffer, Aurora, Colorado

Being Friendly Goes Far

If you are new to a neighborhood and want to help your children make friends, one of the best things you can do is take

baby playdates

Babies and toddlers don't play together like older children do. In fact, get them together for a playgroup and it may seem like a complete bust—they'll probably spend most of the time ignoring each other. But not to worry: While toddlers generally won't interact with each other, this early play is vital to your child's social skills. Here's how to ensure that your littlest one gets the most out of playdates.

✓ Start small. Begin by arranging playdates with one child at a time. Too many other toddlers can overwhelm your child.

✓ Keep it short. Some babies and toddlers will only interact for a few minutes. If your child is cranky or visibly not having a good time, say good-bye and head for home. And don't stop having playdates just because the kids ignore each other; their social skills will eventually develop.

✓ Come prepared. Kids who are well-fed and rested are less likely to have meltdowns, which is why morning playgroups often work best. If you are going to someone else's house, it's also a good idea to bring along a few of your own child's toys.

✓ Set up games. Parents can help lead the play by setting up simple games such as stacking blocks or filling a bucket with balls. Also, provide plenty of containers of small toys that kids can dump and sort—a favorite game of toddlers.

helping new moms find friends, too

For many new and stay-at-home moms, life can become so centered on taking care of the kids that it's easy to forget about their own need for a social life. "Especially in today's society, where extended families are not close by, moms need a network of adult friends for support," says Linda Landsman, executive director of the National Association of Mothers' Centers (NAMC) and a mother of two. The answer for many moms is finding a playgroup: Not only will your child make friends, but you will, too. Here is Landsman's advice for creating a successful playgroup.

Seek out other moms. Try contacting an NAMC Mothers' Center near you by calling (800) 645-3828 or by going to the group's Web site, www.motherscenter.org. If the association doesn't have a center in your area, check the local papers, church bulletins, or the message board at your grocery store for postings from other moms. Or you can put up a note there yourself or introduce yourself to mothers at the park who have children the same age as yours.

Make a plan. Playgroups operate in many different ways; sit down with the other mothers and decide what works best for you. You may want a playgroup where all four moms and their children come together once a week in the park for lunch and playtime. Other groups operate by rotating responsibilities: Two of the mothers might stay at one home with the children while the other two are free for an hour to run errands or go out for coffee together.

Set ground rules. Before you even have your first playdate, it's vital to make decisions as a group. Will only healthy snacks be served? Does a child have to stay home if he has a runny nose? How will you handle it if one child bites another? If you agree to deal with conflict in an open and honest manner, you're less likely to hurt one of the moms' feelings or, worse, end a nice friendship.

your children for walks around your block. Smile and say hello to anyone you see in their yards, and make a point of stopping to chat with neighbors who have kids around the same age as your children. Once you get to know these other parents, find out what activities, such as swimming or preschool, their children participate in. Then, sign your children up for the same activities and try to arrange a carpool.

Carolyn Levitsky, *Westford, Massachusetts*

Be Bookish

Many bookstores and libraries offer storytime, which is a great way for kids to make friends and for moms to meet other moms. And remember, once you start going regularly, you'll probably see the same people, so don't hesitate to start conversations and jot down phone numbers.

Catherine Radler, *Flanders, New Jersey*

Join a Health Club

My son and I met lots of new people when I joined a gym. I had time for myself, and my son got to play with other children his age in the nursery. He's made some nice friendships, and we set up playdates regularly. I've also enjoyed making friends with other moms.

Patricia Flynn, *Foxboro, Massachusetts*

Look into Recreation Centers

I found that community recreation centers are a great source for getting out of the house and giving both mom and children some much-needed interaction with other kids and parents. Our rec center sets up specific times during the day for children ages 1 to 6 years old to play in their gym, so my kids have a chance to meet new friends and release some energy.

Amie Fiedler, *Beaverton, Oregon*

Get a Job

To help my daughter and me get to know more moms and their kids, I got a part-time job at a day care center, working a half-day, 3 days a week. It's a great way to let my daughter play with children her own age. And by working only 12 hours a week, I still have plenty of one-on-one time with my child, not to mention some extra money.

Jennifer Elton, *Austin, Texas*

perfect playdates

Seeing Double

Whenever we have another child over for a playdate with my 3-year-old daughter, I make sure to have two of everything the kids like, including juice boxes and snacks. That way, there's

ask **Peggy Post**

contagious playmates

Q: My daughter, who is 5, has a friend who comes over on playdates when she is obviously ill. Several times, my child has ended up sick as a result. Is there a polite way to ask the mother, whom I don't know well, not to let her child visit when she's sick?

A: Unfortunately, swapping germs is an unavoidable part of growing up. Often, kids are contagious before they even show symptoms. But if a child is obviously sick, it's her parents' responsibility to keep her away from other kids or to ask the other parents' permission before getting them together.

If you're positive that the last time this child came to your house, she passed her cold or some other bug on to your child, you could bring up the subject with her mother. A tactful way of doing so would be to say, "Joanna really loves playing with Lisa, and I don't want to hurt their friendship. But Joanna caught Lisa's cold the last time she was over. Let's make a pact that if my child is sick, I won't bring her to your house, and if your child is sick, you won't bring her to my house." That's evenhanded enough to be inoffensive, and it should do the trick.

no hassle over who had it first. It's also a good idea to have the other child's parent bring a couple of her favorite videos and CDs over, so that we can take turns watching or listening to one child's choice, then the other's.

Crystal Grosenick, Hartford, Wisconsin

Stay Out of It

I've found that the best way to help my 1-year-old son get used to playing with other children is by interfering as little as possible. When he has playdates, I give the kids toys that I know they will both enjoy, then sit back and watch. I've found that when I stay on the floor with them, they both want to play with me, but when I'm not right there, they become curious about each other and start playing together. As time has gone on, my son has become much more adept at playing with other children.

Jodi Carter, Whitehouse, Texas

Get Creative with Playtime

To make sure that my 5-year-old and his friends have fun on playdates at our house, I plan special themes. We've had treasure hunts, decorated paper-plate monster masks, and created a mini Olympics in our backyard with games that focus on fun rather than competition. I also try to encourage play that makes them learn to cooperate. For example, if I notice that

it's my job

best playdate activities

Keeping kids happy on a playdate doesn't mean spending lots of money or having elaborate toys and games on hand. In fact, according to Pennye Pucheu, a kindergarten teacher at Alice Boucher Elementary, in Lafayette, Louisiana, and mother of two children, ages 3 and 8, it's often the littlest things that keep kids content.

Bring a goody bag. Let your child pick out a small bag of toys to share at his playgroup. It doesn't have to include anything special: Crayons, small toys from fast food restaurants, and coloring books work well.

Head outside. When the kids are bursting with energy and the weather is nice, go outside for a game of tag or "Mother may I," or simply to run around. Or entertain them for hours with sidewalk chalk. Keep a variety of colors on hand and watch kids practice their shapes, play hopscotch, or create driveway art.

Have good, cheap fun. Add food coloring to whipped cream, then have kids fingerpaint with it on an old tabletop or plastic tray. Create tambourines by stapling paper plates together with a few beans inside for a little noisy fun. Or, keep strips of crepe paper handy and put on music. Little ones can spend hours dancing and moving their streamers in time with the beat.

Create in the kitchen. "When my son has playdates, we'll give it a *Blue's Clues* theme: First, we read a story or two, then, we make cookies with blue food coloring that can be fashioned into the shape of a paw," says Pucheu. You don't have to be Julia Child to make creative treats. Let kids transform store-bought cookies or snack cakes with jelly beans, M&M's, and icing.

they are playing "fight games" or "superheroes," I'll make an overstuffed paper bag to be a "bad guy" for them. That way, they can both play good guys. Or, if we're doing crafts together, I'll make a really bad version of what they are working on so we can all laugh at mine first rather than argue about which one of theirs is better.

Cathy Shambley, *Hermosa Beach, California*

Fun-Time Snacks

I've found two very different snacks that are big hits when my 4½-year-old son has friends over for playdates. For a healthy alternative, I cut cucumbers into long, thin sticks and serve them with creamy Italian dressing. The kids love dipping the cucumbers, and I like knowing that they are eating something good for them. But, when tensions run high on playdates, there's nothing like ice cream to make everyone happy. Children especially enjoy it—and forget about their squabbles—when you have cones and sprinkles on hand too.

Gigi Berman Aharoni, *Great Neck, New York*

Plan for Every Situation

When my 5-year-old has friends over, I have quiet activities ready in case they get tired: reading a book or giving each child a stuffed animal to cuddle up with. I help head off fights by putting hard-to-share items like tricycles away before my child's friends come over. Otherwise, I may have to listen to nonstop yelling about whose turn it is.

Elena Lewis, *Milford, Connecticut*

share and share alike

Have a Cow

My boys, ages 3 and 6, usually do a good job of sharing. But when they don't, I tell them to get the cow: It's a minute timer in the shape of a cow that moos when time is up. Both of my kids know that if it isn't their turn, they need to play with something else until they hear the moo. Then, it'll be their turn. We've found that setting the timer for sharing sessions of 10 to 15 minutes usually works best.

Kerry Nieman, *Cedar Park, Texas*

grandmother knows best

I have three granddaughters the same age. One is an only child, so getting her to share when she was little was a real challenge. Whenever her cousin reached for one of her toys, she would snatch it away and say, "It's mine!" To help her learn to share toys, I used a two-step approach. First, I would ask her, "How would you feel if your friend wouldn't let you play with her toys at her house?" Then, I would give her a chance to let her cousin play with the toy. If that didn't work, I'd replace the toy that caused the squabble with something that they could share easily: blocks, and so on. They hardly missed the first toy, and my granddaughter learned that she could let her friends share her toys and still have a good time, too.

Mollye Brown,
Fredericton,
New Brunswick, Canada

Sharing Strategies

Whenever my 17-month-old has play-dates, I make it a point to keep an eye on her and interrupt if she's being unfair to another child. If, for example, she grabs a toy away from another toddler, I call attention to the situation, return the toy to the other child, and explain to Logan how it makes the other child feel sad when her toy is taken away. Also, since I know that it's hard to see Mommy giving away her toy to another child, I try to find something just as enticing to replace it. Sharing's a tough subject for toddlers, but with a little help from Mom and Dad, it's a lesson they can learn.

Jennifer Furr, Raleigh, North Carolina

Sing a Song

To help my 3-year-old and 21-month-old learn to take turns, I created "ABC minutes." Each child gets to ride on the swing or play with the toy for the entire length of the ABC song. They know that when it's the end of the song, it's the next child's turn. My oldest happily belts out her ABCs while the youngest hums along, and at the end, they are more than happy to give up their turn.

Vicki Terlap, Reno, Texas

Ask Nicely

My 2½-year-old son is just getting to the "mine" stage. To encourage him to share, we ask him whether his baby sister may borrow his toys or blankets for a while. We point out how much she likes him and mention that it is only for a short period of time. We never force him to give up something that is his, but by asking him nicely, we've never needed to: He makes up his own mind to share his things. Hopefully, this sense of generosity will carry over to sharing with other children too.

Jennifer Duster, Winona, Minnesota

Try a Trading System

Our 2- and 4-year-old children "trade" toys quite often with other children in our neighborhood. We've found that this is a great way to encourage sharing, especially by making it a rule that children must ask the other child—not their mom or dad—for permission to borrow the desired item. It gives the child who owns the toy a sense of control and lets them know that their decision counts. The borrower also knows that in order to get something, they must loan something out in return. When it comes time to trade back, it is the kids'—not the parents'—responsibility to make sure that everyone's property is returned.

Mary Beth Randall, *Franklin, Massachusetts*

Practice On Mommy and Daddy

Our 26-month-old son doesn't have much exposure yet to other tots, so his sharing abilities are still limited. But to pre-

when friends fight

"When you help a child learn to resolve disputes himself, you're giving him an important social skill that he can use for the rest of his life," says Sally Rudoy, a therapist in Montclair, New Jersey. Here are her recommendations.

✓ Teach him to keep cool. You can show children as young as age 4 how to calm themselves down during an argument by counting to 10, reciting a poem, or taking slow, deep breaths. Help your child figure out the strategy that works best for him.

✓ Identify the problem. Ask your child what he and his friend fought over, and listen without offering advice. Give him the opportunity to get his emotions out, even if that means letting him say unkind things about his friend.

✓ Brainstorm solutions. Suggest that your child think of several things that he could say or do to solve the problem. Don't be surprised if he suggests such things as "Call him stupid" or "Beat him up." Remain nonjudgmental. Don't say, "No, that's not nice."

✓ Examine the consequences. Ask your child to think about each solution and ask what may happen if he tries that one. Chances are, he'll figure out on his own that hitting his friend or calling him names won't resolve his dilemma.

✓ Pick a solution to try. Ask your child to try the idea that he thinks would work best. Reassure him that if it doesn't work, he can try something else.

pare him for when he will be around other children, we focus on having him share his toys with his father and me when we're playing. We also try to praise him when he cooperates and does a good job, rather than dwelling on the times when he isn't quite so eager to share.

Dee Dee Bear, Lewisburg, Ohio

Be Consistent

I am currently teaching my 2-year-old how to share. I think that what's most important is to start young and be consistent. Whenever he says, "My book," I'll respond by saying, "Yes, but will you share it with me?" I've also learned that it helps to let him play with his 8-month-old brother's toys—but I first say to him, "It's Charlie's, but he'll share it with you." That way, he understands that sharing is a two-way street.

Renee Gardner, Vernon, New Jersey

Try a Sticker Reward

To help my 2½-year-old understand the importance of sharing, we keep a sticker chart on the wall in her room. Whenever she shares her toys on a playdate and doesn't try to grab them out of another child's hands, she gets to add a sticker to the chart. This little reward has really curbed the "gimmes" on playdates, and she always gets so excited to tell her dad when he gets home from work that she got another sticker for sharing.

Stephanie Olsen, Miami

when kids fight

Resolving Conflicts

Whenever we need to calm everyone down or break up a fight between friends, we have music breaks: Everyone must dance around to work out the bad mood. It also helps to ask my son and his friend what they would like each other to do to make up. Sometimes, each will request that the other child say that he's sorry; other times, we get on a roll with silly things like spinning, singing, jumping, and so on. I have each child do what the other one requested and, in no time, it turns into a fun game much like "Simon says."

Ann Madden, Middleton, Massachusetts

Spell Out the Rules Ahead of Time

Whenever my 4-year-old son Jordan has a friend over, I let him decide which toys he doesn't want to share. He puts those away before the friend arrives and understands that the other toys are fair game. Then, when his friend arrives, I make sure to tell both boys that there is to be no hitting or shoving, no teasing, no name-calling, and no being mean to Jordan's brothers.

Ellen De Money, Boulder, Colorado

Don't Force It

A friend and I had boys who were about the same age. We were both excited for them to be friends, but unfortunately,

? ask Peggy Post

when your child is rude to a friend

Q: Recently, my 5-year-old wouldn't stop teasing another child during a playdate at our house. The mother wasn't due to pick up the girl for another 30 minutes, so I sent my daughter to her room for the rest of the time while her friend watched TV by herself. How could I have handled it better?

A: As you suspected, sending your daughter to her room for 30 minutes was not the best approach. Not only is a half-hour an eternity for a 5-year-old, but it punishes the friend, too. The next time you see your daughter doing something mean to another child, ask to talk to her privately. Once you are out of earshot of the other child, tell her that her behavior is unacceptable and that she must apologize.

It's best not to confront her in front of her friend. If your daughter is unkind to her friend a second time, send her to her room for 5 minutes. But, during that time, stay with the guest to keep her company. After the playdate is over, ask your daughter to think about how she would feel if she were visiting her friend's house and were treated rudely.

By age 5, children are old enough to learn to see another person's point of view and to understand when they have hurt someone's feelings.

her child was very physical and aggressive. When one play session ended with her child biting my son, I realized that it was best to separate them. While we continue to be friends, we've accepted that our children are not. Once they get a little older, we may try again and see what happens.

Holly Barclay, San Antonio

tips and tactics

Try a Toy Swap

I asked the moms who attend our weekly playgroup to bring a bag with five items (toys, videos, or books) that their kids are tired of. The moms exchange bags, and each child has a new set of toys to play with for that week. The kids love the "new" toys and are excited to explore their bags each week. It's fun—and a money saver too.

Lynn Stevens, Hartland, Michigan

Create a Wall of Friends

In order to brighten up a dreary basement playroom, my husband created the "wall of friends." Whenever our 3- and 5-year-old daughters' friends come to our house to visit, we have them put their handprints in colorful paint on our wall, along with their names and ages. Both the kids and their parents love looking at how the prints on the wall have changed.

Sandi Paulik, Wantagh, New York

Trade Off for One-on-One Time

My friend whose twins are nearly the same age as my 3-year-old twins came up with a great idea that lets our children play together—and gives us an opportunity to spend one-on-one time with each child. Once a week, I drop off one of my kids at her house to play with her children. Then, I spend that time with my other child. When we return to my friend's house, we all eat lunch together. The next week, my friend drops off one of her twins at my house and spends time with the other one.

Barbara Krysa, Denville, New Jersey

Playdate Success for Working Moms

I work full-time, so it's often hard to take my 2½-year-old son on playdates; his nanny takes him instead. But because it's important for me to meet his friends' parents and see the environment that my child is playing in, I've come up with a solution. Whenever my son has a playdate with someone I don't know well, I try to schedule it for late in the afternoon. My nanny takes him to the playdate, then I meet them there as soon as I get out of work. That way, I have time to get to know the parents and interact with the kids for a while before we head home for dinner.

Amanda Nadeau, *Brooklyn, New York*

Easing New-House Anxiety

The thought of going to someone new's house for a playdate can be scary for many kids. Whenever my 3-year-old daughter wants to invite a new friend to our home, I speak to the parent in the child's presence, and instead of asking, "Would Breanna like to come over to play tomorrow?," I mention a specific activity, such as "Emily and I are dyeing Easter eggs tomorrow. Would Breanna like to come over?" This gets both children really excited for the next day's activity.

Heather Sibley, *Portland, Oregon*

I can do it myself

from grasping a rattle to setting the table, children of all ages love being able to accomplish things on their own. A big part of your job as a parent is to help your child learn new skills and give her the confidence to do the best she can. It's sometimes hard not to jump in and take over a task, especially when you're in a hurry, but giving your child the time and freedom she needs will help her grow into an increasingly competent person.

Of course, she won't always be eager to do everything you ask—whether it's brushing her teeth or picking up her dirty laundry—but if you follow these smart strategies, she'll be motivated to do more.

first skills

L Is for Left

To teach my 2-year-old daughter, Victoria, left from right, I had her hold her hands in front of her, with fingers spread apart. The thumb and index finger that form an L are on her left hand.

Juliette Saunders, Fullerton, California

All Set to Sit Up

My 5-month-old daughter was beginning to sit up by herself, but I was afraid to leave her alone for even a minute, for fear she would fall backward and hit her head. To give her some independence without destroying my peace of mind, I placed her in a sturdy rectangular wash basket with a few soft toys. She loved her mini-playpen, and I loved that I could take it into the bath-

pediatrician on call

getting little kids to feed themselves

Babies and toddlers like to feed themselves with their hands, but using a spoon is often a different story. According to pediatrician and *Parents* contributing editor Laura Nathanson, M.D., the best way to get your child to use a spoon is to stop feeding him yourself. Otherwise, he has no incentive to use utensils—he'll enjoy both your anxious concern about his food intake and the undivided attention he gets from you as you feed him. Try this strategy.

1. When you sit your child down to eat, casually put two spoons in front of him. Having a choice will give him a feeling of control; you might give him a red spoon and a blue spoon, or two spoons with different cartoon characters on them.
2. Stay in the room, washing dishes or doing other tasks and talking to him occasionally—but don't mention the meal or how much he's eating.
3. If he doesn't use the spoon, don't say anything. Don't make a fuss or feed him. Just cheerfully take him away from the table and go on with the rest of your day.
4. Repeat this process at every meal, and within 5 days to a week, he'll be feeding himself with a spoon.

room while I showered or into the laundry room to switch loads, or put it on the floor of the kitchen while I got dinner ready.

Pamela Neitzel-Garwood, *Riverside, Ohio*

Get Psyched Up

To help boost independence, I told my 3-year-old son the story of the Little Engine That Could. Now, whenever he says that he can't do something like take off his shoes or his coat, I tell him to be like the Little Engine and say "I think I can!" Sometimes, I hear him saying this out loud to himself, even when I haven't reminded him. He is often surprised to realize that he's actually accomplished something he didn't know he could do.

Tara Claeys, *Arlington, Virginia*

Which Shoe Goes Where?

To help my 4-year-old daughter figure out which shoe goes on which foot, I drew one continuous picture on the soles of her shoes with a marker. (I drew the head of a snake on the left shoe and the body on the right.) She puts the picture together to see how to put her shoes on.

Annet Habroun, *Orland, California*

self-sufficient on saturday mornings

If you'd love to sleep later on weekends, but your child bounds into your bedroom at 7:00 A.M., you can help your early bird occupy herself for a while.

✓ Get her a clock radio and set the alarm for 8:00 A.M. Tell her that she needs to wait until the radio comes on before coming into your room ("That's the signal that it's okay to wake Mommy and Daddy").

✓ Put together a basket of wake-up toys, including at least one surprise. (It can be something as simple as a new box of crayons.) Vary what's in her basket each Saturday morning, so it will hold her interest for an hour or so.

✓ To make it easy for your child to fix herself a basic breakfast, set out plastic containers of her favorite cereals and keep a small plastic pitcher of milk on the lowest shelf of the refrigerator. Her "table for one" will be even more appealing if you set out a coloring book or a small game alongside her bowl and spoon.

✓ Teach her to use the VCR, if she doesn't already know how. This is one time when letting her watch a video—quietly—could be a godsend.

No-Slip Bowls

My 1-year-old son had a hard time using a spoon because the bowl would slide away from him. So, I made a place mat out of nonslip drawer liner, available at most grocery stores. I set his bowl on it, and now, he can spoon out the contents easily. Plus, it comes in great colors and is easy to clean.

Crystal Majeski, Elizabethtown, North Carolina

Mistake-Proof Sippy Cups

It seemed that whenever I took my 2-year-old daughter to a playgroup, all the children had the same style of Sippy cup. I didn't want my daughter to drink from the wrong one, so I taped a small picture of her onto the cup. Now, she always looks for her photo before she takes a drink.

Leigh Manor, Manchester, New Jersey

set to get ready

All Tied Up

When my children were learning to tie their shoes, I found that they got frustrated with the tiny laces. To help, I gave them the belt from my bathrobe to practice tying bows around their waists. It worked perfectly: The belt was big enough for their little hands to work with, and I didn't have to untangle lots of knots. In no time, they were tying their shoes with no help from Mom.

Lisa Panchik, Natrona Heights, Pennsylvania

grandmother knows best

Having a job chart works as well at home today as it did when I was a kindergarten teacher. Assign your kids a few tasks that are appropriate for their age, including general responsibilities such as hanging up their coats and putting on their own pajamas, socks, and shoes. Give them a star or sticker when they complete each task. Positive reinforcement is often satisfaction enough, but for extra motivation, you can give them a reward when they have a whole week of stars.

Joan Danoff, Stamford, Connecticut

basic skills made easy

Day care providers count on their young charges to become increasingly independent, and they take steps to make sure that tasks aren't too tough for kids to handle. Here are a few tips from Caryn O'Connor, director of the Innovative Learning Center, in Brooklyn, New York.

Teach your child the "flip method" of putting on her coat:

1. Lay it down on the floor upside down.
2. Put arms in the sleeves.
3. Flip it over the head.

Keep your child's hat and gloves in the sleeves of her coat so that she'll always know where to find them.

Leave paper towels or sponges within reach so that your child can clean up a spill by herself.

Stuck on Velcro

I have a very independent 2-year-old. He's too young to learn how to tie shoelaces, but he takes great pride in putting his shoes on by himself. So, I make sure that I buy only shoes with Velcro closures.

Kerry Moore, *Centerville, Indiana*

Organizing Outfits

I let my daughter Amanda pick out either the shirt or the pants that she wants, and then I choose the other half to make sure that they match.

Jill Lerner, *Framingham, Massachusetts*

It's a Reach

I keep step stools, liquid soap, and Dixie cups in the bathroom so that my 2- and 4-year-old children can wash their hands and brush their teeth. I also place plastic bowls, plates, and Sippy cups in a lower drawer in the kitchen so that they can reach them easily.

Mary Beth Randall, *Franklin, Massachusetts*

Easy Pouring

When my child wants to put milk on his cold cereal by himself, I pour the milk into a small plastic measuring cup, which is easier for him to lift than the whole container and causes less spills. I do the same thing when he wants to pour himself a glass of juice.

Penny Haff, *New York City*

kid-size projects

Puzzle It Out

My 2½-year-old daughter, Lindsay, loves puzzles, but one of her bigger ones was a bit too challenging for her. So, we created the "unpuzzle": We start with the completed puzzle and take turns removing a piece of our choice. The player must describe something they see on the piece they remove ("I see Pooh's arm," for example). Lindsay became so familiar with the pieces and how they fit together that she now can proudly put the puzzle together on her own.

Dawn Gillen, *Hamilton, New Jersey*

How Does Your Garden Grow?

When our 2-year-old outgrew his mini kiddie pool, we turned it into a child-size garden area and planted some vegetables and flowering plants in it. This keeps our son's little garden separate from ours, and he knows which plants are his to water and harvest.

LaRae Moncada, *Tucson*

Cyber Kid

My daughter was fascinated when I showed her what e-mail was, and she was determined to send some herself. I taught her where the tab and return keys were and let her press them for me whenever I needed to. She felt that that was her special role, and now, she's learning where all the letters are.

Diane Debrovner, *New York City*

raising taskmasters

If kids start doing regular chores when they are young, they'll see work as an opportunity to practice new skills and contribute to family life, rather than as drudgery. Here are some ways that you can encourage your kids to help.

✓ Give kids a choice. Make a list of all the tasks that your child can do, and let him choose one weekly and three daily chores.

✓ Focus on the process, not the outcome. Don't expect your child to do the job as well as you could. If your child gives one person two forks and another two knives on the first day he sets the table by himself, praise his willingness to help rather than pointing out his mistakes. He'll learn over time.

✓ Break down tasks. If you tell a young child to clean his room, he won't know where to start. Instead, first ask him to put his clothes in the hamper, then suggest that he put his stuffed animals back on the bed, and so on.

✓ Work together. Even if you're doing different projects, working side by side will help motivate your child as well as keep him company.

mommy's little helper

Sock It to Me!

My 2-year-old daughter Rachel is learning about colors. When I dump the clean clothes onto the bed to sort, she'll jump in and call out, "I found a purple sock!" Then I'll ask, "Can you find another one just like that?" We do that until all her socks are matched, and then she takes pride in putting them away "all by my own."

Kit Seltzer, Des Moines, Iowa

Now We're Cooking

Every Tuesday, I ask one of my boys, ages 6 and 9, to plan the menu for dinner. We shop for the ingredients, spend the

encourage solo play

Young children often depend on you to play with them—and holler whenever you leave to make a phone call, go to the bathroom, or make dinner. However, when your child learns to entertain herself for a period of time, it will not only give you a little break but also increase her creativity and confidence.

One-year-olds, for example, can generally play alone for 10 to 20 minutes at a time in a crib or childproofed area of your home. But they need practice and a gentle nudge from you. Here's how to gradually encourage independence.

1. Engage your child in a favorite activity that can be done by one person (for instance, stacking blocks rather than playing ball).

2. Play with her for a few minutes. Then, stop and simply sit there, talking but not playing.

3. Continue to distance yourself over the next few days. Gradually move farther away, beginning with an arm's length and moving back until you can sit across the room. You can still talk occasionally.

4. Leave the room for a few seconds once your child feels comfortable with that distance. Tell her that you're going away for a moment, then step into the next room. When your child first realizes that you're gone, she may fuss a little. Don't rush back; you might say, "I'm in the kitchen; I'll be right there." Over time, your child should begin to play by herself for increasing lengths of time. Make sure to reassure your toddler nonverbally—patting her back, touching her hair—as you come and go.

afternoon cooking together, and then enjoy the meal. My sons are learning the basics of cooking, and each one looks forward to the two Tuesdays a month when we eat one of his favorite dinners (even if it isn't one of mine!).

Linda Cross, Lake Forest, California

Piece of Cake!

My daughter always wanted to help me when I was baking, but invariably, the ingredients would end up all over her and the floor. So, I now premeasure all the ingredients into cups or bowls and put away the containers before we start. When I call her in to help me, everything is ready to be dumped into the big mixing bowl, and there's less spilling. It goes more quickly, too, so she gets less impatient.

Hannah Williams,
Danbury, Connecticut

Super Shopper

I let my 6-year-old help me with the shopping. Since she reads and writes well already, she writes out the shopping list at home and then reads it while we are at the store. She helps find the items by reading the aisle signs and then locating the groceries in that aisle.

Mary Groezinger, Hanover, Illinois

Lost and Found

To get my sons, ages 2, 4, and 5, to help me find things, I put a "Wanted" poster on the fridge with a picture of the lost item (one of their shoes, for example) and tape on a reward, such as three quarters (they all get the reward, no matter who actually finds the item). Sometimes, the boys even wear their cowboy hats while searching, because the poster reminds them of the Wild West.

Valerie Foley, Plymouth, Massachusetts

it's my job

teaching a positive attitude

"Have a funeral for the words *I can't*," suggests Mimi Knight, a teacher at Covington Christian Preschool in Covington, Louisiana. "We write the words on a poster board and take turns covering them up with dirt. After that, whenever I ask a child to do something new and he's tempted to say 'I can't,' I remind him that we buried those words, and he'll usually say 'I'll try' instead. Nine times out of 10, 'I'll try' turns into 'I can'—but when it doesn't, that's okay too."

no-fuss cleanup

Cleanup Codes

I use games to make cleanup fun for my kids and the other children at my family day care center. We have a race to see who can pick up the most toys. I'll say, "How many toys can you put away while you count to 10? Who can pick up the

what's the appropriate age?

While giving your child the freedom to try and fail is the best way to foster independence, you certainly wouldn't let your toddler use a steak knife or expect your 4-year-old to walk the dog. Even when your child pleads "Me do it!" or "Mom, I'm not a baby!," it can be tough to decide whether it's safe for him to tackle a new task. Here's when experts say your child will be ready for some important childhood milestones.

Going on a sleepover: Many kids can't manage a night away from home until they're well into their grade school years. Others feel comfortable doing it at age 4 or 5. Your child might be ready for a trial run if he has mentioned it several times, has practiced at a relative's house, can eat in various places, and doesn't have a lot of trouble settling down in the evening.

Choosing his own clothes: Most kids can dress themselves by age 4, but parents aren't usually thrilled with the outfits that young children select. Take the conflict out of dressing by letting your child have some input.

Being responsible for a pet: Most experts feel that about 3 is the earliest age for a child to have a pet, because at that point, a child has some self-control and understands what "No, don't pull the kitty's tail" means. There are always age-appropriate ways that a child can participate in animal care, such as measuring out the dog's food or choosing a toy. But children should never be primarily responsible for a pet.

Bathing alone: Most kids are independent enough to handle it by around the age of 6. But deciding whether to let a child scrub in the tub by himself depends not only on his physical skills but also on his good judgment. Even if your 4-year-old is a terrific swimmer, you'd never leave him alone in a pool. Of course, there's less water in a tub, but a child can drown even in a very small amount.

Crossing the street alone: Children under the age of 10 should never cross the street alone. Until then, kids are impulsive and have difficulty judging speed, spatial relations, and distance. Pedestrian injury is the second leading cause of accidental death among children ages 5 to 14.

most crayons?" Some games teach categorizing skills. For example, "Let's pick up everything that's red, and next, we'll put away everything that's blue."

M. J. Coleman, *Brighton, Michigan*

CEO of Cooperation

I'm the mother of four kids, ages 2, 4, 6, and 8, and I've found that shouting "Clean up this mess!" is not an effective motivator. Instead, I have my three older children take 10-minute turns being the boss. They supervise their siblings and ensure that each job is getting done. It's amazing how much more attention they pay to the details when they're in charge; every nook and cranny gets a turn. I'm relieved that I don't have to micromanage their efforts anymore. I have to step in only if anyone on my "staff" gets too bossy—or too insubordinate.

Deirdre Bach, *Indianola, Iowa*

ABCs of reading

23

it's one of the best parts of the day for many kids: story-time. Teach your child to love books and you'll spark her imagination, improve her language development, and give her a gift that will last a lifetime. And it's never too soon to start; even babies as young as 6 months benefit from a daily story, says the American Academy of Pediatrics.

Toddlers adore being read to; and even after kids can read to themselves, they still love snuggling up with Mom or Dad to listen to a good book. Since kids learn by following your example, you should read books, newspapers, and magazines regularly, too. The great advice in this chapter will help you and your children discover all the magic that books have to offer.

starting early

Baby Books

I started reading *Brown Bear, Brown Bear, What Do You See?*, by Bill Martin Jr., to my son every day when he was 2 months old. After a few weeks, he would smile as soon as we sat down together with the book. By 10 months, he seemed to under-stand—and visibly enjoy—his favorite lines in this and other books, and he could even bring me the correct book if I re-cited its first few sentences. I read to him daily, and I know that he is loving every minute of it.

Donya Rhett, *Bronx, New York*

Create a Special Shelf

To instill a love of reading in my infant, I dedicated the bottom two shelves of our living room bookshelf to his things. I put his toys on the bottom shelf and his books above that. From age 10 months on, he would head to the shelf for his toys, then pull all his books onto the floor. I made a game out of putting them

baby bookworms

These steps can help your infant get the most out of storytime.

✓ Talk about the pictures. Babies thrive on hearing your voice. It doesn't matter whether you read the text word-for-word or not.

✓ Keep it short. Don't shoot for intensive reading sessions or continue reading to a baby who is obviously ready to move on to a new activity. Start with 1- to 2-minute reading sessions several times a day, increasing their length over time.

✓ Add movement and touching. Bounce your baby gently in rhythm with your words, or walk your fingers up baby's arm in time with "Itsy Bitsy Spider."

✓ Try interactive books. Introduce books that give him things to do, such as flaps to lift and textures to touch. Encourage 8- to 12-month-olds to hold the book and help turn the pages.

✓ Recite nursery rhymes. From "Little Miss Muffet" to patty-cake, listening and acting out these rhymes introduces a child to a narrative story in a short format. Changing the endings will help boost your child's imagina-tive abilities.

back, or we would stack them like towers or zoom them around on the floor like cars—anything to get him to enjoy interacting with them. He's 3 now and still has his bookshelves— but instead of just pulling books onto the floor, he loves choosing one to look through or have me read to him.

Megan Richardson,
Lacey, Washington

Make It Interactive

Reading is one of my favorite pastimes and I wanted to make sure that my daughter enjoyed it too. In fact, I began reading to her when she was just days old. When she was an infant, I kept her attention by using different voices for each character. When she got a little older, I encouraged her participation by asking her to find familiar objects on the page and point them out. Finally, whether it is a newspaper, magazine, or novel, I make sure that she sees me reading every day.

Susan Loggins, Kernersville, North Carolina

Long-Distance Read-Along

When we were living in Germany, I found a great way to boost my 10-month-old son's interest in books—and help him get to know his grandparents who lived far away. I asked them to video-tape themselves reading children's books and send the tape and books to us. He was mesmerized from the first time he saw them on the TV, and when my parents came to visit 8 months later, my son knew exactly who they were and took out his favorite book for Grandpa to read!

Ann Strand, Lawton, Oklahoma

learning letters and words

Expand Their Vocabulary

To expand my children's vocabulary, I post "words of the week" on our refrigerator. (My mother did this when I was a

librarians choose all-star stories

While there are millions of children's books to choose from, some stand head and shoulders above the rest. For expert advice, we asked Nancy Alcorn, Eloise Schoeppner, and Lisa Estabrook—all librarians at the Newburyport Public Library in Newburyport, Massachusetts—to recommend their favorite books for parents to read with their children.

Birth to Age 2

Pat the Bunny, by Dorothy Kunhardt

The Very Hungry Caterpillar, by Eric Carle

My Very First Mother Goose, edited by Iona Archibald Opie

Do Pigs Have Stripes?, by Melanie Walsh

Ages 2 to 4

The Little Engine That Could, by Watty Piper

Blueberries for Sal, by Robert McCloskey

The Madeline series, by Ludwig Bemelmans

If You Give a Mouse a Cookie, by Laura Joffe Numeroff

Noisy Nora, by Rosemary Wells

Baby Duck and Bad Eyeglasses, by Amy Hest

Ages 4 to 6

Where the Wild Things Are, by Maurice Sendak

Strega Nona: An Old Tale, by Tomie DePaola

Mole Music, by David McPhail

Gingerbread Baby, by Jan Brett

Chocolatina, by Erik Kraft

What! Cried Granny: An Almost Bedtime Story, by Kate Lum

Ages 6 and Up

The Story of Babar, the Little Elephant, by Jean de Brunhoff

Charlotte's Web, by E. B. White

The Amelia Bedelia series, by Peggy Parish

The Nate the Great series, by Marjorie Sharmat

The Magic School Bus series, by Joanna Cole

The Harry Potter series, by J. K. Rowling

Melanie Griffith

"I loved the Eloise books when I was a child. Now, I read them to my daughters, Dakota and Stella. Once, Dakota and I stayed at the Plaza Hotel, in New York City, and she actually thought she was Eloise."

—actress and mother of Alexander, 14; Dakota, 9; and Stella, 3

child.) My kids, ages 5 and 3, are learning to spell and identify these words as they begin to read. They both get excited about each new word and love to practice writing them. I'll continue this game as they get older, making sure to increase the difficulty of the words.

Jane Metcalf, Seattle

Junior Author

When my 8-year-old son was younger, I started writing books with him. Whenever he told me a story, I would write it down. Sometimes, his tales were only a few sentences long; other times, they were quite detailed. The process really helped boost his creativity and language development, and as he got older, he started illustrating his books, too. He loves rereading his early books—and he is still writing stories.

Terri Gross, Commack, New York

Lunchtime Love Notes

When my son began kindergarten, I started leaving short notes in his lunch bag. I kept them simple: "I love you" or "See you at 2:00 P.M." He loved finding his special notes, and they really helped boost his reading skills. Now that he's in the first grade, he'll remind me to write him a lunch note if I forget!

Donna Jansen, Boca Raton, Florida

A Personalized ABC Book

To help my 22-month-old son learn his ABCs, I created an alphabet book for him. I gathered pictures of familiar people and objects, then pasted them on construction paper alongside their corresponding letters. We placed the pages in clear sheet protectors and bound them together. When Trent reads his book, he's learning that *D* is for Daddy—and his little brother Derek.

Joanie Nicholas, Springfield, Virginia

an elementary school teacher's tips for beginning readers

While most children start decoding words and learning to read between the ages of 5 and 6, some children begin identifying letters and basic words as early as 3 years old. To get your child primed to read, follow these suggestions from Beth Dufton, a first grade teacher at West Elementary in Andover, Massachusetts.

Focus on sounds. Practice the alphabet with your child, focusing on the sound that each letter makes. Once he has mastered that, combine letters to make common sounds, such as "sh" or "ch." A great time to practice this is while you're waiting in line at the grocery store, says Dufton. Choose a magazine from the rack and have your child make the sounds of various letters as you point them out.

Isolate words. As you read to your child, pick out easy words, such as *cat*, *dog*, and *rug*. First, sound each one out (for example, "kuh-aa-tuh"); then, have your child repeat it. Pick just one or two words a day, and practice for a few minutes. Let a few nights pass, then see if he remembers the word when you point it out again.

Follow along as you read. When children start reading, they have to master the layout of the page and the proper way to "decode" it. If you use your finger to show them the direction to read in, kids will better understand how letters go together to form words, and words to form sentences.

Give praise often. Whether your child correctly sounds out a word or reads an entire book, encourage his success. Ask him to show off his skills by repeating the word for your spouse, an older sibling, or a grandparent.

Start with what interests them. "Many of the boys in my class are truck fanatics, and they're very eager to learn words that describe trucks," says Dufton. Once your child has had practice and understands some words from a truck or an animal book, take a stab at books on different topics.

Play Word Games

To help my kids, ages 3, 6, and 8, improve their reading and vocabulary skills, I cut words out of magazines. For my oldest child, I cut more complex words; for my youngest, I find large single letters. At breakfast and dinnertime, they pick out a word or letter and we try to read it, make a sentence out of it, or define it. (For my 3-year-old, we discuss the sound of the letter and give words that start with that sound.) They all have fun picking out their words and letters, and their vocabulary skills are growing by leaps and bounds.

Korryn Gonring, *Sylvania, Ohio*

keeping it fun

The Magic Reading Hat

I wanted to encourage the 9- and 6-year-old children I babysit to read more, so I made a "fantasy hat," which they get to wear whenever they read aloud to us. I bought a hard plastic hat at a toy store, then decorated it by gluing on small toys, flowers, feathers, beads, and other things related to stories we have read. The hat makes storytime more fun for everyone—even my husband loves wearing it!

Gail Baillargeon, *Edgewater, Florida*

Raise a Bookworm

To keep my 6-year-old daughter excited about reading last summer, we created Baxter the Bookworm. Whenever she finished reading a book, we wrote the title on a colored paper circle and added it to Baxter, who was taped to the wall. By the time school started again, Baxter was several feet long and Rebecca had read 150 books!

Heather Rayburn, *Salt Lake City*

Give the Gift of Reading

My 4½-year-old daughter loves audio books. So, for Hanukkah, I asked several of the adults in her life to read a story on tape. She was really surprised when she listened to the tapes and heard her preschool teachers, librar-

cd-roms to the rescue!

Today's computer-savvy kids aren't limited to books to boost their reading skills. Each series listed below offers age-specific CD-ROMs that will give your youngster additional reading practice.

✓ *Bailey's Book House*, from the Edmark Corporation

✓ *Reader Rabbit*, from The Learning Company

✓ *Reading Blaster, Knowledge Adventure*, from Havas Interactive

✓ *JumpStart Reading, Knowledge Adventure*, from Havas Interactive

✓ *Arthur's Reading Game*, from The Learning Company

ians, and even a friend from the bakery reading especially for her. I was so impressed with the terrific job each reader did—and I am thrilled by how much Sarah loves following along in her books.

Jill Lubiner, Somerset, New Jersey

Journal Jotting

When my son began second grade, I started writing to him in a notebook three or four times a week. I write about events that happened during the day. I also use it as an opportunity to calm his fears or congratulate him on a special accomplishment. Then, I leave the notebook on his desk when he's asleep. My son loves waking up in the morning and reading his book in private. Besides reinforcing reading and writing skills, his notebook will be a special keepsake for him when he's older.

Teddie LaBar, Cresco, Pennsylvania

Put Your Children in the Story

Whenever I get pictures developed, I always get double prints. After I share these with family and friends, I use the leftovers to make books that I write simple narratives for—starring our family! My books have included *Going to the Zoo*, *The Seasons*, and *My Papa*. My daughter loves looking at her books, and she is learning to read the words that go with each picture.

Laura Cleveland, Westminster, Maryland

help for reluctant readers

Get into Character

Since my 8-year-old son would rather watch television than read, we struck this deal: I allow him to watch an extra half-hour of TV after his homework is done, as long as he turns the volume down and uses closed captioning (available on most new televisions). We sit together and take turns reading the dialogue, mimicking the characters' voices.

Eileen Gonzalez, Caldwell, New Jersey

Make It a Family Event

My 5-year-old son was hesitant to read out loud. To encourage him, we started family reading night. Once a week, our son, our 3½-year-old daughter, and my husband and I bring a book we each would like to read and gather on our bed. Everyone takes turns reading to the family from their book (our daughter "reads" to us by telling us what is happening in the pictures). Our son really enjoys his turn as the reader, and seeing the pride in his face makes it even more special.

Beth Steklac, *Duluth, Georgia*

Spelling Bee

My 8-year-old son hated to work on his spelling words, until we put a chalkboard in his room. I call out his words, and he writes them on the board. Now, he always asks to practice his spelling, and we've discovered that it works great for math problems too!

Tracy Gagnon, *Dieppe, New Brunswick, Canada*

raise a book lover

Some kids are eager to pass the hours with a good book; others need a little encouragement. Try these tips to make reading fun, no matter what stage your child has reached.

✓ Keep reading out loud. The rhythm and cadence of being read to soothes a child and may help relieve anxieties. Because a child's listening comprehension runs ahead of her reading comprehension, reading a book at a level above your child's ability will boost her vocabulary and reasoning skills.

✓ Share the job. Trade off reading parts or passages aloud. Or, if your child is hesitant about her reading skills, read in unison.

✓ Go beyond books. Poems, joke books, comic books, and magazines are all great alternatives to books—and they'll still get your child hooked on the pleasures of reading.

✓ Make it an event. Attend story hours at your local library or bookstore, then go to lunch together. Or, instead of video night at home, try reading night. Have everyone in the family settle in with a bowl of popcorn and their favorite book.

✓ Be creative. If you're going on vacation, have your child help plan activities by reading travel books and brochures with you. When you're cooking, ask your child to join in, and let her read the recipe with you.

A New Approach to Homework

When my son's reading homework starts to become tedious, we take out his children's picture dictionary. He reads a definition to me, and I try to guess the word. We take turns and keep score. It's an easy and fun way for him to put in his daily reading exercises.

Beckie Maschino, Plano, Texas

special tactics

Fill Your House with Books

Have books of every variety available to your kids—and keep them all over the house. We store books in our children's bedrooms, in the car, in the toy box, and on the hearth. Also, keep a basket of books in the bathroom. That way, if you don't have time to read to your kids during the day, you can read aloud while they soak in the tub.

Kim Louria, Gibraltar, Michigan

Hey, That's Me!

After several requests for the same stories, my 3-year-old son often has them memorized. To relieve the monotony of reading the same stories over and over, I recorded him "reading" them himself. He loves to follow along, hearing his own voice—and I get a break too.

Pam Bertilrud, Grandville, Michigan

Discipline by the Books

Every night, I read three books to my toddler. He enjoys this time so much that rather than impose time outs or other punishments if he misbehaves during the day, we threaten to reduce the number of books we'll read that night. His behavior usually improves immediately. Of course, we also reward him for being good—usually with a trip to the bookstore!

Licia Lichliter, Dallas

Sneaky Diaper Change

My 2-year-old son has gotten into the habit of running away and hiding when I need to change his diaper. Coaxing him out of his hiding spot doesn't work, so instead I grab a book, sit down on the floor, and start reading aloud. He's always eager to be read to, so he immediately runs to my lap. Once we finish the story, I ask him questions about it as I change him. This strategy works every time, and if we're in a rush, I just make sure to choose a short book.

Stephanie Sondgeroth, Guilford, Indiana

A Recipe for Reading Success

All three of my daughters—ages 6, 3½, and 2—love books. My husband and I encourage their reading by doing several things. First, our children always have plenty of opportunities to read with us or by themselves. We also try to push the envelope by reading books slightly above their reading level to hold their interest. Finally, we make sure to read their favorite

does your child have a learning disability?

Nearly 15 percent of the American population has a learning disability such as dyslexia. Because each child's reading and writing skills develop differently, spotting a problem can be difficult. But if your child shows several of the warning signs listed below, you may want to call his teacher to find out whether he should be tested. To learn more about learning disabilities, contact the National Center for Learning Disabilities at (888) 575-7373, or the Learning Disabilities Association of America at (888) 300-6710.

✓ He doesn't say several single words by 18 months of age, or he can't put together two- and three-word sentences by 2½.

✓ He still uses baby talk past his third birthday.

✓ He has problems with pronunciation, even with simple words.

✓ He regularly mixes up similar words or sounds, such as saying "bat" instead of "cat" or "ball" instead of "fall."

✓ He cannot rhyme and is older than 4.

✓ He has trouble learning numbers, the alphabet, and the days of the week.

✓ He can't distinguish sounds and syllables in words.

✓ He makes consistent reading and spelling errors, including letter reversals (b/d), inversions (m/w), transpositions ("felt"/"left"), and substitutions ("house"/"home").

books as often as they like. In fact, we read *Goodnight Moon* by Margaret Wise Brown to our middle daughter every night for over a year!

Kathleen Luck, North Olmsted, Ohio

Rotate Stories

My 2½-year-old daughter has tons of books—so many, in fact, that we sometimes go months without reading certain stories. To make sure that we don't forget about any, I pick a theme every other week, such as colors, letters, holidays, or sharing, and put books that fit the theme in a basket next to her book-shelf. When she wants me to read to her, she just brings the basket to me. It really is a great way to rediscover old favorites!

Stacy Maurer, Evansville, Indiana

the well-groomed child

24

keeping your kids neat, clean, and nicely dressed is more than just a daily chore. It's an important way to show your love and concern for their health and to teach them to be proud of their appearance.

Of course, managing the everyday tasks of bathing, dressing, and hair combing doesn't always go according to plan. Dealing with a wiggly baby during bathtime, a preschooler who's still learning to match clothes, or a little girl with perpetually tangled hair are just a few of the grooming challenges that call for creative solutions. The great tips and tricks in this chapter will help you polish your own skills and pass on good grooming habits that will help your child take pride in her self-reliance, as well as what she sees in the mirror.

tub time!

Finding a Comfort Zone

When my son was a newborn, he used to cry during every bath, and I eventually realized that it was because he disliked having his wet skin exposed to the cool air. I started keeping him comfortable by soaking a hand towel in the warm bathwater and covering the areas that I wasn't not washing. When the bath was over, I immediately wrapped him in a hooded towel. He's enjoyed baths ever since.

Esther Lindsey, Philadelphia

Double the Fun

My husband and I used to dread bathtime with my 9-month-old son, Cole, but now it's become one of our favorite activities. One of us gets into the tub with Cole, who enjoys having us laugh and splash with him. We also placed a plastic mirror on the tile above the tub: Cole loves to look at himself

bubble trouble

Little girls love a tub full of bubbles, but the ingredients in the suds can cause vaginal irritation. Girls between the ages of 1 and 8 are especially vulnerable because their vaginal tissue is thinner and more sensitive to these chemicals, says Janet Squires, M.D., associate professor of pediatrics at the University of Texas Southwestern Medical Center at Dallas. If your daughter develops an irritation, follow these helpful tips from Dr. Squires.

✓ If the skin around your daughter's vulva appears redder than usual, or she complains of a burning sensation when she urinates, hold off on the bubbles for a while.

✓ In the meantime, have her bathe in plain water without using soap, and wash your daughter's hair in the sink.

✓ To promote healing, apply an ointment containing vitamins A and D to the affected area after bathing.

✓ Loose-fitting cotton panties are best—nylon ones can trap moisture.

✓ If symptoms don't clear up in 2 to 3 days, call your pediatrician. Your daughter may have a more serious problem, such as a urinary tract infection.

with shampoo bubbles on his head. With a little imagination, we have turned tub time into fun time.

Rayna Mercer, *Brunswick, Maryland*

Safety Step

To make bathtime easier for my 16-month-old son, I have him wear swimming shoes with rubber grips when he's in the tub. It gives him more freedom to play, and I don't have to worry about his slipping.

Sue Cornell, *Washington Island, Wisconsin*

No More Tears

I had a hard time getting my 2-year-old daughter to close her eyes while I rinsed shampoo out of her hair during bathtime. But I came up with a creative "hide-and-seek" solution: After I put shampoo in her hair, I ask Madeline to close her eyes. Then, while

smooth out tangles without tears

A child's fine hair is easily tangled. But yanking a comb or brush through the knots is not the solution. To gently tame tresses, follow these tips from hair and scalp expert Philip Kingsley, author of *Hair: An Owner's Handbook*.

✓ Massage shampoo into your child's scalp, then move from front to back to work suds into the rest of her hair. Don't pile lathered hair on top of your child's head. It may be fun, but hair gets twisted into knots.

✓ After rinsing hair thoroughly, apply conditioner; concentrate on the ends, where hair tends to tangle most. Rinse out most, but not all, of the conditioner.

✓ Don't start combing from the roots—this hurts! Instead, grasp a small section of hair, and starting at the ends, glide the comb through the section with short, downward strokes. When the ends are smoothed out, move up toward the middle of each section. Comb out the hair near the scalp last. Then, rinse out the last traces of conditioner.

✓ If your child's hair tangles up after an active day of play, you can undo knots with a small brush. Look for flexible nylon or plastic bristles with smooth tips. For super-stubborn knots, spritz on a leave-in conditioner before brushing.

I pour water over her head, I hide one of her tub toys under the bubbles for her to find after the rinsing is over. She doesn't want to spoil the game by peeking, so she closes her eyes really tight.

Mary Zwick Nevis, Chicago

Art Smarts

My 2- and 4-year-old boys hated putting their heads back when I rinsed their hair in the bathtub. To hold their interest, I put colorful plastic stickers on the ceiling above the tub. The images encourage them to look up, and I distract them by talking and asking questions about the art on the ceiling. No more tears!

Diane Vyskocil, Baltimore

After-Bath Warmup

My 3-month-old son, Caleb, likes it when I blow-dry his hair and body after a bath. The warm air keeps him from getting cold or fussy, and the sound of the dryer is very soothing. In fact, he relaxes so much that he often falls asleep. The blow-drying session turned out to be a great way to transition between bathtime and naptime.

Melanee Zieman, Reedsport, Oregon

quick cleanups

Mirror Magic

It seemed as if every mealtime ended with a frustrating struggle to wash my toddlers' faces. But cleaning up became a snap after I bought an inexpensive hand mirror. I keep the mirror in the kitchen, and after mealtime, I have the kids hold it up while I transform their faces from messy to clean with a washcloth. They are always so intent on watching the transformation that they sit still the entire time.

Lisa Hess, Bountiful, Utah

So Long, Sticky Fingers!

Our 10-month-old daughter's little hands always get sticky and covered with crumbs during mealtime, but cleaning them was a battle because Emma hated to have her hands wiped. Since she loves bathtime, however, we came up with a solution. After each meal, we give her a "finger bowl"—a large plastic bowl filled with lukewarm water—and let her splash away. She

pediatrician on call

help for nail biters

Does your child have a bad habit of biting his nails? And are you at your wit's end about how to get him to stop? We asked pediatrician and *Parents* contributing editor Laura Nathanson, M.D., the best way to deal with your little nail nibbler.

Keep him busy. Children are more apt to bite when they are passive or tense, especially when watching TV, playing video games, or sitting in the car. Very often, nonbiting times occur when a child is engaged and interacting with others or completely involved in stimulating activities. See what you can do to increase your child's nonbiting activities and decrease the biting ones.

Restrict biting slowly. Tell him that he's allowed to bite the fingernails of only one hand, not both, and remind him when he forgets. After he has restricted the biting to one hand, gradually eliminate biting the nails of one finger at a time. You may need to leave him one lone finger to attack.

Offer a better bite. Giving him something else to do with his teeth can help. Chewing sugarless gum is an option for children 5 and older. Just make sure that he knows to spit it out rather than swallow it!

and the floor get a little wet, but we're just happy that she gets clean without tears!

Kate and John Homan, *Glen Allen, Virginia*

A Safe Way to Clean Ears

My 2-year-old son, Caleb, is now at the age when he wants to do everything himself, including cleaning his own ears. Johnson's has a cotton swab designed with a small tip at the end of a much wider base. The design lets Caleb clean the outermost part of his ears, but the wide base keeps the swab from going into the ear canal.

Amanda Nadeau, *Brooklyn, New York*

Nail Trimming without the Trauma

My 3-year-old son used to hate having his nails trimmed. It was always a battle, until I turned it into a game. Now, we pretend that each finger is a person who is having his hair cut. My son loves telling me stories about who each finger is, and he gets a kick out of it when I pretend that they don't want their hair cut that day.

Stacey Robinson, *Moody, Alabama*

heads up on hair care

Tantrum-Free Trims

Trying to cut our 4-year-old son's hair was always a battle. To end these fights—and have some fun—we play "barbershop." I call him Sir and treat him like a grown-up. After the cut, I shave his face with his play shaving kit. (An ice cream stick and some shaving cream would work just as well.) He pays me with hugs and kisses.

Janet Olson, *Parsons, Kansas*

No More Tangles

Combing my 4-year-old daughter Katie's long hair had become a dreaded morning ritual; it was always full of tangles. To put a stop to this daily battle, I started making two loose braids in her hair at night. In the morning, the comb glides right through, and Katie loves the curls created by the braids.

Amy Cleary, *Temecula, California*

Soak and Snip

I had some reservations about how well my 1-year-old son, Matthew, would sit through a professional haircut, so I opted to try my hand at it. I chose a time when he is most intent on playing: bathtime. He sits and splashes in his tub ring while I trim his hair. He's so involved with his water play that he hardly notices my snipping.

Kristin N. Johnson, *Mosinee, Wisconsin*

---

it's my job

quick fixes for bad hair days

Kids have to cope with hair hassles, too. Here are some simple solutions from Alicia Lyons, manager of Kid-Snips, in Wilmette, Illinois.

✓ Tame a cowlick. Although a cowlick grows in different directions, letting it grow longer can help it lie flat. Another trick: Clip it very short.

✓ Add shine. Dull, dry hair is often the result of too much sun and chlorine. Shampoo and condition your child's hair after every swim. And before every dip, coat hair with a spray-on conditioner.

✓ Get out gum. Rub an ice cube over chewing gum to freeze it. This makes it easier to peel off hair a piece at a time.

how to trim kids' bangs

Want to cut your child's bangs at home? Before you test your talents on a testy (or terrified) tot's head, check out these hints from top New York City hairstylist Ric Pipino.

Step-by-Step Instructions

1. To find the bangs, gather a large section from the crown and tug it a few times. The bangs will fall naturally, forming a triangle.
2. Comb the bangs down and clip back the rest of the hair.
3. Section the bangs in two. With each piece, put ¼ inch of the end between your first two fingers and cut straight across. See below.
4. Take the clips out and let the hair fall naturally. If the bangs still need to be cut shorter, repeat steps 1 through 3.
5. If your child's hair is naturally straight, cut the bangs when her hair is dry. If it's curly or wavy, cut it wet.

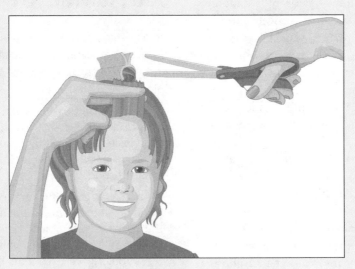

A Home for Barrettes

My daughter Katie has many clip-on bows for her hair, and I was constantly losing track of them. Then, I found an attractive place to store them: a wide-brim straw hat. I looped some ribbon through it and clipped Katie's ribbons and bows along the ribbon. It's a pretty decoration for the back of her door, too.

Sheri O'Quinn, Macon, Georgia

clothes calls

Multipurpose Mittens

My 1-year-old refused to wear mittens. At my wit's end, I put her infant socks with the sewn-in rattles on her hands. She loves shaking them and making them jingle, and I don't have to worry about frozen hands. In fact, I have a hard time getting her to take them off!

Kathy Price, Angoon, Alaska

Mom and Pop Shop

I have three children, so putting on shoes to go somewhere was always a dreaded chore until my husband and I came up with a great way to get our kids to cooperate. We play "shoe store": The kids get to pick out a pair of shoes and socks to try on; then, we check to see if they fit, and finally comment on how nice their "new" shoes are.

Lesley Kubik, Bonita Springs, Florida

Dressing Made Easier

My 3-year-old can dress himself, but the results can be a little strange. To make things easier, I fold a pair of his underwear inside a shirt and then fold them both up into pants. My son just grabs a pack of clothes, and I know he'll match.

Annie Hays, Idaho Falls, Idaho

End Shoe-Tying Hassles

I was getting tired of re-tying my 3-year-old son's shoes every 15 minutes. To make him more independent, I laced his sneakers with a strip of ¼-

grandmother knows best

Keeping clothes clean for four active children was always a chore, but I found a simple way to get out stubborn stains without scrubbing. I filled a big pot with about 4 gallons of water, brought it to a boil on the back burner, and then turned off the stove. Next, I stirred in ½ cup of powdered Snowy Bleach with a wooden spoon. I took any washable clothes (this treatment is not for woolens or silks), threw them in the pot, and let them soak for a few hours before rinsing well and then laundering. This bleach bath worked wonders, even on nasty baby formula stains. Now my daughter Maggie uses this trick to keep her baby daughter's clothes looking like new.

Jeanne D'Alessio,
Brooklyn, New York

super skin smoothers

Teaching your little ones good skin care habits is easier when you make it fun. You can turn one of your favorite standbys, a jar of Vaseline, into three soothing treats for your child. Just follow these tips from busy mother and wellness expert Linda Short, author of *The Complete Idiot's Guide to Self-Healing with Spas and Retreats.*

1. Soften chapped hands. Mix a dab of Vaseline with 1 teaspoon of buttermilk or plain yogurt. Rub well into your child's hands.

2. Smooth rough, ragged hangnails. Blend a little Vaseline with a few drops of olive oil (or try a few drops of blue lavender oil from the health food store—it turns the petroleum jelly a pretty turquoise color). Massage into the nails.

3. Help heal scraped elbows or knees. Mix a dollop of Vaseline with ¼ to ½ teaspoon of sugar, which is a natural healing agent. After cleansing and drying the scraped area, gently smooth the mixture over your child's skin.

inch white elastic and tied the bow into a knot. Now, he can put on his sneakers all by himself by stretching the elastic, and they always stay tied.

Hally Kohls, Cincinnati

Fit to Be Tie-Dyed

My 6-month-old has spit up on almost every one of his outfits. To get more wear out of his stained clothes, I tie-dye them. The stains blend right in with the colorful designs.

Barbara Smith, Minneapolis

Make Jeans Last Longer

My active 3-year-old son, Zachary, wears holes in his jeans very quickly. To make them last a little longer, I iron on patches cut into shapes of things he likes: tools, trucks, and trains. He loves wearing his personalized jeans!

Lisa Patton, Auburn, Illinois

Keep Track of Hats

Our 18-month-old son does not like wearing hats, and keeping one on him is tough. We were constantly losing them when he pulled them off, until my husband fastened one end of a mitten guard (the short elastic strap that attaches mittens to coats) to our son's shirt collar and the other to the back of the hat. The "hat on a leash" never strays far, even when he flips it off his head.

Ellen Woodard-Colletta, Rockton, Illinois

Kid-Friendly Features

Teaching my 4-year-old son and 2-year-old daughter how to dress themselves is easier when I shop for kid-friendly clothes. I buy outfits with large buttons, wide necks, and elastic waistbands. I also look for shoes with Velcro snaps and buckles. Buying clothing that simplifies getting dressed helps my children aspire to dressing themselves.

Mary Beth Randall, Franklin, Massachusetts

Stock Up on Socks

I was getting tired of packing away my infant daughter's outgrown socks almost as often as doing the laundry. I knew that there had to be a better way, so I bought an economy-size pack of socks labeled "24 to 36 months" and just folded the tops down when she wore them. We're still using the same socks 18 months later.

Robin Cox, Fence Lake, New Mexico

cootie control

Shocked (and a bit grossed out) to find lice on your child's head? The good news: These critters rarely pose a health threat, says Victoria McEvoy, M.D., assistant professor of pediatrics at Harvard Medical School. Here's how to get rid of the tiny bugs.

Telltale signs: An itchy scalp accompanied by tiny, white lice eggs, called nits, cemented to the hair shaft.

Best treatment: Use an over-the-counter shampoo that contains permethrin to kill the lice. Nits, which are smaller than sesame seeds, must be removed with a fine-tooth comb and can be loosened with a solution of equal parts vinegar and water. Reapply insecticidal shampoo a week later. Check the rest of the family for nits.

To stop the spread: Wash your child's toys, linens, towels, clothes, and hats in hot water. (Seal objects that can't be washed, such as stuffed animals, in a plastic bag for 2 weeks.) Teach your child not to share hats, brushes, or barrettes.

games
that boost
creativity

you don't have to fill your house with expensive toys and games to encourage your child's creative side. A simple activity such as playing patty-cake with your baby, drawing faces on the sidewalk with your toddler, or making up a story together can open a world of new ideas for your child.

The best games for kids are those that let their imaginations soar, challenge them to develop new skills, force them to think beyond the obvious, and teach them to learn from their mistakes. And playing with your children can help you stretch your own creative muscles as well. If you're stuck for ideas about what to do or how to do it, the innovative, parent-tested tips in this chapter can help you weave creativity into everyday activities.

simple games

Magic Carpet Ride

I play a simple make-believe game with my 4- and 5-year-olds called magic carpet. We sit on a soft rug and I ask them where they want to go. I encourage them to think creatively. If my son says that he wants to go to Africa, I'll ask, "What will we do there?" "Who will we see?" "What kind of animals live there?" "What kind of souvenirs should we bring back?" It's amazing how many places we can travel to in 20 minutes.

Eileen Brown, Novi, Michigan

Beat the Clock

My two young children enjoy playing hide-and-seek. We all like to hide different things and take turns searching and finding. One rainy afternoon, I thought of a simple twist. I wound up the kitchen timer and hid it. It was enormous fun for them to listen for the ticking sound and try to find it.

Michele Hancock, Asheville, North Carolina

Guess Who

"What am I?" is a simple game that I like to play with my children. All I do is make up some easy clues about animals, objects, or people we know. My clues are very specific, so it's fun for young kids. For Pooh Bear, I might say, "I am soft and cuddly; I love honey; Eeyore and Piglet are my friends. Who am I?" Sometimes we switch off so that my kids get to make up a riddle for me to answer.

Louisa Allen, Costa Mesa, California

Picture Puzzles

My kids love this drawing game: I tear out a picture from a magazine, then cut it into large pieces and give one piece to each child. Each child glues his portion to a piece of paper and then fills in the missing parts of the picture with crayons or markers. It's

grandmother knows best

I found an incredibly simple way to encourage my children's creativity when they were young. Each summer, I turned over one side of the garage and a section of the backyard to them. From these empty spaces, they created amazing things. They put together a museum with interactive displays, a neighborhood art show, a carnival, a garden, and even neighborhood plays. During the year, they'd plan the events for the next summer.

Marlene Loecke,
Des Moines, Iowa

creating a costume box

Costumes aren't just for Halloween, says veteran costumer Annie Modesitt, of South Orange, New Jersey, who has designed wardrobes for both theater and television shows. Dressing up is a great way for children to expand their imaginations and take on new identities. "Slip an old cocktail dress over her head, and before you know it, your daughter is a princess," she says. A funny wig and some oversize shoes can transform your son into a circus clown. Here, Modesitt offers advice on creating the ultimate make-believe wardrobe for your child.

Stock up on fabric. Ordinary fabric remnants in a wide array of colors and prints allow children to design their own fashions. For example, a skirt can be made from two pieces of fabric tied together around the waist.

Go for variety. After cleaning out your closets, hit the yard sales and secondhand stores in your area. Look for dresses, skirts, shirts, vests, suit jackets, and pants in a wide range of sizes, colors, and patterns. Be sure to include shoes, wallets, and handbags, too.

Be safe. Before giving children secondhand clothing to play with, check both the pockets and the linings for sharp objects. Replace tiny hook-and-eye closures and buttons with fur hooks (available at fabric stores) that are easier to grasp and too big for children to swallow. Repair torn linings and fix ripped hems.

Accessorize. Stock up on hats, necklaces, and bracelets, which will add authenticity to any costume. (Avoid pieces that could be swallowed by a small child, though.) If you're worried about losing a piece of jewelry, sew it onto a favorite item of clothing.

fun to compare the variety of creative drawings when everyone is finished.

Elizabeth Perkins, Sandusky, Ohio

outdoor fun

Sandbox Alternative

I created a digging spot in our backyard, which has given my three sons (ages 4, 6, and 8) a marvelous chance to develop their imaginations. They take out their farm toys and become farmers. They bring out their construction toys and build roads or dig tunnels. They have even built a track to race their toy cars around. This might not be the most attractive corner of the backyard, but it sure is magical.

Jan Pulido, Oklahoma City

Sidewalk Artist

One day, my 2- and 4-year-olds wanted to draw on the sidewalk. I didn't have any chalk, so I suggested that we try water. I was amazed at how well it worked. I gave each child a bucket of

four ways to choose toys that encourage creative play

"Toy shopping isn't what it used to be," laments Cynthia Gerdes, president of Creative Kidstuff, a Minneapolis-based chain of specialty toy stores. "You really have to look hard to find products that will foster your child's creative side." To simplify your search for well-rounded playthings that won't do the thinking for your child, Gerdes offers the following four pointers that she and her staff use to select the toys in her stores and catalog.

1. Think simple. The more a toy does, the less likely your child will be to use her imagination when playing with it. A basic doll, for example, will lead to more creative play than one that wets, cries, walks, and talks.

2. Opt for open-ended toys. A set of building blocks can be used to create a fanciful castle, the world's tallest skyscraper, or anything else that your child dreams up. Hand puppets are great for acting out a favorite story or a made-up one. "There's no right or wrong way to use these playthings," Gerdes says. "That's the key to their charm."

3. Choose basics that will grow with your child. For example, a wagon with a sturdy handle will help your 12-month-old walk and still provide enjoyment as an imaginary train or construction vehicle once she reaches kindergarten.

4. Think beyond gender. Dishes, pots, and pans can encourage both boys and girls to play house, restaurant, camping, and more. They're also good basics for teaching your child skills that they will need later on as adults.

make-believe boosters

Fantasy play leads to creative thinking. Here are five simple activities that you can do with your preschooler to set his imagination off and running.

✓ Make a fort by draping a blanket or sheet over a table or set of chairs.

✓ Create collaborative artwork. Start with a squiggle and turn it into a complete drawing.

✓ Pretend that you're the child and let your child be the parent.

✓ Place the kitchen chairs in a row, one behind the other, and make believe that you're on a train.

✓ Have a conversation with your child as if you were a character from one of his favorite books.

water and an old paintbrush. I started by painting a tree, and they joined in, each painting a house and a person. They had great fun seeing how long a picture would last before it disappeared.

Sandra Furman, *Greenwich, Connecticut*

On Cloud Nine

The outdoors is a great place to boost creativity. Sometimes, my two young kids and I lie down on the grass and watch the clouds move. We discuss how clouds are formed and what happens when they touch the earth. Then we play, "What does that cloud look like?"

Trona Woods, *Robbinsville, North Carolina*

Get Messy

When the weather is warm, my kids like to take their fingerpaints outside. They can use both their hands and feet to make pictures on construction paper or cement. The best part is cleanup time: They love washing the paint away with the garden hose.

Shayna Seals, *San Angelo, Texas*

Backyard Explorer

My 2-year-old and I like going outside armed with a magnifying glass. We search for interesting things to look at up close, such as a blade of grass, a flower, a stone, bark, a leaf, an ant, and a bird feather. It helps her learn, but it's also tons of fun.

Angie Hillman, Ames, Iowa

creative toys

Block Party

The best toy investment I ever made was a set of oversize cardboard building blocks. They keep my preschoolers occupied for hours. When my children play "office," the blocks become desks and chairs. Sometimes, they use the blocks to build a su-

games babies play

From the moment they're born, babies love to play. Here are the best toys for each stage from birth to 12 months.

Birth to 1 Month

Newborns are most interested in simple black-and-white drawings that resemble faces or geometric patterns, and in objects that are easy to grasp, such as thin, smooth rings.

2 to 3 Months

Gyms and mobiles that dangle above the crib are good for helping a child learn to control her limbs and for developing hand-eye coordination.

4 to 6 Months

Teething toys in a variety of shapes, textures, and tastes are ideal for letting baby explore her mouth. Make sure that all mouthing items are clean—and larger than the opening in a toilet-paper tube, so that they're not choking hazards.

7 to 9 Months

Once a child starts scooting, creeping, and crawling, everything in the house becomes a potential toy. Capture her attention by placing a nonbreakable mirror at crawling height or by giving her objects that can be dropped, thrown, banged, or tossed. Board, foam, and cloth books are also favorites.

10 to 12 Months

Look for toys such as nesting cups and stacking rings that will help your child's perceptual, language, and fine motor skills increase. Babies at this stage also enjoy imitative play with dolls and animals.

permarket and play "store," and other times, they turn the blocks into a car, load it up with their animal friends, and head off to visit Grandma. The fun never ends.

Judy Best, *Westminster, Colorado*

Put On a Show

Puppets are great for creative play. To help my children use their imaginations, I placed a tension rod in a doorway and hung a curtain on it. The children get behind the curtain and put on a show for the rest of the family with their puppets. Sometimes, we even pretend that it's a theater and serve popcorn and snacks.

Amanda Flynn, *Foxboro, Massachusetts*

Boxing Lesson

I save big packing cartons and appliance boxes. On a day when my children don't know what to do, I bring out an empty carton, markers, crayons, paper scraps, scissors, and glue, and see what they can turn the carton into. It might become a dollhouse, a fire truck, a spaceship, a race car, or even a vacation cabin. You might have to help cut a window or door, but the children will have no trouble coming up with creative designs.

Jason Nixon, *Southampton, New York*

cures for cabin fever

Indoor Campground

One rainy weekend, we took my preschoolers on a pretend camping trip. We camped out on the family room floor, where we ate a simple picnic dinner. After dinner, we sang songs, played games, and had make-believe discussions such as "If I were a fireman, I would. . . ." At the end of the evening, my husband and I read stories. Soft music played as we fell asleep in our sleeping bags. I think everyone will remember our indoor camping trip for a long time.

Aleena Woody, *Hewitt, Texas*

Storytime with a Twist

One of my daughter's favorite rainy day activities is making up add-on stories. I like playing it because it's easy, quick, and always full of surprises for both of us. I start a story with some-

the best basics

In today's world of high-tech gizmos, it's nice to know that some toys and games never go out of style. Here's our list of favorites for toddlers and up—toys whose quality and play value have stood the test of time.

For Toddlers

✓ Push and pull toys

✓ Teddy bears

✓ Toy telephones, strollers, and lawn mowers

✓ Jack-in-the-box

For Preschoolers

✓ Fingerpaints and Play-Doh

✓ Classic board games such as Candy Land and Chutes and Ladders

✓ Dolls

✓ Wooden puzzles

For School-Age Kids

✓ Lego blocks, Tinkertoys, and Lincoln Logs

✓ Pick-up sticks, jacks, and yo-yos

✓ Mr. Potato Head

✓ Wiffle ball and bat

thing funny, such as a talking animal. After a few sentences, I point to my daughter or one of her friends to continue. I give everyone a chance to add to the story. After everyone has had at least one turn, I finish the story. The creative possibilities are endless.

Patricia Day, McLean, Virginia

arts and crafts

A Magnetic Attraction to Learning

I always have a surplus of those flexible magnets from advertisers. So, I use them to help my daughter learn her shapes. I just peel off the top layer and attach colored construction paper cut into different shapes. Paige loves playing with them and identifying the different shapes and colors.

Jodie Johnson, Franklin, Wisconsin

Innovative Paper Dolls

We've found a new way to use the catalogs we get each month. My daughters, ages 3 and 5, cut out the clothes, but not the models, and glue them onto construction paper. Then, instead of putting the clothes on the doll, we put the doll on the clothes by drawing a head, arms, and legs. It's a nice change from traditional paper dolls and the results are adorable.

Shari Pulido, Brooklyn, New York

Chalkboard Choo-Choo

I painted a train on the wall of my daughter's playroom with green chalkboard paint. To do it, I used a transparency of a train and projected it onto the wall, then traced it. Anna, 2, loves to draw all kinds of squiggles and shapes on her green train.

Jackie Savage, Louisville

5 cures for the boredom blues

1. Host an art exhibit. Ask everyone in the family to create a work of art. Display the masterpieces on the family room wall or in another prime location where everyone can enjoy them.
2. Take a flashlight walk in the dark. Listen to the night sounds and point out the stars and constellations.
3. Play restaurant. Let kids design a menu, take your order, and prepare your meal, which can be as simple as a bowl of cereal.
4. Start the presses. A neighborhood or family newsletter is cheap, creative, and educational. Your roving reporter can deliver the scoop on everything from new neighbors to a visit from Grandma and Grandpa.
5. Play tourist in your own town. You're bound to find new places that you've never visited before or old ones that you've forgotten about. Have your kids make their own hometown postcards to send to relatives.

pretend friends

Is your child's best friend invisible? If so, there's no cause for worry. In fact, children with lively imaginations often have more advanced language skills, are able to concentrate better, are less likely to complain of being bored, and are more cooperative with their peers, says Jerome Singer, Ph.D., a professor of psychology and child study at Yale University. Here are five key things that you need to know about your child's invisible playmate.

✓ Your child isn't lonely. In fact, says Dr. Singer, research shows that children who have pretend playmates have just as many real friends as children who don't.

✓ Imaginary friends help children express feelings. If a child feels bad about misbehaving, for example, he might scold his imaginary playmate for talking back to Mom or Dad.

✓ Fantasy friends can be stress relievers. If your child is worried about a stressful situation such as starting preschool or visiting the dentist, talking to the imaginary friend can help him cope.

✓ You should never make fun of your child or his friend. But it is okay to set limits, Dr. Singer advises. For example, don't give up your place at the dinner table for his phantom friend.

✓ Always address your child and not his imaginary playmate. This shows that you respect the friend, experts say, but also makes it clear to your child that you understand what's real and what's not.

Buckets of Fun

My mom always kept a scrap bucket full of her leftover sewing and craft materials, and all of us kids were free to go through it and use whatever we liked to create our own masterpieces. Scraps of material and ribbon quickly became doll clothes. It's a great way to encourage creativity and fight boredom.

Melissa Calapp, Sacramento

your
little athlete

26

is your 4-year-old showing an interest in baseball? Can't get your 6-year-old off of the ice rink? Good for them! It's crucial to encourage your children to adopt a healthy lifestyle at an early age.

Exercise certainly builds a stronger body, but it also builds a stronger mind. Children of any age can benefit from participating in sports, whether it's a team sport such as hockey or soccer, an individual activity such as gymnastics or running, or even made-up games in your own backyard. The lessons learned, from new skills to sportsmanship to self-confidence, will last a lifetime.

get active!

Greens Gene

My husband and I love golf. We want it to be a family activity that we can all enjoy. We take our children with us as much as possible. Our oldest now has a "real" children's putter and wedge. We allow her to putt on the course when we do. We don't force it, nor do we give a lot of instruction, because it seems to frustrate her. We simply let her do it her way as long as she is respectful of the course and other golfers.

Lisa Laughlin, Reno

Getting Started

My kids aren't quite old enough for sports yet, but to encourage physical activity, we dance around the house a lot. I play children's tapes and make up little dances to go with the words in the songs. Outside, we pretend to be airplanes or birds and run around the yard.

Janet Phillips, Danville, Virginia

Like Mother, Like Daughter

My daughter started in a "moms and tots" swim program when she was just 7 months old. Not only was it fun, but it's also the only real, formal exercise that children can do at such an early age. I also love field hockey, so when my daughter was just 12 months old, I bought her her own mini field hockey stick. She loves to play in the backyard with me. Needless to say, we have a blast.

Wendy A. Heydon, Silverdale, Washington

Take Advantage Of Local Classes

Our girls, ages 5 and 6, love gymnastics. So, every Monday, after school, they take a gymnastics class at the local health club. Many parents don't know

teaching sportsmanship

We asked Darrell J. Burnett, Ph.D., a youth sports psychologist in Laguna Niguel, California, and author of *Youth, Sports, and Self-Esteem: A Guide for Parents*, how to encourage children to be good sports. Here are his "Eight Great Sportsmanship Traits."

1. Follow your coach's directions.
2. Encourage your teammates.
3. Be a team player.
4. Accept judgment calls.
5. Respect your opponents.
6. Lose without complaining.
7. Win without gloating.
8. Learn from your mistakes.

the competitive child

Most children go through a competitive stage, but some kids are temperamentally more competitive than their peers. One reason is that children mimic what they see at home. "Pay attention to what you say and do," says Greg Prazar, M.D., of the section on developmental and behavioral pediatrics at the American Academy of Pediatrics. "If you act competitively toward your spouse, you may want to curb this kind of behavior."

Also, Dr. Prazar says, if your child says something unpleasant to a teammate, such as "That was a wimpy shot," talk to him about why it's inappropriate later, so that you won't embarrass him. When he makes a general remark about his own prowess, such as "I can throw farther than you," say, "You sure can throw far." It's natural for him to take pride in his accomplishments, and it's fine if you do, too.

that you don't always have to be a member of a health club for your kids to participate in the classes. We also watch sports on TV—usually, the girls and I pick the team with the prettiest uniforms and, of course, my husband cheers on his favorite team. The girls and I usually win!

Jeanette Akright, Dunlap, Illinois

helping reluctant kids

Bubble Batting Practice

My 3½-year-old used to get very frustrated when he'd practice hitting a softball. To encourage him, I thickened ordinary bubble solution by adding dish soap to create larger, longer-lasting bubbles. I blow the bubbles in his direction, and he practices hitting them. He feels more in control this way and is so excited when he hits one. Our 21-month-old daughter also gets a kick out of watching all those bubbles burst, and she cheers him on every time.

Marina DeLeon, San Benito, Texas

Photo Finish

My son is 10 and just started to learn how to swim. He had a hard time getting used to going underwater. I bought him a disposable underwater camera so he could take pictures in the pool. Now, he loves going underwater.

Regina Dolkhart, Elmira, New York

Don't Push It

Team sports are too intense for my young son right now, but he may be interested when he gets older. I've had him try many different things and found that he prefers tap dancing, which, incidentally, he's very good at!

Debbie Hudson, Evergreen, Colorado

Ease into It

My 9-year-old is very shy and introverted. When we started him in youth soccer in kindergarten, all he did for the first 2 years was avoid the ball and talk to his friends. It was no use

how athletes get their kids involved with sports

"I don't want to force my son Jordan to play sports. I hope to teach him by example. At 1, he already loves to play with his own little basketball and to watch me play."

—*Sheryl Swoopes, WNBA star*

"Exercise is a group activity that gives my family the chance to spend time together. My four children naturally have a lot of energy, so it's very easy to keep them active."

—*Sammy Sosa, major league baseball player*

"My two girls travel with the team, which lets them see how positive staying fit is. My daughter Katy doesn't view exercise as work—just more fun and play in the day, like her mom gets to do on the soccer field."

—*Joy Fawcett, member of the 1999 U.S. World Cup champion women's soccer team*

"You can't just tell kids that exercise is fun and hope they'll love it. You have to show them. We play ball with our three boys and go swimming together. When they see you do physical activities, they'll want to do them, too."

—*Chris Evert, tennis legend*

playground games

"The family that plays together stays together," says Opal Dunn, author of *Acka Backa Boo! Playground Games from Around the World*. But playground games are more than just silly chants and jumping around, she adds. "They boost language development, improve physical coordination, and teach winning and losing in a relaxed environment." Here are a few fun, easy games from around the globe that translate into any language.

Tickum-Tackum (Iran)
Stand back-to-back with your child and walk away from each other until you're 10 feet apart. Then shout "Tickum-tackum!" and turn around. Take turns taking steps toward each other, putting heel to toe, you shouting "Tickum!" and your child "Tackum!" as you go. Whoever's foot fills the final gap is the winner.

Ram, Ram, *Rip!* (Indonesia, Malaysia)
Hold out your hand, palm up. Have your child hold her hands on each side of your palm with the tips of her index fingers resting on your palm. Say the following rhyme: "Ram, ram, ram, ram, ram, ram, *rip!*" When you get to *rip!*, close your hand quickly to try to catch a finger while your child tries to get her fingers away. When you do catch a finger, switch and have your child try to catch your finger.

Bounce and Whirl Around (Syria)
Have your child say, "Bounce and whirl around, toes on the ground" as she bounces a ball, then quickly spins around in a circle and tries to catch the ball. She can count how many times she can do it without missing and try to beat the previous score.

to yell and beg him to pay attention, so we just let him have fun. He warmed up to the game by himself and became a great player. Parents also need to participate—not only as chauffeurs to and from the field, but also as cheerleaders.

Ann Morales-Ear, *Staten Island, New York*

Go to the Videotape!
To encourage my daughter to practice gymnastics, I sometimes videotape her. She loves to watch herself, so, turning a prac-

exercise guidelines for kids

How active should a child be? According to the first comprehensive exercise guidelines for kids, issued by the National Association for Sport and Physical Education, children ages 5 to 9 should be getting some sort of exercise for a total of 60 minutes a day. Here are some things that they can do.

Lifestyle activities: Some examples include walking, climbing, kicking, and skipping.

Aerobics: Encourage your child to swim, bicycle, skate, and run around to build her cardiovascular fitness. Let her set her own pace.

Flexibility exercises: Young children don't need formal stretching. Tumbling or hanging from a jungle gym, for example, helps kids become more limber.

Strength exercises: Activities such as climbing on playground equipment or pumping their legs while swinging help children get strong.

tice into a televised performance gives her a real boost. It also helps her see her progress and note any mistakes, and we send a copy to her faraway grandparents.

Jan Kral, Pelham, Alabama

Friendly Persuasion

My 3-year-old is easily inspired by watching older children. We spent several months trying to work with him to learn how to hit a ball with a bat. One day, a 5-year-old from down the street came into our yard and hit the ball into the neighbor's yard. Ever since then, our son has been happy to try. I think he just needed to know that he had a reachable goal.

Laurie Callahan, Boulder, Colorado

be a good sport

Just Try

We emphasize individual effort over winning or losing. Our son is into wrestling; we videotape his matches and point out the moves he used and how well he's mastered his wrestling knowledge, even if he lost the match. We can also point out what his opponents did to succeed.

Tammi Price, Crofton, Maryland

For the Love of the Game

My son was going to be in a race at school and was nervous because he's shorter than the other kids and can't run as fast. I told him how I was the shortest hurdler on my track team, and how, after practicing over and over, I became one of the fastest. More important, I told him that I kept running because I enjoyed it. We talked about how he loves running and about how in the end it didn't matter if he won—just that he had a good time.

Tonya A. Salas, Okinawa, Japan

Positive Role Models

Sports were a big part of my childhood, and I know that it was important for me to have my parents' encouragement. They attended my practices and games, and both my parents coached various teams that I was on. They also talked to me after games and practices about what I could improve on and what I did to encourage others, and they always told me how proud they were. I do the same with my kids.

Jamie Rivington, Monterey, California

active games

Scramble

Our homemade game is really simple, with no rules, but our 3-year-old daughter seems to enjoy it. One person tosses a

a sporting chance

What's the earliest that a child can do a somersault or play Pop Warner football? Here's what you need to know to get your child going in the gym, on the field, or on the ice.

Ice skating: Kids ages 3 and up can learn gliding, stopping, turning, and jumping in place.

Pop Warner football: Kids ages 5 to 7 can play flag football; after that, they learn tackle. Players should wear protection and will be matched by age and weight for safety.

Gymnastics: General gymnastics can start as young as age 3 and can emphasize tumbling, flexibility, balance, and music.

Soccer: Many American Youth Soccer Organization programs give kids 6 and under an excellent introduction to soccer by providing more coaching attention, limiting the number of team players per side, and playing brief games on a short field.

Downhill skiing: Potty-taught preschoolers can enter beginner ski school, where they'll get a half-day of instruction in balancing, stopping, and turning.

softball or balloon up in the air and then everybody tries to scramble for it. If it comes near Mom or Dad, we'll sometimes pretend that we've got it, but then we'll bounce it away again so that our daughter can try for it again.

Bridget Jozwiak, Buffalo

whose dream is it, anyway?

To determine whether your little soccer player or figure skater is fulfilling her goals or yours, ask yourself these questions. If you answer "I do" to all or most, take a hard look at your true motives for developing your child's talent.

✓ When my child wins, who celebrates more?

✓ Who replays the game or my child's performance to friends and relatives?

✓ Who presses for more practice time?

✓ Who collects and dusts the trophies?

✓ Who takes losses harder?

Bill Bradley on the game of life

Getting your children involved in team sports will help them be strong, confident, can-do kids, says Bill Bradley, a former NBA player, U.S. senator, and presidential candidate. Here's what they'll learn.

1. Respect: Kids involved in sports must often remember their goals when other distractions pull them away. To show up to every practice teaches them respect because they have to focus on a goal.

2. Discipline: Learning how hard you have to work to become good at something will help kids succeed elsewhere.

3. Responsibility: Many kids lead chaotic lives and often have a poor sense of time. Abiding by team rules and arriving at practice at a scheduled hour becomes a major obligation.

4. Selflessness: Our society glorifies individualism. Team sports teach a different lesson. Sometimes, an athlete must put his own ego on hold in order to do what's best for the group.

5. Resilience: A team sport is a laboratory for learning how to handle adversity, such as injury or defeat.

The Dandelion Dash

We have made picking bouquets of dandelions a game on our farm. We see who can pick the most for the largest bouquet, or see if we can all make a bigger arrangement than the day before.

Sonia Nelson, *Wetaskiwin, Alberta, Canada*

Get into the Spirit

When our 4-year-old son is playing sports, we try to make the experience fun by goofing around with him. We imitate a sports commentator; we cheer like a crowd and do the "wave." Our son gets a big kick out of it and is having so much fun that he doesn't seem to care whether he scores or not.

Cathy Shambley, *Hermosa Beach, California*

Three Cheers

My 6-year-old daughter invented a game called pom-pom cheers. She gets her father to repeat all of the cheers that she dances to. Boy, is it hilarious to watch my husband!

Susie Higgins, *San Antonio*

building
self-esteem

27

We all want our kids to value their talents and believe in themselves. But no matter how much you encourage your child's self-confidence, there are bound to be challenges ahead.

What do you say when your preschooler is in tears because a playmate rejected him? How do you help a baby feel secure as she explores her world, or urge your young perfectionist to set realistic goals? In this chapter, you'll learn how to turn everyday situations into opportunities to show your child how special she is—and you'll learn how to motivate her to try new things without fear of failure, and how to help her take pride in her successes.

Boosting a child's self-esteem calls for being part cheerleader, part coach. It's a demanding job for any parent, but ultimately, it's one of the most rewarding.

applaud your child's efforts

Celebrate Success

Whether my 2½-year-old daughter has made progress with potty-training or my 6-year-old daughter has received a good report from school, we celebrate a special achievement with "girls' night." We choose an evening when my husband will be working late. The girls get to pick what they want for supper; we rent a movie, make popcorn, and do each other's hair. My daughters love it—our night together is a time to bond and to share in each child's accomplishment.

Mary Groezinger, Hanover, Illinois

Good Sport

My son joined the swim team at school when he was 9 years old. Competition at swim meets was stiff, but I simply wanted him to improve his swimming skills and enjoy the sport without worrying about winning. When he got second and third place ribbons, I would tell him how proud I was. He never won first place, but I think I encouraged his sense of being "good enough" by applauding the fact that he'd done his best.

Tamara Vidos, Springfield, Oregon

The Artist's Way

One day, my 5-year-old daughter Lynnea came home in tears. She and a friend had been drawing pictures and her friend told her that she didn't know how to draw a tree right. I sat her down and told her that no two artists see things the same way and that this is what makes them original. I assured her that drawing the tree the way she thought it should look made her picture beautiful. Now, she loves to draw. Being more confident about her artwork also makes her more comfortable with choices and decisions she makes in other areas of her life.

Cathleen Straley,
Yardley, Pennsylvania

star strategy

☆ Rosie O'Donnell

"Growing up, when people would tell me I was too heavy, too tough, or not pretty enough to succeed, I knew they were wrong. You have to believe in yourself. I really want kids to understand that."

—talk show host and mother of three

shy strategies

The Magic Microphone

To help my 6-year-old daughter open up and talk to us when she's feeling less than chatty, my husband came up with a simple solution. Using a hairbrush as a microphone, he interviews our daughter about her day—what she's feeling, or whatever she wants to talk about. She loves the special attention and even likes to turn the tables by interviewing us.

Molly Stephenson, *Glendale, Missouri*

Pillow Talk

My 7-year-old daughter often has a hard time telling us why she is upset. So, I made a pillow for her bed with a pocket on the back. I told her that if there was ever anything that she didn't want to say out loud, she could leave me a note in the pocket, and I would read it and then write back to her. The pillow works wonders—it's really helping us communicate as my daughter grows up.

Laurie Martinchek, *Newington, Connecticut*

it's my job

letting kids make mistakes

You want your children to do their best. But when you step in to "fix" or "tidy up" an imperfect job, it can backfire. "If you redust the spot she missed or rewipe the kitchen counter, you're telling your child that what she did wasn't good enough," says mother and parenting workshop leader Karin Ireland, author of *Boost Your Child's Self-Esteem*. "Unfortunately, kids can begin to believe that they are not good enough." This 10-second strategy from Ireland will help your child feel more successful. Next time you're tempted to touch up your child's work, ask yourself:

✓ Is there a health or safety issue involved?

✓ Will this matter 10 years from now?

✓ Just this once, can I let go of my need for things to be perfect?

easing frustration

Vote of Confidence

One day, my 6-year-old daughter came home from school devastated that her teacher had reprimanded her twice. She usually gets along with her teacher very well, and their relationship means a lot to her. But she was so humiliated that she didn't want to go back to school. I reassured her that being reprimanded didn't mean that her teacher didn't like her, but that I would speak with her teacher the next day. Knowing that I was on her side gave her the confidence to return to school.

Holly Reich, *New York City*

Try, Try Again

My 2½-year-old gets frustrated easily when he's building with blocks or playing with trains, and he often wants to give up on a difficult task, such as attaching two trains together. Instead of

it's my job

teaching children to succeed

Laurie Rausch Andrews, who teaches fourth grade at P.S. 9 in New York City, has some winning strategies to help kids achieve success in the classroom. What works for her and her students at school can also be applied at home.

✓ Don't just say "Good job" when a child has made progress toward a goal or mastered a skill. It helps to be more specific, to point out the details that you find impressive. Saying "I like the way that you described the hero in your book report" is more meaningful than a rote pat on the back.

✓ Do let a child correct your mistakes. "If you accept a correction with good grace and a sense of humor, it can help a child see that taking criticism doesn't have to result in humiliation," explains Andrews. Realizing that an authority figure is human, too, is also a big relief for a young child.

✓ Don't overdo the reward system. "I don't give out gold stars," says Andrews. "I used to hand out prizes every Friday, but it got to the point that the kids were more focused on the reward than on getting satisfaction from doing well." Instead, give positive feedback. Let your children know how great it is when they succeed.

doing it for him, we take the time to talk him through his problem. If he sticks with it, then he feels good that he was able to finally do it himself.

Jennifer Duster, Winona, Minnesota

One Step at a Time

When my daughter Anna was 4 years old, she began to take violin lessons. Because so many other things came easily to her, she would get discouraged when she couldn't play perfectly. I reminded her that when she was a baby, she couldn't walk—that first, she had to learn how to crawl and then, little by little, become strong enough to walk. Realizing that she could also learn to play violin a "baby step" at a time helped her believe in her ability to pick up new skills—and it helped her enjoy her music lessons.

Janet Hurley, Iselin, New Jersey

how to say "you're great!"

Spinning Compliments

During my 3-year-old's quiet time, I play a CD for him called *You Are Special*, by Mister Rogers. I listened to the album when I was growing up and it helped me feel better about myself. It seems to be having the same wonderful influence on my son.

Tara Claeys, Arlington, Virginia

No Comparison

My three sons have all gone through stages comparing themselves with each other. To keep any one of them from feeling that he doesn't "measure up," I've always stressed that what makes them so different from each other also makes them unique and interesting. Knowing that my husband and I accept each child for who they are has helped our boys pursue goals that they enjoy and that help set them apart as individuals.

Pamela Straley, Columbus, Ohio

Ways to Say Thank You

I not only praise my 4-year-old son for his successes, I also compliment him on his good behavior. This way, he knows that I'm paying attention to his efforts to please. I'll say,

"Thank you for cleaning up without being asked." Or, "I'm so glad that you hung up your clothes." Or, "You were so well-behaved in the restaurant today." This positive reinforcement encourages him to try to do his best.

Diane Rocheny, New York City

No Teasing, Please

To teach our 6- and 8-year-old daughters self-respect, we never tease them or let them tease each other. If other kids make fun of them, we try to explain that those children may just be lonely or afraid of making friends. We hope they're learning that they should always expect to be treated well.

Anne and Ben McLaughlin, Cheshire, Connecticut

feeling important

Decisions, Decisions

I let my daughter, Gracie, make decisions for and by herself. She's only 2½, but every morning she picks out her own

build baby's self-esteem

It's never too early to help your little one feel secure in her ever-changing world. Here are three ways to boost your baby's confidence in her first year of life.

1. Give tons of hugs and kisses. Research has shown that much of a baby's emotional and physical health depends on the tender, loving touches that she receives from a parent or caregiver. All your hugs, kisses, and cuddling go a long way. "Contact" games such as patty-cake are also delightful ways to stay in touch.

2. Speak up. Your baby may not understand your words, but the tone of your voice will speak volumes each time you tell her "I love you so much!" or "You're terrific!" Sending these little messages on a regular basis reassures your little one that you are there to meet her needs.

3. Applause, applause. Each time your baby accomplishes something new—figuring out a new way to play with a toy, or exploring a different corner of her room—clap your hands to show her how pleased you are. Your encouragement makes it easier for her to take the next important steps in discovering more about her world.

grandmother knows best

When my youngest child was in third grade, he still felt like a baby. And no wonder! His older brother and sister were continually caring for him, constantly telling him what to do, when to do it, and how to do it. To show my son that I trusted that he could act responsibly, I decided to let him adopt a puppy that he could care for as his own "child." Having his own pet promoted my son's self-confidence, and he became more assertive. Now that they're all parents with families of their own, each of my children has adopted dogs to help their own sons and daughters feel grown up, too.

Ethel Weisberg, *West Orange, New Jersey*

clothes and even puts them on by herself. Often, the colors clash. Sometimes, she'll put on pants and a dress, but unless we're going somewhere special and she really has to dress nicely, I try not to override her choices. I think this makes her feel like her opinions count.

Sally Lee, *Hoboken, New Jersey*

"I Made It Myself!"

My 5- and 4-year-old sons love to help their dad with carpentry work. One of their latest projects was building a birdcage. It doesn't exactly fit my vision of what a birdcage should look like, but it doesn't matter whether your child's efforts turn out the way you'd like them to. Letting kids accomplish tasks on their own is a richer reward. My boys are proud of their imperfect birdcage because they built it themselves.

Regina Daly, *Summit, New Jersey*

let them shine

The Supper Club

One day, my 5-year-old daughter came home from preschool with a cookbook for kids that featured easy recipes such as happy-face bagels, sandwich roll-ups, and fruit kabobs. I thought that it would be fun to let her pick the menu one night a week. My daughter and her 3½-year-old brother put the meal together. Even my 21-month-old daughter can help (she likes putting raisins on the bagels). We talk about measurements and ingredients as we fix the meal. The kids are always very proud that they made our dinner.

Kathleen Caggiano, *Bethesda, Maryland*

Show, Not Tell

Showing a keen interest in my children's schoolwork lets them know that how they spent their day is important to me. From the time Joshua and Marisa were in preschool, I would ask them to show me something that they'd done in class that day. Whether they were learning their numbers, colors, or the alphabet, they would delight in the opportunity to teach Mom what they knew. This strategy also helped to reinforce their school lessons in a way that was fun for everyone.

Lynette Hamara, *Flemington, New Jersey*

4 things never to say in front of your daughter

A positive body image can be an important source of a young girl's self-esteem. But any griping that you do about your own size or shape can ultimately influence the way your daughter sees herself. Here are some phrases to avoid.

1. "Do I look fat in this outfit?" If you want your daughter's opinion about an outfit, it's okay to ask, "Do you like the color of my dress?" or "Doesn't this sweater feel soft?" You want her to see clothing as fun and functional, not as a source of anxiety.

2. "I hate my stomach." A healthy body image is not just about appearance. You need to acknowledge your natural grace, strength, or athletic ability. Say, "Wow! I ran 3 miles today." This helps your daughter value her abilities rather than fixate on her looks.

3. "I wish I were as pretty as that woman." Comparing yourself with other women may push your daughter to check the mirror for her own shortcomings.

4. "Don't eat that or you'll grow up to be fat." Even a mild suggestion that your daughter might want to lose a few pounds sends a message that the only acceptable body is a slender one. Less talk about appearance and more praise for achievements will help boost your child's self-confidence.

Read-Aloud Family Time

Every day, we take time as a family to read to each other. Our 6-year-old daughter excels at reading in school, so we like to give her the opportunity to show us her skills. She knows how much we enjoy listening to the stories she chooses, which enhances her self-confidence. Our daughter would rather give up a playdate than miss this special time together.

Janet DeWitt, Kerhonkson, New York

Keeping Secrets

My 5-year-old daughter, Lauren, likes to tell me secrets. For example, she'll confide what she's planning to bring to show-and-tell at school when she wants it to be a surprise. I promise that I'll keep her thoughts locked up in my heart. This assures her that it is a private matter between just the two of us. Keeping her secret safe helps my daughter know that her thoughts are important and that her feelings matter.

Kathy Straley, Hampton, New Jersey

how to ease hurt feelings

At the ages of 5 and 6, kids are especially vulnerable to the emotional blows that come from their friends. Name-calling can feel as painful as sticks and stones. When your child's playmate hurts her feelings, try these strategies from pediatrician Edward Schor, M.D., who practices in Des Moines, Iowa.

Be reassuring. You want to turn around your child's pain and make her feel better about herself. Tell her how much you love her and what you think makes her so special. If your child feels accepted, she's less likely to take another child's mean words or thoughtless actions personally.

Be objective. Try to help your child understand why her playmate may have behaved badly. Say, "I don't think Erica meant what she said. She's just not in a good mood today."

love your body

Here's Looking at You

My 7½-month-old son, Evan, loves it when I sit him in front of the full-length mirror in our bedroom and point out his eyes, nose, mouth, and feet. I also describe what he's wearing. Recognizing himself in the mirror makes him smile, laugh, and play. I do this once a day to promote positive self-awareness, but Evan is just having fun getting to know himself.

Bari Seiden, New York City

boys have body image issues, too

Although some boys do worry about being overweight, a far greater number are concerned that they may be too skinny. "A boy looks into the mirror and sees himself as puny," says Roberto Olivardia, a doctoral candidate in clinical psychology at the University of Massachusetts, Boston. "Boys as young as 10 and 11 are visiting bodybuilding Web sites on the Internet and asking for advice on steroid use."

What can a parent do? Follow these guidelines from Olivardia.

✓ Boost his self-image as you would with a daughter, by praising him for his achievements and encouraging him to set realistic goals.

✓ Educate him about steroid use. Explain that steroids are drugs and that they can have very harmful effects.

✓ Get help if you notice that your son is excessively preoccupied with his body. Your pediatrician can direct you to a therapist who specializes in eating disorders.

Barbie's Not Perfect

When my daughter Hannah was 3 years old, I gave in to her request for a Barbie doll. But from time to time, I made sure to comment on how Barbie did not look healthy to me. I said that her tummy looked too small to hold any food. Then I might add that her feet looked bent from wearing such high heels, and how could they possibly work? Hannah loved Barbie for 2 years and then the fascination was over. I think that my remarks about her doll helped my daughter realize that what her own body can do is far more important than what it looks like.

Renee Smith, *Baton Rouge, Louisiana*

Stand Tall

By the time my daughter Genevieve was in the second grade, she had gotten into the bad habit of slouching. I didn't want to constantly nag and nudge her to stand up straight; instead, I enrolled her in ballet classes. Learning to dance made her feel more confident. At the same time, she learned how to maintain good posture, which makes her look more self-assured, too.

Jane Gyulavary, *Warwick, New York*

school time

28

Whether they're just starting out or they're old pros in the classroom, kids look forward to school with a mix of excitement and nervous anticipation. Besides learning brand-new things every day, your child will also make friends, bond with his teacher, pick up new hobbies, and grow more independent.

A parent's world changes each September, too: Suddenly, you have to load up on school supplies, adjust to stricter bedtimes, make lunches, organize after-school playdates, and deal with homework dilemmas. The time-tested tips in this chapter will help make the school year less stressful and more rewarding for everyone in your family.

school supplies

Cheaper by the Dozen

My children's schools strongly encourage reading at home—just like I do. But with four kids, buying new paperbacks can get pretty expensive. To save money, I take my kids to bookstores and let them point out all the books they're interested in. Then, I go hunting at garage sales and used-book shops for the 25- to 50-cent versions.

Kimberley Hirschi, *San Diego*

Bargain Hunting

Each year, several weeks before school starts, I consult my sons' teachers and make a list of all the school supplies they'll need. Then, I gather the various local stores' fliers and compare prices. Finally, we all head out and make our selections. My sons love being able to choose their own supplies, but I still have control over how much we pay.

Mary Vourlias, *Brooklyn, New York*

how to handle a perfectionist

Some children won't take anything less than the best when it comes to their own performance in school. How do you deal with your child when he won't let up on himself? Here's what the experts advise.

✓ Explain how mistakes help. Perfectionists need to realize that mistakes teach lessons and stimulate growth. Emphasize that it's not about being the best but about being at one's own best. You can demonstrate this by stressing teacher comments over grades or the creativity of a project over its rank in the science fair.

✓ Be a good example. If you berate yourself for making mistakes, most likely, your child will follow your lead. Likewise, if you're a little more forgiving of yourself, your child will likely adopt a similar attitude.

✓ Lighten the load. If your child is overscheduled with activities and becoming stressed by all the demands, suggest that he give up his least favorite activity so that he's not spread so thin.

✓ Encourage relaxation. Help your child learn how to relax when he's feeling overwhelmed or anxious. Deep breathing exercises, time alone, cuddling with a pet, and your loving words can all help. Perfectionist kids also thrive on routines and predictable schedules.

helping parents be better classroom volunteers

Whether you chaperone a field trip or spend an hour in the classroom reading to the kids, helping out at your child's school is important. Not only do over-worked teachers rely on parents to lend a hand, but volunteering is also a key way for you to stay more involved with your child's education.

"Volunteers show students how teachers and parents link together to help kids learn," says Greg Lawler, a third grade teacher at the Findley School in Beaverton, Oregon. We asked him how parents can make the most of their time in the classroom.

Don't be a spy. If you just want to check up on your kid in class, you're not volunteering for the right reason. "I tell parents that if they're going to be in the classroom, I really need them to do something productive," says Lawler.

Offer your expertise. Are you artistic? Do you play an instrument? Then lead a special crafts project or teach the kids a new song. You can help out behind the scenes, too: If you're an organization whiz or savvy with computers, offer to order new books over the Internet, send out letters to other parents, or file papers.

Don't be distracted by your child. No doubt, your child will be thrilled that you're in the classroom. Let him enjoy having you there—but make sure that he doesn't get too clingy. Other kids will need your attention, too.

Give what you can. If you work full-time and can't afford to spend an hour or two in your child's class during the day, there are other ways to help. Volunteer to bake cupcakes for a school party, help out at a Saturday morning fair, or design decorations for bulletin boards.

Finding the Perfect Pack

When my three daughters choose backpacks, I let them pick ones that they think are "cool"—as long as they fit most of my requirements. To hold all of their stuff, each bag has to have a wide opening at the top and a deep space, plus only a couple of smaller pockets, since things get lost if there are too many pockets. For high-priority items, I also buy them each a special wallet that can be clipped to the pack.

Celena Perkins, Cokesbury, New Jersey

parent participation

Lend a Hand

Because my son attends a cooperative preschool, all parents are required to volunteer to help out at least once a month. Even though I work full-time, I try to go in for my half-day session as often as I can. On my days at the school, I get to sit with him and lead his first activity of the day. It gives me great insight into what he does at school.

Vicki Rolens, *Edwardsville, Illinois*

Fabulous Field Trips

My husband and I like to chaperone both of our kids' field trips as frequently as we can. In addition to the thrill we get from spending more time with our kids, our children

it's my job

calming first-day-of-school jitters

The long hallways, the crowds of strangers, the questions, the homework, all the new adults: The first day of school can be extremely overwhelming and nerve-racking for a kid. What advice does a seasoned teacher have for making kids feel comfortable on day one? We asked Cheryl Curbishley, a fifth grade teacher at G. E. Wilson Elementary School in Hamilton Township, New Jersey.

Teacher tactics: "I smile a lot and use plenty of open and friendly body language to show kids that they're welcome," she says. "I also make sure that I'm well-organized, because children are more at ease and comfortable when they see a routine in progress and realize that they will become part of it. The first day, we do plenty of introductions and we set classroom rules, too, so they know what's expected of them. Eliminating that guessing game eases a lot of their fears as well."

Parental pointers: Make sure that your child gets enough sleep before the first day, says Curbishley. Tell her what she can expect on the first day and reassure her that everything will be fine, even fun. Tell her not to be afraid to approach the teacher with any questions. "It's very helpful for one or both parents to come in and meet the teacher on the first day," says Curbishley.

learn that we're really interested in what they do during school hours and, as a result, they become more interested themselves.

Sharron McDonald, *Springdale, Arizona*

Chaperone Rules

After serving as a chaperone for many of my daughters' field trips, I am now equipped with my own set of rules. First, I make colored name tags for each of the students, since it's easier to see a color than a name or a face from a distance. I bring extra snacks, sandwiches, and drinks for kids who may have forgotten theirs. When I first have my group together, I pair everyone up with a buddy so they don't wander away without anyone noticing. I tell them the times when we will be taking bathroom and snack breaks. And finally, I order them to have fun!

Lynette Kittle, *Hilo, Hawaii*

rough days

Too Sick for School?

When my daughter was in kindergarten, she suddenly started playing sick during the school day. So, I told her the story about the little boy who cried wolf, and I explained that if you lie about something enough, people will eventually stop believing you. Fairly soon after, I received another call from the school nurse. I asked that my daughter be put on the phone, and I reminded her of that little boy. I told the nurse that unless my daughter was running a temperature or vomiting, she should stay put. Realizing that she wouldn't get to come home, she didn't play sick again.

Brenda Gautreaux, *Houma, Louisiana*

Quick Cure

When one of my three kids claims to be sick and I really don't believe that it's true, I remind him or her of what the day at home will consist of: no television, no games, no outside play, and plenty of boring rest. With all the fun taken out of the day, they can't stand being home and usually start to feel much better in a matter of seconds!

Julie Menghini, *Pittsburg, Kansas*

Parent-Teacher Powwow

As a teacher and parent, I've learned that going in to have a friendly conversation with your child's teacher can do wonders for the relationship between the two of them. If the child sees the two adults getting along, he'll feel more comfortable and be able to trust his teacher. That's why I go into the classroom during school hours at the start of each school year and again intermittently throughout the year—especially if problems come up.

Deborah Beaucaire, *East Bridgewater, Massachusetts*

Communication Is Key

When I started getting reports from my son's teacher that he was being disruptive in class and not completing his homework, we developed a team approach to improve his behavior. I spoke with her at school and on the phone every week until we saw some progress. We asked my son to bring home a homework schedule each day, which I'd review, sign, and then

when is your child ready for kindergarten?

Generally, kids should only be enrolled in kindergarten when they meet the age requirements for the school district. But if you must err on one side or the other, it's better to enroll a child who's a bit younger rather than a bit older than his classmates.

If your child is the youngest in the class because of a late birthday, his teachers can work with him to address any problems that arise from the age difference. "There's a lot of variability in kindergarten-age children, and schools should be able to accommodate individual differences," says Barbara Willer, spokesperson for the National Association for the Education of Young Children.

Holding your child back so that he has some kind of age advantage may only backfire. One study reported that 19 percent of students who were old for their grade had behavior problems during their adolescent years—possibly because they were bored or somehow considered different by their peers.

A child's first days at a brand-new school can be quite stressful, especially if you have moved recently and she doesn't know any other children yet. To ease her anxiety, "acquaint your child with school as early as possible," advises Lindsey Bergman, Ph.D., associate director of the UCLA Child and Adolescent Anxiety Program.

Go into the school, take a tour, and visit her new classroom so that she'll know where she's going and not get completely lost on her first day. If possible, call the school and find out the names and contact information of some of her classmates. Then, you can try to set up playdates so that your child will see some friendly faces when she walks into the classroom on day one.

return. Once my son understood that he couldn't pit one of us against the other, he started to get into line.

Diana Berry, *Smithfield, Kentucky*

teaching tools for home

Unforgettable Fortune Cookies

When my daughters were in elementary school, they would often bring home vocabulary and spelling lists. Sitting down each week to review them with me became a chore for them, so I decided to make it a little more fun. I found an easy recipe for fortune cookies and mixed a batch up. Then, I wrote their spelling and vocabulary words (complete with definitions on the reverse sides) on small pieces of paper. Finally, I folded and baked the papers right into the cookies. My kids had such a great time learning their words that we'd do it as a special treat every couple of months.

Sharian Fulper, *Glen Gardner, New Jersey*

Edible ABCs

I used to have a hard time getting my 4-year-old son, Alec, to eat his breakfast. He loves trains, so I decided to make "fun pancakes" by using a turkey baster to draw train shapes with the batter. I'll even mix in some letters and have Alec

pediatrician on call

heavy-backpack hazards

It seems like kids these days carry everything but the kitchen sink in their backpacks. Could such a heavy load harm your child?

"It won't hurt her posture, but it can definitely cause muscle strain and pain in her shoulders and back," says pediatrician and *Parents* contributing editor Laura Nathanson, M.D. Here are her tips for helping your child carry her books safely.

Step on the scale. Experts say that a child shouldn't carry more than about 15 percent of her body weight. So, if your child weighs 50 pounds, her pack should be 7 pounds or less. (Weigh her with the pack on and then without it to figure out how heavy the pack is.)

Make sure that she wears both straps. Slinging the bag over one shoulder puts too much strain on her joints. Make sure that the bag is properly adjusted as well, so that the bottom of it falls just above your child's waist and the top is no higher than her upper shoulder blades.

Trim the load. Have your child go through her pack weekly to see whether there are books she can leave at school, sweaters or sneakers she doesn't need, or toys she can live without.

spell out the words that go with the shapes. He doesn't realize that he's practicing his ABCs, and even better, he eats every last bite.

Dolly Boliver, *Rochester, Minnesota*

storing school creations

Display All That Artwork

My 4-year-old daughter creates a lot of artwork at preschool, and we needed a simple way to display it. I threaded small binder clips onto a piece of clothesline and secured the clothesline to the wall with small screws. It's easy to change the artwork as new drawings come in, and Kaylee is able to show off a lot more of her creations.

Kimberly Emerson, *Cardiff by the Sea, California*

Holiday Handouts

My three kids bring home plenty of artwork. My husband and I like to have at least one piece of artwork from them on the refrigerator at all times, but we were never sure what to do with the rest. Then, I thought up the idea of using them as presents. I sit down with the kids before holidays, we decide which friend or relative is going to receive which picture, and we cut out cardboard frames for each drawing. The kids love the project, and the relatives like the presentation and effort we put into each gift.

Janine Leaver, Califon, New Jersey

Art by Mail

Here's another thing to do with all the wonderful artwork that your children bring home from school. We place all the pic-

10 preschool number games

1. Sing counting songs, such as "This Old Man," "The Ants Go Marching," and "(We're Gonna) Rock around the Clock."

2. Practice chants and rhymes, such as "One, two, buckle my shoe" and "One potato, two potato."

3. Count things everywhere you go, including cars, cans, people, and signs.

4. Do body math by helping your child count how many eyes, ears, toes, elbows, or teeth she has.

5. Point out numbers on everyday objects such as signs, license plates, and calendars.

6. Provide blocks as play toys—and as great examples of size, area, space, dimension, and shape.

7. Encourage categorization by telling your child to place objects in groups by certain characteristics, such as color, shape, and size.

8. Teach your child how to use a ruler, and ask for her assistance in measuring any number of household objects.

9. Bake together: It's a great time to discuss measurements, amounts, and numbers required for ingredients, and the sizes of the bowls and baking sheets.

10. Play classics such as "go fish," dominoes, and number-guessing games in which you give hints as to whether the number is "higher" or "lower" than the one your child says.

1. Time management: Show your child how to make a list, broken down into her different assignments, and decide how much time each task warrants. Set a final deadline each night for when her homework needs to be done.

2. Organization: Help her figure out which organizational system works best for her (pencil box or pouch, folder or binder), and establish routines based around homework time.

3. Focus: Encourage short breaks after every 15 or 20 minutes of homework so that she can maintain her energy and attention span. Allow her to decide how she works best—sitting at a desk in a totally quiet room or sitting on the floor with quiet music in the background.

tures in a huge wicker basket in our daughter's bedroom, and whenever we send letters or packages to family and friends, we ask our daughter to choose the perfect masterpiece to include in the mailing. She enjoys letting us know exactly which drawing Grandma would love to receive.

Guy Stehley, *Libertyville, Illinois*

Recycling Dioramas

My son Matthew is continuously making dioramas for his various school projects. But each time he makes one, the project that he has put hours of hard work into is returned home, placed on a shelf, and left to gather dust—never to be looked at by Matthew again. One day, I noticed my younger son, Brett, pointing curiously at Matthew's most recent diorama on different kinds of snakes. I had Matthew give a short presentation of his project to Brett, and then, after asking for Matthew's okay, I removed any tiny pieces and handed it to Brett. He played with that diorama until it fell apart.

Bonnie Smith, *Lebanon Township, New Jersey*

tips and tactics

Get Ready in a Snap

To help my preschooler get his act together in the morning, we clipped pictures of all the things he needs to put on to get ready, plus a picture of a bed (to remind him to make his!). We also included a label from a jar of peanut butter, his morning fare. We affixed each picture to a piece of poster board and called it "Joshua Is Ready." Each morning, my son consults his list so that he knows what he has to do.

Kathy Baer, *Oswego, New York*

Picture Perfect

Several days a week, I pick up my daughter, Sarah, from kindergarten; on the other days, she takes the bus. To eliminate confusion, I cut out one picture of a school bus and another of a minivan and glued them onto separate index cards. Each morning, she slips the appropriate card into her backpack to remind her.

Jacqueline Kremer, *Bozrah, Connecticut*

Guess What, Mom!

My 3-year-old started preschool this year, and I always want to know what she does during her day. It's hard for her to remember all the activities, so we play a guessing game on our drive home from school. I start by guessing something that she did that day. (She's always impressed when I get it right.) Then, it's her turn to guess something that I did, and so on. We both feel good about sharing our new experiences together.

Susan Hamburger, *Cedar Grove, New Jersey*

Cooperative Carpooling

We joined a baby-sitting co-op with 14 other families, spread over three elementary schools. There's always someone who can do a pickup from school and a playdate. The best part: It doesn't cost a cent.

Deborah Hartwick, *Vancouver, Canada*

star strategy
stylish stars

Three actors recall their most memorable first-day-of-school outfits.

"I remember fighting my mom the first day of kindergarten. She wanted to put me in short overalls, and I wanted to wear long pants. I was very upset because I was ready to be a man. I didn't win the argument."

—**Thomas Gibson,**
of Dharma and Greg

"We had a dress code in high school: a tie, a collared shirt, and a jacket. So I wore a tie with a Lacoste shirt instead of a button-down oxford. I just wanted to be comfortable."

—**David Duchovny,**
of The X-Files

"The first day of third grade, I wore a brand-new pair of white flat shoes with a buckle that fastened behind the heel so they could be worn as slip-ons. They made me feel like a grown-up."

—**Cheryl Ladd,** *TV movie star*

fantastic crafts and holiday fun

29

is your refrigerator a rotating art gallery on which you proudly display your child's artwork? Do your kids look forward to decorating your front door at Halloween or making ornaments at Christmas?

Doing arts and crafts is a great way for families to spend time together. As your child cuts, pounds, spreads, and presses materials like paper, paint, and clay, he'll also stretch his creative muscles, develop important motor skills, and boost his self-esteem. Studies on schools with arts-rich programs have even shown that students who take art classes test better in other subjects.

In this chapter, we'll show you dozens of ways to expand your child's creativity. We've gathered fantastic ideas for setting up a crafts corner in your home, transforming everyday household items into works of art, making great holiday projects, teaching your kids to sew, and more.

less-mess crafting

Marker Cap Holder

I grew tired of losing the caps to my children's markers, so I created a unique holder for them. I poured plaster of paris into a tuna can and pushed the caps into it until just the opening was visible. Then, I let it harden for about 30 minutes. Now, the caps stay in one spot and my kids can just push the markers into them.

Alice Harding, Lemoore, California

Sticky Situation

My 3-year-old loves using glue when she makes crafts, but I can't stand the mess. So, I put some glue into an empty baby food jar and give her a paintbrush. Painting the glue on is easier than squirting it, and it makes much less of a mess.

Tami Grundy, Inver Grove Heights, Minnesota

think outside the box

To open up new horizons for your kids, have them try these twists on favorite craft projects, courtesy of Carol Scheffler, mother of three and arts and crafts editor of *Parents* magazine.

If your kids like to draw pictures: Give them markers and a piece of paper cut into a circle. Watch how a shape other than a rectangle unleashes their creativity.

If your kids like to fingerpaint: Mix equal parts shaving cream and white glue, add a few drops of color, and let them sculpt on paper with the mixture. It retains its dimension when it dries.

If your kids like to thread beads: Let them put pony beads (or any small bead with a good-size hole) onto pipe cleaners. They can twist them into all sorts of shapes.

If your kids like to cut paper: Fold strips of paper accordion-style and have the kids cut along the folds with decorative scissors. Unfold the paper to reveal lacy patterns.

If your kids like to play with puzzles: Cut out pictures of people and animals from magazines. Cut the heads and legs off of the bodies and tell your kids to reassemble them any way they like.

Pudding Paint

Our 1-year-old daughter wanted to paint with her older sister, but I was worried that she'd try to eat the paint. Not wanting her to miss the fun, we gave her a pudding cup and let her fingerpaint with the pudding. It worked perfectly: She had fun, and I didn't have to worry if she had a taste while she worked.

Jennifer Von Bergen, Welches, Oregon

Dough Play

We discovered a great alternative to fingerpaint: pizza dough! My kids and I made a batch and added food coloring. It's thicker and easier to work with than gooey fingerpaint. They love creating unique pictures by smearing it onto paper.

Donna Naggar, Fort Polk, Louisiana

Mess Mat

My two sons, ages 5 and 2, love making things with modeling clay. But I hate the ground-in mess they leave on our carpet. To eliminate this cleanup hassle, I use an old plastic shower curtain for a mat. The boys know to keep their cutters, rolling pins, and other tools—as well as the clay itself—on the mat. When the boys are done, we shake out the curtain and store it in the closet.

Chris Lightner, Smethport, Pennsylvania

Art Table

We set up a permanent arts and crafts table at our house that we stock with crayons, markers, paints and brushes, paper, coloring books, stickers, and clay. Our 4-year-old, Cally, loves painting and coloring and goes to the table whenever she's feeling creative. It also saves me the hassle of constant cleanup and gives me peace of mind that there won't be messes all over the house.

Denise Gustafson, Valley Springs, California

No More Paint Wars

When my two preschoolers began painting with brushes, they would fight over the containers and colors. Now, I put four colors of their choice on each side of a muffin pan. They set it between them and have their own sides. It's a breeze to rinse and reuse, too.

Sheryl Butterfield, Dallas

Tray Smart

Instead of throwing away the trays that Lunchables come in, I found a great way to recycle them: using them as paint palettes. The trays are shallow enough that my two young children can get the paint out of them. When they're finished, I put the trays in a resealable bag and save them for next time.

Kathe Ingle, *Mooresville, North Carolina*

Just Dishy

My two daughters love to fingerpaint, but it can be such a hassle to clean. To keep things tidy, I let them use the inside of the dishwasher door as a painting surface. It saves paper and cleans up with the next load of dishes.

Juliette Saunders, *Fullerton, California*

Smear-Free Handprints

We wanted to preserve our baby's handprints but didn't want to use ink to stamp them into his baby book. Instead, we took two pictures: one with Parker's hand in mine and the other with his hand in his dad's hand. The photos look great and are a lasting reminder of how tiny our son once was.

Leigh Davis, *Des Moines, Iowa*

cheap and chic recycling

Magnetic Gifts

My daughters came up with a fun gift to make from frozen-juice lids: magnet art. They each glue their picture in the center of a lid and arrange petals cut out of construction paper around the edges. They attach a magnet to the back, and voilà!

Amy Shearer, *Hillsboro, Oregon*

Clothes Call

Many of my 3½-year-old daughter's clothes are covered with impossible-to-remove stains. I didn't want to throw them away since they still fit her, so I started letting her paint them.

---

most popular projects for kids

1. Drawing and painting
2. Beading and making jewelry
3. Folding and cutting paper
4. Rubber stamping
5. Making candles

SOURCE: American Hobby Association

Whenever a solid white or light-colored shirt becomes too stained to wear, I sit her down with fabric paints and let her draw away. She loves wearing her creations, and the activity gives her a great artistic outlet.

Kathryn Presnell, Boone, North Carolina

Framed!

While my daughter and I were playing with Lego blocks one day, I discovered that I could use them to make great picture frames. Just attach the blocks to create a rectangle that's two blocks thick and the size of a 4-by-6 or 5-by-7 photo. Then, use a glue gun to fasten the blocks together securely. The pieces come in both primary and pastel colors, so I can customize the frames to match a room.

Kim George, Petaluma, California

Crayon Cooking

I turn my child's broken crayons into giant rainbow crayons. I spray a muffin tin with nonstick cooking spray, and I peel the paper wrapping off the crayon bits and place them in the tin.

sew much fun

You can teach children as young as 7 the basics of sewing by hand; once they reach 10 or 11, they're old enough to use a sewing machine. Here are some tips on getting started.

✓ Involve him from the beginning. Let your child pick out fabrics and trims at the store. This will stimulate creativity and teach him about different textures.

✓ Focus on fun. Teach your child not to expect straight stitches at first. He'll have his share of knotted threads and crooked lines, which are all part of the learning process.

✓ Review equipment and safety. Talk about the safe way to handle needles, pins, and scissors. If your child will be using a sewing machine, make sure that he knows how to turn it off and how to keep his fingers out of the way of the needle.

✓ Start with an easy project. Practice sewing lines, circles, and squares drawn on paper. Good beginning projects include sewing a patch on a T-shirt or jeans, or making a drawstring tote bag, a pillow sham, or a Christmas stocking.

crafts for all ages

What are appropriate crafts for toddlers? At what age can kids start using scissors or be trusted with paint? We asked Cindy Groom-Harry, an elementary art teacher in Ireton, Iowa, and author of 40 how-to books on making crafts with kids, for the scoop.

Age (years)	Materials	Projects
2	Precut paper, paste	Collages
3	Washable paints and markers, chalk, play clay with fun tools	Painting, drawing, sculpting
4	Scissors	Cutting along lines, paper chains
5 and 6	Icing, charcoal pencils, fabric scraps, yarn	Cake decorating, textured rubbings of leaves, weaving and braiding
7 and up	Yarn, special paints with glitter, blank journals	Crocheting and knitting, decorating T-shirts, scrapbooking

Then, I heat the crayons in a warm oven (200° to 250°F) until they've completely melted, and I let them cool overnight.

Karma Bombe, *Laguna Beach, California*

Pillow Power

When you've gathered a pile of clothes that no longer fit your child, turn them into a gigantic pillow. Sew together two rectangular pieces of fabric, leaving one end open. Then, stuff the old clothes in and sew up the end. Use it as a decoration or as a "kid catcher" at the end of the bed to cushion any falls. When you have your next baby, just cut one end and take out the clothes.

Cheryl Borowski, *Toms River, New Jersey*

Thrifty Solution

My 5-year-old daughter loves to play dress-up. But the dress-up clothes sold in toy stores can be very expensive and often don't hold up well. So, I began to shop at thrift stores, where I found things such as bridesmaids' dresses for as little as a dollar each. My daughter loves the dresses and thinks that she's the belle of the ball when she wears them.

Allison Uehling, Glenside, Pennsylvania

Card Trick

Instead of throwing away birthday and holiday cards, my 3-year-old daughter and I make puppets out of them. We simply cut out the animal, flower, or cute ornament on the cover and glue it onto craft sticks. She loves playing with them. They also store easily in a shoe box.

Josephine Romano, Rocky Point, New York

Safer Sandbox

Our 16-month-old son loves to play in the sandbox in our yard, so, in the winter, we decided to make one for his room. Instead of sand, we used rice and beans. We poured them into a big plastic tub and added some sandbox toys such as shovels and trucks. When he's had enough, we simply push it under his bed.

Susan Biffinger, East Granby, Connecticut

creative christmas projects

A Tree for Tots

Rather than put up just one big Christmas tree for the family last year, we added a small cedar tree for our children. They spent hours making their own decorations for it out of magazine pictures, wrapping paper, and ribbon, and they strung popcorn on it too. On Christmas morning, they had a ball handing out presents from under their own tree.

Cathy Bates, Blue Ridge, Texas

Snow Smiles

If there's snow at Christmastime, my kids enjoy making "tree faces." We pat snow on the tree trunks to make eyes, eyebrows, noses, and mouths and create various expressions. Their creations stay intact while it remains cold, and our holiday guests are greeted with smiling faces.

Dawn Ulmer Morrison, Fulton, Michigan

Book of Carols

Last Christmas, my 3-year-old daughter kept asking me to sing carols to her. The only problem? I didn't know all of the words. So, I typed up her favorite hymns and songs on our computer. We printed the songs, decorated each page with cutouts from Christmas cards, and put them inside page protectors in a binder. Now, Mallory loves looking through the songbook and following along when I sing to her.

Cassie Felch, Laurel, Maryland

Double-Duty Gifts

My mom has an early-December birthday, so my three daughters made her a Christmas-tree skirt. On one side, it has a Christmas print, and the other has their handprints. Grandma loves her unique gift.

Tracy Nickelson, Winters, California

Foiled Again

My 2-year-old son, Spencer, loves to help me wrap gifts, but he gets frustrated that he can't do it himself. I figured out an easy way for him to wrap his own small gifts: with aluminum foil. Now, he has no trouble wrapping boxes, and it stays in place without tape. Spencer then decorates the foil with holiday stickers. The best part is that I can get my wrapping done at the same time!

Heidi Douglas, Gainesville, Florida

Picture-Perfect Ornaments

We always receive photo greeting cards from friends and relatives during the holiday season. Instead of filing them away, I turn the cards into little ornaments. I cut them into different shapes, adorn them with glitter and trim, and attach a ribbon to the top. We keep some for next year's tree and return others to the senders as keepsake gifts.

Helen Murdock–Prep, Huntington, New York

hearts and crafts for valentine's day

There are so many ways to say "I love you." Here are some favorites from *Parents* magazine.

The "I Love You" frame: Create a conversation piece for photos by gluing candy hearts onto a wooden picture frame. Even a young child can paint the frame pink and glue on the candies.

Heartfelt cushions: Cut out two hearts of felt in pink and purple. Sew or glue the edges together, leaving a small hole along one edge for inserting cotton balls. Fill with cotton and decorate by piping on a message or a design with fabric paint.

Rosy glasses: Decorate a pair of kids' sunglasses with rhinestones and faux jewels. Use tacky glue and squeeze paint to attach the charming details. Let the glasses dry overnight before wearing them.

Recipes from the heart: Turn a wooden recipe box into a decorative file filled with favorite family recipes. Paint the box red with acrylic paints. When it's dry, add heart-shaped paper cutouts using Mod-Podge sealer.

Love is in the air: Catch the breeze with a wind sock. Cut a 6-inch by 12-inch rectangle from a piece of craft foam (available at craft stores), roll it into a tube, and staple the edges together. Decorate it with small purple and pink pom-pom balls, and tape strips of crepe paper streamers to the bottom. Punch two holes on opposite sides at the top, and attach a string for hanging.

1. Roll foam rectangle into tube and staple.

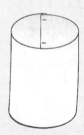

2. Stapled edge

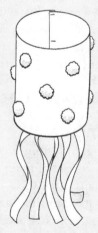

3. Attach pom-pom balls and streamers.

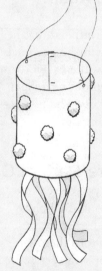

4. Punch hole in opposite sides of top to attach string.

Hearts and flowers: An oversize tissue-paper flower is one way to show your never-fading love. Take three sheets of red or pink tissue paper and cut them in half. Stack the six sheets on top of each other and use pinking shears to trim all of the edges. Gather in the center and fluff into a flower. Wrap green pipe cleaners around the base for the stem.

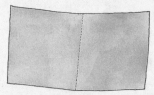

1. Cut tissue paper in half.

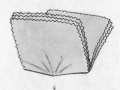

2. Stack all pieces, and trim edges with pinking shears. (side view)

3. Grab stack at middle and pull middle down through opposite hand. Twist gathered sheets to create stem base.

4. Fluff out sheets into flower. Attach one pipe cleaner at stem base; use another to make a leaf.

Book of love: Fold several small sheets of white paper between red or purple construction paper. Punch holes along the folded side and stitch it together with red yarn or twine. Inside, add pictures and messages from friends and loved ones.

You've got mail: Make a little mailbox just for your valentines. Using scissors or a craft knife, carefully cut a slit in the top of a shoe box. Then, wrap the box and its lid in red wrapping paper. Add a label with your name on it, and use the box to store special cards and letters.

Making Snowflakes

We create a winter wonderland in our own home by making paper snowflakes. Just fold a square piece of paper in half and then into quarters. Next, fold diagonally so you have a triangle shape and round off the side where no folds are showing so that you have a cone shape. Then, cut little triangles and squiggles from all the edges, and cut off the tip. When you unfold this, you'll have a snowflake—and as in nature, no two will be the same.

Beth Murphy, Wilmington, Delaware

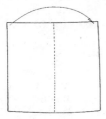
1. Fold square sheet.

2. Fold again.

3. Fold on a diagonal.

4. Cut open end so it's rounded.

5. Cut out little shapes along edges, then cut off tip.

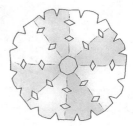
6. Open up into a snowflake.

valentine's day fun

A Heartwarming Treasure Hunt

My 4-year-old son loves treasure hunts, so, on Valentine's morning, I left a trail of Hershey's Kisses from his bed to the breakfast table. There, we shared heart-shaped pancakes before I had him look under his plate for the next clue. At the end of the trail, my son found a ticket to spend the next Saturday with me doing whatever he wanted. We had a great time at the roller rink. It was the perfect way to make Valentine's Day fun last a little bit longer.

Stacey Faubion, Indianapolis

Can-Do

My 4-month-old son was too young to make a gift for his grandparents, so I made one from an empty formula can. First, I removed the paper. Then, I painted it red, for Valentine's Day. I added hearts and dots with a permanent marker and wrote, "I love my Grandma and Grandpa." I stuck a Styrofoam ball inside and inserted fake flowers in the ball. They loved it and can use it every year. It's easy to change colors and themes with the seasons and specific holidays.

Alisa Nachtigal,
Chamberlain, South Carolina

other holidays

Easter Bunny Sacks

I use a small, white paper bag (bakery bags are ideal) to create an adorable bunny sack for Easter treats. To make one, keep the bag folded and mark a big V starting about an inch from the top corners and ending one-third of the way down. Cut out the V with scissors and you will see the bunny ears. Use markers and scrap paper to make the bunny's face and whiskers. Glue a cotton ball on the back of the bag and you have a bunny. We fill ours with Easter grass and goodies.

Nancy Jeager, Stillwater, Oklahoma

Father's Day Keepsake

To help my 5-year-old better understand the meaning of Father's Day, I had her draw a picture and write, "I love you because. . . ." Then, I asked her to name things she loves about her dad and things she'd like to do with him. I wrote down her answers, which ranged from "because you're silly and you make me laugh" to "because you're teaching me how to play baseball." She gained a greater appreciation for all that her dad does, and he received a treasured keepsake on his special day.

Kelly King Alexander, Baton Rouge, Louisiana

Thanksgiving Leaf Book

When we know which family members won't make it to Thanksgiving, we make them a special book. We collect colorful autumn leaves from the canyon where we live and press them in a book. Then, we take pictures of our children in seasonal locations such as a pumpkin patch or a pile of leaves. When the pressed leaves have dried, we glue them into a small booklet with the photographs and send them off. Our children love making these, and our relatives feel closer as a result.

Tara Stenhoff, Logan, Utah

summer crafts

Bigger Bubbles

To create giant, inexpensive bubble wands, just cut out the centers of plastic tub lids (from margarine containers), place

---

it's my job

teaching music to young children

For more than 30 years, Karin Warner of Newburgh, New York, has been teaching violin to kids as young as 3 years old. We asked her for her advice on getting kids interested in playing a new instrument.

✓ Listen to the pros. "From the beginning, I encourage my students and their parents to listen to recordings of classical music in general, as well as recordings of the piece they are going to play," she says. "I start my students out with nursery rhymes, folk songs, and baroque melodies."

✓ Get involved. Like other subjects, music has homework. Parents need to become the home teacher and practice together with the child.

✓ Play games. You can adapt "Simon says" and even some board games to teach music. Reward charts with stickers are another great way to motivate young children.

✓ Take recitals seriously. Children learn poise and self-confidence when there is an audience. They love to show what they have learned to proud parents and grandparents.

bubble solution in a bowl, dip the rims in, and wave the wands through the air. Kids love them!

Lori Maunsell, *Calgary, Alberta, Canada*

Shell Surprise
When we go on vacation, our daughter loves to collect shells. Not knowing what to do with all of them, I decided to mix them in with the sand in her sandbox. She loves rediscovering her hidden treasures.

Dawn Neuberger, *Lake Mills, Wisconsin*

Water "Colors"
When I'm outdoors barbecuing or gardening, I give my 3-year-old son a bucket of water and a paintbrush and set him up along a wall of our house. He then paints along the foundation, bricks, and siding. He also enjoys attacking the patio furniture with his brush.

Lisa Petsche, *Stoney Creek, Ontario, Canada*

living in a high-tech world

30

turn off the TV and go outside!"

Sound like something you've said before? If you're like most parents, you have a love-hate relationship with the television . . . and the computer . . . and the video game console. On one hand, they're great forms of entertainment— and these days, they can be very educational if you help your kids make smart choices. But too much of any one of them can make your child less social, cut into his homework time, squelch his creativity, and even affect his health.

Making peace with multimedia can be a challenge, but the great tips in this chapter will help you do just that. From setting limits on TV time to choosing quality kids' Web sites, you'll learn how your family can get the most from today's technology.

setting limits

Must-Read TV

My 9-year-old son loves playing video games, so we worked out a trade-off system to limit the amount of time that he spends playing and to encourage him to read. Each school day, he's allowed to play Nintendo for 30 minutes, but in return, he must read for 30 minutes. If he reads for an additional amount of time, it gets added to the next day's playing time, or he can save it for the weekend.

Ashley DeWitte, Roeland Park, Kansas

Let Each Child Choose a Show

We're pretty strict about TV during the school week. My kids can each choose a half-hour show a night, and it's usually on

it's my job

choosing a good TV show for your kids

Allison Joseph, project coordinator for the Children's Television Workshop (the creator of *Sesame Street*) in New York City, knows what it takes to keep kids entertained while they learn. We asked her what makes a quality kids' TV show.

- ✓ It's diverse. The cast should be multiracial or include characters with disabilities or kids living in different parts of the country. It's important for children to be exposed to people who do—and don't—look like them.

- ✓ It teaches well. Some children learn visually, and some learn by repeating concepts out loud. The program should teach in more than one way. "For example, on *Sesame Street*, they may flash the big letter *A* but then may also have a song about it. Repetition is important since it reinforces ideas and concepts," Joseph says.

- ✓ It boosts imagination. The show should include plenty of storytelling and fantasy.

- ✓ It helps kids overcome fear. "*Sesame Street* knows that kids are afraid of monsters. The Muppets have shown kids that monsters aren't always scary—that sometimes, they're just like you or me," says Joseph.

Nickelodeon. I only let them watch shows that I've seen, so I know that the content is appropriate. On weekends, we're usually too busy for TV, but sometimes on Saturday nights we'll rent a video for them.

Linda Fears, Chappaqua, New York

Monkey See, Monkey Do

I found that the best way to keep my five kids from watching television is to not watch it myself. On school nights, I keep the television off after 5:30 P.M.—no exceptions. It's too tempting for them to sneak a peek while trying to do their homework, and it's very unfair for me to expect them to be doing work when I'm not setting a good example.

Judith Heckman, Englewood, Ohio

Certificates for Success

My 7-year-old son got into the habit of watching too much television. To help him learn to better budget his time, I created TV-time coupons. Each week, I give Derek coupons that are each worth a half-hour of television. Every time he wants to watch TV, he has to give me one. When he runs out of coupons, that's it for the week. The coupons have worked well: We don't argue about the television, and Derek has learned how to save his coupons for things he really wants to watch.

Christine Payne, North Hills, California

Timing Is Everything

My 9- and 5-year-old boys love playing video games, but I don't let them play for more than an hour each day. To save me the hassle of reminding them that their hour is up, I use the sleep timer on the television. The TV automatically turns off after 60 minutes, and it even warns them when time is running out, so that they can save their game.

Patty Shirey, Womelsdorf, Pennsylvania

A Puzzling Distraction

My 3-year-old son had come to prefer watching TV to doing just about anything else. To break him of this habit, I created a new routine. I told him that he had to put a puzzle or two together before he could turn on the television. Within a

TV health alert

Can watching too much TV make your child sick? Well, not exactly, but it can compromise his health. Here's the latest.

Babies and TV: The American Academy of Pediatrics discourages parents from letting children under the age of 2 stare at the tube. Although the brightly colored shapes and movements are intriguing, babies learn more from interacting with their peers, parents, and siblings, and watching television is too passive an activity to encourage learning. If you do need to distract a little one for a few minutes while you're doing a task nearby, make sure that what you choose isn't too loud or jarring.

Sleep problems: If your child is having trouble falling asleep or staying alert in school, too much TV may be the culprit. One report found that children who watch a lot of television—especially close to bedtime or on a set in their bedroom—are more likely to resist going to bed, have trouble falling asleep, wake up during the night, and sleep less overall. Some TV is fine, but don't make it part of your child's bedtime routine. Leave 20 minutes of downtime for reading, talking, or taking a bath.

week and a half, he was actually looking forward to doing the puzzles and would even remind me about it. Within a month, he had become a puzzle master!

Kathryn Berg, Woodbury, Minnesota

quality shows and games

Make It a Family Outing

I go with my kids to the video store when they want to buy a new game. We spend about an hour trying out the games, reading the covers, and narrowing our selections to the one perfect game. That way, I know that the game will be both fun and appropriate.

Tony Aiello, San Ramon, California

Get with the Program

When choosing television programs for my kids, I usually watch the show first. I figure that if I get upset, they will, too. I also make sure to read up on shows in magazines and ask about them at my son's day care. When it comes to limiting their

Parents' favorite kid videos

For Toddlers

Are You My Mother?

Babe

Barney's Great Adventure

Bugs Bunny Classics

The Jungle Book

Lady and the Tramp

The Robert McCloskey Library

Snoopy Come Home

For Preschoolers

The Adventures of Milo and Otis

Aladdin

The Brave Little Toaster

Charlotte's Web

Lady and the Tramp

The Land Before Time

The Mouse and the Motorcycle

Preschool Power (Jacket Flips and Other Tips)

Road Construction Ahead

viewing time, I usually let them know in advance how much time they have, but I don't tell them in minutes. Instead, I say, "We're stopping after the next commercial."

Jen Salberg, *Denville, New Jersey*

Gentle Viewing

I always look for gentle programs when choosing what my daughter can watch. Usually, anything on PBS is great, and we never miss *Teletubbies* or *Dragon Tales*.

Rebecca Delatorre,
Port Angeles, Washington

Bookish Endeavors

I approve of any TV show derived from a book series, such as Arthur or Little Bear. But if there's a program that our daughter really wants to watch, and we're not sure, I usually ask her friends' parents first what they think of it. If they seem to be okay with it, then my daughter and I sit down together to watch it the first time. We talk about any questionable behavior that comes up, and then I ask her if she thinks that she should continue watching it. I am proud of her whenever she tells me that she turned off a television program because it wasn't right for her.

Stephanie Caputo,
Oceanport, New Jersey

Interactive Programming

I love children's shows where the main character really interacts with the child. For example, I definitely allow my son to watch *Blue's Clues* because Steve is always so involved with the children on the show. Usually, instead of just turning on the television, I pop in a *Blue's Clues* video either in the morning

pediatrician on call

computer health tips

Even if your child uses the computer just for games, adult-size equipment can force him into poor posture. Easy adjustment can reduce his risk of neck, shoulder, and back strain. We asked pediatrician and *Parents* contributing editor Laura Nathanson, M.D., for advice on helping your child sit healthier.

✓ The top of the computer screen should be at eye level and 18 to 26 inches away. If necessary, have your child sit on a phone book.

✓ Keep the mouse within easy reach and level with the keyboard.

✓ Encourage stretching breaks every 20 to 30 minutes.

✓ Support his feet with a pile of books, a backpack, or a footrest.

✓ Support his lower back with a rolled-up towel.

or in the evening, but I try to keep total viewing time to 2 hours a day maximum.

Pam Mortensen, *Pocatello, Idaho*

Scary News Flashes

I try to limit the amount of offensive language or violence my kids are exposed to on TV, and that includes the evening news, which can be just as violent as any movie. But if my kids mistakenly see something disturbing on television, we always make sure to discuss it afterward.

JoAnn Glenn-Lewin, *Camden, Delaware*

carefree computing

Mousing Around

To keep our 16-month-old son happy while his 3-year-old brother is using the computer, we give him a spare, unconnected mouse and a mouse pad to use. He clicks on it right along with his older brother, as if he were playing, too.

This also works great when I'm using the computer. It makes computer time a much more enjoyable experience for the whole family.

Deanne Jones, Charleroi, Pennsylvania

Don't Make It a Habit

My 4-year-old loves playing on the computer, and it used to be very difficult to get him to stop. What has helped me is that he now stays with his grandma during the day while I'm at work, and she doesn't have a computer—or a VCR, for that matter! He's learned how to keep himself busy without it, and at night, between dinner, bathtime, and bedtime, we're able to limit his computer time to an acceptable amount.

Jaymey Boston, Goodman, Montana

it's my job

picking out the perfect computer program

There are lots of excellent software programs for kids, says Ellen Wolock, managing editor of *Children's Software Review* in Flemington, New Jersey. Although store shelves are stocked with over 1,000 new kids' titles each year, looking for these four important features will help you choose the right one.

1. Instant gratification. When an image or word is selected on-screen, the related activity should snap to life. The best programs don't make children wait.

2. Simplicity. Even very young children should be able to navigate the program by themselves. If the software is designed for nonreaders, for example, the menu should consist of pictures rather than words.

3. Fun design. A great program automatically adjusts to the child's ability level, making the learning experience neither too easy nor too hard. The content should also change as your child progresses so that enthusiasm doesn't turn to frustration.

4. Variety. Components of the game should change each time kids play. Math or reading programs should present fresh problems to solve, and adventure games need to offer new mysteries.

creative technology

Play It Again, Mom!

My 3-year-old daughter's favorite videos are musicals, but since she is too young to appreciate the entire movie, she generally watches only the songs. She was constantly asking me to find specific songs, which was time-consuming. So, using a second VCR, I copied all her favorite songs and scenes onto her own videotape. Now, she can play *Rachel's Favorite Songs* to her heart's content! As a result, we are both less frustrated, and she has learned the lyrics to many Broadway songs as well!

Terri Gross, Commack, New York

Be a Borrower

My 3-year-old son gets fixated on one video for weeks at a time, but then he's ready to move on. To save money, I borrow videos about his favorite subject, trucks, from the library. After 2 weeks, the video is due back and he's ready for a new one.

Catherine Ley, Chicago

cyber tots

In this increasingly technological age, are you worried that your toddler or preschooler isn't keeping up with the Joneses.com? Though you shouldn't expect your child to be an expert Web surfer just yet, she can learn a lot from the latest educational software. Here are answers to your frequently asked questions.

What's the best age to begin? Whenever she seems interested. Pop a kiddie CD-ROM into the computer and start playing yourself. Your child will probably be curious and want to join in.

Which software is appropriate? For your toddler, look for titles that introduce such basic concepts as distinguishing and matching colors, shapes, sizes, and sounds. A preschooler may be able to handle more sophisticated puzzles and games.

How long should I let her play? Thirty minutes max, though she'll probably lose interest before then.

Madonna

"To be plopped in front of a television instead of being read to or talked to or encouraged to interact with other human beings is a huge mistake. I think limiting Lourdes's TV time shows her that I love her, because it's me reading or talking with her instead."

—*pop star and mother of Lourdes*

Friendlier Flying

Thanks to my husband's ingenuity, our first airplane trip with our 17-month-old son was a breeze. Using our camcorder's VCR adapter and two VCRs, he recorded several of Skyler's favorite videos onto cassettes. Then, we played them back on the camera's internal screen throughout the 6-hour flight. It made the flight go faster—and more smoothly—for all of us.

Laura Fortgang, *Verona, New Jersey*

Easy-Access Videos

I record all of my sons' favorite TV shows, but I have trouble figuring out which program they want to watch. To make it easier to find the right one, I put stickers of a character from each show on the tapes. My sons can now choose the videos on their own.

Julie Saltman, *Peoria, Arizona*

family-friendly web sites

Surf the Internet with your child and you'll discover new ideas and explore parts of the world you've never seen, all with the click of a button. Try these *Parents*-tested Web sites.

✓ www.discovery.com. Read up on interesting science news, and take a sneak peek at various animals, from sea otters to bats.

✓ www.muppetworld.com. Get up close and personal with Miss Piggy and Kermit at this exciting Henson site.

✓ www.mamamedia.com. Kids will love the variety of activities, from sending an electronic card to playing a game.

✓ www.homeworkcentral.com. If your little scholar is stuck on his school assignment, make sure to check out this Web site. It even gives parents tips for helping kids study more effectively.

Make Her the Star

When my 2-year-old daughter goes to a babysitter's house, I don't want her to feel far away from her mommy and daddy. So, we put a series of home videos onto a VCR tape for our daughter to take along with her. She loves watching herself on TV, and the movies of her family and friends help her feel more at home.

Jennifer Thesing, San Jose, California

all in the family

finding a
great caregiver

31

Choosing child care for your baby is one of the most important decisions you'll make as a new parent. And even if your children are preschoolers or older, you still want to be absolutely sure that they're in good hands while you're at work—or at the movies on a Saturday night.

There are many factors that you need to consider when deciding what type of care will work best for you. But whether you're looking for a day care center, a nanny, or a teen sitter from the neighborhood, taking the time and effort to weigh your options carefully will be well worth it in the long run, both for your peace of mind and for your child's well-being. Although many parents say that going with your gut instinct is the best way to choose a caregiver, the following tips from moms and dads who've been there will make your decision less daunting.

be a day care detective

Careful Observation
If you like a certain center, visit more than once. Try to go during a morning dropoff or afternoon pickup time, and also after the kids are settled in. It's helpful to see how caregivers greet each child, as well as how they play with them.

Nancy Burrows, Corpus Christi, Texas

Stick to a Schedule
A day care class should have a daily and/or weekly schedule, even for babies, because consistency is important. When you visit, check the schedule to see if they're actually following it. Caregivers aren't always on time, but they should keep to the schedule as much as possible. If your child is older, knowing what goes on in school also gives you details so that you can talk about his day.

Tracie Beidman, Miami

day care safety checklist

When you visit prospective day care centers or family day care homes, look for the following things:

- ✓ Clean toys in good condition with no sharp edges
- ✓ Diapering area separate from children's play areas
- ✓ Perishable food refrigerated
- ✓ Cleaning supplies and other toxic materials in locked cabinet
- ✓ Easily accessible first-aid kit and posted emergency numbers
- ✓ Electrical outlets covered with protective caps
- ✓ Security gates at top and bottom of stairs
- ✓ Window guards on all windows except designated fire exits
- ✓ Smoke alarms and fire extinguishers
- ✓ All outside play areas enclosed; soft surfaces under all equipment
- ✓ An emergency evacuation plan

an expert's tip for picking a center

Faith Wohl, president of the Child Care Action Campaign, a nonprofit advocacy organization in New York City, is a pro when it comes to finding a great day care center. Her smartest tip? "When you observe children playing in a center, focus on one child instead of all of them at once. This will give you a better sense of what your child's experience might be like. Ask yourself: 'How busy is that child?' 'How does he interact with others?' 'Who comes to help when he needs it?'"

Another Pair of Eyes

To find the best day care, I visited 10 different centers in my area. Since my husband was working, I took a friend with me so that I could see things from two different perspectives. That way, I knew that I wouldn't miss anything.

Jennifer Salberg, *Denville, New Jersey*

Safe and Sound

A day care center should always have good security. My son's center always has someone at the office desk, which is in front of the building. In order to enter, we must punch in a code, which is changed about three times a year.

Carrie Augustine, *Dublin, Ohio*

Listen Up

Pay attention to how noisy a center is. If it's too loud, the caregivers may not be able to control the kids. On the other hand, if it's too quiet, the kids may not have enough to do.

Elizabeth Melican,
Stamford, Connecticut

recommended ratios

In order to assure that your child receives the attention and supervision he needs at a day care center, there should be one caregiver for every:

✓ 3 or 4 infants or toddlers

✓ 4 to 6 2-year-olds

✓ 7 to 8 3- or 4-year-olds

✓ 8 to 10 5-year-olds

The Doctors' Choice

Investigate whether a local hospital has its own child care center. The providers at these centers are often particularly well-trained. They usually give preference to hospital employees, but there may be extra spaces.

Bonnie Bratt, *Providence, Rhode Island*

family day care you can trust

Location, Location

I found an at-home caregiver who lived close to my office, so that I could go to her house and breastfeed my son during my lunch break.

Kerry Moore, *Centerville, Indiana*

Parents' ideal interview questions

When meeting with day care directors or caregivers, don't be afraid to ask as many questions as you need to in order to feel comfortable. It's a good idea to have a written list with you so that you don't forget a key query.

At a Day Care Center

✓ Do caregivers have first-aid/CPR and child development training?

✓ Is each child assigned to a primary caregiver?

✓ How many children do you serve, and what are their ages?

✓ What is the range of activities in which the children participate?

✓ How large is the center? (There should be 35 square feet per child in order for each child to have enough room to play comfortably.)

✓ Is the center licensed?

✓ What happens if I need to bring my child early or pick him up late?

✓ Do you let kids attend if they're not potty-trained or if they have a runny nose or a cough?

✓ How do you discipline kids?

✓ Is there an outside play area? Do kids use it every day?

✓ Do you ever take children on outings off-site?

Senior Sense

I had to go back to work 6 weeks after my daughter was born. What helped me most was to find a licensed, experienced, grandmotherly woman who watched my daughter in her home. I considered her to be less of a babysitter and more of my partner, and she considered herself to be another grandmother to my daughter.

Kathy Walker, Oklahoma City

Neatness Counts, But . . .

Of course you want to find a home that's clean, but if a caregiver's home looks too perfect, she might spend more time cleaning than playing with the kids in her care.

Virginia Weeks, Dayton, Ohio

✓ Will I be charged if I take a vacation or my child is sick?

✓ Will you let me know if my child has had a bad day for any reason?

At a Family Day Care

✓ How long have you been providing care?

✓ Do you have first-aid/CPR and child development training?

✓ Do you have a current state license or registration?

✓ How many children do you care for? What are their ages?

✓ Do you care for the same group of kids every day?

✓ What is a typical day like for the children? How much time do they spend outside?

✓ What meals and supplies do I need to provide?

✓ Can I drop my child off early or pick him up late sometimes?

✓ Can you give me an example of how you discipline children?

✓ What happens if you are ill?

✓ If my child gets sick, would you give him medication?

✓ If my child misses a day, do I still have to pay?

✓ Do you let children watch TV?

Who's at Home?

If the provider has a child of her own, look to see whether he or she is well-behaved. And bear in mind that if her child seems unhappy, he might try to take attention away from your child.

Stacy Cummings, Long Beach, New York

nanny know-how

Be Age-Appropriate

Make sure that a babysitter has experience taking care of kids who are the same age as your child. The demands of taking care of a school-age child, for example, are very different from taking care of a toddler. If a woman has only taken care of babies, it's possible that she might want to look for another job once your baby grows up.

Diane Debrovner, New York City

Creative Questions

When you interview a caregiver, ask her what she would do in various hypothetical situations, such as: your child refuses to eat; your child falls and hits his head; a storm hits and your child is afraid of thunder and lightning. The way she answers these types of questions can be very enlightening.

Marcy Johnson, Edison, New Jersey

Mom to the Rescue

I would love to be a stay-at-home mom, but I knew that we could not survive financially without my income. What helped me was having my mother take care of the children in my home while I worked. I knew that if I couldn't be with them, she was the next best thing.

Lorie Rogers, Dyer, Indiana

grandmother knows best

Local newspapers and community bulletin boards often have advertisements placed by nannies who are looking for jobs. Look for ads that were written by a nanny's former employer. They often say something like "We no longer need our loving, responsible babysitter who has taken care of our children for 5 years" and offer their phone number to call as a reference. That's how my daughter found a great babysitter she knew she could trust. When another parent takes the time and effort to help her nanny find a new position, you know that the woman is an excellent caregiver.

Patricia Bruder,
New York City

helping your child settle in

It may take a week or so for a toddler or preschooler to get used to his new surroundings. Here's a day-by-day guide to making a smooth transition, from Diane Lusk of the Meeting House Childcare Center in Newton, Massachusetts.

First morning: Come prepared to stay until lunchtime. Then, take your child home and give him lunch and a nap there before returning.

Second morning: Stay for an hour or so, leave for a brief time, then return. Take your child home before lunch again. You're showing him that this is a place that people leave and come back to.

Third morning: Stay for about 45 minutes in the morning; leave; then return when your child will be waking up from his nap, and take him home.

Fourth morning: Let him get settled, then say goodbye. If he fusses when you leave, ask for the caregiver's help. Your child may be upset for a few minutes, but by now, he will be familiar enough with the day care center that he will rebound quickly.

Chore Conversation

Before you hire her, talk to your potential sitter about which specific household chores you expect her to do. Will she just be responsible for picking up after the children and keeping the kitchen neat? Do you also want her to do laundry or occasional vacuuming or ironing when the kids are napping? If you make it very clear from the start, there will be fewer misunderstandings on both sides later on.

Dan Lawler, Brooklyn, New York

making the transition

Familiar Faces

To help our 22-month-old daughter, Nicole, adjust to her new day care center, we visited a few weeks prior to her first day and asked her future caregivers to pose for a photo with her. We then displayed the pictures on our refrigerator and pointed them out to our daughter on a regular basis. By the time Nicole

sitter do's and don'ts

Here are some great tips to help you have a better working relationship with your full-time in-home babysitter.

Do compliment her work or praise her for handling a difficult situation with aplomb; she takes pride in her job.

Do give her an annual tip at the holidays (1 week's salary is standard).

Do offer to pay her carfare to get home when she works late.

Do give her major holidays off when you don't have to work.

Do give her a raise after a year.

Do make sure that there's food in the house for lunch that she likes to eat.

Don't ask her to do chores that you haven't agreed upon from the start, such as walking the dog.

Don't drop hints when she's done something that upsets you; be honest about the situation.

Don't come home late without letting her know in advance.

Don't expect that she'll be a gourmet cook.

Don't expect that she's free to work on the weekends if you need her to.

Don't expect that your live-in nanny is on duty all the time.

started day care, she was familiar with Miss Vicki and Miss Ginny, which made the transition a little bit easier for all of us.

MaryAnn Billmeyer, *St. Louis*

Preventing Morning Mayhem

I pack of all of my daughter's things for day care and my bag for work the night before, so that all I have to do in the morning is pick up a couple of bags and go. The last thing you want to do is run around like a crazy woman when you are already stressed about leaving your baby. You can spend the time you save giving extra attention to your child before you go.

Michelle DeBlois, *Greene, Maine*

Look on the Bright Side

I felt guilty about going back to work after 5 months home with my baby. Then, I decided to change my attitude. I began to view my return to work as a chance to reconnect with the adult world, which I had missed. I also thought that it would be a good experience for my son to be with other children. My son is now 1 year old, and he's a wonderfully social child.

Amy Miller, *Buffalo*

missing the kids

In Your Heart

I wear a locket with my children's pictures in it. That way, they're always close to me, and I can take a peek at their adorable faces anytime.

Gloria Pantell, *Howard Beach, New York*

Baby Mouse

I took a favorite photo of my daughter and had it made into a mouse pad at a local photo store. I work at the computer all day, so it's a constant reminder of her.

Lisa Skyer, *Overland Park, Kansas*

Lunch Dates

I asked my babysitter to bring my baby and my 3-year-old to meet me for lunch once a week. These midday reunions help all of us cope.

Jane Pianetto, *Barrington, Illinois*

it's my job

finding a great teen sitter

Many responsible teen sitters have completed the Babysitter's Training course offered by local chapters of the Red Cross, says Sarah Lang, director of training at the American Red Cross in Greater New York. The 8- to 11-hour course covers CPR, first-aid, diapering and feeding, bedtime issues, and safe and age-appropriate toys and games.

Although the Red Cross won't give out names of teens who have completed the course, they'll probably give you the names of babysitter instructors, who may have suggestions about reliable sitters, says Lang. If you have already found a teen sitter who came highly recommended, you might offer to pay her to take the course, or pay her a higher hourly rate upon completion.

Dropping By

It was helpful for me to drop by our son's day care center in the middle of the day whenever possible, just to reassure myself that we chose the best center. My husband stops by occasionally, too. This way, we know that our son is comfortable and happy with his caregivers.

Marcie Roberts, *Cape Girardeau, Missouri*

it's my job

what babysitters wish they could tell you

We asked experienced high school babysitters what their biggest gripe is with their neighborhood clients.

"Make sure to tell each child his bedtime in front of the babysitter so that the kids can't argue about it later."

—Ofra Paul, 13

"Don't ask a babysitter to bathe your child. It's uncomfortable for both the child and the sitter."

—Hanna Hopfinger, 15

"Tell your kids to clean up their toys before they go to bed. And don't ask me to make sure that they clean their room. I can't even clean my own room."

—Dan Goren, 15

"Don't let your kids eat junk food when the babysitter comes. If they eat stuff that's loaded with sugar, it's impossible to get them to go to sleep an hour later."

—Dvora Gaultieri, 13

"Come home at the time you promise. Especially on a school night, it's not fair to the sitter to come in late. And if you are late, pay the sitter for the extra time—not everyone does that."

—Kate Hebert, 17

"Make it clear to your children that the babysitter is in charge. After parents leave, there are some kids who think they can get away with anything."

—Arielle Bloom, 15

saturday night sitters

Network with Teens

Make friends with teens who attend your church or synagogue. I try to start a conversation with some of the girls while my three kids are right there, so that the girls can meet them and see what they're like. Then, I eventually get around to asking if they ever babysit and take down their names and numbers.

Casey Hirsch, Merion, Pennsylvania

Don't Ban Boys

A teenage boy is the only one who can keep up with my three sons, ages 4, 8, and 10. We use a 15-year-old boy who plays soccer and baseball with them in the yard. He knows all about the video games they play, and he doesn't seem to mind their squabbling as much as some of the girl babysitters.

Sara Rapuano, Penn Valley, Pennsylvania

Pay Fairly

I found a great babysitter once who was working in a local toy store. But she was making $7 an hour in the toy store, so I had to match her wage to entice her away. Older kids have lots of activities—after-school sports and part-time jobs. You have to make babysitting an attractive option.

Wendy Beizer, Scarsdale, New York

smart strategies
for working moms

balancing work and family is one of the greatest challenges facing parents today. Now, more than ever, parents want to spend more time with their kids and be satisfied with their careers.

No matter how much you enjoy your job, it's hard not to feel guilty about time spent away from your kids. And every working parent—whether full-time or part-time—has experienced the mad race to get ready in the morning and the inevitable exhaustion at night. In this chapter, we'll offer you ways to cope with everything from figuring out your benefits package to connecting with your kids during the day.

kid-friendly jobs

Write Away

I've created a successful home-based business that produces newsletters and provides word processing services. I'm at home with my 2½-year-old and 6-month-old, and I have a new career that I really like.

Rondi Oldham, *Kennewick, Washington*

Make Child Care Your Career

Start a state-licensed day care center. I did, and now I'm able to stay at home with my children, be my own boss, and set my own hours. Call your local department of social services for licensing information.

Rhena Groters, *Grand Rapids, Michigan*

Phone It In

My boss agreed to telecommuting and provided me with a computer, modem, and fax. I work as an executive assistant from home 2 days a week, and I'm in the office 3 days. My husband works 10 hours 4 days a week, which means that our daughter only needs care 2 days a week.

Kathie Turner,
Upper Marlboro, Maryland

Share and Share Alike

Request a job share. I now work as a secretary 2 days one week and 3 the next. This arrangement allowed me to keep my insurance and half my salary—and spend more time with my child.

Karen Sharp, *Liverpool, New York*

star strategy

Cindy Crawford

"To help strike a balance between work and caring for my new son, I've rearranged my priorities. I'm still going to act and model, but my number one job now is being a mom. I also want to make life easier and more convenient for working moms everywhere, so I've recently launched Cindy's Corner, a monthly column of fashion tips, beauty tips, and baby product recommendations on www.babystyle.com."

—supermodel and mother of Presley Walker

mommy, why do you work?

No question conjures up more confusion—or guilt. Here's how to explain to your child why work is such an important part of your life.

✓ Don't dodge the question. Talking to your child about your job teaches her about the roles of women, the value of contributing financially to your family, and the importance of getting recognition for doing something that you enjoy.

✓ Keep it simple. Explain just the basics. If you work in real estate, for example, tell your kids that you help people find houses and apartments for their families.

✓ Focus on the positive. Don't say things like "I get in trouble if I'm late." You don't want your child to feel that you're working against your will. An upbeat attitude will positively affect your child's feelings about work in the future.

✓ Talk about money. Tell your child that one of the reasons you work is to make money. Make sure, however, that the information is tempered with why you value your work. If you're a lawyer, for example, you could say, "I went to law school to learn how to help people when a crime is committed, and it makes me feel good to do that. I also like to make money so that we can have nice things."

maximize family time

Banish Stress

Don't waste precious hours on meals and housework; share dinner-making detail with your husband, and cook a lot of one-pot meals. To keep that "messy house stress" at bay, we hired a housekeeper to come in twice a month. Yes, it's yet another expense, but the time I gain with my son is worth it.

Liz Hobbs, *Signal Mountain, Tennessee*

Call a Time Out

In order to make sure that my husband and I have enough time to relax and reenergize while we deal with the challenges of work and parenthood, we created "bubble time" for when one of us needs a break. It's a 15-minute period when you can't be disturbed by your spouse, your children, or the ringing phone. It's been a great sanity preserver.

Susan Zenk, *Greeley, Colorado*

Clip Coupons

My kids felt that I was spending too much time at work. So, I gave them each a gift for Mother's Day: coupon books. Each one contained tickets redeemable for something special from me. Sometimes, it was dinner at their favorite restaurant or a trip to the movies; other times, it was homework help or reading a book together. The kids loved it, and it helped me reevaluate my priorities.

Judi Barnes, Plantation, Florida

Break for Lunch

As a stay-at-home dad, I'm always looking for ways for our family to spend more time together. My wife works an extra

it's my job

how to get more quality time with your family

Organization expert Stephanie Winston, author of *Getting Out from Under: Redefining Your Priorities in an Overwhelming World*, offers tips on how to stop wasting precious family time when you're balancing work and kids.

- ✓ Don't be a superparent. It's perfectly fine to ask your spouse and kids for help around the house so that you can spend more time together. Even a 4-year-old can fix himself a bowl of cereal, leaving your whole family time to have breakfast together.

- ✓ Just say no. You don't have to cook for every bake sale or attend every single PTA meeting. Volunteer for one activity that you love and spend the extra hours with your family.

- ✓ Leave work at work. If you must bring work home, don't do it during family time. Ignore the phone and e-mail until your children are asleep.

- ✓ Give up on perfectionism. Your bed doesn't have to be made every morning. Tomorrow, leave the sheets in a pile and read your child a story before school instead.

- ✓ Remember that time is money. Think about how long certain chores, such as raking leaves or washing the car, would take—and how much it would cost to hire the kid down the block to do it. Think about which is the bigger bargain.

half-hour each day so that she can come home for a 90-minute lunch break and squeeze in some extra family time. My 6-month-old and I also take lots of outings (hiking, trips to the park) to help make the days easier and more fun.

George Bond, Rahway, New Jersey

stay close during the workday

Say Cheese

Help your child see you during the day by laminating family photos that he can play with safely. After all, your desk at work is probably full of photos of him, so why shouldn't he have some of you at home?

Jackie Beaupre, Pembroke, Ontario, Canada

Phone Home

Keep in touch, even by just calling your child once a day. As he gets older, leave notes in silly places (such as the refrigerator) or prepare heart-shaped sandwiches for lunch. Your nanny can help by talking about you and pointing out photos.

Pam Weiss, Danbury, Connecticut

Get the Ball Rolling

Start an activity that your caregiver can continue, so you can share in the fun. We bake cutout cookies with our sons in the evening, and they frost them the next day with our caregiver. I start building a block tower or playing their favorite music before I leave for work, so I'm part of the activity that begins their day.

Peggy A. Laughlin, Waterford, Pennsylvania

Family Secrets

Don't miss those firsts. We asked our caregivers not to tell us if our daughter took a step or said a word under their care. Then, if she does it again later, it's a first for us.

Mindie Taylor, New Eagle, Pennsylvania

Keep a Record

You don't have to miss a precious moment of your child's day, even if you can't be there in person. Have your caregiver keep a journal of the day's events for you to read when you return

managing maternity leave

Getting ready for your new baby can be stressful enough without having to worry about the technicalities of your maternity leave. Claudia St. John, a health care and group benefits consultant for William M. Mercer, an employee benefits consulting company, recommends the following steps for a smooth transition.

Study the policy. Some companies offer leave as its own benefit; others count it as short-term disability. This will have a direct impact on the length of time you're allowed to take. You'll also need to find out how much of your salary you'll receive: Some companies offer full compensation; others provide none.

Discuss benefits. Ask whether or not you'll accrue vacation time, and whether you must pay premiums on your medical, dental, and life insurance while you're away.

Decide on a return date. If you plan on changing your work arrangements—you'd like to switch to a job share after the birth of your baby, for example—discuss these options with your employer and put the terms in writing.

Get organized. Before you go, leave your desk as neat as possible and leave written instructions for your replacement. E-mail your contacts to let them know that you'll be away, and let them know who they can speak to in your absence.

from work. As your child gets older, he can add pictures or notes.

Sherry K. Markwell, Plainfield, Illinois

Share a Story

While struggling to juggle my career and my family, I came up with this idea for when I wasn't home. I took my children's favorite books and recorded the stories on cassette tapes. Then, I glued an envelope onto the back of each book and placed the corresponding tape inside. When the children popped a tape into the recorder, they heard my voice telling them the story. This seemed to ease the pain of separation and gave me some peace of mind at the same time.

Sherry Lavender, Weatherford, Texas

dealing with guilt

Shed Your Doubts

Don't feel guilty if you can't stay home. I felt awful when I first returned to work after my daughter was born, but I realize now that it is the best thing for our family. We are able to give her more, and she enjoys spending the extra time with both sets of grandparents, who help care for her. (And she speaks three languages as a result!)

Dimitra Kanellopoulos, *Laval, Quebec, Canada*

Go Part-Time

I took a part-time job because I missed working, and I enrolled my son in preschool. We're both happier: I'm not responsible for him all day, I can keep up with my computer skills, I have more time with adults, and my son loves school. Now, I have more patience when I'm with him.

Karen Willis, *San Marino, California*

make flextime work for you

A growing number of companies offer flextime: flexible work arrangements that allow parents to share jobs, work from home part-time, or telecommute. Here are tips to think about if you're considering a flextime work arrangement.

✓ Assess whether you have the right temperament to share work or work from home. If you have trouble delegating responsibilities, need control over your own projects, or are easily distracted, it might not work for you.

✓ Ask yourself whether you can create a good working environment in your home. Will you have enough space and privacy? Can you make the proper child care arrangements?

✓ If you're considering a job share, find a suitable partner to share your duties, and make sure that you work well together before you commit to the arrangement.

✓ If your flexible work arrangement requires that you cut some hours from your job, ask about how your pay and benefits will be distributed. You may need to change your insurance policy.

when dad stays home

Lend a Hand
I help out around the house, just as I would expect my husband to if I were the at-home parent. Marriage is a partnership; it doesn't matter which member of the team works outside the home.

Denise Sharrow, Drexel Hill, Pennsylvania

Get a Reality Check
When I'm about to give my husband advice, I ask myself, "Are the children safe? Are their needs being met?" If the answer is yes (which it almost always is), I keep quiet.

Ann Feltch, Newtown, Connecticut

creative scheduling

Be an Early Bird
I work from 7:30 A.M. to 1:30 P.M. This way, I can spend afternoons and evenings with my daughter. To me, it feels like the best of both worlds.

Deb Kramer, La Crosse, Wisconsin

Timing Is Everything
My husband works days and I work nights, so one of us is always home with our 5-month-old daughter. We don't see each other as much as we'd like, but the time we do have together is that much more precious. I earn more money working the night shift, too.

Kerri Clark, Duluth, Georgia

Work around Their Schedule
I work a 3:00-to-11:00 shift. That way, I'm home to see my daughter off to school and to greet her when she gets home. I'm also able to prepare dinner during the day, so I know that she's getting a nutritious meal.

Judy Fox, Sarasota, Florida

bone up on your benefits package

Does your benefits plan work for your family? Here are some things to look for.

Health care: Low premiums aren't necessarily a bargain. If you choose an HMO, your trusted family doctor may not be in the network, so find out how much it will cost to go outside the plan. If you're planning to have more children, review your prenatal coverage; many HMOs limit hospital choices, which has a direct affect on services such as delivery procedures. Ask, too, about preventive care, such as well-baby visits. Some plans offer them for free, while others don't cover them at all.

Time off: If parental leave is in your future, find out about your company's short-term disability policy, which is typically how paid leave is funded. The Family Medical Leave Act provides 12 weeks of unpaid leave for employees of large companies, but only a few states offer paid family leave. Many employers offer their own paid leave benefits, however, so ask about them.

Child care: Though companies aren't required to give you time off to care for a child with the flu, some will make an occasional exception, so ask about your company's unofficial policy. Many companies also allow you to set aside up to $5,000 in a pretax flexible spending account for child care, which could save you thousands. But the money must be used by the end of the calendar year.

back-to-work tactics

Do a Practice Run

I took my baby to her babysitter for half-days 2 weeks prior to my return to work. This helped me adjust to the separation from my daughter and helped her get comfortable with her babysitter in small doses. I also practiced getting ready for work with her. These strategies helped the transition go well for both of us.

Kristi Martin, Kingwood, Texas

Use Your Benefits

I work for an advertising agency that has an on-site day care center for employees. To aid in the transition from maternity leave to full-time working mom, my company lets us spend 1 hour per day in the center during business hours. I check in on my son and get a good snuggle in when things get stressed. I find that I don't miss my son when I'm not with him because I know that I can pop in on him whenever I want.

Cammy Wagner, Phoenix

Start Early

I arranged for our daytime nanny to start 1 week early. It helped her learn my parenting style and assured me that we had hired a caring person. In addition, I scheduled needed doctor, dentist, and hairdresser appointments for myself, and shopped for some work clothes that fit my postpregnancy size. It was a wonderful way to transition back to work with a minimum of hassle, and to test out our child care arrangement.

Nancy Durie, New York City

taking your kids to work

Is it okay to occasionally tote your tot to work? Yes, if you follow some commonsense rules, says Paula Dubeck of the Kunz Center for the Study of Work and Family at the University of Cincinnati.

✓ Set aside a day when nothing is pressing, or one that's typically slow, such as Friday. Then ask your boss and alert any coworkers who need to know before you take your child in.

✓ Don't expect a high-productivity day. Even the most self-possessed child won't be able to amuse herself for long stretches, and toddlers and infants will need your full attention. Ideally, your child should stay with you for only half a day.

✓ If your child is a preschooler or older, set some ground rules before you go. Start off by saying, "I know you'll do a great job acting like a big girl at my office." Then, let her know that she can't run around or speak in a loud voice.

✓ Pack a bag full of snacks, drinks, and quiet playthings such as coloring books or picture books. Make work fun by having your child sharpen pencils, sort paper, or deliver messages.

making
family
time count

33

every parent wants to create memories and traditions that her child will cherish in years to come. But when every day seems to be a never-ending round of diapers, laundry, cooking, and errands, it can be hard to find the time and energy for another item on the agenda. The best solution is to make memorable moments for your children out of simple, ordinary events. Whether it's building a fort on a Saturday morning, calling Grandma out of the blue just to say hi, or having a pretend tea party, it's the little things that stick with children and end up being the most meaningful. Read on for creative advice on how to sneak some of those special bonding moments into your daily routine.

finding the time

Special Delivery

I work 3 evenings a week as a registered nurse, so on those days, I'm not home when my 8-year-old son, Corey, gets out of school. To help him feel closer to me, we've worked out a letter system. After school, he writes me a note either on paper or on the chalkboard in his room. When I come in late to check on him, I read his letter and find out about his day. I always write back, and when he wakes up in the morning, he reads what I've written. The letters help us stay connected, and they also give Corey a chance to practice his reading and writing skills.

Debra Landry, Forrestdale, Massachusetts

Perfect Picnics

I wanted my 1- and 3-year-old sons to see more of their father, who has to work a lot and always felt that he was missing out on their development. As a solution, we started lunchtime family picnics. The boys and I make lunch, then pick up Dad at his office and head to the park to eat. Not only is it a great stress reliever for my husband, but the kids also really enjoy spending this time with him. And they're usually so worn out afterward from running around that they take a nice, long nap!

Michelle Graack, Carlsbad, California

Dinner Dates

My husband works during the day and I go to school at night, so we're not often home at the same time. Despite our hectic schedules, we try to have dinner with our four young kids every night. I know it might sound ordinary, but it's become a really special time for all of us. It's easier to deal with stress when I feel connected to my family.

Jennifer Reagan, Moline, Illinois

Snooze to Me

I work a graveyard shift, so I catch a nap when my baby wants to! He loves to lie on his back with his head burrowed into my side. I love it, too—it makes us both feel peaceful and close.

Angela Williams, Winston-Salem, North Carolina

building strong families

"Living in a family is about 90 percent chaos," says Donna Erickson, host of the TV program *Donna's Day* and a *Parents* magazine contributing editor. "The trick to spending quality time with your kids is finding a little order in the confusion." Here, Erickson offers ways for families to bond.

It's the little things. Kids remember the ordinary stuff, like playing catch with Mom or jumping in a pile of leaves together.

Take advantage of chore time. Include a child in your everyday routines: sorting socks, polishing the car, screwing in a lightbulb.

Seize the moment. Take time with your children to appreciate the joy and wonder in the world. Watch a sunset, smell a flower—it doesn't take much to make an ordinary day special.

Share what you love. You're an expert. Teach your special talent to your kids, whether that's cooking, gardening, knitting, or carpentry.

Learn from them. When it comes to parent-child relationships, learning is a two-way street. Have your children teach you how to inline skate, play with a yo-yo, or play hopscotch.

Make traditions matter. Family rituals are the line that connects us through generations. Bring out that heirloom candlestick or cook Grandma's special Yorkshire pudding recipe at least once a year. If you don't like the traditions you were raised with, create some new ones.

Lounge Lizards

When my daughter was an infant and I was on maternity leave, now and then I'd take a day off from doing the chores and just lounge around with her. That made it easier for me to feel fully focused on her and to discover who she was.

Sarah Mahoney, *Queens, New York*

family traditions

Antiquing Antics

My son, Jimmy, and I roam estate and tag sales every Saturday morning. It's great buddy time, and we've picked up some terrific furniture and toys.

Jeffrey Johnstone, *Wilmington, Massachusetts*

Treasure Hunt

My sister and I both have preschoolers who can't read, so we created a "treasure hunt" for them. For clues, we glued pictures from magazines onto cards: A photo of diapers led them to the baby's changing table, one of a toothbrush led them to the bathroom, and so on. At the end of the road, their treasure is foil-wrapped chocolate coins.

Sharron Lehnert, Kenosha, Wisconsin

Gone Fishing

My son, Davis, and I are learning how to fly-fish together. It's great for both of us to watch the other master something new and fun.

Tony Tilford, Driftwood, Texas

Tea for Two

My daughter and I dress up in my grandmother's old flowered hats and mink stoles and sit at her little table, where two dolls have donned their finest to join us for tea. The table is set with silver pieces that I inherited, and my daughter pours ice water or air tea—it doesn't matter; it's the ritual that counts.

Theresa Coronado, Denver

Barking up the Right Tree

My sons and I walk the dogs together. It's great exercise—for us and for the dogs—and there is something very relaxing and companionable about those walks.

Philip Perkins, Havana, Illinois

Manicure Moments

My daughter and I sit side by side at the beauty salon, getting manicures, two "ladies" being groomed and pampered for a while. And I let her pick whatever nail color she wants—it's usually something wild!

Michelle Schonauer, Larchmont, New York

grandmother knows best

I only get to see my 5-year-old grandson Buster a few times a year because he lives so far away. But we've come up with a creative way to keep in touch. I call it the ABC Postcard game. I started by sending him a postcard with a picture of an apple, which begins with the letter A. The next week, he sent me a postcard with a picture of a baseball, for the letter B, and so on, back and forth, until we get to Z. I can't wait to see what pictures he will pick out to send to me next, and when I visit him, we have a wonderful time looking back at all of the pictures we've sent each other. Not only is our game a special bond between us, it's also a great way to help him learn the alphabet!

Linda Baer,
Chicago

5 ways to connect with your kids

1. Crack open separate books and curl up to read side by side.
2. Leaf through old family albums, telling stories as you look at the pictures.
3. Act out the classic fairy tales.
4. Put on a CD and have a dancefest.
5. Lie on the grass and spot shapes in the clouds.

Training Them Well

Once a week, my 5-year-old son Mason and I go to a local park and ride the open-air minitrain. The engineers all know him by name, and they always let him start the ride by shouting "All aboard!"

Lisa Dillard, *Austin, Texas*

The Apple of His Eye

Every October, my son and I go to our favorite orchard to pick apples, then come home and make a pie together. He especially loves helping with the dough for the crust.

Ted Conklin, *Sag Harbor, New York*

☆ star strategy

Leeza Gibbons

"One thing I've learned is that when I'm home with my children, I'm truly with them. I'm not answering the phone, opening mail, or scurrying around. I listen to them not only with my ears but with my eyes as well."

—*talk show host and mother of Lexi, Troy, and Nathan*

Just My Style

My two oldest kids brush my hair for me every morning. It's relaxing for me, and it's a great time to talk.

Jerry Valley, *Galesville, Wisconsin*

Matinee Madness

Ever since the arrival of our new baby, my daughter and I go to the Saturday matinee at least every 2 weeks. We sit in the middle of the theater and share a soda and popcorn.

John Dillenbeck, *Orem, Utah*

Ride Share

After dinner most nights, I take one of my older kids for a bike ride. We go around the block a few times, enjoying our time together.

Gary Walz, Harvey, Louisiana

bad weather, good times

Picture Perfect

When it's too cold to go outside, my sons and I have our own photo shoots. They have a ball picking out themes, finding props, and going through wardrobe changes, and I wind up with some treasured photographs. A recent Winnie the Pooh shoot yielded such great pictures that we had them made into wallet-size photos to give to family and friends.

Julie Papin, Sainte Genevieve, Missouri

it's my job

Bill Nye on rainy day boredom busters

Inclement weather is the perfect time to conduct fun, easy science experiments, says Bill Nye the Science Guy, the popular kids' TV host. And your own home is teeming with natural wonders. Try these.

- ✓ Create a tidal wave in the bathtub. Go ahead and let your kids make a mess. Everything may get wet, but that's part of the fun.

- ✓ Look at all things big and small. Get out the magnifying glass or a microscope if you have one and look at dirt, a pencil point, even the face of a watch. This will help your children understand the exquisite detail of the universe.

- ✓ Discover your surroundings. Ask them questions about the world around them and encourage them to use resources such as the dictionary and the Internet to find the answers.

- ✓ Color your world. Use food dye to make rainbows, or investigate what happens when you mix colors.

Birthday Wishes

When my kids are restless and the weather outside is awful, I host an "un-birthday" party. I gather all the party hats, plates, napkins, noisemakers, and candles left over from previous birthday parties; then, I bake and decorate a cake, and we sing, "A very merry un-birthday to you. . . ." Sometimes, I even wrap small, inexpensive gifts for the kids to open. It's a great way to beat those bad-weather blues.

Mary Sullivan, Sunnyvale, California

Indoor Picnics

On cold, rainy days, when the kids can't go outside, I plan indoor family picnics. My three children, ages 4 to 8, love to spread out a sheet on the living room floor and dine on hot dogs, pretzels, and potato salad. It's a great way to liven up a dreary afternoon—and it allows me to spend some special time with my kids.

Adrienne Pakal, Petaluma, California

grandparents

The Greatest Gift

My son likes to make special gifts for his grandparents for birthdays and holidays. One of his favorites was a plain cotton tote bag that he decorated with his handprints (you just press them on with fabric paint). We added "Grandma's Bag" and my son's name at the bottom. He's looking forward to making some for other relatives this year.

Judy Bartels, La Porte, Indiana

Picture Pals

My 2-year-old daughter enrolled her faraway grandparents in her personal "Picture of the Month" club. We sent them a decorated 11- by 14-inch photo mat with magnetic strips on the back, labeled "Nicole's Picture of the Month." Once a month, our daughter mails a new

---

★ star strategy

Connie Selleca

"I try to give my children some of the love my parents gave me through their traditions. I put on Italian music, including a lot of Frank Sinatra, and cook up some spaghetti sauce from my mother's recipe."

—actress and mother of Gib and Prima

---

why traditions matter

"Rituals strengthen family bonds, and they also forge a link between the family you came from and the new one you're creating," says Robin Chernoff, M.D., director of the Family/Behavior Clinic at Johns Hopkins Children's Center, in Baltimore. In addition, they slow us down and help us focus on the here and now. More surprising is that traditions are also important for your child's development.

They create character. Whether you play charades every Sunday after dinner or act out your own game show for the video camera, your traditions create a unique family style, one that helps children form self-identity and shape their own characters.

They provide security. Just as babies thrive on daily routines, older children need the predictability of rituals. They find security in the familiar, which is especially important in times of stress or important transitions.

They foster maturity. Kids use rituals to mark their growth in the family. A child who watches a parent or older sibling hang a special ornament on the tree each year will feel very grown up and competent when she is old enough to take over that important task.

---

picture to her grandparents, which they proudly display in the frame on their refrigerator.

Karla Ethier, Huntington Beach, California

Hop on Pop-Pop

When my five grandchildren visit us at our beach house in the summer, I tell their parents to sleep in each morning and let the kids come wake me up early. We goof off together for a few hours on our own, bouncing on the bed, making pancakes, and playing games. My grandkids really look forward to their "mornings with Pop-Pop"—and so do I.

Traugott Lawler, Hamden, Connecticut

She's Got a New Album

To keep in touch with her grandchildren, my mother creates themed scrapbooks for them from old photographs and greeting cards. She's made books about the seasons, colors, holidays, and animals. My 18-month-old twins really enjoy looking through them.

Ellen Gardner, Aurora, Colorado

timesaving strategies

Ever wish that you could have just an hour more with your kids each day? Try these timesaving tactics.

✓ Set the table for breakfast the night before, after the kids go to sleep.

✓ Take the phone off the hook during meals.

✓ Hire a cleaning service. They're more affordable than you think, and they save you time and sanity.

✓ Tape your favorite TV shows and watch them after the kids have gone to sleep.

✓ Time your children's chores. Say, "Let's see if we can all make our beds within 15 minutes! Go!" The competition will leave less room for dawdling.

✓ Make a week of dinners on Sunday.

Nature Walks

I often take walks around the neighborhood with my 3-year-old daughter and 1½-year-old son. My daughter loves to collect treasures as we walk, such as stones, pinecones, twigs, and leaves. I didn't know what to do with all of her finds until we started making pictures with them using glue and construction paper. Now, she sends her creations as gifts to her grandparents.

Sarah Underwood, Battle Creek, Michigan

Grammy's Shopping Day

I have 11 grandchildren, and though I see them often in big groups, I rarely get to spend one-on-one time with any of them. So, each year at Christmas, I take each child, alone, on a shopping trip so that he can pick out a small gift for his parents. Afterward, we go for hot chocolate.

Mary Loftus, Nyack, New York

traveling
with kids

34

Some of a family's most treasured memories are made on vacations. But to ensure a relaxing and fun trip, you have got to budget well and make your plans ahead of time. You'll need to figure out everything from how to get all of your baby's gear in one car—or worse, one suitcase—to trying to keep a toddler entertained on a long journey.

The tips in this chapter offer practical advice on what to bring, where to go, and how to keep kids entertained.

before you go

Vacation Countdown

Our 3½-year-old son, Sean, was impatiently awaiting our vacation, but he doesn't have a good sense of time yet. So, we came up with a simple way to help him gauge how long it would be until we left. With 2 weeks to go, we made a poster with pictures of our destination (we cut them out of a brochure). Then, we crafted a chain of paper links, with one for each day until the trip. Each night, he removed one of the links, and we'd count how many days were left.

Kathleen Brown, *Westminster, Colorado*

Make a List and Check It Twice

When you're traveling with children, leaving an important item at home can be a major inconvenience. So, we created a master packing list of everything we need that we refer to when we pack for any trip.

Jacqueline Kremer, *Bozrah, Connecticut*

Simplify Packing

To pack for our recent vacation, we used 20-gallon hard rubber storage bins (like the kind Rubbermaid makes) for all

baby carrier buying tips

Soft baby carriers are great for traveling: They allow you to tote your baby on your back or in front of you, freeing up your hands so you can check out a map while sight-seeing or carry a suitcase in the airport. To buy a safe and comfortable carrier, follow these tips from consumer expert Sandy Jones, author of the *Consumer Reports Guide to Baby Products*.

✓ Test snaps and straps to make sure that they can't work loose. Buckles and belts should have backup security, such as plastic stops or double loops.

✓ Look for sturdy, washable fabric that won't scratch your baby's tender skin. Seams should be well-finished with double stitching at stress points.

✓ Read the manufacturer's age and weight recommendations.

✓ For your own comfort, choose a sling with a cushioned shoulder and neck, or a soft carrier with thick, padded straps and a strong waist belt.

of our clothes and toys. It eliminated suitcases in the car and made it much easier to pack and unpack.

Kimberly Klein, Somerville, New Jersey

The Suite-est Things

Always reserve a suite in a moderately priced hotel rather than a standard room in an expensive hotel. Not only will you enjoy a little privacy and be able to turn on the lights and TV whenever you want, but both you and your baby will also sleep better.

Marsha Stein, Sewickley, Pennsylvania

Crib Notes

If you are buying or borrowing a portable crib to take on vacation, put your baby to bed in it for a couple of nights before you leave to make sure he'll sleep in it.

Tori Gleiberman, Los Feliz, California

You Gotta Keep 'em Separated

With two children, we've learned the wisdom of packing each child's belongings in a different bag. That greatly cuts down on confusion—and fighting.

Lisa Findley, Cincinnati

don't leave home without it

Travel Light

I always pack a night-light in my luggage when I travel with my kids. If they awaken in a strange room, they're not as frightened when they can see where I am and get to me without stumbling around in the dark.

Marilyn Lawrence, *Monticello, Iowa*

Powder Plus

I always make sure to carry baby powder in my beach bag. After a day at the shore, I sprinkle the powder all over my 3-year-old daughter (and myself), and the sand brushes off like magic. No more uncomfortable, messy rides home.

Naomi Lamb, *Flushing, New York*

Stick to It

If you take along a stain remover stick, you can pack fewer clothes for yourself and your baby. It's the answer to chocolate ice cream, ketchup, and spit-up.

Bette Blau, *New York City*

is it safe to travel when you're pregnant?

Yes, if you take a few precautions, says Boston obstetrician Hope Ricciotti, M.D. Here are her four rules for a stress-free trip when you're expecting.

1. Travel during the second trimester. You'll be at lower risk of miscarriage and you won't have third-trimester discomfort from weight, back pain, and sheer exhaustion. If you have a high risk of preterm delivery or a history of pregnancy-induced hypertension, however, your doctor will likely advise you not to travel.

2. Avoid high-altitude destinations. The decreased oxygen levels may be harmful to your fetus. Thinner air can also make you dizzy, which increases your risk of falling.

3. Travel within the United States. This will ensure the best available medical care for you and your baby.

4. Stay close to home near the end. Do not travel farther than 2 hours from your hospital after 36 weeks, in case you go into labor.

Feedings on the Go

When we're staying at a hotel or visiting friends, high chairs aren't always available. Without someplace secure, it's hard to get my 1-year-old to sit still long enough to eat. Our solution: taking the swivel bath seat along. We suction it to a countertop or sturdy table. This makes for easy feeding and cleanup on the go. [Editor's note: Never leave your baby unattended while doing this.]

Kelli Jackson, Bessemer, Alabama

Keep Kids Cool—and Safe

When we head to the beach, we bring along an inflatable wading pool for our 3-year-old daughter. We fill it with water and put an umbrella over it. She has fun while staying close by, and the shade offers extra sun protection.

Pat Wood, Amsterdam, New York

Road Remedy

Bring along some ginger candy (available at stores that sell Asian foods). It helps when your child feels sick in the car or in flight.

Lily Hou, New York City

Sticky Situations

Always carry a roll of duct tape with you. It has helped us out more times than I can remember, repairing everything from a stroller handle or a ripped high chair seat to broken luggage at the airport.

Murray Lampert, Toronto, Canada

A Portable Bed

When we travel, we take along our pool raft to use as a toddler bed. The deflated raft and the pump fit easily into our suitcase. [Editor's note: Inflatable beds should not be used by children under 1 year old; they can increase the risk of sudden infant death syndrome (SIDS).]

Aleena Headrick, Waynesboro, Georgia

in-flight advice

Keep Little Travelers Busy

I've discovered that a disposable camera helps keep my children occupied while we wait for a flight; they especially enjoy taking pictures at the airport. It's also interesting for me to see what people and things they choose to photograph.

LaVonne Feigeles, *Montville, New Jersey*

Entertainment for Long Trips

When we fly, I worry about keeping my 2½-year-old daughter busy for such a long period of time. My husband suggested recording some of her favorite videos onto 8-millimeter tapes so that she could watch them on our camcorder's tiny video screen. She plugs her headphones into the camera, leaving us with nice, long stretches of quiet time.

Susan Russo, *Riverview, Florida*

Plane Games

We live abroad, so, when we travel, we have to prepare for very long plane trips. I pack a special surprise bag for each

---

it's my job

helping kids overcome airplane fears

"There are a lot of reasons why children are afraid to fly," says Carol Cott Gross, director of Travel and Fly without Fear, a self-help and education program in New York City. "Air turbulence can be very scary; many kids also become anxious because they've seen plane crashes on the news and in the movies." To ease your child's anxieties, Gross recommends the following tactics.

✓ Do some research beforehand. A child may fear airplanes because he doesn't understand how they operate. Together, look up the plane's configuration on Web sites such as Travelocity (www.travelocity.com) and read books about how planes fly. When you board, have your child meet the flight crew.

✓ Think positively. Help your child create a flight log that's illustrated with upbeat pictures, stories, and poems about the future journey. Picturing how happy he'll be onboard helps counteract "what if" worries.

✓ Change your attitude. Kids often pick up on their parents' fears. If you do things such as wear a lucky sweater when you fly, grip your seat tightly and squeeze your eyes shut when you take off, or breathe a sigh of relief when you land, you send a negative message to your child.

junior jet lag

Did you know that babies can suffer from jet lag, too? To help your little one adjust to changing times, try these tips.

✓ Slowly alter your baby's schedule to suit the new time zone. For example, if the time difference at your destination is 3 hours later, start moving naptimes, feedings, and bedtime from 7:00 P.M. to 10:00 P.M. 3 days before you leave, with a 1-hour increase each day.

✓ When you arrive at your destination, continue all the usual bedtime rituals, whether it's reading your baby a favorite story or letting him sleep with a beloved blankie.

✓ Give your baby a lot of light exposure in the morning, and keep lights dim in the evening.

child, containing snacks and individually wrapped games. We also take along glue sticks and scissors, since one of our favorite activities is cutting up magazines and making puppets out of the airsickness bags.

Ellen Shankman, Rehovot, Israel

Car Seat Saver

Most airlines have large, heavy-duty plastic bags for car seats that are checked as baggage. Ask for one at check-in to protect your car seat from inclement weather and dirty baggage carts.

Cindy Finsie, Newnan, Georgia

A Change Will Do You Good

Make sure that your carry-on has a spare T-shirt handy for every person who's traveling, in case of spills or accidents.

Robin Aronow, New York City

on the road again

Brainy Car Games

To help my 4-year-old son learn to identify letters and numbers, we play this license plate game while we're in the car. When he identifies all the letters and numbers on a

safe flying with a newborn

Before you book: Wait until your baby is at least 6 weeks old. Because of their immature immune systems, newborns are more vulnerable to germs from the plane's recirculated air.

When you book: Buy your baby his own ticket. Children under age 2 fly free when they sit on a parent's lap, but air turbulence injures or kills about 58 babies each year. The Federal Aviation Administration recommends securing a baby who weighs less than 40 pounds in a car seat.

After you board: Breast- or bottlefeed your baby during takeoff and landing. Changing air pressure during takeoff, landing, and climbing is the reason that ears pop. Give your baby a pacifier or a bottle or breastfeed him to prevent painful earaches.

license plate, he gets a point. After 12 points, he gets a prize—either an extra story at bedtime, a movie rental, or a snack treat.

Catherine Brown, Dallas

Picturing a Trip

Last year, we took our first family vacation with Amy, our 18-month-old daughter. It was a 4-hour car trip, and I wasn't sure how she would do. I made a photo album with pictures of suitcases, the belongings we would pack, photos from the hotel brochure, and the tourist sights we were going to see. Amy loved looking at it, and it helped her to be more comfortable with all the new situations.

Carol Phillips,
Egg Harbor Township, New Jersey

Window Dressing

When traveling on long car trips, I always bring along pressure-sensitive window decals (available at retail and classroom supply stores) that my kids can apply to the car windows. Since the stickers are removable, my kids can play and make new scenes again and again.

Amy Butler Barsanti,
Nags Head, North Carolina

Private Screenings

Keeping our children occupied during our 8-hour drive to Florida is quite a task. We invested in a small TV/VCR designed to be plugged into the cigarette lighter of a car, and we bought two sets of headphones so the kids can watch and listen quietly. To secure the TV, we strap it firmly between the front seats on the console. When we aren't traveling, I use the TV in the kitchen.

Kim Turner, Cordova, Tennessee

Edible Jewelry

Food always makes my 2-year-old happy on long trips. I take a length of licorice and string it with Froot Loops, Cheerios, and such. Then, I tie the licorice ends together, making a necklace or bracelet for him. Just be sure to have some wipes handy for a quick cleanup.

Laurie VanAnnan-Johnson, Duncan, South Carolina

Midnight Express

On long trips, we leave during the night so that our kids will sleep almost the entire trip. Traveling while it's dark also helps to ease my daughter's motion sickness.

Kelley Fultz, Terra Alta, West Virginia

Story Tapes

To make car trips with my 6-year-old daughter, Carolyn, more entertaining, we've recorded our own books-on-tape series. We chose books and then recorded the stories on cassette

friendly excursions

Traveling with another family can be a great way to share costs and good times, but it can also be the worst mistake you've ever made, says Nadine Nardi Davidson, author of *Travel with Others without Wishing They'd Stayed Home*. She recommends that you consider these questions before you plan your journey.

✓ Are your families compatible? Personality traits that are tolerable in the short run may become insufferable on a long trip. Think long and hard about spending a week with a Dennis the Menace, a spoiled child, or a notoriously frugal couple.

✓ Are your budgets compatible? Don't assume that because you have the same income bracket you like to spend money the same way. This can be especially problematic when scheduling activities (free beach versus pricey theme park) and making dinner reservations (family-style versus four-star).

✓ How well do the children get along? We all know that kids can form cliques, gang up, or in general tease each other. Be aware of alliances forged between the children. If one of yours always seems to be the odd man out, there will be little fun for him—or you—on your vacation.

tapes, adding sound effects and changing voices for different characters. Making the tapes was just as much fun as listening to them on the road.

Fran VanBrocklin, Olney, Maryland

Picture This

When getting ready for the 4-hour drive to Grandma's house, I buy a box of my kids' favorite crackers and a can of Cheez Whiz. I use the cheese to print letters on the crackers for my 5-year-old and small pictures of dogs, houses, trees, and so forth for my 2-year-old. The kids have fun guessing the cracker pictures and then eating a snack that keeps them going a little longer in the car.

Cindy Endres, Rosemount, Minnesota

All Mapped Out

Whenever we drive into a new state, we stop at the first rest stop and pick up a map for each of our kids. They enjoy plotting the trip and following the route with a crayon or marker. Our oldest also tracks the miles to the next major city or attraction.

Joan Caskey, Baltimore

Fun in a Box

To keep my toddler, Benjamin, busy on the road, I pack a metal, hinged Band-Aid box and a bag of interesting items, such as crinkly tissue paper; a large, empty thread spool; a large craft pom-pom; and pretzel sticks. When Benjamin gets cranky, I put an item in the box, close the lid, and hand it to him. He loves shaking the box, figuring out how to open it, and playing with the surprise.

Jacqueline Kremer, Bozrah, Connecticut

Backseat Comfort for Baby

I know that a rear-facing seat placed in the backseat of a car is safest for my baby daughter. To make the view more interesting, I sewed Katie's favorite cloth doll to the backseat; now, she has a friendly face to look at while we travel. I just made a few stitches, easily removable without damaging the car or the doll.

Jennifer Coburn, San Diego

pediatrician on call

how to curb car sickness

A child gets carsick because she can't see (or isn't looking at) the rapidly changing landscape out the window but can sense the motion of the car. Her brain gets conflicting signals from her inner ears (which regulate balance) and her eyes. She feels queasy and nauseated at first; her brain may eventually activate a response that makes her throw up. Although there's no magic cure for car sickness, we asked pediatrician and *Parents* contributing editor Laura Nathanson, M.D., for tips that might help.

- ✓ Let your child sit next to a backseat window, and encourage her to look outside. A child who is tall enough to see out the windshield from the back can try sitting in the middle of the backseat, since images seen from the windshield don't appear to change as rapidly as they do out of a side window.

- ✓ Discourage your child from reading or playing games while the car is moving. Looking down at something motionless will only make her feel worse. Opening the window a bit, so that she gets fresh air, can also help ease her queasiness.

- ✓ Try Dramamine, an over-the-counter motion sickness medication. This anti-histamine also makes kids sleepy, which can help them tolerate longer trips. The over-the-counter drug Bonine is a bit stronger; however, the FDA has not yet approved it for children under age 12.

- ✓ Give her a light snack before you start your trip. Hunger pangs can exacer-bate car-sickness symptoms in some children.

- ✓ Make frequent stops. If your child is nauseated, pull over as soon as you can, get out of the car with her, and walk around until she feels better.

planning the perfect itinerary

Big Apple, Big Fun

Our kids just loved New York City. We went without much of a schedule; there was one planned activity each day, like seeing the Statue of Liberty. The rest of the time, we walked around at our leisure. We also made sure to get to our hotel at

hotel room safety

To protect your child when you travel, you must childproof your hotel room. Follow these guidelines from the National Safe Kids Campaign.

- ✓ Come prepared. Make sure to pack a child's night-light, corner guards for furniture, plastic cups, inflatable faucet covers, and outlet covers.
- ✓ Call ahead. When you book your reservations, ask for a room with window and balcony guards, a crib that meets federal safety standards, and faucets and shower heads equipped with anti-scald devices.
- ✓ Check it out. Once you arrive, make sure that the room is clear of hazards such as matches, ashtrays, breakable drinking glasses, hard candies, coins, pins, and dangling drapery cords.

least once a day to freshen up and rest. A big city can be tiring for kids—and their parents.

Michael De Boer, *Milwaukee*

Sight-Seeing Suggestion

We usually restrict excursions such as sight-seeing, visiting museums, or shopping to the few hours between breakfast and lunch; kids can't really handle more than that. After lunch, we try to do something active, such as swimming or tennis. This gives everyone in the family something to look forward to during the day.

Anne Sweeney, *Grosse Pointe, Michigan*

Resort Rewards

When my wife was pregnant with our second child, we decided to take our daughter on a long weekend, so that the three of us could have a special time together before she became a big sister. We chose an all-inclusive resort in Jamaica, and it couldn't have worked out better. My wife got some much-needed pampering, our daughter adored the children's program, and we all got to spend a lot of time with each other in a beautiful place.

Bill McCoy, *Cranbury, New Jersey*

Mountain Highlight

The smartest vacation we ever took was when we went skiing at a western resort. We shared a house with a couple whose kids were around the same age as ours. Then, we traded off child care—the younger kids would play in the yard while the older ones went to ski school. In the evenings, we cooked dinner instead of going out to restaurants.

Lisa Kridos, *Woodland Hills, California*

Go Your Own Way

To avoid disagreements over what everyone wants to do each day on a family trip, have your spouse take half the group out sight-seeing while you take the other half to the beach or pool. We find that it's easier to keep things moving and keep people from getting crabby if we break up into smaller groups.

Linda Pedersen, *Tampa*

Disney on a dime

Do It Yourself

Book your Disney World vacation online. I've done a lot of comparison shopping and have always found the cheapest rates by booking each component—air, ground transportation, and hotel—myself. The best site that I've found is www.disney info.com. Disney's own Web site, www.disneyworld.com, is also a good source of information.

Carrie Bullock, *Foothill Ranch, California*

Membership Has Its Rewards

Before planning your vacation, ask your company's human resources office or your credit union if they are members of the Magic Kingdom Club. The Club Card entitles you to discounts on Park Hopper and Length of Stay passes and Disney dining, hotels, and merchandise. If your employer is not a member, call (714) 781-1550 to request an application. For a small fee, you can receive a 2-year membership.

Joan Caskey, *Baltimore*

Persistence Pays Off

After booking your hotel, call back every month or so to ask whether there are any upcoming promotions. At Disney resorts, these deals are offered throughout the year, but you have to be flexible with your travel dates and weigh the advantages of locking in a cheap airfare against the amount you may save with a last-minute discount.

Cathy Shambley, *Hermosa Beach, California*

Parents' favorite national parks for families

The Grand Canyon is spectacular, but it's not the only place to go to show your kids the great outdoors. Check out these equally gorgeous national parks.

Assateague Island National Seashore This 18,000-acre barrier island off the shores of Maryland and Virginia is most famous for the herd of 150 horses that run wild and free. Kids love pitching a tent in the sand next to the ocean, crabbing, and digging for clams. Contact info: (410) 641-1441, or www.nps.gov/asis.

Indiana Dunes National Park For kids, being here is like playing in the best, most gigantic sandlot ever created. Fifteen thousand acres on the southern curve of Lake Michigan provide miles of beaches, bogs, wetlands, and forests. The dunes are multistory mountains of sand; kids love scrambling to the top, surveying the horizon for ships, and sliding down. Contact info: (219) 926-7561, or www.nps.gov/indu.

Mammoth Cave National Park A whole secret world underneath the ground? Even today's kids, raised on Hollywood special effects, are awed by the longest recorded and mapped cave system in the world (350 miles), located in Kentucky. Kids who love getting dirty will really enjoy donning hard hats and headlights to crawl with rangers into crannies of the cave that their parents never see. Contact info: (270) 758-2251, or www.nps.gov/maca.

Mesa Verde National Park In A.D. 550, ancestral Pueblo people made their homes in the canyons, cliffs, and mesas of the Southern Colorado Rocky Mountains. Today, their architecture is not only intact but stunning—and it makes for an outstanding learning vacation. Visitors climb up and down ladders, edge along narrow shelves of rock, and wiggle through small tunnels to explore the networks of cavelike dwellings. Contact info: (970) 529-4465, or www.nps.gov/meve.

Yellowstone National Park Old Faithful is the most famous attraction here in Wyoming, but there's far more to see—including 2 million acres of wilderness to explore and amazing geological features left over from a massive volcanic eruption aeons ago. Kids love the odiferous Dragon's Mouth, the putrid Sour Lake, and the spewing Mud Volcano. Contact info: (307) 344-7381, or www.nps.gov/yell.

A Star Is Born

We could afford the convenience and services of a Disney resort by booking a package vacation at Walt Disney World's least expensive property, the All-Star Resort. As AAA (American Automobile Association) members, we were entitled to an additional discount on our already affordable off-season lodging and multiday admission package. For less than $70 a night, we enjoyed shuttles, a pool, a game room, and a food court.

Sally and Jake Doran, *Centerville, Ohio*

It's in the Card

Contact the Orlando/Orange County Convention and Visitors Bureau at (800) 551-0181 or www.go2orlando.com, and request the Orlando Magicard. The card saved us $45 a night on a hotel and entitled us to discounts on a rental car.

Venus D. Smalley, *Lake Parsippany, New Jersey*

Midday Feast

Eat your largest meal of the day at lunchtime, since restaurant prices are lower then than they are at dinner.

Kimberly Ripley, *Portsmouth, New Hampshire*

Do the Splits

Share your meals. The sit-down restaurants at the parks serve such large portions that we always ordered one meal for two and requested an extra plate. Occasionally, a restaurant will charge a dollar or two for the privilege of sharing, but most were happy to oblige.

Carey S. Gregg, *Spring, Texas*

Eat In

Eating breakfast and lunch in your room is relaxing and saves lots of money. Try to book a room with a refrigerator (or you can rent one inexpensively) and stock it with goods from a nearby grocery store. By midday, our kids needed a break anyway, and then we would return to the park refreshed and well-fed.

Sheri Opper, *Wilmington, North Carolina*

Don't Act Your Age

Adults can easily order a children's meal at any counter service restaurant. You get a generous meal and drink at half the price.

Christine Mann, *Coplay, Pennsylvania*

keeping your child safe in a crowd

The crowds at any large theme park, carnival, or summer concert can be terrifying for a parent. Who hasn't had that nightmare where you turn your head for a split second and your child is lost in a sea of people? For smart tips, we asked someone who helps frantic parents find their lost kids every day: Gary Daniels, manager of guest relations for Magic Kingdom at Walt Disney World in Orlando, Florida.

✓ Dress your family in similar clothes—a special, brightly colored T-shirt or baseball hat—to make everyone easy to spot in a crowded area.

✓ Make information tags for young children that they can wear under their shirts. The tags should not be visible because it's a potential danger if strangers know their names.

✓ As soon as you enter the gates of the park or carnival, designate a meeting location in case you get separated (for instance, the information booth or a prominent statue or landmark).

✓ Tell your child that if he can't find you, he should find a park employee right away. Point out the uniform that the employees wear so that your child will know who to look for.

✓ Upon arrival, find out whether the park has a messaging service that allows you to leave a new meeting location or a change of plans.

Cheap, Filling, and Good for You

Don't miss Pizza Planet at MGM. It's a blast, and a small pizza only costs about $5. You also can't beat the fruit stands around the park for a healthy and inexpensive snack. Carrots, apples, pears, and oranges are 85 cents.

Angelia Tuttle, *Tobaccoville, North Carolina*

The Best Things in Life Are Free

The best way to cut your costs is to take a day off from the parks. Visit Disney's resort hotels, tour the grounds, admire the gardens and architecture, and listen to the music. Visit the petting zoo at Fort Wilderness. Check out the playground there and play checkers in front of the general store.

Barbara Thornton, *Somerville, New Jersey*

Set a Souvenir Budget

Although we were on a shoestring budget, we felt that our son should be able to bring home a souvenir or two. So we only bought for our son, not ourselves, and limited him to about $25 for the whole trip. For him, just having something small like a Mickey Mouse pen was a thrill.

Penny Singleton, Cut Off, Louisiana

Autographs—a Bargain!

Your kids are going to want to have memories of all of the Disney characters they meet. The best souvenir in the park is an autograph book. They're sold everywhere and only cost $6.

Karen Madigan, Green River, Wyoming

Bring Your Own Wheels

Bring your own stroller. Not only will you save the $5 a day on stroller rental, you also won't have to wait on line or worry about the park running out of them.

The Classey family, Westerly, Rhode Island

organize
your home

35

Statistics show that on average, we wear about 20 percent of our clothing, listen to 20 percent of our CDs, and read 20 percent of our books. In short, we use only 20 percent of the things we own, leaving the remaining 80 percent to create chaos in our closets and clutter in our lives.

This probably goes double for parents, who feel compelled to save ancient baby toys and puzzles missing three key pieces. Kids are also natural pack rats: Most of them have no idea what's at the bottom of that toy box (but whatever it is, it's vital to their happiness).

Organizing your family's possessions is a guaranteed way to improve your disposition and your mental health. And once it's done, you'll feel more in control—and save on cleaning and upkeep to boot. The tips in this chapter will help you devise a successful plan of attack.

toy time

Everything in Its Place

My toddler couldn't seem to keep his toys in any kind of order. Annoyed with the constant mess, I searched furniture stores and catalogs for toy racks and shelves, but everything I saw was too expensive. Then, one day, I mentioned my dilemma to a friend, who passed on an idea that worked for her: Get an unfinished wooden shoe storage rack that has cubbies, get some baskets that fit the cubbyholes, and label the baskets for books, cars, building blocks, and so forth. I tried this and it worked like a charm. Now, when it's time to set the table, I just bring a few baskets to the kitchen to clear off the toys. A bonus: Because the bins are labeled, my son is becoming familiar with new words every time he cleans up.

Lynda Hassick, Whitehall, Pennsylvania

Eggs-ellent Solution

We've finally found a way to organize the many tiny figures we've accumulated: We store them in empty egg cartons. Our son enjoys rearranging them in their little homes, and it's a great way to recycle egg cartons.

Mary Clare LaCaria, Algonquin, Illinois

Bath Mates

My 2-year-old son loves to play with toys while he bathes, but it was quite a task to drain the water from them and store them. Now, I load the toys into a plastic, open-hole crate and leave them to drain in the tub. I store the crate—with the toys in it—near the tub to reduce clutter.

Suzanne Robards, Charlotte, North Carolina

A Formula for Storage

Empty formula cans are a great place to store the tiny cars and other small toys that kids love to collect. Just remove the label, wash the can, cover it with pictures from magazines, and then seal it with clear Con-Tact paper. Attach a label to the plastic lid of each can to indicate the contents. The cans look cute, and they make it easy for my son to find the toys he wants.

Katie Nelson, Murray, Utah

Solving the Puzzle

My 3-year-old son loves puzzles, but I hate dealing with broken boxes and missing pieces. To solve this problem, we put each puzzle in its own resealable plastic bag. We cut the picture of the puzzle from the box and include it in the bag so that he knows which puzzle is which.

Mary Jane Dye, *New Castle, Indiana*

Barbie Overload

My 3- and 6-year-old daughters had so many Barbie dolls that I didn't know how to store them. So, I purchased an inexpensive pocket shoe organizer (the kind that hangs on a closet door) and put the dolls in the pockets. It works perfectly.

Linda Abrams, *Huntington Station, New York*

it's my job

cleaning closets

These great tips from Doreen Tuman, a professional closet organizer and owner of The Closet Lady, a design business based in New York City, will help you put an end to time-consuming searches by bringing order to any closet in your house.

✓ Evaluate your storage space. Decide what needs to reside in the closet and what can be stored elsewhere in the room. Make an inventory of everything that's going to go into the closet to determine whether you need to buy more shoe racks and other storage pieces.

✓ If you don't use it, lose it. Give away or store any article of clothing that hasn't been worn in 3 years (less for kids, of course, who outgrow things quickly).

✓ Make closets kid-friendly. If possible, make the poles, shelves, and racks in your child's closet easily accessible.

✓ Stock up on baskets. They'll help organize items that don't go on hangers, such as T-shirts, sweaters, and baseball caps. The less effort it takes to put something away, the more likely it is that you—or your children—will do it.

✓ Make sure that everything in your closet applies to your life now. While it's fine to keep items that you cherish but don't often use, says Tuman, they should probably go in the attic, not your closet.

Doll Closet

I discovered a wonderful way to organize my 6-year-old daughter's doll clothes. I inserted a tension rod across the lower shelf of a bookcase. Clothes on baby-size hangers go on the rod, accessories go on the shelf below the clothes, and the dolls go on the shelf above.

Kathy Edelstein, Caldwell, New Jersey

Wagon Works

An old wagon can do wonders when it comes to organizing collections of toys. For example, a red wagon that I picked up at a garage sale works great for keeping my 9-year-old daughter's stuffed animal collection in order. An old wheelbarrow keeps my 5-year-old son's collection of Tonka trucks in order, and storing my son's construction toys in the wheelbarrow makes it easy to take them outside for playtime and back in at the end of the day.

Julie Alvarez, Sparks, Nevada

Baskets of Fun

After our son was born, our house was quickly overrun with toys and baby items. To help keep order, I made attractive toy holders for each room. I took large, inexpensive baskets and decorated them with ribbons to match each room's decor. The baskets look great, my son's toys are much easier to put away, and I don't feel the need to rearrange everything each time we have company.

Janet Borosak, Crestwood, Illinois

clothes call

It's in the Box

I use a simple system to help me locate old baby clothes for reuse. I bought pretty cardboard storage boxes and labeled them "zero to 3 months," "3 to 6 months," and so on. I stacked the boxes in the closet, and as my older daughter outgrows an item, I wash and fold it and place it in the appropriate box. When my second child was born, I was able to find the clothes in her size quickly—I didn't have to sift through bags of clothes. And my closet is neat and organized.

Jaclynn Brennan, Anaheim Hills, California

organizing videos, toys, and more

Family life doesn't have to be chaotic, says professional organizer Julie Morgenstern. The key, she explains, is creating a systematic plan of attack. Here, Morgenstern, owner of Task Master, a New York–based consulting firm, and author of *Organizing from the Inside Out*, shares her four-step foolproof formula for whipping your cluttered family room into shape.

1. Sort. If you're sorting a collection of videos, put all of the comedy selections in one pile, all of the drama in another.

2. Purge. Weed out duplicates, triplicates, broken or stained items, and things you simply no longer want.

3. Assign. Find a home for each of the groups of items that you'll be keeping. Depending on the size of the collection, videos might be stored in a basket that fits on a shelf underneath the TV.

4. Equalize. To keep your newly ordered room in tip-top shape, Morgenstern suggests setting aside a minimal amount of time (say, 5 minutes) at the end of each day to put everything back in its place. Then, once a year, reevaluate your organization system to ensure that it remains current with your needs, priorities, and interests.

Mug Shots

A mug rack is an inexpensive way for young children to organize a variety of possessions. My 7–year-old son uses one to keep his collection of baseball caps in order. My 10–year-old daughter uses hers to keep hair ribbons and jewelry neat. With a little paint and a few other personal touches, these racks can even look artful hanging on a bedroom wall.

Darlene Cantwell, West Caldwell, New Jersey

We've Got It Pegged

In the winter, our hall closet is bursting with cold-weather gear. So, we added two decorative peg holders to the inside of the closet door to hang up our children's coats. This frees up much-needed hanger space for larger and heavier clothes, and the boys (ages 2 and 3½) can easily reach the low pegs to hang up their own jackets.

Lorraine Galkowski, Apex, New York

clutter control

Coupon Storage

I've discovered that the best method for controlling coupon chaos is to sort them by category in a recipe file box. Not only does this system keep my coupons in order but it also helps control the number that I save, since I have to weed them out regularly in order to add new ones.

Amy Johnson, *Kansas City, Missouri*

Pack Rat Gallery

My daughter is a collector—she squirrels away everything from party hats to backpacks—so I was soon faced with a sizable storage problem. To solve it, I hung a large Peg-Board on my daughter's wall, at a height she can easily reach, so she can arrange and rearrange her collections on the hooks. Not only does the board provide ample storage space but it also makes an ever-changing and interesting wall hanging.

Sheila Lucia, *Hutchinson, Kansas*

kids and clutter

Here are four easy ways to cut back on kid-related clutter while teaching your children valuable organizing skills.

✓ Snap away. Take pictures of special things that you want to remember but don't have room to keep. For example, photograph an award-winning science project that your child displayed at school, and then get rid of the project.

✓ Give kids control. Make your children responsible for things that they want to keep. If your son won't let you get rid of a painting he made in art class, hang it in his room. He can decide when he's tired of it and wants to throw it away.

✓ Sell it. Organize a garage sale and offer your children a cut of the proceeds. You'll be surprised how quickly they will part with "important" toys, books, and other possessions when there's a chance of making some spending money.

✓ Weed regularly. Establish a filing system for school papers, art projects, and report cards. (A crate with hanging file folders works well.) Once a month, sit down with your child and sort through the folder, weeding out what is no longer important.

Mudroom Madness

I put my mudroom in order with one long, low wooden bench. The kids sit on it to remove their shoes and boots, which they then tuck beneath the seat. Hooks on the wall above the bench keep hats and coats off the floor. School bags can sit on the bench until the next morning. It's a simple but effective solution that eliminates the hectic morning search for shoes and schoolwork.

Kate Anderson, *Madison, Wisconsin*

make cleanup fun

Photo Finish

I wanted to encourage my two young sons (ages 2 and 3) to hang up their bath towels, which they usually discard somewhere between the bathroom and the bedroom. I wasn't making any progress until I bought two big hooks and hung them low on the wall where they could reach. Then, I framed a smiling photo of each child and hung it above his hook. The

family albums

Stop tossing family photos into shoe boxes, and create a scrapbook instead. They're a great way to preserve cherished mementos from important events. Here's how to do it.

1. Gather scrapbooking supplies. An album with acid-free paper is essential to keep your book from deteriorating with time. Other must haves include glue, scissors, and thin markers for writing identifications. Dress things up with colored or patterned paper for backgrounds and borders; rubber stamps; templates; and stickers.

2. Put it together. Make color copies of photos that you don't want to cut up or glue permanently in place. To save space, tape photos together to make an accordion pullout. Add personal notes to help you remember the good times.

3. Go beyond photos. Glue certificates, tickets, growth charts, ribbons, letters, and other memorabilia into albums, too, or stash them in accordion-style folders.

4. Store the rest. Put photos that won't fit in your scrapbook according to theme in labeled and dated photo boxes. File negatives with their accompanying photos in case you need to make reprints.

home office ideas

Whether you have the luxury of an at-home office or can barely eke out a corner for a desk, setting up systems for family files and daily schedules keeps everything—and everyone—running smoothly. Here are three ways to create a central work and communication area in your home.

Build a computer corner. To maximize limited space, create storage areas both on and under the desk. Colorful cardboard files are great for organizing magazines, bills, and clippings. A wooden chest with pull-out drawers will hold CD-ROMs, floppy disks, or art and writing supplies. A freestanding file cabinet or drawer that slides under the table can be used for files and paper.

Make a bedroom home office. Start with a desk or table large enough to hold a computer. To keep clutter to a minimum, use the computer to track daily schedules, shopping lists, school notices, and other essential information. Organize stationery, mail, and other supplies in stacking drawers that fit neatly on the desktop. Use file boxes that match the room's decor to hide folders for bills, receipts, and other important documents.

Consider the kitchen. If you don't have room for a freestanding desk, simply designate a section of counter space. Stacked filing trays will keep mail, school notices, and homework papers in one easy-to-access place. Artwork, once it has run its course on the refrigerator, can be stashed in a spare drawer. Use an easy-to-read desktop calendar to track family members' schedules.

---

photo tells them which hook is theirs, and they are now happy to cooperate—most of the time.

Carol Alexander, *Baton Rouge, Louisiana*

Choice of Chores

To get cleaning done, we have a Saturday job jar filled with slips of paper describing various household chores, and we leave some slips blank. If one of our kids chooses a blank one, he has to look around and find a task that hasn't been assigned, such as bagging newspapers or watering plants. We think that it encourages independent thinking and initiative.

Ann Elwell, *Nixa, Missouri*

Good Night, Toys

I've created an easy way to motivate my kids to pick up their toys. Before bedtime, I tell them that their toys are sleepy and need to be tucked into the toy box. They're delighted to bid each toy good night and tuck it in—and it brings out their nurturing side, too.

Rima Menchaca, *Leming, Texas*

Pyramid Scheme

I've found a way for my sons, ages 5 and 6, to have fun on a rainy day while getting their room clean at the same time. We start by taking a look at what kinds of toys and games are scattered around. Then, I draw a pyramid with different categories of things that need to be put away, such as wood and plastic or different colors, shapes, and sizes. They then try to find things to fit each category and come to me to check off when they've completed a "level." The game helps them hone their reasoning skills because some items don't fit clearly into just one category. It also gives me time to do something else while they're busy.

Cindy Woody, *Hewitt, Texas*

Cleanup Contest

When many toys are spread out around the house, I enlist the entire family for a pickup race. Everyone guesses how long it will take. One minute? Six? Fifteen? When I say "Go!," everyone starts picking up and putting things where they belong. (No fair shoving it under the sofa or behind a door.) There are no prizes except the satisfaction of a job well done. It takes just a few of these races to realize that picking up isn't such a terrible job.

Pat Berna, *Kansas City, Missouri*

information, please

The Ideas File

It's a chore to search through magazines to find an article I want to refer to, so I use binders to organize them. I keep one for cooking ideas and another for crafts and activities. I place articles I'd like to save inside a plastic page protector. Now, anytime I need a new recipe or a fun thing to do with my kids, I know exactly where to look.

Amy Martz, *Laguna Niguel, California*

Cyber Gallery

It seemed like our house was overrun with my 4-year-old daughter's drawings and paintings. To get rid of the clutter, I

lighten the load

Paring down possessions that you no longer need is the often the hardest part of the organizing process. Here, organization experts offer three simple tips guaranteed to ease the pain of parting with your sometimes cherished belongings.

1. Adopt a charity. By donating your unwanted clothing, books, and other household items to a charitable organization such as the Salvation Army, you help not only yourself but others as well.

2. Start a neighborhood exchange. Have friends and neighbors bring their unwanted possessions—books, toys, small appliances, and household goods—to your home and swap. (Just don't bring home more than you get rid of!)

3. Rent an off-site storage space. This will allow you to experience life in a clutter-free environment without the trauma of permanently parting with your belongings all at once. After 6 months, go through the storage facility with your family and reevaluate your choices, tossing anything that you feel is no longer relevant to the way you live.

started scanning them into our computer to digitally preserve them. It worked so well that I posted some on a Web site for friends and family to see.

Amy Perry, *Fayetteville, North Carolina*

Storing School Memories

When my daughter started day care, I needed a way to organize her many projects and drawings. Loose-leaf binders with clear sheet protectors were the perfect solution. At the end of each week, I sort through her creations and slide them into transparent sleeves. The books are easy to label by year and take up little space, and Kathryn loves looking back on her work.

Susan Kelly Taylor, *Greenville, South Carolina*

Saving Sweet Sentiments

My sons love the cards they receive at their Valentine's Day parties at school. So, I found a way to keep them in good shape and cut down on the clutter. I make Valentine's place mats by arranging the cards between two layers of clear Con-Tact paper. It's a great way to display the cards, and my kids love looking at them year after year and remembering their friends.

Kim Wardean, *Durand, Wisconsin*

Childhood Collections

I finally came up with a solution for keeping small collectibles such as baseball cards and postage stamps in order. I have my son keep the bulk of his sports card collection in labeled photo albums. His favorites go in simple picture frames that hang on his bedroom wall, and he can exchange them for other cards in his collection whenever he likes.

Deni Murphy, Rolla, Missouri

how long should I keep it?

The big question when cleaning out a den or a home office area isn't where to file tax forms, insurance policies, and other important documents, but how long to hold on to them. Here's a general guide from organizing experts on what to keep and how long to store it.

Appointment books: One to 10 years, depending on whether you use them for tax records, reference, or memorabilia.

ATM slips: If needed for tax records, hold for 6 years. Otherwise, toss once your next bank statement arrives.

Automobile records: For as long as you own your vehicle.

Bank statements: If needed for tax records, for 6 years. If not, toss after a year.

Credit card statements: If the statement lists a tax-related purchase, keep for 6 years; if you get an annual statement, save these and discard the monthly statements at the end of the year.

Insurance policies: With auto, homeowners', and liability policies that have been cancelled, hold the policy until the statute of limitations on late claims is up. For disability, medical, life, personal property, and other similar policies, keep only as long as the policies are in force.

Tax returns: Keep the current year, plus 6 prior years.

Never toss adoption papers, birth and death certificates, citizenship papers, copyrights or patents, marriage certificates, divorce decrees, medical illness and vaccination records, passports, Social Security records, and wills.

birthday bashes

36

remember how exciting your birthday was when you were a kid? No doubt, your own child looks forward to the big day with just as much anticipation.

Few events in a kid's life are as exciting as the day when he proudly turns a year older, has a party, and gets to be the center of attention. Naturally, you want to create the perfect birthday bash—but you also want to have some energy left after planning it to snap pictures, relax, and enjoy the treasured moments. In this chapter, we've gathered dozens of tips from parents and experts on everything from inexpensive gift wrapping to sending invitations to throwing a fantastic celebration. Party on!

birthdays made easier

Posting Party Invites

I always attach a little magnet on the back of the party invitations I send. This makes it easier for guests to post them on the refrigerator so that they have the info handy when the special day comes around.

Stacy Brown, Lubbock, Texas

Picture This

When my 4½-year-old daughter is invited to a birthday party, I often give an inexpensive camera as a gift. I let the parents know ahead of time so that the child can open this gift first to capture the rest of the fun. This way, the birthday child can take pictures of her special day.

Kelly Fekette, Fayetteville, North Carolina

A Picture Says . . .

A friend clued me in to this trick. To keep track of which kid gives your child which birthday present, let your camera do the work. When it comes time to open the gifts, set up two chairs, one for your child and the other for his friend. Take a picture of the two of them with the opened gift. It's a great reminder when you're writing thank-you notes, and you can include the snapshot as a memento.

Darlene Esposito, West Caldwell, New Jersey

Keeping Track of Guests

When I was planning my son Reed's sixth birthday party at a busy kids' restaurant, I worried about keeping track of all the children. Before the party, I bought 2 yards of bright yellow smiley-face fabric and cut it into triangles (32 inches diagonally) for the guests to wear as bandannas. The kids loved them, and it was easy for me to spot them in the crowd. My husband and I also wore them so that the kids could find us, too.

Pharma Woodyard, Oklahoma City

Takes the Cake

Planning a party for preschoolers is tough, but keeping eager fingers from sampling the frosting on the cake is even tougher. To avoid this, I covered my table with edible sprinkles. It was

Parents' birthday party planner

The best way to ensure that your child's birthday party is nonstop fun is to organize. Here's the plan.

Four Weeks Before

✓ Choose a theme and set the date. If your child is old enough, he can help pick the theme.

✓ Book any entertainment or party location.

✓ Prepare the guest list. A good rule of thumb: Add 1 to your child's age, and use that as the ideal number of kids to invite.

Two Weeks Before

✓ Make a menu and a shopping list of all the supplies and groceries you'll need.

✓ Buy tabletop paper goods, decorations, and party favors.

✓ Try shopping online. Party supply Web sites such as www.iparty.com and www.celebrateexpress.com can save you time and money.

✓ Make a list of fun party activities—you can never have too many. Make sure that you have the same number of high-activity games and quiet ones, so you can alternate.

One Week Before

✓ Double-check attendance and call any parent who hasn't yet responded.

✓ Enlist other parents or older siblings to help out.

✓ Make sure that you have plenty of film for your camera. Do a test run with your camcorder.

✓ Order the cake if you're not making it yourself.

The Day Before

✓ Buy the groceries and party snacks, and prepare any make-ahead food.

✓ Bake and decorate the cake if you are doing your own.

✓ Decorate the room and table. Fill the goody bags.

✓ Assemble any arts and crafts materials.

When the Big Day Arrives

✓ Make the food. Chill extra juice, soda, or milk. Make coffee and tea for parents.

✓ Blow up balloons and set up activity or craft stations.

✓ Tape a party schedule up on the fridge so you can refer to it.

fun and decorative—and the kids concentrated on munching these, leaving the cake intact.

Cheryl Rohrscheib, Anchorage

A Teddy Bear Tea

My daughter is very attached to her stuffed animals, so, on her last birthday, we had a teddy bear tea party. We asked all the guests to bring their favorite teddy bear, and we gave out prizes for the oldest, biggest, smallest, and funniest. We also played a teddy bear relay game and frosted and decorated teddy-bear-shaped sugar cookies. My daughter still remembers it as one of her best parties.

Janet Crowe, Papillion, Nebraska

Patchwork Party

At my 9-year-old daughter's birthday, I had the girls create special birthday quilt squares. Each child was given a square of felt to decorate with fabric paint, sequins, and other art supplies. The kids had a lot of fun—and my daughter loved the colorful mementos from her birthday, which we later sewed into a quilt.

Mary Montella, San Francisco

Share the Birthday Blowout

Whenever my children have a birthday party, I make a cupcake with a candle on it for each guest, in addition to the cake for the birthday child. When it's time to blow out the candles, every child has one right in front of him to huff and puff at. The kids love it, and the birthday child doesn't get any unwanted help when he blows out his candles.

Marla Bellina, Lebanon, Illinois

Beauty-full Birthday Kits

I created "beauty parlor" kits for my 10-year-old niece (who lives far away) and her friends. I began with empty paint cans (available at home-improvement stores) and made labels on my computer. Then, I filled the cans with mascara, lipstick and gloss, glitter, nail polish, and hair doodads—you name it! I even included purple inflatable chairs for them to sit on while they played beautician. I also sent my niece a disposable camera so they could capture the magic for me.

Suzy Moco-Williams, Isle of Palms, South Carolina

cake decorating tips

Whether you have an innovative cake shape in mind, such as a clown or a puppy, or you simply want to spell out "Happy Birthday," decorating your homemade cake can be a messy job if you're not careful. These tricks from the pros will help.

1. If you're cutting the cake into a shape, freeze it for an hour first. Insert toothpicks an inch apart to mark where you will need to cut, then use a sharp, serrated knife. Sweep away any crumbs with a pastry brush or a new, unused paintbrush.

2. Create the colors you want by adding food coloring to canned vanilla frosting or your own recipe. Add one drop at a time and mix until you obtain the desired shade.

3. Apply frosting with a metal spatula. Dip the spatula in hot water so that the frosting spreads more easily. Begin by icing the sides, then ice the top.

4. To pipe the cake with letters or designs in different colors, use disposable pastry bags with screw-on tips. Practice first on a sheet of waxed paper.

5. Scratch guidelines into the frosting with a toothpick before you pipe on letters. If your initial spacing is off, flatten the frosting and rescratch the guidelines.

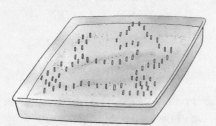

Insert toothpicks 1 inch apart to mark shape you want to cut.

After frosting cake, use toothpick to lightly scratch locations of letters you want to use.

a house of cards

Clever Hang-Up

I have always enjoyed displaying my kids' birthday cards, but they take up so much space. My solution is to hang them from the dining room chandelier. I simply punch a hole in each card, then string curly ribbon through it and tie it to the fixture. The kids love to see their festive cards floating around, and it takes up almost no space.

Suesan Larsen, Carlsbad, California

Picture-Perfect Cards

I hated to throw out all of the cards my son received on his first birthday, so I turned them into a picture frame. I cut up the cards and glued the pieces into a collage on a piece of poster board. Then, I laminated it and cut a hole out for his photo.

Nicole Messenger, Edmonton, Alberta, Canada

december birthdays

The Birthday Tree

Our 3-year-old daughter's birthday is on December 19, so, when we put up our Christmas tree after Thanksgiving, we decorate it with birthday items such as balloons and streamers. After her birthday festivities are over, we redecorate the tree for Christmas.

Melanie Jacobs, Sheridan, Wyoming

great party venues

Off-site parties are a lot of fun for kids and parents alike. They're also a good alternative to hosting a crowd at home. Don't be fooled, though: These events take just as much organizing, and you're still the host. Always find out whether you will need a reservation, whether they have a party room, and whether there's a group discount. Keep refreshments simple, and if you're planning an outdoor event, have a "plan B" in case it rains. Here are some of our favorites.

✓ Zoo or aquarium

✓ Local museum or sculpture garden

✓ Ice-skating rink

✓ Fire station

✓ Movie theater or playhouse

✓ Do-it-yourself arts and crafts center (bead or pottery shop)

✓ Tea parlor

✓ Amusement park (indoors or out)

safe celebrations

To keep birthday parties safe, the National Safe Kids Campaign suggests that you take the following advice.

Childproof. Remove valuable and breakable items, tape down electrical cords, gate stairways, and rearrange furniture so that there's more space for guests.

Have plenty of adult supervision. You'll need one adult for every three children 2 and younger, one adult for every four children 2 to 3, and one adult for every eight children 3 years and older.

Beware of choking hazards. Use Mylar balloons instead of traditional rubber ones, which can burst and break into small pieces, presenting a choking hazard. For children under 4 years of age, watch out for small or breakable toy parts when choosing party favors, and don't serve small, round foods such as nuts, cut-up hot dogs, and hard candies.

Be prepared. Make sure that you have all the parents' phone numbers in one place, and keep a first-aid kit handy in case a child gets hurt.

Setting the Scene

Choose a party site that's not decorated for the holidays, such as a roller rink or an indoor playground. At my 2½-year-old daughter's last party, we made a rule that the word *Christmas* could not be mentioned. We really want her to grow up knowing that there's a difference between her birthday and the "other" holiday.

Nichole Startup, Salt Lake City

Celebrate at Thanksgiving

Since our entire family is gathered for the day, it's a perfect time to make our December daughter the center of attention. We serve her birthday cake after dinner, along with the pumpkin pie. She loves it, and we don't have to worry about trying to squeeze in a party a few weeks later.

Linda De Angelis, Churchville, New York

Salute the Flag

To make our daughter feel special, I replace our Christmas flag with a birthday flag the day before her birthday and leave it up for 3 days. I also have a birthday plate and mug that she uses only during that time.

Mary Anne Haynes, Augusta, Georgia

Birthday Budget

Celebrating a birthday in conjunction with Christmas can be tough on your wallet. I make it a habit to look for gifts throughout the year and put them away, to ease the financial burden later.

Len Bjorgo, Lubbock, Texas

Celebration Weekend

Our family has several December and January birthdays, so we decided to have a family weekend in the summer to celebrate all of our birthdays. (For example, one year, we rented a cabin by the beach.) We give our kids cake and ice cream on their actual birthdays and save the presents for the big party. It's like a second Christmas.

Lana Hackbardt, Howard City, Michigan

first birthday memories

Preserve the Pleasure

For my child's first birthday party, I bought a blank videotape and filmed the big event. Then, I set the tape aside to use only for recording birthdays each year. Instead of having to forward through hours of tapes to find these precious memories, I have them all in one place. I'm looking forward to showing my daughter the birthday tape on her 18th birthday.

Kimberly Lind, Canyon Country, California

Create a Time Capsule

I have twins, a boy and a girl. I celebrated their first birthday with a dinner party. I invited family and friends who had helped support me and my family through the first year. I asked everyone not to bring a gift. Instead, I gathered my babies' birth announcements, hospital caps, first outfits, shoes, socks, pacifiers, photos, and a lock of their hair, and I arranged them in shadow boxes—one with a pink mat, the other with blue. Then, I had my guests sign books with special messages for each twin, which I placed inside the shadow boxes. It is a time capsule that I know they will cherish in the years to come.

Parish R. Cromer, Charleston, South Carolina

Time for Teletubbies

I wanted my son Malcomb's first birthday to be very special for him, even though he will not remember it. Because he loves *Teletubbies*, I had a Teletubby-themed party. I ordered a Teletubby cake, and I made loot bags for the kids out of colored paper bags decorated with squares of tinfoil and pipe cleaner closures to match the characters. The day was perfect, and my son had a ball. We videotaped the whole day and took lots of pictures.

Susan Nemchin, *Toronto, Canada*

A Magical Day

We took our youngest daughter, Marina, to Disney World for her first birthday, and we chose to have lunch in the Crystal Palace, in the Magic Kingdom. We told the staff ahead of time that it was her first birthday, and they brought out a cake with a candle. Pooh, Tigger, and Eeyore sang happy birthday to her and gave her a card signed by all of them. Everybody had a wonderful time!

Leslie Ritacco, *Middletown, New York*

Scrapbook Party

When our little girl, Renae, had her first birthday, we invited our friends, family, and neighbors and took a picture of each of them. During the party, everyone wrote a little blurb about Renae and how much she is loved. I spent a few days after her birthday putting everything together in a scrapbook—the pictures, the guest list, the loving little blurbs, and all her cards—so that when she's older, she can look back on a time when memory was short but love was long and deep.

Yvette Nemec, *Mitchell, South Dakota*

See How They Grow!

Every month throughout my son's first year, I took a picture of him in the same setting with a small sign displaying his age. Then, at his first birthday party, I pasted these pictures in chronological order on a decorated poster board, which I hung on the wall for friends and family to see. Everyone was enter-

birthday facts

✓ Seventy-eight percent of all birthday parties for children under the age of 10 are held at home (the parents' or someone else's). Only 12 percent are held at a restaurant.

✓ On average, children's birthday parties include eight other children.

✓ Virtually all birthday parties are celebrated with a cake (98 percent) and ice cream (87 percent).

✓ Most babies are born in July (9 percent), August (9 percent), or May (9 percent).

party entertainment

Aaron Hsu-Flanders, a world-renowned balloon sculptor based in Cambridge, Massachusetts, and the bestselling author of *Balloon Animals*, has taken part in many a birthday celebration. We asked him what parents should look for when they hire a performer. Here's his advice.

Think twice about hiring a clown. "I've found that the costume and makeup can be frightening for young kids," says Hsu-Flanders. "They also create a distance between the audience and the performer. It's more important to be yourself."

Choose someone who lets the kids help. Kids get more out of a demonstration if they can try the trick out themselves. "For my balloon act, I enlist parents to help if the children are younger than 5," he says.

Get everyone in on the act. Even if there are a lot of kids, it's important that the performer spend a few minutes one-on-one with each of them.

Make sure to honor the birthday child. "I always do a little something extra for the birthday child, such as make an animal hat or use several balloons with different colors," he says. Just don't forget to tell the performer whose birthday it is!

tained by the display and remembered special times with Jacob throughout the year.

Brenda Wilson, *Saginaw, Michigan*

Birthday Blanket

Because our extended family lives in different states, getting them to our daughter's first birthday party was impossible. So, we sent each relative a square of fabric, paint, and markers, and asked them to make a handprint and write their names and ages below it. We also included postage-paid return envelopes so they could send the squares back to us easily. At home, we made our own squares, including our daughter's handprint and our two dogs' pawprints! When all the squares arrived, I sewed them together to make a birthday blanket with my daughter's handprints in the center, and her name and birth date embroidered on it. When she's older, she'll know that her first birthday was a very special event for the whole family.

Elizabeth Meador, *Dallas*

it's a wrap

Wrap Artist

My 4-year-old daughter loves helping me wrap presents, but using paper and tape can be difficult for her, so I let her create gift bags using paints and brown paper bags with handles. We save money on wrapping paper, and Kassie loves delivering the presents in her original artwork.

Kim Bauer, South Elgin, Ilinois

traditional birth-month symbols

Month	Flower	Birthstone
January	Carnation	Garnet
February	Violet	Amethyst
March	Jonquil	Aquamarine
April	Sweet pea	Diamond
May	Lily of the valley	Emerald
June	Rose	Pearl
July	Larkspur	Ruby
August	Gladiolus	Peridot
September	Aster	Sapphire
October	Calendula	Opal
November	Chrysanthemum	Topaz
December	Narcissus	Turquoise

A Handmade Card

I was wrapping a birthday gift for my daughter's friend when I realized that we didn't have a card. After some quick thinking, I found a handprint that my daughter had made with fingerpaint. I cut out the hand, wrote "Happy Birthday" on it, and attached it to the gift. It worked great—and she was proud of the personal touch.

Terri Gaulkin, Watertown, Connecticut

Happy Birth Day

I wrap presents for newborns in the front page of the newspaper from the day when the baby was born. The parents can put the paper in the baby book, and when the child is older, he can look back to see what was going on in the world at the time of his birth.

Annemarie Scobey-Polacheck, Glendale, Wisconsin

baby showers

Double-Duty Wrapping

When I hosted a baby shower for a friend who enjoys quilting, I asked the guests to wrap their gifts in 1 yard of baby-friendly fabric instead of wrapping paper. The gifts looked great, and the guest of honor was thrilled with the variety of material. She used it to create a beautiful blanket for her new baby.

Mildred Winslow, Fort Drum, New York

Say It with Flowers

I've come up with a great shower gift for friends who know that they're having a son. Simply buy a colorful toy dump truck and place a flowering plant in it. New parents love the flowers, and they use the truck to decorate their son's room until he's old enough to play with it. It's a gift that everyone gets to enjoy—and you don't even have to wrap it.

Catherine Brown, Dallas

The Perfect Thank-You

I received so many beautiful outfits at my daughter Nicole's shower. So, whenever she wears one for the first time, I take a

ask **Peggy Post**

invitation etiquette

Q: How do I decide who to invite to my 6-year-old's birthday party? She has a lot of kids in her class, plus lots of friends in the neighborhood.

A: Consider making the preliminary list yourself rather than asking your child. Perhaps you'd like to invite the whole kindergarten class, but realistically, you just can't handle 25 or 30 kids. That's fine. To narrow down the number, think in terms of kids with whom your child is likely to have a special relationship. For example, you might decide to include only those friends and neighbors she's had playdates with outside school. You might also ask your child's teacher which children she plays with in class. Or you might limit the invitation to just the girls or just the boys in the class. By using positive criteria rather than eliminating children your child doesn't like, you're less likely to hurt anyone's feelings.

When you've nearly reached your total, show your child the list and ask if there's any special friend you've missed. This is also a good time to explain to her the concept of discretion—at age 6, she's old enough to empathize with those who are not invited. Don't distribute your invitations or thank-you notes at school, and ask your child to try not to discuss the party there.

photograph of her and send a duplicate to the person who gave it to her. All our friends and relatives enjoy seeing Nicole in "their" outfits.

Michelle Grobowski-Ray, Chatsworth, California

Give Your Favorite Advice

One of the most thoughtful gifts a mom-to-be can receive is good advice from a trusted friend. I've found that attaching a list of tips and tricks to baby shower gifts is most appreciated. After all, what may seem like common sense to an experienced mom can save a new mom from learning something the hard way. Just think of all the little things that make your life easier, type them, add a blue or pink ribbon, and voilà! You've made a new mom's life easier.

Daria Rowe, Baltimore

Postbirth Shower

My baby shower was held after my son Bradley was born, so that faraway friends and family members wouldn't have to make the trip twice. To give the party a focus, we asked everyone to bring a toy or a book that started with the first initial of their last name. Many of our guests commented that this was a good way to shop for a gift. It also provided Bradley with a library of books and toys that he can grow up with. I stored them by age range, and we are still enjoying their gifts.

Cathy Gorman, Grand Rapids, Michigan

resources

organizations to contact

Childbearing and Infancy

Adoption and Infertility Treatments
RESOLVE: 1310 Broadway, Somerville, MA 02144; (617) 623-0744; www.resolve.org

Adoption Literature
Adoptive Families magazine: 2472 Broadway, Suite 377, New York, NY 10025; (212) 877-1839; www.adoptivefam.com

Childbirth
International Childbirth Education Association: P.O. Box 20048, Minneapolis, MN 55420; (952) 854-8660; www.icea.org

La Leche League: 1400 North Meacham Road, Schaumburg, IL 60173; (800) 525-3243; www.lalecheleague.org

Multiple Births
Mothers of Supertwins: P.O. Box 951, Brentwood, NY 11717; (631) 859-1110; www.mostonline.org

National Organization of Mothers of Twins Clubs: P.O. Box 4388, Thompson Station, TN 37179; (877) 540-2200; www.nomotc.org

The Triplet Connection: P.O. Box 99571, Stockton, CA 95209; (209) 474-0885; www.tripletconnection.org

Twin Services: P.O. Box 10066, Berkeley, CA 94709; (510) 524-0863

Premature Infants
International Childbirth Education Association Book Center: (800) 624-4934; www.icea.org/book.htm

The Preemie Store and More!/TLC Clothing: (800) 676-8469; www.preemie.com

Child Care

AuPairCare: 455 Market Street, 17th Floor, San Francisco, CA 94105; (800) 428-7247; www.aupaircare.com

Au Pair in America: 102 Greenwich Avenue, Greenwich, CT 06830; (800) 727-2437; www.aifs.com.aupair/index.htm

EF Au Pair: One Education Street, Cambridge, MA 02141; (800) 333-6056 www.efaupair.org

EurAupair: 210 North Lee Street, Alexandria, VA 22314; (800) 333-3804; www.euraupair.com

National Association of Childcare Resource and Referral Agencies: 1319 F Street NW, Suite 500, Washington, DC 20004; (202) 393-5501; www.naccrra.net

Education

General Information
National Association for the Education of Young Children: 1509 16th Street NW, Washington, DC 20036; (800) 424-2460; www.naeyc.org

Learning Disabilities
Learning Disabilities Association of America: 4156 Library Road, Pittsburgh, PA 15234; (412) 341-1515; www.ldanatl.org

National Center for Learning Disabilities: 381 Park Avenue South, Suite 1401, New York, NY 10016; (888) 575-7373; www.ncld.org

Sensory Integration International: 1514 Cabrillo Avenue, Torrance, CA 90501; (310) 320-2335; www.sensoryint.com

Medical Issues and Information

General Information
American Academy of Family Physicians: 11400 Tomahawk Creek Parkway, Leawood, KS 66211; (913) 906-6000; www.aafp.org/family/patient.html

American Academy of Pediatrics: 141 Northwest Point Boulevard, Elk Grove Village, IL 60007; www.aap.org

American Board of Medical Specialties: 1007 Church Street, Suite 404, Evanston, IL 60201; (866) 275-2267; www.abms.org

American Dietetic Association: 216 W. Jackson Boulevard, Chicago, IL 60606; (800) 877-1600; www.eatright.org

American Heart Association: 7272 Greenville Avenue, Dallas, TX 75231; (800) 242-8721; www.americanheart.org

Food and Drug Administration: HFI-40, Rockville, MD 20857; (888) 463-6332; www.fda.gov

MedicAlert: (800) 432-5378; www.medicalert.org

National Clearinghouse for Alcohol and Drug Information: P.O. Box 2345, Rockville, MD 20847; (800) 729-6686; www.health.org

National Immunization Information Hotline: Centers for Disease Control and Prevention, 1600 Clifton Road, Mailstop E-05, Atlanta, GA 30333; (800) 232-2522

Allergies and Asthma
Allergy/Asthma Information Association (AAIA): Suite 424, 130 Bridgeland Avenue, Toronto, ON M6A 1Z4; (416) 679-9521; www.cadvision.com/allergy

Allergy and Asthma Network/Mothers of Asthmatics: 2751 Prosperity Avenue, Suite 150, Fairfax, VA 22031; (800) 878-4403; www.aanma.org

Allergy Control Products: 96 Danbury Road, Ridgefield, CT 06877; (800) 422-3878; www.allergycontrol.com

Allergy-Free: 905 Gemini, Houston, TX 77508; (800) 255-3749; www.allergy-free.com

American Academy of Allergy, Asthma, and Immunology: 611 East Wells Street, Milwaukee, WI 53202; (800) 976-5536; www.aaaai.org

American Lung Association: 1740 Broadway, NY, NY 10019; (800) 586-4872; www.lungusa.org

Asthma and Allergy Foundation of America Information Helpline: 1233 20th Street NW, Suite 403, Washington, DC 20036; (800) 727-8462; www.aafa.org

The Lung Line Information Service: National Jewish Medical and Research Center, 1400 Jackson Street, Denver, CO 80206; (800) 222-5864; www.nationaljewish.org

Cancer
American Cancer Society: (800) 227-2345; www.cancer.org

Candlelighters Childhood Cancer Foundation: 3910 Warner Street, Kensington, MD 20895; (800) 366-2223; www.candlelighters.org

Children's Leukemia Research Association: 585 Stewart Avenue, Suite 536, Garden City, NY 11530; (516) 222-1944; www.childrensleukemia.org

Leukemia and Lymphoma Society: 1311 Mamaroneck Avenue, White Plains, NY 10605; (800) 955-4572; www.leukemia.org

National Cancer Institute, Cancer Information Service: Building 31, Room 10A03, 31 Center Drive, MSC 2580, Bethesda, MD 20892; (800) 422-6237; www.nci.nih.gov

National Children's Cancer Society: 1015 Locust, Suite 1040, St. Louis, MO 63101; (800) 532-6459; www.children-cancer.com

Diabetes

American Diabetes Association: 1701 North Beauregard Street, Alexandria, VA 22311; (800) 342-2383; www.diabetes.org

Juvenile Diabetes Foundation International/Diabetes Research Foundation: 120 Wall Street, 19th Floor, New York, NY 10005; (800) 533-2873; www.jdf.org

National Diabetes Information Clearinghouse: 1 Information Way, Bethesda, MD 20892; (301) 654-3327; www.aoa.dhhs.gov/aoa/dir/153.html

Family Support for Children with Medical Problems

Children's Hospice International: 2202 Mount Vernon Avenue, Suite 3C, Alexandria, VA 22301; (800) 242-4453; www.chionline.org

Federation for Children with Special Needs: 1135 Tremont Street, Suite 420, Boston, MA 02120; (800) 331-0688; www.fcsn.org

National Easter Seal Society: 230 West Monroe Street, Suite 1800, Chicago, IL 60606; (800) 221-6827; www.easter-seals.org

Ronald McDonald House Charities: One Kroc Drive, Oak Brook, IL 60523; (630) 623-7048; www.rmhc.com

Hearing Disorders

American Academy of Audiology: 8300 Greensboro Drive, Suite 750, McLean, VA 22102; (800) 222-2336; www.audiology.org

American Association of the Deaf-Blind: 814 Thayer Avenue, Silver Spring, MD 20910; (800) 735-2258; www.tr.wou.edu/dblink/aadb.htm

American Society for Deaf Children: P.O. Box 3355, Gettysburg, PA 17325; (800) 942-2732; http://deafchildren.org

American Speech-Language Hearing Association: 10801 Rockville Pike, Rockville, MD 20852; (888) 321-2742; www.asha.org

Better Hearing Institute: 5021-B Backlick Road, Annandale, VA 22003; (800) 327-9355; www.betterhearing.org

HIV/AIDS

Elizabeth Glaser Pediatric AIDS Foundation: 2950 31st Street, #125, Santa Monica, CA 90405; (888) 499-4673; www.pedaids.org

HIV/AIDS Treatment Information Service: P.O. Box 6303, Rockville, MD 20849; (800) 448-0440; www.hivatis.org

National Pediatric and Family HIV Resource Center: University of Medicine and Dentistry of New Jersey, 30 Bergen Street, ADMC #4, Newark, NJ 07103; (800) 362-0071; www.pedhivaids.org

Injuries

Brain Injury Association: 105 North Alfred Street, Alexandria, VA 22314; (703) 236-6000; www.biausa.org

National Spinal Cord Injury Association: 8701 Georgia Avenue, Suite 500, Silver Spring, MD 20851; (800) 962-9629; www.spinalcord.org

Mental Health

American Academy of Child and Adolescent Psychiatry: 3615 Wisconsin Avenue NW, Washington, DC 20016; (800) 333-7636; www.aacap.org

American Psychiatric Association: 1400 K Street NW, Washington, DC 20005; (888) 357-7924; www.psych.org

Autism Society of America: 7910 Woodmont Avenue, Suite 300, Bethesda, MD 20814; (800) 328-8476, extension 150; www.autism-society.org

Center for Mental Health Services/Knowledge Exchange Network: P.O. Box 42490, Washington, DC 20015; (800) 789-2647; www.mentalhealth.org

Indiana Resource Center for Autism: 2853 East 10th Street, Bloomington, IN 47408; (812) 855-6508; www.iidc.indiana.edu/~irca

National Institute of Mental Health: 6001 Executive Boulevard, Room 8184, MSC 9663, Bethesda, MD 20892; (301) 443-4513; www.nimh.nih.gov

National Mental Health Association: 1021 Prince Street, Alexandria, VA 22314; (800) 969-6642; www.nmha.org

Obsessive-Compulsive Foundation: 337 Notch Hill Road, North Branford, CT 06471; (203) 315-2190; www.ocfoundation.org

Organ/Marrow/Tissue Donor Organizations

Children's Organ Transplant Association: 2501 COTA Drive, Bloomington, IN 47403; (800) 366-2682; www.cota.org

National Marrow Donor Program: 3433 Broadway Street NE, Suite 500, Minneapolis, MN 55413; (800) 627-7692; www.marrow.org

National Heart, Lung, and Blood Institute: NHLBI Information Center, P.O. Box 30105, Bethesda, MD 20824; (301) 592-8573; www.nhlbi.nih.gov/index.htm

Other Diseases and Chronic Illnesses

American Lyme Disease Foundation: Mill Pond Offices, 293 Route 100, Somers, NY 10589; (914) 277-6970; www.aldf.com

Children's PKU [Phenylketonuria] Network: (800) 377-6677; www.pkunetwork.org

Cystic Fibrosis Foundation: 6931 Arlington Road, Second Floor, Bethesda, MD 20814; (800) 344-4823; www.cff.org

Epilepsy Foundation: 4351 Garden City Drive, Landover, MD 20785; (800) 332-1000; www.efa.org

Muscular Dystrophy Association: 3300 East Sunrise Drive, Tucson, AZ 85718; (800) 572-1717; www.mdausa.org

National Brain Tumor Foundation: 414 13th Street, Suite 700, Oakland, CA 94612; (800) 934-2873; www.braintumor.org

National Hemophilia Foundation: 116 West 32nd Street, 11th Floor, New York, NY 10001; (800) 424-2634; www.hemophilia.org

Sickle Cell Disease Association of America: 3345 Wilshire Boulevard, Suite 1106, Los Angeles, CA 90010; (800) 421-8453; http://sicklecelldisease.org

Spina Bifida Association of America: 4590 MacArthur Boulevard NW, Suite 250, Washington, DC 20007; (800) 621-3141; www.sbaa.org

Physical Disabilities

American Association on Mental Retardation: 444 North Capitol Street NW, Suite 848, Washington, DC 20001; (800) 424-3688; www.aamr.org

Arthritis Foundation and the American Juvenile Arthritis Foundation: 1330 West Peachtree Street, Atlanta, GA 30309; (800) 283-7800; www.arthritis.org

Cleft Palate Foundation: 104 South Estes Drive, Suite 204, Chapel Hill, NC 27514; (800) 242-5338; www.cleftline.org

Council for Exceptional Children: P.O. Box 79206, Baltimore, MD 21279; (888) 232-7733; www.cec.sped.org

March of Dimes: 1275 Mamaroneck Avenue, White Plains, NY 10605; (888) 663-4637; www.modimes.org

National Down Syndrome Congress: 7000 Peachtree-Dunwoody Road NE, Lake Ridge 400 Office Park, Building #5, Suite 100, Atlanta, GA 30328; (800) 232-6372; www.ndsccenter.org

National Down Syndrome Society: 666 Broadway, New York, NY 10012; (800) 221-4602; www.ndss.org

National Fragile X Foundation: P.O. Box 190488, San Francisco, CA 94119; (800) 688-8765; www.fragilex.org

National Information Center for Children and Youth with Disabilities: P.O. Box 1492, Washington, DC 20013; (800) 695-0285; www.nichcy.org

Special Olympics: 1325 G Street NW, Suite 500, Washington, DC 20005; (202) 628-3630; www.specialolympics.org

United Cerebral Palsy Association: 1660 L Street NW, Suite 600, Washington, DC 20036; (800) 872-5827; www.ucpa.org

Skin Problems

American Academy of Dermatology: (888) 462-3376; www.aad.org

National Psoriasis Foundation: (503) 244-7404; www.psoriasis.org

Vision Disorders

American Council of the Blind: 1155 15th Street NW, Suite 1004, Washington, DC 20005; (202) 467-5081; www.acb.org

American Foundation for the Blind: 11 Penn Plaza, Suite 300, New York, NY 10001; (800) 232-5463; www.afb.org

National Association for Parents of Children with Visual Impairments: P.O. Box 317, Watertown, MA 02272; (800) 562-6265; www.spedex.com/napvi

National Association for Visually Handicapped: 22 West 21st Street, New York, NY 10010; (212) 889-3141; www.navh.org

National Federation of the Blind: 1800 Johnson Street, Baltimore, MD 21230; (410) 659-9314; www.nfb.org

Web Sites

www.kidshealth.org:
Children's health information from the Nemours Foundation

www.americasdoctor.com:
Medical advice from a virtual doctor

www.centerwatch.com:
Keeps a close watch on clinical trials, listed by condition and geographic location

www.drkoop.com:
Former U.S. Surgeon General C. Everett Koop has medical information and a drug interaction checker

http://hopkinsmedicine.org: Medical Web site of Johns Hopkins University

www.intelihealth.com: Medical questions answered by doctors at Johns Hopkins University and Aetna U.S. Healthcare

www.mayohealth.org: General info from the Mayo Clinic

www.mediconsult.com: A virtual medical center with information tailored to patients' needs

www.navigator.tufts.edu: Nutrition information from Tufts University

www.nih.gov/health: The National Institutes of Health's home page, offering links to several more-specific sites

www.pedinfo.com: An online pediatric information library

www.reutershealth.com: Health news from Reuters

Parenting

General Information

www.parentcare.com:
Advice for parents

www.parents.com:
Web site for *Parents* magazine

www.parentsoup.com:
A fun discussion forum for parents (or parents-to-be) about kids of all ages

www.thelaboroflove.com:
Online pregnancy and parenting support with feature articles and interactive bulletin boards for discussions

Single Parents

Parents Without Partners:
1650 South Dixie Highway, Suite 510, Boca Raton, FL 33432; (800) 637-7974; www.parentswithoutpartners.org

Single Mothers Online:
P.O. Box 68, Midland, NC 28107; www.singlemothers.org

Safety

General Information

U.S. Consumer Product Safety Commission
Hotline: (800) 638-2772; www.cpsc.gov

Federal Auto-Safety Hotline:
(800) 424-9393; www.nhtsa.dot.gov

Juvenile Products Manufacturers Association:
www.jpma.org

National Safe Kids Campaign:
(202) 662-0600; www.safekids.org

Household Pollution

Environmental Protection Agency (EPA) Safe
Drinking Water Hotline: (800) 426-4791

EPA Toxic Substance Information Service:
(202) 554-1404

Indoor Air Quality Association:
(301) 962-3805; www.iaqa.org

National Lead Information Center:
(800) 424-5323; www.nsc.org/ehc/lead.htm

your child's medical diary

you'll spend a large part of your child's first years talking about facts and figures: how much she weighs, when she first started to walk, how tall she is, and how many colds she's gotten.

Some of this information is fun to jot down so you can look back and remember important milestones. But facts about your child's medical history can be vital to her health if she needs to be treated by a new doctor who's not familiar with her.

This medical diary will help you track your child's growth, record immunizations, and note specifics about major and minor diseases. You can fill in these pages right here in the book or photocopy them several times so you can keep a separate record for each of your children.

_____'s Medical History

Birth Information

Date of birth: _____

Weight at birth: _____ lb _____ oz (or _____ g)

Length at birth: _____ in (or _____ cm)

Feeding Guidelines

Breastfeeding: _____

Formula feeding: _____

Supplements: _____

Record of Immunizations

Vaccination	Date	Reactions
Chicken pox (12–18 months)		
Diphtheria, tetanus, pertussis (DTP or DTaP), first shot (2 months)		
DTP or DTaP, second shot (4 months)		
DTP or DTaP, third shot (6 months)		
DTP or DTaP, fourth shot (15–18 months)		
DTP or DTaP, fifth shot (4–6 years)		
Diphtheria (11–16 years)		
Haemophilus influenzae type b (Hib), first shot (2 months)		

Vaccination	Date	Reactions
Hib, second shot (4 months)		
Hib, third shot (6 months)		
Hib, fourth shot (12–15 months)		
Hepatitis A (2–12 years, required in selected states only)		
Hepatitis B, first shot (Birth–2 months)		
Hepatitis B, second shot (1–4 months)		
Hepatitis B, third shot (6–18 months)		
Hepatitis B, fourth shot (11–12 years)		
Measles, mumps, rubella (MMR), first shot (12–15 months)		
MMR, second shot (4–6 years)		
MMR, third shot (11–12 years)		
Polio, first shot (2 months)		
Polio, second shot (4 months)		
Polio, third shot (6–18 months)		
Polio, fourth shot (4–6 years)		
Tetanus (11–16 years)		
Others		

History of Diseases

Disease	Date(s)	Comments
Anemia		
Chicken pox		
Ear infections		
Measles		
Mumps		
Pneumonia		
Rheumatic fever		
Rubella		
Scarlet fever		
Tuberculosis		
Whooping cough (pertussis)		
Other		
Other		

History of Other Illnesses

Illness	Dates/Duration	Symptoms	Medications
	to		
	to		
	to		
	to		
	to		
	to		
	to		
	to		
	to		
	to		

Allergies

Type	Date(s)	Symptoms	Treatment
Animals			
Environmental (molds, dust, etc.)			
Foods			
Medications			
Seasonal (ragweed, pollen, etc.)			

Accidents/Major Injuries

_____

_____

_____

_____

_____

Hospitalizations/Operations

_____

_____

_____

_____

_____

Prenatal Care

Pregnancy problems: _____

Doctor's name: _____

Notes from doctor visits: _____

_____

Medications taken during pregnancy: _____

Baby's First Office Visit

Date: _____ Height: _____ Weight: _____

Head circumference: _____ Questions: _____

_____

Notes (medications prescribed, dosages, doctor's directions, etc.): _____

_____

Doctor's name: _____

3-Month Visit

Date: _____ Height: _____ Weight: _____

Head circumference: _____ Questions: _____

_____

Notes (medications prescribed, dosages, doctor's directions, etc.): _____

_____

Doctor's name: _____

6-Month Visit

Date: _____ Height: _____ Weight: _____

Head circumference: _____ Questions: _____

_____

Notes (medications prescribed, dosages, doctor's directions, etc.): _____

_____

Doctor's name: _____

1-Year Visit

Date: _____ Height: _____ Weight: _____

Head circumference: _____ Questions: _____

_____

Notes (medications prescribed, dosages, doctor's directions, etc.): _____

_____

Doctor's name: _____

2-Year Visit

Date: _____ Height: _____ Weight: _____

Questions: _____

_____

Notes (medications prescribed, dosages, doctor's directions, etc.): _____

_____

Doctor's name: _____

3-Year Visit

Date: _____ Height: _____ Weight: _____

Questions: _____

_____

Notes (medications prescribed, dosages, doctor's directions, etc.): _____

_____

Doctor's name: _____

4-Year Visit

Date: _____ Height: _____ Weight: _____

Questions: _____

_____

Notes (medications prescribed, dosages, doctor's directions, etc.): _____

_____

Doctor's name: _____

5-Year Visit

Date: _____ Height: _____ Weight: _____

Questions: _____

_____

Notes (medications prescribed, dosages, doctor's directions, etc.): _____

_____

Doctor's name: _____

6-Year Visit

Date: _____ Height: _____ Weight: _____

Questions: _____

_____

Notes (medications prescribed, dosages, doctor's directions, etc.): _____

_____

Doctor's name: _____

Growth and Development

Date	Age	Milestone
		(rolling over, sleeping through night, walking, etc.)

_____

_____

_____

_____

_____

_____

_____

_____

_____

_____

Family Medical History

	Mother	Father	Other
Allergies, adult			
Allergies, childhood			
Cause of death			
Chronic conditions			
Exposure to harmful substances (asbestos, radiation, toxins, etc.)			
Hospitalizations			
Illnesses, serious childhood			
Operations			
Reactions to medications			

growth charts and body mass index

While growth charts like those on pages 440 to 443 measure your child's weight and height compared with other children, the government's Body Mass Index (BMI) tracks your child's height and weight in relation to each other. Figuring out your child's BMI is especially helpful if you're worried that he is overweight. To determine your child's BMI:

- Multiply his weight in pounds by 703;
- divide that number by his height in inches;
- divide that number by his height in inches again.

The answer is his BMI.

Once you've figured out his BMI, check the table on page 444, which gives BMI cutoffs for overweight and obese conditions, according to a child's age. If your child's BMI is below the figures in the "Moderately Overweight" column, he is fine. If his BMI is at or above the numbers in either column, talk to your pediatrician about how you can help your child lose weight.

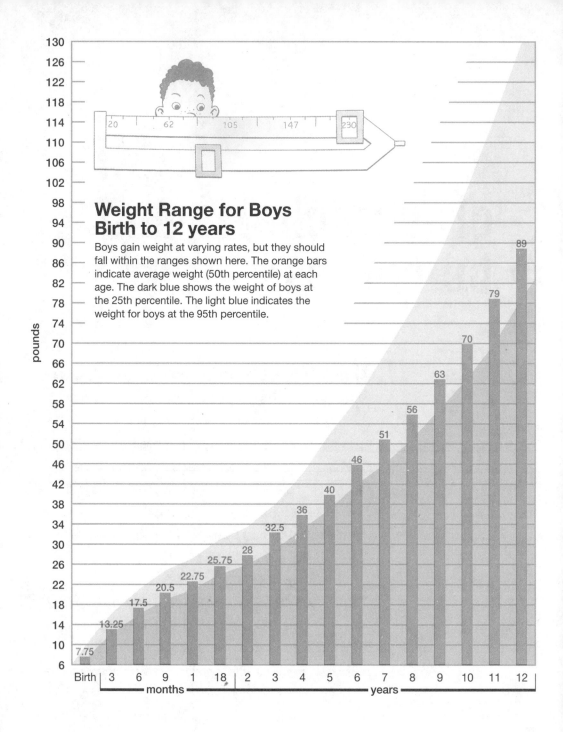

Weight Range for Boys
Birth to 12 years

Boys gain weight at varying rates, but they should fall within the ranges shown here. The orange bars indicate average weight (50th percentile) at each age. The dark blue shows the weight of boys at the 25th percentile. The light blue indicates the weight for boys at the 95th percentile.

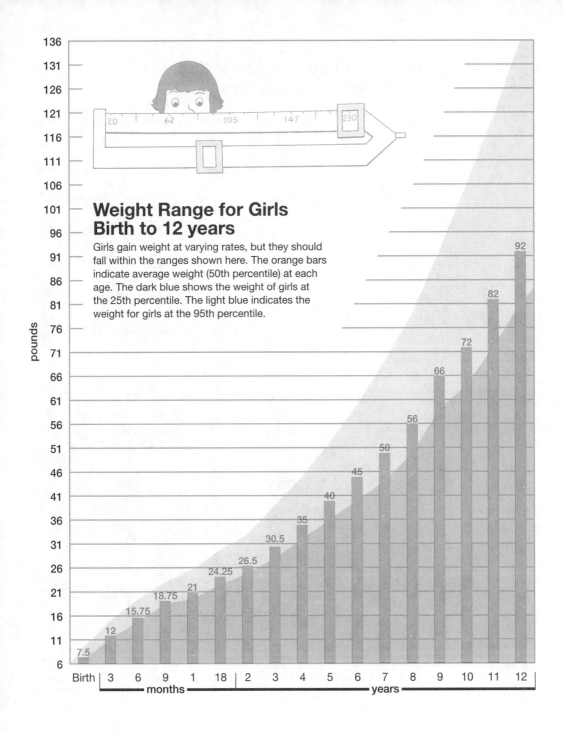

Weight Range for Girls Birth to 12 years

Girls gain weight at varying rates, but they should fall within the ranges shown here. The orange bars indicate average weight (50th percentile) at each age. The dark blue shows the weight of girls at the 25th percentile. The light blue indicates the weight for girls at the 95th percentile.

pounds

136
131
126
121
116
111
106
101
96
91
86
81
76
71
66
61
56
51
46
41
36
31
26
21
16
11
6

7.5 · 12 · 15.75 · 18.75 · 21 · 24.25 · 26.5 · 30.5 · 35 · 40 · 45 · 50 · 56 · 66 · 72 · 82 · 92

Birth | 3 | 6 | 9 | 1 | 18 | 2 | 3 | 4 | 5 | 6 | 7 | 8 | 9 | 10 | 11 | 12

months — years

Source: Developed by the National Center for Health Statistics in collaboration with the National Center for Chronic Disease Prevention and Health Promotion (2000).

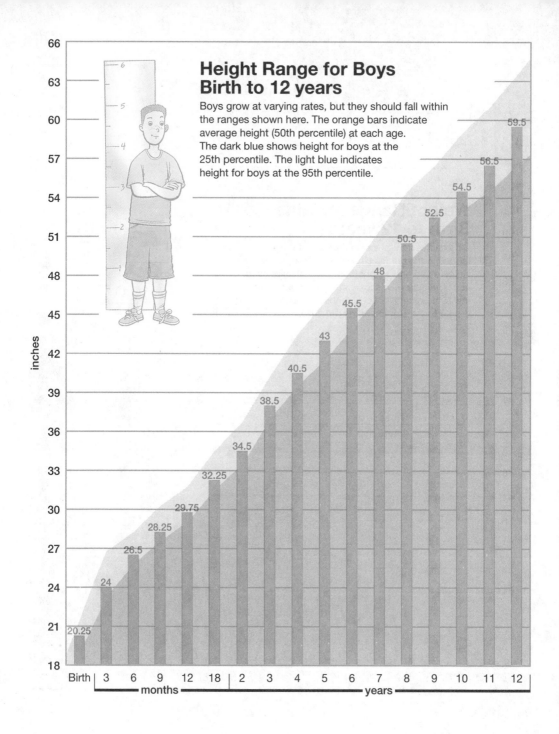

Height Range for Boys
Birth to 12 years

Boys grow at varying rates, but they should fall within
the ranges shown here. The orange bars indicate
average height (50th percentile) at each age.
The dark blue shows height for boys at the
25th percentile. The light blue indicates
height for boys at the 95th percentile.

inches

66
63
60
57
54
51
48
45
42
39
36
33
30
27
24
21
18

59.5
56.5
54.5
52.5
50.5
48
45.5
43
40.5
38.5
34.5
32.25
29.75
28.25
26.5
24
20.25

Birth 3 6 9 12 18 | 2 3 4 5 6 7 8 9 10 11 12
months | years

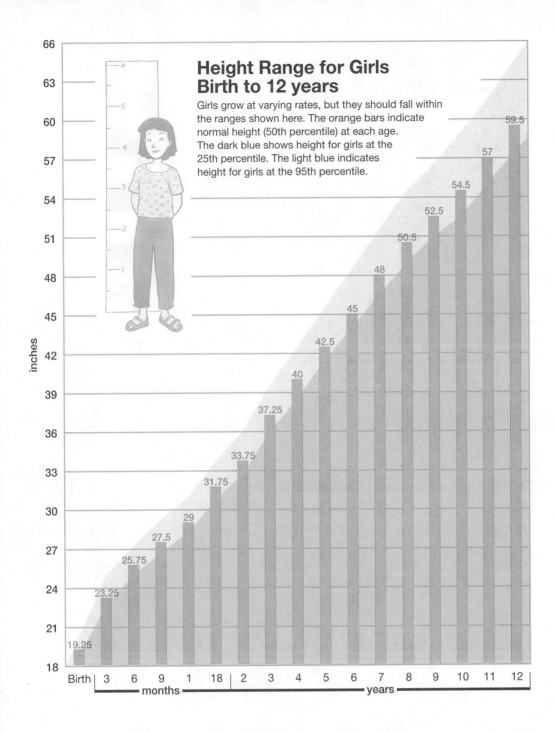

Height Range for Girls Birth to 12 years

Girls grow at varying rates, but they should fall within the ranges shown here. The orange bars indicate normal height (50th percentile) at each age. The dark blue shows height for girls at the 25th percentile. The light blue indicates height for girls at the 95th percentile.

inches

66
63
60
57
54
51
48
45
42
39
36
33
30
27
24
21
18

19.25 · 23.25 · 25.75 · 27.5 · 29 · 31.75 · 33.75 · 37.25 · 40 · 42.5 · 45 · 48 · 50.5 · 52.5 · 54.5 · 57 · 59.5

Birth | 3 · 6 · 9 · 1 · 18 | 2 · 3 · 4 · 5 · 6 · 7 · 8 · 9 · 10 · 11 · 12 |
months · years

SOURCE: Developed by the National Center for Health Statistics in collaboration with the National Center for Chronic Disease Prevention and Health Promotion (2000).

Body Mass Index for Children Ages 2 to 17

Age (years)	Moderately Overweight		Severely Overweight	
	Boys (BMI)	Girls (BMI)	Boys (BMI)	Girls (BMI)
2	18.41	18.02	20.09	19.81
2½	18.13	17.76	19.8	19.55
3	17.89	17.56	19.57	19.36
3½	17.69	17.4	19.39	19.23
4	17.55	17.28	19.29	19.15
4½	17.47	17.19	19.26	19.12
5	17.42	17.15	19.3	19.17
5½	17.45	17.2	19.47	19.34
6	17.55	17.34	19.78	19.65
6½	17.71	17.53	20.23	20.08
7	17.92	17.75	20.63	20.51
7½	18.16	18.03	21.09	21.01
8	18.44	18.35	21.6	21.57
8½	18.76	18.69	22.17	22.18
9	19.1	19.07	22.77	22.81
9½	19.46	19.45	23.39	23.46

Age (years)	Moderately Overweight Boys (BMI)	Moderately Overweight Girls (BMI)	Severely Overweight Boys (BMI)	Severely Overweight Girls (BMI)
10	19.84	19.86	24	24.11
10½	20.2	20.29	24.57	24.77
11	20.55	20.74	25.1	25.42
11½	20.89	21.2	25.58	26.05
12	21.22	21.68	26.02	26.67
12½	21.56	22.14	26.43	27.24
13	21.91	22.58	26.84	27.76
13½	22.27	22.98	27.25	28.2
14	22.62	23.34	27.63	28.57
14½	22.96	23.66	27.98	28.87
15	23.29	23.94	28.3	29.11
15½	23.6	24.17	28.6	29.29
16	23.9	24.37	28.88	29.43
16½	24.19	24.54	29.14	29.56
17	24.26	23.7	29.41	29.69

index

Boldface page references indicate illustrations. Underscored references indicate boxed text.

Dressing
baby, 7–9, <u>8</u>
in crib, 7
in high chair, 8
independence and, 255–56, <u>256</u>, 283
tantrums over, 198
toddlers and older children, 281–83
Driveway safety, <u>112</u>
Drugs. *See* Medications
Dry sink as changing table, 9

E

Ear infection, <u>102</u>, <u>104</u>
Ears, cleaning, 278
Easter arts and crafts, 335
Eating
choices and, giving children, 57
habits, healthy, 57–59
independence and, <u>253</u>, 255
mirrors to encourage, 51
parent as role model for healthy, 64
rewards for healthy, 59–60, 63–64
Elderly, helping, 226, 228, 230–31
Electrical cord safety, 109–10
Emergency medical care, <u>92</u>, <u>149</u>
Engorgement, 15–16, <u>15</u>
Etiquette. *See* Manners
Exercise. *See also* Outdoor activity
competitive child and, <u>296</u>
encouraging children to engage in, 296–300, <u>297</u>, <u>300</u>
equipment safety in home and, 113
guidelines, <u>299</u>
importance of, 294
for overweight children, <u>61</u>
playground games, <u>298</u>
role modeling by parents and, 300
sports
effort in, applauding, 304
life skills and, <u>302</u>
parental goals in, <u>301</u>
readiness for, <u>301</u>

sportsmanship and, teaching, <u>295</u>
team, 297
starting, 295–96
videotaping, 298–99
Eye contact, 168

F

Fabric softener sheets for diaper pail odor, <u>10</u>
Family
activities for bonding, 374–77, <u>374</u>, <u>375</u>, <u>376</u>
albums, <u>404</u>
co-sleeping, 182–84, <u>182</u>
mealtime, with baby, 43
as priority, 235–36
time, 372–80
connecting with children during, tips for, <u>376</u>
grandparents and, 378–80
importance of, 372
indoor activities and, 377–78, <u>377</u>
morning, <u>157</u>, 322–23, 358
photographs and, 377
reading during, 311
scheduling, 373–74
strategies for increasing, <u>380</u>
strong families and, <u>374</u>
working mothers and, maximizing, 364–66, <u>365</u>
traditions, 374–77, <u>374</u>, <u>375</u>, <u>379</u>
Fantasy, as creativity booster, <u>288</u>
Fast food, <u>54</u>
Fat. *See* Dietary fat; Weight problems
Fathers
breastfeeding and, <u>16</u>
stay-at-home, 369
Father's Day arts and crafts, 335
Fear
of airplane, <u>386</u>
of dentist, 134–35
of monsters, 182–84
of needles, 147

Hurt and upset feelings, soothing, 154, <u>311</u>

Hygiene. *See also* Grooming
    with baby, 32–34, <u>32</u>
    for cuts and wounds, 83
    medical care and, 103
    teaching proper, 277–79

Hypothermia, <u>120</u>

I

Ice cream cones, eating, 69

Ice skating, <u>301</u>

Ice treatments, 85, 87

Identification bracelet, 131

Illnesses. *See* Medical care; *specific types*

Imaginary friends, <u>293</u>

Immune system, 94

Immunizations, <u>146</u>, 147

Independence
    ages for activities promoting, <u>260</u>
    bathroom routines and, 256
    baths and, <u>260</u>
    book about, 254
    chores and, <u>255</u>, <u>257</u>, 258–59
    cleanup and, 260–61
    clingy children and, 161
    clothing choices and, <u>260</u>, 309–10
    cooking and, 259, 309–10
    day care and, <u>256</u>
    dressing and, 255–56, <u>256</u>, 283
    eating and, <u>253</u>, 255
    games and projects promoting, 256–57,
        309
    importance of, 252
    morning, <u>254</u>
    pet care and, <u>260</u>
    playing alone and, <u>258</u>
    pouring milk and, 256
    self-esteem and, 308–9
    separation anxiety and, 161–62
    shoes and, putting on own, 254, 283
    skills for, first, 253–55
    sleepovers and, <u>260</u>
    street crossing and, <u>260</u>
    time alone and, <u>258</u>

Indiana Dunes National Park, <u>394</u>

Individuality, nurturing, <u>211</u>

Indoor activity, 377–78, <u>377</u>. *See also* Arts
    and crafts

Information and paper, organizing, 406–8,
    <u>408</u>

Insect protection, 123–24, <u>123</u>

Instant axillary thermometer, <u>33</u>

Instincts
    breastfeeding and, 14–15
    medical care and parental, 97

International games, <u>298</u>

Internet, family-friendly sites on, <u>346</u>

Interruptions to conversation,
    discouraging, 216

Introductions, teaching proper, <u>221</u>

Invitation etiquette, <u>421</u>

Iodine, <u>52</u>

Iron, <u>52</u>

J

Jeans, extending life of, 282

Jet lag, <u>387</u>

Job sharing, 363

Journals. *See* Writing activities

Juice, fruit and vegetable, <u>42</u>, 53, 133

Junk food, avoiding, <u>61</u>

K

Kicking during tantrums, <u>197</u>

Kindergarten
    readiness for, <u>318</u>
    separation anxiety and, <u>161</u>

Kitchen safety, <u>76</u>, <u>108</u>

L

Lactation. *See* Breastfeeding

Lamaze breathing, breastfeeding and, 14

Laundry bag
    for baby, 9
    for chores, 258

Learning disability, <u>272</u>

Leaves, making book of, 336

Letters, teaching, 264, 266–68

to national parks, <u>394</u>
to New York City, 391–92
with other families, <u>389</u>
resort, 392
sight-seeing, 392–93
Vaccinations, <u>146</u>, 147
Valentine's Day arts and crafts, **332–33**, 332–33, 334–35
Values, teaching, 234–36, <u>236</u>
Vaseline, 31, <u>282</u>
Vegetables
dental care and, 139
dips for, 60–61
disguising, <u>64</u>
feeding baby, <u>44</u>, 48–49
frozen vs. fresh, <u>60</u>
increasing intake of, 59
juice, 53
purées, 56–57
questions about, frequently asked, <u>60</u>
Velcro, 256, 283
Videotapes
borrowing other people's, 345
organizing home, <u>402</u>
physician office visits and, 147
reading books on, by grandparents, 264
of sports and exercise events, 298–99
technology management and, 345–47
for toddlers and older children, list of favorite, <u>342</u>
as travel distractions, 386
Virus, 32–34, <u>32</u>, <u>36</u>
Vitamins. *See specific types*
Vitamin A, <u>52</u>
Vitamin C, <u>52</u>, 103–4
Vitamin D, <u>52</u>
Vitamin E, <u>52</u>
Vitamin K, <u>52</u>
Vocabulary, teaching, 264, 266–68
Volunteering. *See also* Charity
book about, <u>227</u>
in community, 226–31, <u>227</u>, <u>228</u>, <u>229</u>
during holidays, 229

opportunities for, <u>229</u>
at school, <u>315</u>, 316–17
Vomit, baby's, <u>36</u>

W

Waking from sleep, 180–81
Walks
for bonding with children, 375, 380
with dog, 375
for making friends, 240–41
nature, 380
with stroller and toddler, 129
Water intake
of baby, <u>22</u>
in hot weather, <u>121</u>, 122
increasing with food coloring, 51
at night, 177–78
for overweight children, <u>61</u>
of toddlers and older children, 51
Web sites, family-friendly, <u>346</u>
Weight problems, 50, <u>58</u>, 61–64, <u>61</u>
White noise for colic, 28
Word games, 267–68
Words, teaching, 264, 266–68
Working mothers
back-to-work tactics for, 370–71
benefits package of, <u>370</u>
bond with children and, 20, 366–67
breastfeeding and, 20–21, <u>20</u>
challenge facing, 362
children at work with, <u>371</u>
explaining job to child and, <u>364</u>
family time and, maximizing, 364–66, 365
father at home and, 369
flextime and, <u>368</u>
guilt of, managing, 368
job sharing, 363
jobs for, child-friendly, 363–64
maternity leave and, <u>367</u>
multitasking and, 20–21
part-time work and, 242, 368
playdates and, 250–51
scheduling and, creative, 369

Working mothers *(cont.)*
   telecommuting and, 363
   telephone and, 366
Wounds, 82–85, <u>88</u>
Wrapping paper as drawer liner, 9
Wrapping presents, 331, 419–20
Wrestling, 299
Writing activities
   for caregiver, 366–67
   as disciplinary measure, 173
   journal-keeping for children, 269
   letters for easing separation anxiety,
     155–56
   notes in promoting good manners, 214,
     221

   schedules of breastfeeding, 19
   stories by children, 266

Y

Yard safety, <u>109</u>, <u>114</u>, 115–16, <u>117</u>
Yelling, alternatives to, 167–70
Yellowstone National Park, <u>394</u>
"Yuck" lists, 57

Z

Zinc, <u>52</u>
Zinc oxide formulas, 30